Perspectives on Legal Education

This edited collection offers a critical overview of the major debates in legal education set in the context of the Lord Upjohn Lectures, the annual event that draws together legal educators and professionals in the United Kingdom to consider the major debates and changes in the field.

Presented in a unique format that reproduces classic lectures alongside contemporary responses from legal education experts, this book offers both an historical overview of how these debates have developed and an up-to-date critical commentary on the state of legal education today. As the full impact of the introduction of university fees, the Legal Education and Training Review and the regulators' responses are felt in law departments across England and Wales, this collection offers a timely reflection on legal education's legacy, as well as critical debate on how it will develop in the future.

Chris Ashford is Professor of Law and Society at Northumbria University. He is Editor of *The Law Teacher* and Chair of the Association of Law Teachers.

Nigel Duncan is Professor of Legal Education at City University and a Principal Fellow of the Higher Education Academy. He is convenor of *Teaching Legal Ethics UK* and Consultant Editor of *The Law Teacher.*

Jessica Guth is Head of Law at the University of Bradford School of Law. She is Deputy Editor of *The Law Teacher* and Vice Chair of the Association of Law Teachers.

Perspectives on Legal Education

Contemporary Responses to the Lord Upjohn Lectures

Edited by
Chris Ashford, Nigel Duncan and Jessica Guth

Routledge
Taylor & Francis Group
LONDON AND NEW YORK

First published 2016
by Routledge
2 Park Square, Milton Park, Abingdon, Oxon, OX14 4RN

and by Routledge
711 Third Avenue, New York, NY 10017

Routledge is an imprint of the Taylor & Francis Group, an informa business

British Library Cataloguing in Publication Data
A catalogue record for this book is available from the British Library

Library of Congress Cataloging-in-Publication Data
Perspectives on legal education : contemporary responses to the Upjohn Lectures / Edited by Chris Ashford, Nigel Duncan and Jessica Guth.
pages cm
Includes bibliographical references and index.
ISBN 978-1-138-81258-1 (hbk) – ISBN 978-1-315-74873-3 (ebk)
1. Law–Study and teaching–Great Britain. I. Ashford, Chris, editor. II. Duncan, Nigel editor. III. Guth, Jessica, editor.
KD432.P39 2016
340.071'141–dc23
2015023567

ISBN: 978-1-138-81258-1 (hbk)
ISBN: 978-1-315-74873-3 (ebk)

Typeset in Baskerville
by Apex CoVantage, LLC

Contents

Foreword viii
PATRICIA LEIGHTON
Notes on Contributors x

1 The Lord Upjohn Lectures and Legal Education 1
CHRIS ASHFORD, NIGEL DUNCAN AND JESSICA GUTH

2 The Rt. Hon. Lord Upjohn, C.B.E., D.L.: Honorary President of the Association of Law Teachers, 1966–1971: An Appreciation 8
SIR I. H. JACOB Q.C.

3 Forty-first Lord Upjohn Lecture 2012: Reforming Legal Education 10
LORD NEUBERGER OF ABBOTSBURY

4 Response: A Tale of Two Cities: Reflecting on Lord Neuberger's 'Reforming Legal Education' 24
JULIAN WEBB

5 Fortieth Lord Upjohn Lecture 2011: Widening Participation in a Changing Educational Landscape 43
WES STREETING

6 Response: Transformation by Education 54
GRAEME BROADBENT

7 Thirty-ninth Lord Upjohn Lecture 2010: Training the Lawyers of the Future – A Regulator's View 72
DAVID EDMONDS

8 Response: Of Competence, Confidence and the Last Chance Saloon 85
STEPHEN MAYSON

9 Twenty-ninth Lord Upjohn Lecture 2000: The Education, the Justice System Requires Today 97
LORD WOOLF C.J.

10 Response: Education in Times of Developing Law and Civil Procedure 104
HON. SIR VIVIAN RAMSEY

11 Fourth Lord Upjohn Lecture 1974: Fact-finding: Art or Science? 113
LORD JUSTICE ORMROD

12 Response: Preparation for Practice: Developing Effective Advocates in a Changing World of Adversarial Civil Justice 121
NIGEL DUNCAN

13 Thirty-eighth Lord Upjohn Lecture 2009: The Student Contract 135
BARONESS RUTH DEECH D.B.E.

14 Response: Changing Terms: A Response to Professor Deech 145
REBECCA HUXLEY-BINNS

15 Sixth Lord Upjohn Lecture 1977: The Law as Taught and the Law as Practised 155
HON. SIR ROBERT GOFF

16 Response: How Well Are We Moving Forward in the Teaching v Practice Debate in Law? 162
SUSAN BLAKE

17 Tenth Lord Upjohn Lecture 1980: Legal Education and the Needs of the Legal Profession 171
SIR FREDERICK LAWTON P.C.

18 Response: The Needs of the Legal Profession and the Liberal Law School: (Re)negotiating Boundaries 177
CHRIS ASHFORD

19 Twenty-second Lord Upjohn Lecture 1993: The Lord Chancellor's Advisory Committee on Legal Education and the Legal Profession 188
LORD GRIFFITHS OF GOVILON M.C.

20 Response: From Gavotte to Techno – But the Dance Goes On 196
JOHN HODGSON

21 Eleventh Lord Upjohn Lecture 1981: The Teaching of the Law and Politics 207
J. A. G. GRIFFITH

22 Response: But It Still Goes On: The Teaching of Law and Politics in 2015 219
ANTHONY BRADNEY

23 Twenty-fifth Lord Upjohn Lecture 1996: The Integration of Teaching and Research in the Law Department 228
DAWN OLIVER Q.C.

24 Response: Fostering Curiosity: The Importance of Research and Teaching in Law Schools 240
JESSICA GUTH

Index 253

Foreword

This is an extremely timely book, coming as it does when legal education is facing some major challenges and controversies. These include structural and cultural changes in the provision of legal professional services, and the questioning of the notions of professionalism and consumerism as drivers of reform. In the academy, we have tensions between teaching law and researching law, mounting pressures on resources, along with concerns over the costs of legal education and their impact on access to it.

The book has an excellent and innovative format. The device is that of contemporary experts in legal education commenting on specific Lord Upjohn Lectures. This provides a unique opportunity for reflection and critique, looking at topics through different lenses and perspectives. The Lord Upjohn Lectures themselves span nearly 50 years, which have seen many important developments in legal education, not least its major expansion. At the same time, the book illustrates that some topics remain complex, constant and unresolved. Perhaps the most constant topic of all is what is the essential role of law studies themselves, especially the LLB? The debates that pre-occupied late-nineteenth-century jurists as to whether law is truly an academic subject and the relationship between so-called 'academic' and 'vocational' law continue as fiercely today.

The Lord Upjohn Lectures, to a marked extent, reflect the evolution of the Association of Law Teachers itself. Early lectures, frequently delivered by judges focused on doctrinal rather than educative issues, illustrated the early and positive links between the Association and the profession. Gradually, wider and more educational issues surfaced, reflecting also changes in the content and priorities of the Association's Journal *The Law Teacher*. Law students and their aspirations, but also their problems, began to merit attention, as part of changed emphases in higher education itself. Many of the Lord Upjohn Lecturers dealt, some bravely, with highly controversial topics, not least concerning the recent Legal Education and Training Review (LETR), and it is good to see many of these represented in the book and subject to critique.

Taking together the contributions of both Lord Upjohn Lecturers and their respondents in the book, one can also see other features of legal education more clearly. When I look back on these lectures I also note the topics that have not been addressed, which is not intended as a criticism but merely an observation.

Legal education emerges still closely aligned to the legal profession and its bodies but curiously detached from its higher education context. It also seems curiously detached from developments in other academic disciplines, especially those with professional/vocational links. International and EU developments and issues are also somewhat neglected, as have been developments in legal education outside higher education. Legal education, at least as seen from the Lord Upjohn Lectures, can emerge as perhaps isolated or ring-fenced. There is evidence of the impact of external forces, not least the nature and culture of the common law in the content and delivery of legal education, but perhaps less evidence of drawing on and benefiting from 'non-law' experiences.

This book is a thought-provoking read. The task of bringing together the excellent team of respondents is much appreciated and their individual contributions confirm what a fascinating and lively topic legal education is!

Professor Patricia Leighton,
University of South Wales.

Notes on Contributors

Chris Ashford

Chris Ashford is Professor of Law and Society at Northumbria University. He is Chair of the Association of Law Teachers, Editor of *The Law Teacher: the International Journal of Legal Education*, and Editor-in-Chief of *The International Journal of Gender, Sexuality and Law*. *Pink News* named Chris as twenty-sixth in the top 50 Twitter users who influenced LGBT lives the most in 2011. He is also a member of the Society of Legal Scholars Legal Education Committee and a former Executive Committee member of the Socio-Legal Studies Association.

Susan Blake

Susan Blake is Associate Dean at The City Law School, City University, London. She was a member of the group which designed the Bar Vocational Course, and Programme Director for several years, going on to develop master's level courses focussed on legal professional practice. She is now Convener of the Centre for the Study of Legal Professional Practice at City Law School. Her research and publications focus on alternative dispute resolution, mediation and civil litigation, and she is an author of The Jackson ADR Handbook and other books published by Oxford University Press.

Anthony Bradney

Anthony Bradney is Professor of Law at Keele University. He is also a member of the Advisory Editorial Board of the *Journal of Law and Society* and a Board Member of the Research Group on the Legal Professions (International Sociological Association). He is a member of the Legal Education Research Network and the Law and Religion Scholars Network. Between 2005 and 2012 he was editor of the Web Journal of the Current Legal Issues.

Graeme Broadbent

Graeme Broadbent is Senior Lecturer in Law at Kingston University. He joined Kingston Law School in September 2002. He teaches criminal law and remedies, as well as teaching law to students on social work courses. His main research interests lie in legal education and criminal law. He is a former Reviews Editor and member of the Editorial Board of *The Law Teacher: the International Journal of Legal Education.*

Ruth Deech

Baroness Ruth Deech D.B.E. is a Crossbench member of the House of Lords. In 2015 she was elected Chair of the House of Lords Equality Act 2010 and Disability Select Committee. She was the first Independent Adjudicator for Higher Education from 2004 to 2008. She was Principal of St. Anne's College from 1991 to 2004 and former Fellow and Tutor in Law of that college, specialising in Family and Property Law. From 1994 to 2002 she was Chair of the UK Human Fertilisation and Embryology Authority. She was a member of the Committee of Inquiry into Equal Opportunities on the Bar Vocational Course from 1993 to 1994.

She was a Governor of the BBC from 2002 to 2006, a Rhodes Trustee from 1996 to 2006, and is an Honorary Bencher of the Inner Temple. She is a member of the Executive Committee of the International Society of Family Law, a member of the Editorial Board of *Child and Family Law Quarterly* and an Honorary Fellow of the Society for Advanced Legal Studies.

Nigel Duncan

Nigel Duncan is Professor of Legal Education at The City Law School, City University, London and Principal Fellow of the Higher Education Academy. He is Course Director of the LLM in Professional Legal Skills and Convenor of Teaching Legal Ethics UK, a community of practice including members from many different law schools and some practitioners, which holds regular workshops. He is a Director of the International Association of Legal Ethics and an Honorary Fellow of the Society for Advanced Legal Studies. He is Consultant Editor of *The Law Teacher: the International Journal of Legal Education* and former Editor. He is also a former Chair of the Association of Law Teachers.

David Edmonds

David Edmonds was appointed as the inaugural Chair of the Legal Services Board (LSB) on 1 May 2008 and served in that role until 2014. After a career in the senior civil service and as Chief Executive of the Housing Corporation, he spent seven years as a Managing Director within the NatWest Group. David's regulatory experience includes five years as Director General of Telecommunications for the United Kingdom, and two years as a founding member of the Board of Ofcom. He was the Chair of the Board of NHS Direct from 2003 to 2008. He was a Commissioner at the Legal Services Commission for four years.

Robert Goff

Known as Mr Justice Goff at the time of his Lord Upjohn Lecture, Hon. Sir Robert Goff retired in 1998 as Senior Law Lord. He is the President of the British Institute of International and Comparative Law and a patron of the *Oxford University Commonwealth Law Journal.*

John Griffith

J. A. G. Griffith died in 2010 at the age of 91. He is regarded by many as a leading public law scholar, noted for his work on the judiciary.

Hugh Griffiths

Lord Griffiths of Govilon M.C. died in 2015 at the age of 91. Between 1980 and 1985 he was Lord Justice of Appeal, and between 1985 and 1993 Lord of Appeal in Ordinary. He was made a life peer in 1985.

Jessica Guth

Dr Jessica Guth is Head of University of Bradford School of Law. She is Deputy Editor of *The Law Teacher: the International Journal of Legal Education* and Vice Chair of the Association of Law Teachers. She is also a member of the Socio-Legal Studies Association Executive and a member of the Society of Legal Scholars Legal Education Committee.

John Hodgson

John Hodgson is a Reader in the Law School at Nottingham Trent University. He was formerly a solicitor in private practice as a partner and consultant, and also formerly an academic review chair and academic auditor for QAA. John is a committee member (formerly Secretary and Chair) of the Association of Law Teachers.

Rebecca Huxley-Binns

Rebecca Huxley-Binns is Vice Provost and Professor at the University of Law. She is a former Chair of the Association of Law Teachers and won the accolade of Law Teacher of the Year in 2010 and a National Teaching Fellowship in 2012. She is Chair of the 2015 QAA Subject Benchmark Statement for Law, and a member of *The Law Teacher: the International Journal of Legal Education* Editorial Board.

Jack Jacob

Sir I. H. Jacob Q.C. has been described as 'England's leading proceduralist'. Jacob sat on many government committees concerned with court reform, including those on personal injuries litigation (1968) and on the enforcement of judgment debts (1969). He was Master and Senior Master of the High Court (1957–80) and Senior Master and Queen's Remembrancer (1975–80). He died in 2000 at the age of 92.

Frederick Lawton

Sir Frederick Lawton P.C. is a former Lord Justice of Appeal who died in 2001 at the age of 89. A high profile and sometimes controversial judge, he also contributed to a series of significant judgments, notably in *Rose v Plenty* and *Spartan Steel & Alloys Ltd v Martin & Co (Contractors) Ltd.*

Stephen Mayson

Stephen Mayson is Professor of legal services regulation at The University of Law, and Honorary Professor of Law in the Faculty of Laws at University College London, working particularly with the Centre for Ethics and Law. He serves as a non-executive director or trustee with a variety of plc, limited company, LLP, ABS and charitable bodies. He is also the former director of the Legal Services Institute (a charitable think-tank originally established by The College of Law).

David Neuberger

Lord Neuberger of Abbotsbury is President of the Supreme Court of the United Kingdom. Between 2006 and 2007, he led an investigation for the Bar Council into widening access to the Bar. He also served on the Panel on Fair Access to the Professions, led by former Health Secretary Alan Milburn, which reported in July 2009.

Dawn Oliver

Dawn Oliver Q.C. is Emeritus Professor of Constitutional Law at University College London. She served as Dean of the Faculty from 1993 to 1998 and in 2007. She was editor of *Public Law* from 1993 to 2002. Professor Oliver was also Member of the Royal Commission on Reform of the House of Lords, 1999–2000, Member of the Fabian Society Commission on the Future of the Monarchy, 2002–3, Chair of the UK Constitutional Law Group, 2005–10 and a member of the Executive Committee of the International Association of Constitutional Law, 2007–10.

Roger Ormrod

Lord Justice Ormrod was a Privy Councillor and Lord Justice of Appeal (1974–82). He Chaired the landmark 1968 Lord Chancellor's Committee on Legal Education (known as the 'Ormrod Review').

Vivian Ramsey

Hon. Sir Vivian Ramsey is a former High Court judge. Appointed to the High Court Bench in 2005, Sir Vivian Ramsey was voted Construction Silk of the Year by Chambers Directory. He served as Head of Chambers from 2002 until his appointment to the Bench, where he is a judge in the Technology and Construction Court. He continues as joint editor, with Stephen Furst Q.C., of the seventh, eighth and ninth editions of *Keating on Construction Contracts*.

Wes Streeting

Wes Streeting was elected Member of Parliament for Ilford North in the 2015 General Election. He was President of the National Union of Students from 2008 to 2010. In March 2009 *Pink News* listed him as the thirty-third most powerful LGBT politician in the United Kingdom. He was previously Head of Education at Stonewall, where he led their 'Education for All' campaign to tackle homophobia in schools, and also previously served as Chief Executive of the Helena Kennedy Foundation.

Julian Webb

Julian Webb is Professor of Law at the University of Melbourne, Australia, Honorary Professor of Law at the University of Exeter, and a Visiting Professor at Derby Law School. He has previously held chairs at the Universities of Warwick and Westminster in the UK, and between 2006–11 was Director of the UK Centre for Legal Education. He has published extensively on legal education policy and practice, on the legal profession and on lawyers' ethics and regulation. From 1998 to 2008, he was a founding editor of the international journal *Legal Ethics*. He has been involved in a range of legal education reform projects across the UK, Australia and New Zealand since the 1990s, and is co-author (with Professors Jane Ching, Paul Maharg and Avrom Sherr) of *Setting Standards*, the report on the research phase of the BSB/IPS/SRA Legal Education and Training Review (2013).

Harry Woolf

Lord Woolf C.J. was Master of the Rolls from 1996 until 2000 and Lord Chief Justice of England and Wales from 2000 until 2005. His committee work in the 1990s led to the Civil Procedure Rules 1998 and a significant modernisation of the civil litigation process.

1 The Lord Upjohn Lectures and Legal Education

Chris Ashford, Nigel Duncan and Jessica Guth

Lord Upjohn was the first President of the Association of Law Teachers (ALT), serving from 1966 until his untimely death in 1971. An appreciation of Lord Upjohn by Sir Jack Jacob[1] appears below. The first Lord Upjohn Lecture was delivered by Lord Diplock in December 1971 at Gray's Inn before an audience including Lady Upjohn, Lord Denning, Lord Morris, the President of the Law Society, a large number of judges from the High Court and the Court of Appeal amongst many others.[2] His subject was 'The Common Market and the Common Law'.[3] This and many of the subsequent lectures were published in the Association's journal, *The Law Teacher*, where they can be found in the archive maintained by Routledge.[4] The lectures covered a wide variety of topics of interest to members of the Association. In addition, many focused directly on issues of legal education. We have chosen 11 of those lectures to form the backbone of this book. In each case we have asked a current expert in the relevant field to provide a contemporary commentary. Some of the lectures exceeded the length permissible for inclusion in this volume and have been edited. The full versions are, of course, available from the Routledge archive.

The lectures reflect the focus of the ALT in promoting excellence in legal education, bringing together scholars, practitioners, policy-makers and other key stakeholders to debate and reflect on legal education discourse. In 2015, the Association celebrated its fiftieth anniversary. It was born into the radicalism and idealism of 1960s' education and activism. In looking back at these lectures, we are able to document not just the historical debates of legal education policy and pedagogy but to draw upon contemporary legal education voices to reconsider these arguments and to offer fresh reflections. Taken as a whole, this collection looks back to our history and forward to our future.

1 Originally published as 'The Rt. Hon. Lord Upjohn, C.B.E., D.L., Honorary President of the Association of Law Teachers 1966–1971: An appreciation', 1971, 5, 1, *Law Teacher*, 1.

2 Stan Marsh, *A History of the Association of Law Teachers, the First Twenty Five Years*, 1990, Sweet & Maxwell, 24.

3 Rt. Hon. Lord Diplock P.C., 'The Common Market and the Common Law', 1972, 6, 1, *Law Teacher*, 3.

4 See <http://www.tandfonline.com/loi/ralt20#.VTDcpy5ChHY>, accessed 17 April 2015.

In doing so, the editors hope that this collection enables readers in some way to reconnect with the ambition and radicalism that characterised our foundation. We hope that it will enable legal education scholarship to move beyond the well-worn grooves of discourse that too-often characterise scholarship in this field. Binary debate, whether it is vocationalism verses liberal arts, technology verses 'tradition', creative versus rigour in pedagogic practice, or other such binary choices, have had their value, but there is a need to move beyond these well-rehearsed and too familiar discussions. Recent years have seen greater reliance on empirical work alongside greater sophistication in the application of theory to legal education scholarship. Yet, there remains a need to deepen our scholarship and to engage with broader literature.[5]

We have been fortunate in our authors. The Lord Upjohn Lecturers themselves include senior judges, experienced academics, professional regulators and those who have experience in more than one of those fields. Their lectures have come at key points in their work. Thus Lord Woolf wrote at the point of introducing the 'Woolf reforms' of civil litigation. David Edmonds, then Chair of the Legal Services Board, used his Lord Upjohn Lecture to introduce the Legal Education and Training Review (LETR), the key event in legal education policy development in England and Wales. Lord Neuberger, then President of the Supreme Court, introduced themes he was developing elsewhere in his speeches and writing to respond to the LETR, which was at that time shortly due to report. Our contemporary commentators are, we hope you will agree, equally well-chosen. For example, Sir Vivian Ramsey, who responds to Lord Woolf's lecture, was, in 2012, appointed to lead the implementation of the 'Jackson reforms' which built on Woolf and are changing practice in the civil justice system as we write. Professor Stephen Mayson, a key commentator on the consequences of the Legal Services Act 2007, addresses the views of David Edmonds. Professor Julian Webb, Lead Researcher of LETR and lead author of its report,[6] provides a response to Lord Neuberger's Lecture.

The lectures are not presented in chronological order. We start with Lord Neuberger, the most recent of our Lord Upjohn Lecturers, and Julian Webb. Being such a recent lecture there was little need for Webb to update us. Instead, he chooses to set out the context of historical attempts to improve legal education before directly addressing Lord Neuberger's arguments. This provides a useful overview and places much of what follows in this book in context. Webb's historical overview covers some two centuries, and demonstrates a compromise flowing through the changes which have occurred, with vested interests a factor in that compromise. He criticises Neuberger for repeating that compromise, although he

5 J Ching, P Maharg, A Sherr and J Webb, Lord Upjohn Lecture 2014, 'An overture for well-tempered regulators: four variations on a LETR theme', 2015, *Law Teacher*, DOI:10.1080/03069400.2015.1035866.

6 LETR, *Setting Standards: The future of legal services education and training in England and Wales*, 2013, <http://letr.org.uk/>, accessed 8 June 2015.

recognises that the same is true of the LETR Report. Webb makes more radical suggestions. Might training for the Bar, for example, not be a post-qualification matter, as it is in Scotland? A more fundamental critique is the limited reference to access to justice. Do we allow too much focus on the needs of the corporate sector? This cannot be resolved by changes to legal education alone; instead we need to think about the design of rule of law systems. The contributions by Sir Vivian Ramsey and Nigel Duncan give some indication of the interaction between changes in the justice system and the legal education that prepares people for it, but Webb proposes a more open inquiry. He reiterates the need for a Legal Education Council to make progress with this.

The next four contributions address significant legal education policy areas. Wes Streeting's lecture, based on his experience as President of the National Union of Students and subsequently as Chief Executive of the Helena Kennedy Foundation, addressed widening participation. He identified *desiderata* and made practical proposals as to how they might be addressed. Graeme Broadbent's response develops Streeting's own arguments and places them in a historical context. He draws on the scholarship of widening participation in respect of higher education generally, but applies it particularly to legal education. He recognises that access is insufficient if students are not adequately prepared for all aspects of the experience of higher legal education and that retention is equally important. A key element to this is the information available to aspiring law students. He looks critically at the official information available through the NSS[7] and the KIS[8] and then develops his argument through an exploration of the plethora of conflicting advice available through universities' own websites, social networks and personal connections. Through this analysis he shows how those intended to benefit from widening participation continue to suffer from structural and informational disadvantages.

David Edmonds's lecture, as mentioned above, introduced the LETR with a series of challenges to legal educators and the legal professions. Stephen Mayson analyses the Report of that Review pointing out the limited extent to which it met Edmonds's aspirations for it. He identifies specific shortcomings with the Report, flowing largely, in his view, from a failure to step away from the existing framework of major professional bodies. He proposes, instead, that ensuring the competence and ethics of those providing legal services must be disconnected from awarding a title. Further attention must be paid to a number of interrelated central challenges. Much legal work is non-reserved activities and may be provided by solicitors or barristers, or by practitioners who are not subject to similar levels of regulation. Within solicitors' firms as well as the new alternative business structures there are those whose central role is service provision and

7 Ipsos MORI, 'The National Student Survey', http://www.thestudentsurvey.com/about.php, accessed 8 June 2015.

8 Higher Education Statistics Agency, 'Key Information Sets', <https://www.hesa.ac.uk/index.php?option=com_studrec&Itemid=232&mnl=15061>, accessed 8 June 2015.

others whose central role is owning and managing the business. The interaction between individual regulation and entity needs further work. Mayson then identifies five key areas where practitioners may fail to meet the desired standards and five specific aspects of the processes of preparing lawyers for practice which need to be developed. Ultimately, his concern is that the current review process is too tied into the existing professional structure to respond effectively to the rapidly changing legal services marketplace.

Four contributions address the specific demands of preparing lawyers for the process of litigation, particularly in the civil sphere. Lord Woolf's Lord Upjohn Lecture explained the 'Woolf Reforms',[9] their implementation and their implications for legal education. This focused on the professional stage of legal education and training. These reforms have been a qualified success, having effectively encouraged greater use of ADR and thus diverted many cases from expensive and time-consuming court hearings, but have done less to control costs. As a result, Sir Rupert Jackson was asked to undertake a further review. His report[10] develops court management powers and focuses in particular on the costs of the litigation process. Sir Vivian Ramsey explains how these reforms are being implemented in practice. He focuses on the way in which the concept of proportionality has been entrenched, drawing attention, as he does so, to the dialectical process whereby its introduction in the Woolf reforms appeared to be undermined by the decision of *Lownds v Home Office*[11] (a decision of Lord Woolf himself) and has now been reinforced with a statutory definition that gives more power to the judges in their attempts to control costs. He also considers the impact of the Human Rights Act, new legislation at the time of Lord Woolf's lecture, with its potential for conflict between legislature and judiciary, and concludes with a survey of the way in which legal education has responded to these changes.

Sir Roger Ormrod, writing a quarter of a century earlier than Lord Woolf, explained the consequences for solicitors and advocates of the then recent changes in court practices and procedures. These continued to create problems which he identified and placed in the context of changes to education and training for the Bar which had developed in the light of his own Report[12] of a few years earlier. Nigel Duncan adopts an historical perspective to draw attention to two developments. One is the changes in the civil justice system referred to above by Lord Woolf and Sir Vivian Ramsey which he summarises to show how the various strands interact. The second development is that in education for the Bar. He explains the way in which a modern Bar Professional Training Course integrates the different areas of learning that students must achieve and uses a particular example from the course at his own School. This is supported by the results of

9 *Access to Justice, Final Report.* HMSO, July 1996 ('Access to Justice').

10 Sir Rupert Jackson, *Final Report on Civil Litigation Costs*, December 2009.

11 *Lownds v Home Office* [2002] EWCA Civ 365.

12 Ormrod Report (1971), *Report of the Committee on Legal Education*, Cmnd No 4595. London: HMSO.

an evaluation recently undertaken into student responses to this element of their learning. It is indicative of the strides that have been made in constructing professional programmes which focus on preparing people for practice in a changing environment.

Two contributions then focus specifically on students. Ruth Deech, in her Lord Upjohn Lecture, considered student contracts as a way of regulating the relationship between universities and students. She noted that contracts which set out duties on both sides highlight that education cannot simply be delivered to a passive audience, but she also noted that education is a life event which does not easily lend itself to contractual regulation and that the relationship between student and university is rather more complex. Rebecca Huxley-Binns takes up this notion of complexity in her response to Deech. She reminds us that students starting university now have very different experiences and expectations than we did when we started and that we must therefore challenge some of the assumptions (such as the distinction between knowledge and skills) made by Deech. Huxley-Binns conceptualises the relationship between university and student more as a psychological rather than a legal contract and encourages us to remember that we teach better when we understand that our students learn differently to how we did.

Mr Justice Goff (as he then was, before elevation through the Court of Appeal to become the Senior Law Lord) chose as his topic the then course of professional training for the Bar. As Chairman of the Council of Legal Education he understood well the pressures on students and the provider and used that experience to suggest seven lessons for the future. He also pointed out how an effective professional course liberates the academic stage from the need to prepare students for practice. Susan Blake responds to these themes. She challenges his assertion that standards of scholarship are often higher in the Inns of Court than in the universities, pointing out the essential difference in focus. While Mr Justice Goff sought a middle way between analytical and sociological jurisprudence, Blake suggests that the current focus on commercial law has made that balance harder to achieve. She also considers the impact of the changes to the funding of higher education and the current changes in regulation for the academy. Looking to the future she proposes six developments which will be key: the limited range of reserved activities; the developing use of technology in the courts; the development of alternative business structures; the withering of public funding for litigation; the growth of ADR; and the impact of globalisation.

Lord Justice Lawton's tenth Lord Upjohn Lecture in 1980 reflected on the legal education needs of the legal profession, whilst looking back and criticising aspects of his own 1930s' legal education: 'I had no tutorials and no opportunity of discussing legal problems with any knowledgeable persons' save for his time at Cambridge University. Looking back upon his own 50 years in the legal profession, Lawton argued for a 'good education' with a focus upon a mastery of the English language. Lawton did not merely look back in his lecture. He noted the increased use of technology within legal practice and the increased internationalisation of law, advocating graduates fit for the modern world of legal practice. Chris Ashford notes that Lawton's view of legal education and the needs of the profession are inevitably shaped by his background as well as his position. The lack of diversity in the profession then, as now, is striking and differences within and between legal professions as well as Law Schools are not sufficiently recognised and acknowledged. Ashford notes the impact this has on the 'tug of war' between law as an academic discipline and Law Schools as training schools for the professions. He raises questions about how well the profession knows what it needs and suggest that it cannot help but perpetuate that which has always been as it reflects its past into the future.

Lord Griffith, giving his lecture in 1993, was embarking on the major initiative of the Lord Chancellor's Advisory Committee on Legal Education and Conduct (ACLEC). This detailed consultation and analysis of legal education and the profession is discussed in many of the chapters in this book, even though, in the end, its recommendations were never implemented. John Hodgson places Lord Griffiths's arguments in a historical context in order to bring our understanding of how regulation of legal education has changed over 20 years. This explains the way in which the Clementi Report and the Legal Services Act 2007 have established a completely new approach, with extra layers of regulator, but a more limited perspective on regulation. He then explores the way in which the Solicitors' Regulation Authority has approached its task. His critique covers the methodology used and a lack of transparency in the ways in which conclusions are reached. This is in significant contrast to the working methods of ACLEC. Most significantly, perhaps, is a concern for the apparent goals of the exercise. Identifying the contrasting approaches in Lord Upjohn Lectures by David Edmonds and Lord Neuberger, Hodgson warns of the consequences if the regulators abandon a concern for the values of quality legal education in its own right.

J.A.G. Griffith's 1981 lecture sought to focus upon the teaching of law and politics. Griffith challenged a narrative that considered socio-legal or the sociology of law to be a new approach to the study of law. He noted his own legal education of the late 1930s and early 1940s in which he was taught by Kahn-Freund, Robson, Ivor Jennings and Harold Laski. His education was one in which teaching placed law in the context of politics and society. He dealt with the reception to his text *The Politics of the Judiciary*, which continues to be a key reference point for contemporary students of public law, and in a final teasing section, Griffith called for the abolition of the binary distinction between universities and polytechnics, appropriately fusing law and politics to conclude his lecture. Anthony Bradney seeks to address Griffiths directly 33 years on. 'Thirty-three years after Griffith's lecture matters should be different; 33 years later they are different', he opens. He challenges Griffith's assumptions about socio-legal studies, noting Griffith's own education at the London School of Economics and the unique approach to law until the 1970s that the LSE offered. Griffith's experience – Bradney suggests – was far from typical. He notes the transformation within socio-legal studies since the original lecture but also notes a growing chasm between the research of public law which is more likely to engage with theory and a broader context, whilst 'teaching law and politics is still stuck in the past', and noting that if public law texts are 'books about law and politics, and many are, they are more about law than they are about politics'.

Dawn Oliver delivered her Lord Upjohn Lecture in May 1996 as Law School submissions for the Research Assessment Exercise had been sent off and results were awaited. She commented on the difficulties of managing both teaching and research activity in Law Schools and noted that it is not realistic to expect all Law Schools to receive research funding, considering the relationship between research and teaching as one which is in tension. She expressed concern that we, as legal academics, are being turned into 'teaching and research machines' and the impact that this is likely to have on the 'world of intellectual responsibility and intellectual discovery'[13] which we inhabit. Jessica Guth's response to Oliver is characterised by surprise at how contemporary Oliver's lecture seems, almost two decades on, commenting that 'the debates may not have changed but they have become more nuanced and our understanding of what legal education is, what research is, and what teaching is has also developed'. Guth asks why our teaching should be influenced by research, and vice versa. She goes on to advocate and explore the importance of research-informed and research-led teaching, positioning research at the centre of the teaching of law, rather than at the periphery of the Law School or as an alternative to law teaching.

Brought together, these chapters provide a context for our current review of how we best conduct legal education and training and ideas as to how it might best be taken forward. They are drawn from different perspectives and express, sometimes, conflicting views. You will find analyses to challenge your own, but also material to develop your own thinking. We hope that you will find it a useful contribution and will stimulate a more fruitful debate. What is clearly needed is an effective forum for that debate to be taken forward and to develop resources and understanding. The LETR Report called for a Legal Education Council to do this and to advise the regulators.[14] William Twining has argued cogently for a 'national institute for legal education and training to replace UKCLE as a cross-sector meeting ground for all interested in LET . . . and as a centre for research and development on all aspects of legal education and training'.[15] The need for some such body is now urgent and is a matter on which all interested in the quality and effectiveness of legal education and training should be able to agree upon.

13 Dawn Oliver, 'The Integration of Teaching and Research in the Law Department', 1996, 30, 2, *Law Teacher*, 133, 149.

14 LETR (n 6), Recommendation 25.

15 William Twining, 'LETR: the role of academics in legal education and training: 10 theses', 2014, 48, 1, *Law Teacher*, 94, at 103.

2 The Rt. Hon. Lord Upjohn, C.B.E., D.L.

Honorary President of the Association of Law Teachers, 1966–1971: An Appreciation

Sir I. H. Jacob Q.C.

THE untimely death of Lord Upjohn at the age of sixty-seven has grievously robbed the law of one of its outstanding figures and has sadly deprived the Association of Law Teachers of its first President.

Gerald Upjohn had as distinguished a legal career as anyone in the annals of the law, a career which took him in a natural, almost inevitable, progression to the House of Lords. In 1929, at the age of twenty-five, he was called to the Bar by Lincoln's Inn, of which he became a Bencher in 1948 and Treasurer in 1965. He enjoyed a busy practice at the Chancery Bar, competing with other front-ranking practitioners of the time, as a Junior before the war and, taking silk in 1943, as a silk after the war. (In parentheses, one may recall that in consultation he was incisive as well as decisive, so that the client, above all others, knew exactly where he stood.) In 1951, at the age of forty-eight, he was appointed a judge of the Chancery Division, and he served for four years in the Restrictive Practices Court. In 1960 he was promoted to the Court of Appeal, and in 1963 he became a Lord of Appeal in Ordinary and sat regularly on appeals to the House of Lords and frequently on appeals to the Judicial Committee of the Privy Council. His work as a judge for a period of nearly twenty years made him, it has been said, one of the best Chancery judges of our time, and, perhaps one may say, of this century. As a judge, he was courteous and patient, yet quick and anxious to get to the heart of the case. He was passionately as well as intellectually imbued with the principles of equity, not as a body of outdated doctrines and technicalities, but as a living concept of fairness, honest dealing and even-balanced justice. He greatly enriched the life of the law and our jurisprudence with his clear, careful, wise, discerning, polished judgments, very few of which can be faulted and most of which will long endure not only as authorities but as models of expression.

Lord Upjohn applied his exceptional talents without stint to many fields of public service and to his varied interests outside the law. In the war, he joined the Welsh Guards, rose to the rank of Brigadier, and served as Vice-President of the Allied Control Commission. After the war he served on a number of tribunals and inquiries, the most well known of which was the Lynskey Tribunal which inquired into the Stanley affair. He was a member of the celebrated Evershed

Committee on Supreme Court Practice and Procedure. He was Chairman of the St. George's Hospital Medical School, and he was a prominent Freemason. Not surprisingly, in 1945 he was made a C.B.E. and in 1946 he was appointed to be an officer of the Legion of Merit.

Looking back over six years, a period of time small in measure but vast in growth, it is difficult to believe how tentative, even perhaps speculative, were the beginnings of the Association of Law Teachers. That it has now, more rapidly than might have been the case, come to be accepted as a well-based, important, influential and flourishing Association, and not only in the field of legal education, may be largely due to the act of faith made by Lord Upjohn in joining up with what might have been regarded as a body of break-away law teachers seeking, as it were, 'a local habitation and a name', a new identity. By becoming its President in 1966, Lord Upjohn gave the new Association status as well as stature, and at the same time he infused the early pioneers with new hope and encouragement. As its first President, he seemed, as it were, to be conferring on the new Association not only acceptability or even respectability but also authority. The Association thereafter became a viable institution, able to live out and develop its own life as an independent body. The extraordinary growth of the Association since these early days is palpable proof that Lord Upjohn's instinct as well as his judgment was right.

As President, Lord Upjohn took an active interest in the affairs of the Association. He regularly attended its Annual Dinners, at which he presided with enormous charm and aplomb, reporting, as though to an annual meeting of shareholders, the main work accomplished by their President in the previous year in the House of Lords and the Judicial Committee of the Privy Council. He particularly delighted in describing the latest state of play in the game centred around the deserted wife's 'equity' in the matrimonial home. It was a great disappointment, as much to him as to all the members of the Association, that illness prevented him from presiding at last year's Annual Dinner, which was held in the Great Hall of Trinity College, Cambridge, which he had himself gone to so much trouble to obtain as a venue for the occasion.

In the afternoon of Lord Upjohn's sudden death on January 27, 1971, the Lord Chancellor, Lord Hailsham, described him to the Appellate Committee of the House of Lords as 'a superlative judge'.

We mourn him as a superlative friend of the Association of Law Teachers, which owes him an eternal debt of gratitude. To Lady Upjohn, who so signally supported him and added so much by her grace and charm to the gatherings of the Association which she attended with him, we extend our heartfelt sorrow at the passing of so great and so gentle a man.

3 Forty-first Lord Upjohn Lecture 2012

Reforming Legal Education*

Lord Neuberger of Abbotsbury

Introduction[1]

It is an honour, albeit something of a daunting honour, to have been asked to give the Lord Upjohn Lecture, at this important time for legal education. It is two years since David Edmonds, who chairs the Legal Services Board (the LSB), delivered this lecture, which was, as he put it, based on a hypothesis. That hypothesis was simple: that the '*dialogue and interplay* [between legal practice and education] *isn't happening at the level it should*'. He went on to suggest that '*some people*' went further than this hypothesis and believed that the current framework for legal education and training was '*simply not fit for purpose*'.[2]

Since June 2011, the Legal Education and Training Review (the LETR) team, led by four Professors of legal education, has been testing that hypothesis.[3] Although perhaps partly inspired by those thoughts, the LETR was not established by the LSB. It was established as a joint venture by the 'professional regulators': the Solicitors Regulation Authority (SRA), Bar Standards Board (BSB) and the Chartered Institute of Legal Executives Professional Standards (IPS). These professional regulators, all of which can be said to sit under the LSB, are responsible for ensuring that legal education is 'fit for purpose'. In that connection, the LSB's role is essentially subsidiary: if asked, it must assist the professional regulators in maintaining standards of legal education and training of lawyers.[4]

The LETR is due to report next month. When it does, the professional regulators will no doubt carefully scrutinise the quality and statistical reliability of its evidence, the soundness of its underpinning assumptions (including its understanding of the professional environment), and the validity of its conclusions.

* This lecture was delivered as the forty-first Lord Upjohn Lecture at City Law School on 15 November 2012.

1 I wish to thank John Sorabji for all his help in preparing this lecture.

2 D. Edmonds, *Training the lawyers of the future – a regulator's view* (Lord Upjohn Lecture 2010) (2011) 45 *Law Teacher*, 4, <http://www.legalservicesboard.org.uk/news_publications/speeches_presentations/2010/de_lord_upjohn_lec.pdf>.

3 See <http://letr.org.uk/about/research-team/>.

4 Legal Services Act 2007, s 4.

Having considered such matters, and made their consequent assessment of the validity of any resulting recommendations, the professional regulators will then have to decide on the next step in the review process.

I suggest that it may well make sense to institute a second phase to the review – a phase which is practical and professional, to complement the report's initial, academic-based phase. One of the complaints made about previous reform efforts was that they have been too focused on professional experience, ignoring educational theory.[5] We should not now make the opposite mistake and proceed without taking into account practical, professional experience. It is, of course, true to say that the Review has carried out consultations, but it has necessarily done so from a single perspective. It must be right to combine the educative expertise, experience and theory with the professional expertise, experience and requirements.

Any such second phase should be the product of collaborative work by representatives of the professions, the judiciary, and consumer groups, including the Legal Services Consumer Panel and the Legal Ombudsman. They all have a direct interest in the development of education and training, as well as being able to provide practical insights. The judiciary in particular brings both practical and principled insights. The judges have many years of accumulated legal practice, are quasi-consumers of legal services in court, represent the branch of the state which upholds and enforces the rule of law, and constitute the ultimate disciplinary appeal body of the legal profession. Consumer groups also offer fundamentally important insights, born of the need to secure good quality legal advice and assistance at proportionate cost, in a market place where an increasing number of business models are being developed by lawyers, as well as individuals who are not part of the regulated professions.

A preliminary call for open minds

I should emphasise that, in my view, it remains an open question whether the hypothesis that the present system is not fit for purpose is anything other than assertion, whether it is made generally or in respect of aspects of the system. There is real reason for doubting whether there is that much wrong. UK lawyers enjoy a high worldwide reputation. Places on our university law degrees, at both undergraduate and postgraduate level, are highly sought after. Research and publications of academics in our universities are of high value and enjoy international recognition. Our courts and our substantive law are prized throughout the world – not only by those who seek to litigate in our courts, but also by those who seek our judges and lawyers out to assist them in the development of their laws and justice systems. Some of these points may largely apply to the more

5 LETR, *Draft Literature Review*, at [71], <http://letr.org.uk/wp-content/uploads/2011/06/LR-chapter-2.pdf >

financially rewarding end of the profession. Nonetheless, they do firmly shift the onus on to those asserting education and training is unfit for purpose.

However, the main issue is not whether the legal education and training system can in any way be described as not fit for purpose: it is what reforms should sensibly be made. It would be absurdly complacent to pretend that there are no improvements to be made to the system. But if we can properly marry the educational, professional, judicial and consumer perspectives, we are far more likely to identify in what way they could be improved and the nature of any appropriate improvement.

I cannot share the view which David Edmonds was reported in *The Guardian* as expressing in March this year, namely that he would be '*extremely disappointed*' if the LETR only made minor recommendations.[6] That suggests a conclusion that major reform is both necessary and proportionate, reached in the absence of any evidence and analysis. But surely we should wait for the evidence, the analysis of that evidence, and the conclusions drawn from that analysis, before we start talking of disappointment or the nature of the appropriate recommendations. We should all be surely approaching the Review and its outcome with an open mind. So, at best, Mr Edmonds's statement should be taken as a hypothesis not a conclusion, and perhaps that is what it was meant to be.

A little parable

Before I consider some issues which might well be relevant to any consideration of the LETR's report, with a view to testing the hypothesis rather than advancing any premature conclusion, let us take a short detour to Bruges. In *The Undercover Economist*, Tim Harford recounts the development of that city from the end of the 9th century. Having been a small city in the Zwin estuary, Bruges grew into the capital of Flanders and the centre of the Hanseatic League.

Prosperity brought with it the development of the diamond-cutting industry, and the creation of nascent stock exchanges in the taverns owned by the Van der Beurs family, from which it is suggested the modern continental Bourses take their name today.[7] Innovation brought with it further prosperity, which continued unabated for nearly six hundred years. But then, as Harford explains,

> '*something strange began to happen. The Zwin began to silt up. The great ships could no longer reach the docks of Bruges. The Hanseatic League moved up the coast to Antwerp. Bruges quickly and literally became a backwater. So lifeless did it become that it was nicknamed "Bruges-La-Morte". Today it is a quaint museum piece . . .*'[8]

6 D. Edmonds cited in N. Rose, *Forget Tesco Law, this legal education review will transform the legal market* (*The Guardian*, 19 March 2012), <http://www.guardian.co.uk/law/2012/mar/19/review-legal-education-change-market>

7 T. Harford, *The Undercover Economist* (Abacus) (2006) at 203–4.

8 T. Harford, ibid. at 204.

The success of Bruges stemmed from one feature: the Zwin, and the burghers of Bruges either forgot their city's raison d'être, or they simply failed to protect it.

The first question for the professional regulators, when considering the reform of legal education, is this: what is the legal profession's raison d'être? Before we embark on reform, we need to be clear what that purpose is. And that also requires us to have in the forefront of our minds the raison d'être for the legal profession. If we are not clear about these issues, we are no better than the burghers of Bruges. We may in fact be worse: they did nothing to stop the river silting up. We may end up actually silting up the river if we embark on misguided reform.

The purpose of education and training according to the LETR

What then is the purpose of legal education and training? The LETR suggested an answer to that question,

> *'The primary objective of the Review is to ensure that England and Wales has a legal education and training system which advances the regulatory objectives contained in the Legal Services Act 2007, and particularly the need to protect and promote the interests of consumers and to ensure an independent, strong, diverse and effective legal profession.'*[9]

I am afraid that that is not a good start. It is true that legal education and training should be consistent with the regulatory objectives specified in the 2007 Act. But those objectives also include improving access to justice, promoting competition in the provision of legal activities, increasing public understanding of the citizen's legal rights and duties, and promoting and maintaining adherence to the professional principles, which include acting in the best interests of clients, and independence in the interests of justice.[10] It is worrying that the Review decided to describe its fundamental aim as directed to only two of the regulatory objectives: the interests of consumers, and a diverse and effective legal profession.

By singling out two of the regulatory objectives in this way, the Review team may well have provided themselves with a deformed theodolite through which to survey the field. Its report into the case for reform may therefore be unbalanced or worse. Any proper assessment of the case for reform must primarily take account of what I would suggest are the two fundamental regulatory objectives specified in the 2007 Act:[11] the need to protect and promote the public interest, and the need to support the constitutional principle of the rule of law.

Parliament did not specify an order of precedence amongst the regulatory objectives, but it is clear that the two objectives singled out by the LETR are a significant aspect, but nonetheless only an aspect, of the two fundamental

9 <http://letr.org.uk/about/what-is-letr/>.
10 Legal Services Act 2007, ss 1(1)–(3).
11 Legal Services Act 2007, s 1(1).

objectives. Improving access to justice and promotion of competition, serve both to protect and promote the public interest and to support the rule of law. Like the other statutory objectives, they thereby support the two fundamental objectives. In other words, there are the two fundamental objectives, and there are the other objectives (including the two singled out by the LETR) which facilitate the achievement of the fundamental objectives. And they are limited by the fundamental objectives: promoting competition, diversity, and consumer interest are only valid aims to the extent that they are compatible with protecting and promoting the public interest and with the rule of law.

What is the purpose of legal education and training?

This leads me directly to the question of the purpose of the legal profession. A vibrant, independent legal profession is an essential element of any democratic society committed to the rule of law. It is not merely another form of business, solely aimed at maximising profit whilst providing a competitive service to consumers. I am far from suggesting that lawyers ought not to seek to maximise their profits, or ought not to provide a competitive service. What I am saying is that lawyers also owe overriding specific duties to the court and to society, duties which go beyond the maximisation of profit and which may require lawyers to act to their own detriment, and to that of their clients.

The duty to the court, to conduct litigation honestly and strictly in accordance with the rules of court, may well require a lawyer to act to his or her client's detriment. The duty to disclose to the court, and one's opponent, a document or an authority which goes against one's case is hardly in one's client's best interests. It is, however, firmly in the public interest. It is essential if we are properly committed to the rule of law, rather than the rule of unscrupulous lawyers who wish to win at all costs.

Asking and answering the question whether legal education and training is fit for purpose, or the more measured question of how it could be improved, must begin with an assessment of whether it properly equips those entering the profession with the knowledge, skills, integrity and sense of independence which will enable them to play their proper role in maintaining the rule of law. It is within that overarching framework that other considerations, such as those in the facilitative regulatory objectives, gain their value and meaning.

This point was not lost on the Carnegie Foundation for the Advancement of Teaching, when, in 2007, it published the results of a two-year study into legal education in the United States, which included a number of recommendations for the reform of legal education.[12] In a short summary at the start of the report, the authors make the following point,

12 W. Sullivan, A Colby, J. Welch Wegner, L. Bond, L. Shulman, *Educating Lawyers – Preparation for the Profession of Law* (2007) (Wiley).

> *'The profession of law is fundamental to the flourishing of American democracy* [one could omit the word 'American']. *Today, however, critics of the legal profession, both from within and without, have pointed to a great profession suffering from varying degrees of confusion and demoralisation.'*[13]

The profession of law is fundamental to democracy, because it is through good quality legal advice and good quality legal representation that citizens can effectively enforce their private rights in courts and tribunals, can gain a proper understanding of their rights and duties, can order their affairs lawfully, and can hold the powerful executive to account. The starting point for any review of legal education and training is how it can best equip those who enter the profession to fulfil this role. If we exclusively focus on promoting consumer interests, on the development of law as a trade, by treating the provision of legal services as any old commodity, we cast aside its fundamental role and purpose, its raison d'être, and we undermine the rule of law and our democracy.

The Carnegie Foundation report is particularly in point given that some people suggest we might well adopt a US-style approach to legal education here. There is, of course, the fundamental point, borne out by many misconceived reforms in many fields, that it is unwise for us to adopt a system which has developed in a legal, social and political culture which, whilst similar to ours in some ways, is profoundly different in others. But it is even more unwise to be advocating the adoption of a foreign system which is being operated by people who are seeking to reform it in the light of its serious weaknesses.

To return to Bruges, if, and I emphasise the 'if', the Zwin is silting up, it is because legal education and training has lost sight of the fact that it is intended to produce professionals who have the necessary knowledge, skills, integrity and independence to serve the rule of law. I now want to turn to some of the issues on which the professional regulators may want to focus when they consider the LETR's report.

Three forms of apprenticeship

The Carnegie Foundation report suggests that there are '*three conceptual apprenticeships*'[14] involved in legal education. They are,

13 W. Sullivan, A Colby, J. Welch Wegner, L. Bond, L. Shulman, *Educating Lawyers – Preparation for the Profession of Law: Summary and Recommendations* (2007) (The Carnegie Foundation for the Advancement of Teaching) at 3, <http://www.carnegiefoundation.org/sites/default/files/publications/elibrary_pdf_632.pdf>.

14 For a short discussion see J. Welch Wegner, *The Carnegie Foundation's Educating Lawyers: Four Questions for Bar Examiners* (The Bar Examiner, June 2011) at 14, <http://law.ubalt.edu/academics/pdfs/Carnegie%20Report%20article_final.pdf>.

> *'the cognitive apprenticeship that relates to ways of thinking in the context of relevant subject matter*
>
> *the apprenticeship of skills and practice that relates to developing an ability to do or produce what professionals in a given field must do or produce, and to act in a way that those professionals must act*
>
> *an apprenticeship of professional identity and values that concerns an emerging professional's capacity to navigate the relationship between his or her personal and professional values and ways of being in the world.'*[15]

This seems to me to be an unexceptionable, if perhaps rather analytical and particulate, approach which is equally valid for our legal system. After all, the profession of law can be said to be taught in England and Wales through the same three conceptual stages.

The cognitive apprenticeship is undergone when aspiring solicitors or barristers are undergoing their university degree or Graduate Diploma in Law, or, in the case of legal executives, whilst they are doing their CILEX Diploma. The cognitive apprenticeship is further refined at the same time as the apprenticeship of skills and practice, at the LPC, BPTC, or CILEX Diploma stages. Although the first two forms are not then discarded, the third form of apprenticeship is honed through a solicitor's training contract, a barrister's pupillage, and the legal executive's employment.

If either of the first two aspects of apprenticeship, degree and qualification would benefit from change, which they very probably could to some extent, I would take a lot of persuading that root and branch reform is needed. It seems to me that such reform is normally expensive, disruptive, morale-undermining, and, courtesy of the law of unintended consequences, productive of a host of unexpected problems. The present system is one which produces many high quality lawyers, and radical reform may pose a threat to that. Accordingly, in the absence of very clear and cogent evidence of widespread and deep-rooted inadequacy in the present system, radical reform, as opposed to appropriate, targeted reform, should be avoided.

A common non-university route into the profession?

Serious thought may have to be given to the relationship between the manner in which CILEX carries out its apprenticeship and entry into the profession as a whole. CILEX qualification already provides a non-university route into qualification, and, for some, into the solicitors' profession. The cognitive, skills and practice apprenticeships experiences by CILEX fellows are roughly equivalent to the university degree, LPC, training contract route of entry to the solicitors' profession. CILEX fellows can already, following further training, qualify as advocates who can appear in a number of courts and tribunals.

15 Ibid.

It seems to me that a possible reform might be to develop the existing relationship between solicitors and legal executives and to extend that relationship to the Bar. Greater co-operation between the SRA and IPS could further facilitate the use of CILEX qualification as a route to qualification as a solicitor. Equally, the IPS and BSB could properly develop a similar qualification route via CILEX qualification to the Bar. The CILEX model of qualification as a solicitor could with some thought form the basis of a distinctive route not just to CILEX qualification in its own right, but to entry into the other two branches of the profession.

This is a step which the profession could possibly take to achieve greater diversity in a world where university education is becoming increasingly expensive. It may soon (if it does not already) cost in the region of £100,000 (if one includes living expenses) to qualify as a solicitor or barrister through the university route to qualification.[16] Increased cost of the university route is likely to pose a real danger to the promotion of diversity in the profession; a less diverse profession is an impoverished one, one less able to reflect and support a flourishing democracy committed to the rule of law. While the professional regulators plainly cannot ameliorate any adverse effects which might stem from increasing university tuition fees or compensate for any inequalities which arise through the education system, they can ensure that there is an effective, straightforward route to qualification into the three branches of the profession for non-graduates. There is more than one way to secure high quality cognitive, skills and practice apprenticeships and ensure that the excellence for which our legal profession is known is maintained, and enhanced, in the years to come. Building on the present CILEX route into the profession appears to me to be a good model.

Knowledge and skills

There could be a number of simple and effective improvements which could be considered to the first two forms of apprenticeship – the cognitive apprenticeship, and the apprenticeship of skills and practice.

It may well be worth considering reform of the content of qualifying law degrees, and of the Graduate Diploma in Law (GDL), which is itself a key means of facilitating diversity within the profession as it enables non-law graduates and those who seek career changes to enter the profession. As the law and society develop, so should legal education and training. Strong arguments can be made for adding civil procedure and human rights law to the list of core subjects on any qualifying law degree. Others may be able to stake their claim. A principled reconsideration of the core subjects is perhaps overdue. In any such reconsideration, it would be important not to cram too much into the qualifying law degree.

16 Assuming a three-year law degree, with tuition fees of £9,000 per year, a one-year LPC or BPTC at £15,000, and in those cases where a non-law degree requires a GDL to be undertaken, another £15,000. Figures approximate and exclude living expenses.

Any subjects considered core will have to go into an already overcrowded GDL. Further, there is the risk of limiting the freedom of universities to develop their own academic interests outside the core subjects, such as in legal history, jurisprudence, or Roman law, to name but a few.

It is also important that we do not lose sight of the need to ensure that the knowledge component of the university route through apprenticeship is not diluted. That said, it seems to me that both university and non-university legal education should develop what may be characterised as professional skills to a fuller degree than currently. I have in mind topics such as professional ethics, client dealing, understanding how institutions (such as the police and prisons) work and how to deal with them, and understanding business and finance. I believe that there is real scope for the development of such skills programmes as part of a law degree, similar to the clinical training already found in many existing degree courses.

Skills-training through applied practical work is not uncommon in university degrees in other subjects, and there is no reason why the professional regulators could not work with the universities to develop a practical skills curriculum to complement the academic core subjects of a law degree. Such courses would not only begin to develop the practical skills which would then be honed during the LPC and BPTC at an earlier stage, but enabling the skills courses on the vocational courses to be pitched at a higher level might better prepare trainees as they enter their pupillage and training contracts. They would also complement the academic subjects, enhancing students' ability to analyse the law, discern and apply and its principles.

The introduction of mandatory skills requirements in each year of an undergraduate degree would bring more practising lawyers into the university. Greater collaboration between academia and practice would benefit course design and delivery, as it would foster the exchange of ideas between the academic and practical aspects of law. Teaching wider skills also would enable law students to gain valuable experience through taking part in clinical education programmes. In the first year these could be virtual programmes, such as those developed by Professor Maharg, who is one of the LETR review team, for the Diploma in Legal Practice (the Scottish equivalent to the LPC) offered by Strathclyde University.[17] In the second and third years these could, under appropriate supervision, be clinical programmes which provide pro bono advice to members of the public, similar to those which are already in place on the vocational courses and in some universities. Such programmes could also usefully help students to become familiar with the practical reality of the court system, procedural law, and ADR. It could also begin to teach law through developing negotiation skills, drafting skills, and practical problem-solving skills, whilst embedding legal research skills.

17 See R. Susskind, *Briefing Paper – Provocations and Perspectives* (October 2012) at 20, <http://letr.org.uk/wp-content/uploads/2012/10/Susskind-LETR-final-Oct-2012.pdf>.

The third benefit which could flow from the development of greater skills training takes me to the third aspect of apprenticeship: of professional identity and values.

Professional identity and values

An important aspect of university education is to develop students as individuals during the course of their studies. If a compulsory skills component, along the lines I have suggested, were to be introduced into all qualifying law degrees, we could start to develop the professional identity of lawyers of the future at a much earlier stage than we do now. Equally, it would broaden the experiences of those students who do not aspire to enter the profession. Through a compulsory skills element we could teach professional ethics and the values which inform the profession. First, the teaching of skills through clinical programmes would enable students to appreciate their clients' concerns, the impact of their professional decisions, and the ethical challenges which will arise in practice. Second, the provision of pro bono assistance through such programmes would give a practical, direct, insight into the public value of legal work. Third, the students would thereby gain an early appreciation of professional values. In the brave new world of alternative business structures, where enhancing shareholder value may not naturally or always coincide with the professional's duty to the court, or the public interest, and outcome-focused regulation, these aspects will be increasingly important.

Professional ethics should not stop there. Through introducing ethics teaching in universities we can then improve the way in which it is taught on the vocational courses. All this would provide a strong mechanism to instil professional values into aspiring lawyers. Rather than being taught at entry level courses at that second stage, ethics training could be carried out at a higher level. Further, if clinical programmes are undertaken at university, clinical programmes on the vocational course – which might usefully be mandatory – could be carried out at a higher level, involving more complex, albeit still supervised work.

Diversity

Professional identity also includes valuing diversity. No discussion of the legal profession, or almost any other profession, function or calling, can be complete without considering this important topic. Legal education and training, and indeed entry into the legal profession, has much to be happy about so far as women are concerned and not that much to be unhappy about with regard to ethnic minorities. The problem there, of course, lies at the later stage, that of progression through the profession. The proportion of women and ethnic minorities decreases as one goes up the ladder, and the fact that the higher up the ladder one goes, the more one is looking at historic intakes, is nothing like a complete explanation. There is something, but I suspect a very limited amount, which legal education and training can do about this problem. In so far as it is attributable to societal or inherent factors, there is little one can expect specifically legal education and training to do about it. However, in so far as it is due to attitudes and cultures within chambers or law firms, it would be wholly right for the wider education and training which I am calling for to cover the topic with a view to changing things, within the bounds of propriety and practicality.

The big diversity problem for legal education and training is, of course, that those with more privileged social, educational and economic backgrounds are disproportionately represented in the universities, on the professional qualification courses, in pupillage and traineeships and as junior barristers and solicitors. The Milburn committee, of which I was a member, in its 2009 report, said that the professions should be doing more to encourage and include the less privileged.[18] I would make three points about that. First, I agree that the professions have that duty, and the legal profession, with its commitment to justice and the rule of law, has a particular duty. Second, the duty has to be circumscribed by practicality: solicitors and barristers are working in an increasingly challenging time nationally, following the 2007 Act, and internationally, in the light of increased globalisation of legal services, and even more in the present economic climate. Third, the professions cannot and should not be the whipping boys and girls to whom the Government transfers the blame for the inherent inequalities and dysfunctionalities of society.

Having said that, any proposed reforms to the structures or contents of legal education and training must take into account the need to improve diversity, both in those actually undergoing the education and training, and in terms of the contents of the education and training they receive. I am not in a position to say in exactly what way education could be restructured so as to improve access for the underprivileged, but to the extent to which it can be done without reducing quality, it should be. Nor can I say precisely how one can inculcate a different approach to the practice of law, or the structure of firms or chambers, so as to improve diversity both at entry and in relation to progression, but, again, anything which can help achieve this should be part of any set of recommendations.

The need for vocational training

I turn now to the third stage of training, vocational training. As with the first two stages, in the absence of clear and convincing evidence suggesting something more radical is needed, an approach of targeted, of relatively discrete, focused reforms is likely to be the optimum approach to take to vocational training.

One must begin by acknowledging the reforms which followed the detailed, evidence-based review into what is now the BPTC and pupillage produced by Derek Wood Q.C. But they do not mean that we should close our minds to further reforms.

18 *Unleashing Aspiration: The Final Report of the Panel on Fair Access to the Professions* <http://www.cabinetoffice.gov.uk/media/227102/fair-access.pdf>.

It is said by some that we should move to the US system where there is no pupillage or training contract requirement, which would have the benefit of enabling more students to move from the academic and vocational stages of training to practice. I cannot accept that such a reform could be consistent with maintaining quality standards within the profession, or even with maintaining the idea that the practice of law is a profession. Training and mentoring before an aspiring lawyer can practise independently are an essential means, not only to hone practical skills in the working environment, but they also serve to embed a professional ethos.

The best plumbers or electricians will not merely have gone on courses and got qualifications: they will have been apprentices. The same applies to lawyers. The best way to learn to be a good lawyer is by getting direct experience, that is by doing the job oneself. But it is wholly unfair on clients, if one learns at their expense any more than is strictly necessary. Spending time first closely working with an experienced lawyer – watching and listening to him or her at work, benefitting from his or her experience – is essential.

For trainee advocates, this is important because of their direct and immediate introduction to court appearances on behalf of their clients as soon as they can practise. For trainee solicitors, the training contract also provides an ideal period to teach what are becoming ever more essential skills: managerial skills, marketing skills, and business advisory skills.

Possible changes to vocational training

Simmons & Simmons introduced an optional MBA course for their trainees in 2009. This is shortly to become a compulsory aspect of the LPC which its trainees are to undertake followed by further training during the training contract.[19] This seems to me to demonstrate two things.

First, that there is innovation within vocational training and that it is being driven by the market within the framework set by the SRA. Contrary to what some say, vocational training is developing consistently with the needs of the legal profession today and in the future, and it is doing so on a demand-led basis, subject to the rigorous demands of the regulatory framework set by the 2007 Act. The second thing this shows is that the skills taught before the training contract can be further developed during the training contract. If the Simmons & Simmons approach is adopted more widely, which may be a good idea, such skills could be taught as part of bespoke LPCs and then consolidated during the training contract.

On a rather different tack, David Barnard has suggested a common start for all lawyers.[20] His idea is that all would-be lawyers should undertake a common

19 See <http://l2b.thelawyer.com/simmons-to-put-all-trainees-through-bespoke-mba-course/1013114.article>.

20 D. Barnard, 'Legal Education – A Common Start For Everybody', response to LETR Discussion paper 01/2012, <http://letr.org.uk/wp-content/uploads/2012/11/D-Barnard-.pdf>.

course and a common examination. They should then begin their careers as salaried employees in barristers' chambers, solicitors' offices, the CPS, in-house legal departments, and the new alternative business structures. At any time after three years as 'trainee lawyers', it should be open to any person who has got so far to take a course, leading to being called to the Bar. After spending three or more years in legal practice, the idea is that lawyers have a better idea of their skills and weaknesses, and will better understand their fitness for the Bar, based on their real experience and understanding.

Mr Barnard's suggestion is, in part, based on his view that the number of students paying to sit the BPTC, but who do not obtain pupillage, is a matter of a scandal. That is a view shared by others, but there is a contrary perspective. More, probably many more, students complete the BPTC than will obtain pupillage, but, provided that those students are aware of the realities they face, should we interfere with their personal autonomy? Further, we should not discount the likelihood that the BPTC will assist in obtaining other forms of employment.

That point apart, I see the attraction of Mr Barnard's proposal, but I wonder whether it is one of those seductive ideas, which has the attraction of simplicity and novelty, but which, when implemented, makes one realise, all too late, what a valuable system has been lost, and how much more sensible it is to make small practical changes rather than grand gestures. I suspect that there may well be a strong case for more radical reform of the LPC, but that is no reason for subsuming into a new LPC the BPTC. First, the BPTC has been overhauled recently; second, if significant change is needed to the LPC, it strikes me as probably unwise to overload the change agenda with a substantial and unnecessary additional feature.

Finally on vocational training, I consider that the review should not seek, or appear to seek, to unify solicitors' and barristers' training as a means of achieving fusion of the two professions. Any open-minded person can see that there are serious arguments for and against fusion of the two branches of the profession. However, if that is a suitable subject for discussion or a report, it should be discussed and reported on openly and fully as a separate topic. The fact that fusion may be thought by some to be a good idea does not justify the present review of legal education and training being used as a stalking horse for advancing it. Any attempt to use this review as a means of taking forward fusion would, I suspect, result in any proposals being discredited in many peoples' eyes, and understandably so.

Conclusion

I have only been able to touch upon some of the issues which might be relevant to the development of legal education and training over the coming years. Much more could be said, and it will be interesting to see what the LETR report adds to the debate. The professional regulators will need to scrutinise it carefully. And they should approach the scrutiny with the same open mind that should inform the minds of all its other readers, whether barristers, solicitors, CILEX fellows, lay people, the Bar Council, the Law Society, or CILEX. And, having read it, I hope that the professional regulators will then draw on the views of those bodies and a wide-range of practitioners, judges and consumer groups.

In looking to reform, we should take great care not to undermine either the present generally high standard of entry into the profession and of those practising law in the UK, or the undoubted many good qualities of our legal education and training. No system is ideal. Improvements can always be made, not least in a changing environment, and our legal environment is certainly a changing one at present.

I return to Bruges. If there is evidence that the Zwin is silting up, we will need to take steps to remedy that problem. But, before doing so, we must have convincing evidence that it is indeed silting up. We must then properly identify the cause and an effective solution. I think it unlikely that evidence will uncover much silting up. Nevertheless it is likely that there are a number of targeted reforms which we can put in place to make Bruges a more attractive harbour – to improve legal education and training to increase standards and skills. Most importantly, I think there are steps we can take to reinvigorate the profession of law in the public interest and in the interest of ensuring that our democracy, in which the rule of law is so deeply embedded, continues to flourish.

Thank you.

DAVID NEUBERGER

4 Response: A Tale of Two Cities

Reflecting on Lord Neuberger's 'Reforming Legal Education'[1]

Julian Webb

Introduction

Since the first Lord Upjohn Lecture was delivered by Lord Diplock in 1971,[2] a further 16 have been offered by judges (or former judges) of the senior courts. Of these only five have chosen legal education as their sole or primary subject; Lord Neuberger is thus the latest of a small and distinguished group.[3] This by itself makes his lecture of interest to legal educationalists. That the intervention comes from no less than the President of the UK Supreme Court must also place a certain institutional call on our attention.

My aim is to place Lord Neuberger's lecture in the context of the earlier reviews of legal education and training. It will be apparent from this that I am more interested in what Lord Neuberger's intervention adds to our understanding of the 'politics' of legal education,[4] than in what it said about the Legal Education and Training Review (LETR) specifically.[5] The LETR has inevitably moved on.[6] A number of Lord Neuberger's specific concerns have thus been addressed

1 Rt. Hon. Lord Neuberger of Abbotsbury, 'Lord Upjohn Lecture 2012: Reforming Legal Education' (2013) 47 *Law Teacher* 4–17 (hereafter '*RLE*').

2 Rt. Hon. Lord Diplock, 'The Common Market and the Common Law' (1972) 6 *Law Teacher* 3–16.

3 The others are: Mr Justice Goff, 'The Law as Taught and the Law as Practised' (1977) 11 *Law Teacher* 75–88; Sir Frederick Lawton, 'Legal Education and the Needs of the Legal Profession' (1980) 14 *Law Teacher* 163–7; Rt. Hon. Lord Griffiths, 'The Lord Chancellor's Advisory Committee on Legal Education and the Legal Profession' (1994) 28 *Law Teacher* 4–12; Rt. Hon. Lord Woolf CJ, 'The Education, the Justice System Requires Today' (2000) 34 *Law Teacher* 263–70.

4 'Politics' here is used in a broad sense to characterise the values and processes involved in institutionalised policy- and decision-making by those in established authority.

5 Please note that the views expressed in this chapter are personal to the author and do not necessarily reflect the opinions of any other (former) member of the LETR Research Team, or of the regulatory bodies that commissioned the LETR.

6 See Julian Webb, 'The LETRs (Still) in the Post: The Legal Education and Training Review and the Reform of Legal Services Education and Training – A Personal (Re)view' in Hilary Sommerlad *et al* (eds), *The Futures of Legal Education and the Legal Profession* (Oxford, Hart, 2014).

in the first phase report,[7] while others have been largely overtaken by events.[8] Some, it may be said, were somewhat misplaced even at the time of publication, but that is another story.[9]

A short history of English legal education reform

The modern legal education system in England and Wales has been shaped in part by a series of reform processes that began only in the mid-nineteenth century. In the early 1800s legal education and training in England was almost non-existent. The Inns of Court and the ancient universities were virtually moribund as teaching institutions.[10] No examination was required before call to the Bar; solicitors' articled clerks were not required to take any initial examination before admission until 1836. Moreover, neither the ancient universities nor the Inns appeared willing of their own volition to take remedial action.[11] In 1846 government finally acceded to demands to create a formal commission of inquiry, and a Parliamentary Select Committee was established for that purpose.[12] This, then,

7 For example, discussion regarding the move to common legal training for solicitors and barristers – *RLE*, 16; see Julian Webb *et al*, *Setting Standards: Regulating Legal Services Education and Training* (Legal Education and Training Review, 2013), available at http://letr.org.uk (hereafter '*LETR Report*'), paras 5.54–5.58.

8 For example, Lord Neuberger's call for a second phase to the LETR (*RLE*, 5), which is underway, and was, so far as I am aware, always intended.

9 Notably the concern that the research team was selectively privileging the consumer interest and the need to 'ensure an independent, strong, diverse and effective legal profession' over the other regulatory objectives laid down by s. 1 of the Legal Services Act 2007, see *RLE*, 7–8; cp LETR, *Discussion Paper 02/2012: Key Issues (I): Call for Evidence*, paras 44–45, available at http://letr.org.uk/wp-content/uploads/Discussion-Paper-012012.pdf (accessed 18 September 2015); LETR, *Key Issues (II): Developing the Detail* (August 2012), para. 109, available at http://letr.org.uk/wp-content/uploads/Discussion-Paper-02_2012final2.pdf (accessed 18 September 2015). See also Richard Moorhead, 'Lord Neuberger and the LETR', *Lawyer Watch* blog, 20 November 2012, available at http://lawyerwatch.wordpress.com/2012/11/20/lord-neuberger-and-the-letr (accessed 18 September 2015).

10 Indeed 'professional' education in the universities (ie, in medicine, law and divinity) generally was in a very poor state: see, eg, W.H.G. Armytage, 'The Conflict of Ideas in English University Education – 1850–1867' (1953) 3 *Educational Theory* 327, 328 and 329; Peter Searby, *A History of the University of Cambridge: Volume III, 1750–1870* (Cambridge University Press, 1997), 464.

11 Brian Abel-Smith and Robert Stevens, *Lawyers and the Courts: A Sociological Study of the English Legal System, 1750–1965* (London, Heinemann, 1967), 63; Keith Vernon, *Universities and the State in England, 1850–1939* (Abingdon, RoutledgeFalmer, 2004), 20–4; Christopher W. Brooks and Michael Lobban, 'Apprenticeship or Academy? The Idea of a Law University, 1830–1860' in Jonathan A. Bush and Alain Wijffels, *Learning the Law: Teaching and the Transmission of Law in England 1150–1900* (London, Hambledon Press, 1988), 353.

12 *Report from the Select Committee on Legal Education*, 25 August 1846, H of C No. 686 (hereafter '1846 Committee').

was the first of six major 'reviews' of legal education preceding the LETR.[13] The others reported in 1934,[14] 1971,[15] 1979,[16] 1988[17] and 1996–7.[18]

The story of these various reports has been told extensively elsewhere.[19] Collectively, these reports tracked and to some extent shaped a number of important features of the modern legal education system, notably:

- the emergence and consolidation of (English) law as an academic discipline in its own right;
- the construction of discrete stages of education and training which have created distinct spheres of influence for the different stakeholders;
- the maintenance of a structure which has both marginalised university law schools in the process of professional formation and assured that professional bodies retain ultimate regulatory control over access to professional titles;

13 This figure does not include the significant number of other reports which either addressed legal education as part of a wider higher education remit (such as the 1913 Haldane Commission on university education in London), or focused on training for one branch of the profession only or some sub-part thereof. The latter group includes the Law Society's Training Framework Review (TFR) and the numerous committees set up by the Bar since the Bar Vocational Course was established in 1989.

14 *Report of the Legal Education Committee*, Cmd. 4663 (London, HMSO, 1934) (hereafter 'Atkin Committee').

15 *Report of the Committee on Legal Education*, Cmnd. 4595 (London, HMSO, 1971) (hereafter 'Ormrod Report').

16 *Royal Commission on Legal Services, Final Report,* Cm. 7648 (London, HMSO, 1979) (hereafter 'Benson Report'). Legal education was not a major focus of the Benson Report. As Twining commented at the time, the Commission had more than enough on its plate without reopening the structural issues that had been addressed by Ormrod. Its approach therefore was, in Twining's words, 'selective, gradualist, largely exhortatory and strikingly parochial': see William Twining, 'The Benson Report and Legal Education: A Personal View' in Philip Thomas (ed), *Law in the Balance: Legal Services in the Eighties* (Oxford, Martin Robertson, 1982), 186.

17 *A Time for Change: Report of the Committee on the Future of the Legal Profession* (London, General Council of the Bar/The Law Society, 1988) (hereafter 'Marre Committee').

18 Lord Chancellor's Advisory Committee on Legal Education and Conduct, *First Report on Legal Education and Training* (London, ACLEC, 1996) (hereafter 'ACLEC'). A second and far less detailed report on continuing professional development was published in 1997 but is not considered substantively in this chapter.

19 See, eg, Abel-Smith and Stevens, n. 11, 63–76 and Chs 7, 13; William Twining, *Blackstone's Tower: The English Law School* (London, Sweet and Maxwell, 1994), Ch. 2; Andrew Boon and Julian Webb, 'Legal Education and Training in England and Wales: Back to the Future' (2008) 58 *Journal of Legal Education* 12. The Ormrod Report itself also offers a useful overview of the earlier reports.

- a formalisation of vocational training, involving differentiation both from academic stage education, and, increasingly, between the training of solicitors and barristers.[20]

But they were also individually flawed and collectively less impactful than their authors undoubtedly would have hoped. Indeed, some have struggled to make any lasting impression at all.[21] Much of this is, of course, already well known, and my aim is not to go over well-trodden ground. Rather, in the remainder of this section I highlight a number of seemingly important, recurrent and often interrelated themes. Taken together, these go some way to explain why these formal review processes have been of limited effect. This is not to say they have been of no value, but I do suggest that the story of legal education reform can largely be summarised as, 'two steps forward, one step back'. The reasons for this are both structural and conceptual.

A reliance on external triggers for change

The history of legal education policy can be characterised as one in which periods of benign neglect have been interspersed with and punctuated by shorter periods of more or less intense navel-gazing. These latter interventions have not, on the whole, been initiated or led by those actually engaged in legal education and have seldom been actuated by a simple desire to build a superior system of education and training. Rather, they have been political engagements triggered by state or

20 This has been despite a persistent debate about common legal education. The Bar's introduction of its new Vocational Course in 1989 can be seen as a critical turning point, and part of a deliberate strategy of market differentiation by the Bar: see, eg, Lord Hoffmann, 'Common Professional Education' in ACLEC, *Review of Legal Education: Report of the Third Consultative Conference*, 10 July 1995 (London, ACLEC, 1995), 1, on file with the author (Lord Hoffmann was Chairman of the Council of Legal Education at the time and chaired the committee responsible for proposing the new Bar Vocational Course). Within the solicitors' profession some element of intra-professional differentiation has emerged following creation of the 'City LPC' and subsequent moves to more bespoke LPC offerings: see Andy Boon and Julian Webb, 'The Legal Profession as Stakeholders in the Academy in England and Wales' in Fiona Cownie (ed.), *Stakeholders in the Law School* (Oxford, Hart, 2010), 78; Philip Hoult, 'Controversial City LPC Consortium Splits as Firms Opt for Different Providers', *Law Society Gazette*, 25 March 2004, available at http://www.lawgazette.co.uk/news/controversial-city-lpc-consortium-splits-as-firms-opt-for-different-providers/41684.fullarticle (accessed 18 September 2015).

21 Most notably the Atkin Committee's report which, though welcomed at the time, failed to engage with core weaknesses in the system, despite the efforts of Harold Laski to get people on the Committee 'who are likely to do a real job' – Mark DeWolfe (ed.), *Holmes–Laski Letters: The Correspondence of Mr Justice Holmes and Harold J. Laski, 1916–1935* (Cambridge, MA, Harvard University Press, 1953), vol. 2, 1156. Cp L.C.B. Gower, 'English Legal Training: A Critical Survey' (1950) 13 *Modern Law Review* 137, 147 (describing the report as a 'thoroughly disappointing document').

profession in response to perceived 'problems'.[22] The trigger events have tended to manifest outside the education and training system itself, usually occurring as a threat or challenge to what, in political economy terms, might be called the 'material base'[23] of the legal profession, or to its regulatory authority or autonomy. Thus, to put it more concretely, legal education and training reform has tended to be mooted at points where the *profession* has been facing a particular challenge: over recruitment (either too few or too many, or possibly just the 'wrong type'),[24] or market,[25] or one of the periodic debates about competence or probity,[26] or over its ability to manage its affairs in the public interest,[27] or, latterly, where a new regulatory body is seeking to establish its jurisdiction,[28] or, frequently, some combination of these. This has had a number of significant consequences.

First, it has meant that the reform agenda has tended to be shaped by the profession and, to some extent, the state, not the educators. As a consequence

22 Following Ormrod, Thomas and Mungham argued that the failure of any of the major reviews up to that time to initiate major structural rather than incremental change indicated that law had yet to experience the kind of 'identity crisis' that had led to a more dramatic redesign of training in professions like medicine, teaching or social work: Philip A. Thomas and Geoff M. Mungham, 'English Legal Education: A Commentary on the Ormrod Report' (1972) 7 *Valparaiso University Law Review* 87, 125. The conservatism of the Benson Report, the institutional resistance of the Bar to change, and the failure of ACLEC and the TFR to persuade the profession of a need for major reforms suggest that the underlying complacency of both the profession and the educational establishment has survived relatively intact.

23 Z. Bankowski and G. Mungham, 'A Political Economy of Legal Education' (1978) 32 *New University Quarterly* 448.

24 This was a factor in both the Ormrod and ACLEC Reports. It has also tended to be a recurrent theme of more localised, profession-led, reviews, see, eg, the influence of the 'recruitment crisis' on the Law Society's thinking in the run-up to the development and launch of the Legal Practice Course, discussed in Andrew Boon, 'History is Past Politics: A Critique of the Legal Skills Movement in England and Wales' (1998) 25 *Journal of Law & Society* 151, 154. It has particularly dominated much of the debate at the Bar over the last decade or more, with numerous reports seeking to address access and diversity (including Lord Neuberger's 2007 Report on *Entry to the Bar*), the need for alternative pupillages, and the cost of training.

25 See, most notably, the Benson Commission and Marre Committee. Note also the extent to which the opening up of the advocacy market influenced Law Society thinking on vocational training in the late 1980s – Boon, ibid.

26 Eg, the transition from the Law Society Finals to the Legal Practice Course was in large part predicated on the need to respond to widespread concerns about solicitors' communication and client care skills, highlighted by the Marre Committee: see Law Society, *Training Tomorrow's Solicitors* (London, The Law Society, 1990); also Vivien Shrubsall, 'Training Tomorrow's Solicitors – The Legal Practice Course and Beyond' (1995) 27 *Bracton Law Journal* 16, 17. Note also the focus on standards of ethics and professionalism in the ACLEC Report and the TFR – see Andrew Boon, 'Ethics in Legal Education and Training: Four Reports, Three Jurisdictions and a Prospectus' (2002) 5 *Legal Ethics* 34, and subsequently the proposals put forward by Kim Economides and Justine Rogers, *Preparatory Ethics Training for Future Solicitors* (London, The Law Society, 2009).

27 The 1846 Select Committee; the Marre Committee; the Law Society's TFR.

28 The ACLEC Review and the LETR itself.

reviews have tended to show marked signs of professional influence in the scope of their remit and in various other features. 'Legal education and training' has thus been treated, until the LETR, by default as education for the traditional professions. Postgraduate academic legal education, law in schools and public legal education, and even education and training for other legal service providers have largely been disregarded.[29] There has been little serious acknowledgment of, let alone debate about, the epistemological, methodological and even ideological differences between academic and vocational education, and the extent to which those differences are 'real' or imagined. Approaches to curriculum content and design have consequently been instrumentalist. Evidence-gathering has been sporadic and unsystematised, and the need to build a body of discipline-specific pedagogic research to inform instructional design has also gone largely unrecognised.[30]

Second, the diffusion of control over legal education has also meant that many of the economic, political and institutional problems of the law schools have tended to be played out within the universities, rather than as part of a more 'public' debate about their role in education and training. This may have insulated the law schools from undue external interference, but potentially at some cost. In particular it has left the academic law schools largely unsupported in arguing for resources and funding. It has arguably helped create an environment in which divisions between public and private higher education have been able to flourish. It may have left law schools even more exposed to competing pressures to meet the needs of their various actual or proclaimed stakeholders, particularly given the commoditised, neo-liberal, agenda for higher education increasingly imposed by the state.[31]

Last, it has meant that many of the apparent problems that have been the impetus for review (absence of common training, poor co-ordination, access to the profession) have not necessarily been about education as such, but about the professional political economy. To that extent legal education reform reflects a more generalised policy tendency towards the 'educationalisation' of (other) social and economic problems: that is, the practice of policy actors to shift responsibility for larger problems onto educational institutions, often as a way of

29 The Ormrod Report was the first and, until the LETR, only review to consider the training of legal executives, which it did in less than two pages. See n. 15, paras 180–3.

30 Though the UK Centre for Legal Education during its existence took steps to narrow the research gap, it faced an uphill task. The level of funding was insufficient for much in the way of large projects; activity was hindered by limited educational research skills and doubts about the value (for research audit purposes) of pedagogic research in the subject community, while priorities were also increasingly determined by Higher Education Academy institutional, and hence funding council, objectives, rather than the needs of the subject community.

31 Fiona Cownie, 'Introduction: Contextualising Stakeholders in the Law School' in Cownie (ed), *Stakeholders in the Law School* (Oxford, Hart, 2010), 1, 12–13; Margaret Thornton, *Privatising the Public University: The Case of Law* (Abingdon, Routledge, 2012).

being seen to do something, even though such institutions may be incapable of delivering the desired change.[32]

This dependence on external change agents to drive agendas and processes of itself may go some way to explain both the tendency of the Anglo-Welsh legal education system to develop by happenstance rather than design, and the recurrence of certain, seemingly irresolvable, issues across successive reviews.

Fragmentation into stages and fiefdoms

As noted already, the relatively sharp separation between academic and professional legal education is a distinctive feature of the Anglo-Welsh tradition. It can largely be traced back to the 1846 Committee Report. This saw the universities as central to raising educational standards amongst entrants to the profession. However, because the Committee also doubted the universities' ability or willingness to take on preparation for professional practice, it also identified the need for the Bar and solicitors' profession to revive and/or develop their educational role, and this became increasingly institutionalised in examination and also, ultimately, separate teaching arrangements.[33]

The reluctance of the professions to provide formal exemptions to law graduates also meant that for many years the professions and the universities provided overlapping qualifications for what gradually came to be recognised as the initial stage of education and training. The Atkin Committee in 1936 suggested that the distinction between professional and academic education was in danger of being overdrawn, arguing that the difference was primarily one of emphasis rather than something more fundamental. However, by pushing for greater professional recognition of the law degree, the Atkin Committee gave its own imprimatur to this idea of separate but overlapping fiefdoms.[34] Ormrod similarly, in seeking to establish the law degree as the normal academic stage, further institutionalised

32 David Bridges, 'Educationalisation: On the Appropriateness of Asking Educational Institutions to Solve Social and Economic Problems' (2008) 58 *Educational Theory* 461, 461–2.

33 Notably by the Inns' establishment of the Council of Legal Education (CLE) in 1852, and the eventual foundation of the Law Society's School of Law in 1903, though the Law Society never established a teaching monopoly over its Finals course in the way that the Bar did (up until the devolution of the Bar Vocational Course to approved providers in the 1990s).

34 See Atkin Committee, n. 14, para. 10: 'Your Committee accept fully the principle that it is for the professional bodies alone to decide what degree of professional knowledge shall qualify for admission to the profession, and to determine the tests by which that proficiency shall be ascertained. It is inherent in the differentiation of function of University and professional body that the teaching and examination in such a subject as law should to some extent differ. . . . The University function is more concerned with the teaching of law as part of the *universitas* of knowledge; it will necessarily emphasize principles and, as far as it can, will develop the scientific side of its subject. Nevertheless it would be a mistake to exaggerate the distinction between academic and professional teaching of law'.

the divide by formalising the adoption of the three-stage (academic-vocational-continuing) model of legal education.[35] Even ACLEC, whilst trying to break down some of the rigid distinctions that had developed between the stages, could be seen, in its message to trust the universities with the law degree, to be reinforcing the degree's essential separateness from professional education and training.[36]

This tendency to treat academic and professional education as largely independent territories has also created, or at least has not resolved, a range of co-ordination, accountability and implementation problems.

Consistency and co-ordination problems

The stratification of legal education and training post-1846 has inevitably created consistency and co-ordination problems, given the historical absence of a rational distribution of functions, and continuing tensions between different stakeholders. The need for greater consistency and a proper development of the 'science of law' had been highlighted by the 1846 Committee. A number of unsuccessful attempts were made to unify the first stage of training in the second half of the nineteenth century, particularly by the Legal Education Association and its founder, Sir Roundell Palmer.[37] The failure to create a unified model heightened the need for co-ordination. This was recognised by the Atkin Committee, which recommended the creation of a standing 'Advisory Committee'.[38] However, despite tantalising early signs of action,[39] by 1947 no committee had met, and the government peremptorily decided that the new body's proposed functions were being adequately performed by the professional associations.[40]

35 Ormrod Report, n. 15, para. 100. Though note Hepple's doubts that the Committee intended this to be a 'rigid demarcation': Bob Hepple, 'The Renewal of the Liberal Law Degree' (1996) 55 *Cambridge Law Journal* 470, 477.

36 ACLEC, n. 18, para. 2.2.

37 Widely regarded as 'the *decus et tutamen*' of the English Bar ('Leaders of the Bar in England', *Sydney Morning Herald*, 28 May 1872, p. 6), and, as Lord Selbourne, twice Lord Chancellor under Gladstone. See notably Sir Roundell Palmer Q.C., *A Speech Delivered in the House of Commons on Tuesday, July 11, 1871 on Moving Resolutions for the Establishment of a General School of Law* (Westminster, J B Nichols & Sons, 1871) (British Library; Accession No 6147. Bb. 28). See also Abel-Smith and Stevens, n. 11, 72–4.

38 The proposed committee was to provide non-binding advice on proposals for professional exemption; on the level of general education required for admission to the profession, and could assist in co-ordinating distribution of teaching of so-called 'special options' within the professional courses, especially across London: Atkin Committee, n. 14, paras 17–20.

39 The Attorney-General thus told the House of Commons that 'steps have been taken to set up a Standing Advisory Committee to which questions relating to legal education can be referred': *Hansard* (HC Deb) (Written Answers) 17 December 1935, vol 307, c 1576W. Membership nominations were also sought by the Lord Chancellor's Department: see 'The Society of Public Teachers of Law: Report of the General Committee 1935–36' (1936) *Journal of the Society of Public Teachers of Law* 58.

40 *Hansard* (HC Deb) (Written Answers) 15 May 1947, vol. 437, c 189W.

In the early 1960s, pressure for co-ordination and change to legal education began to increase once more. This reflected various factors:[41] dissatisfaction with the apprenticeship system of training continued, and debate about common initial training for the Law Society and Bar was also renewed. More particularly, with the emergence of an increasingly interventionist state, new areas of both commercial and social welfare practice were emerging, and the legal profession was consequently growing and needing to assure a sufficient supply of recruits with the appropriate skills and knowledge.[42] For some, these issues were all part of a wider need to overhaul a legal system that was insufficiently responsive to problems of access to justice.[43] Within higher education too, change was in the air. Increased state funding had already aligned the university law schools' financial interests increasingly with those of the wider university,[44] while the Robbins Committee's interest in what we would now call widening participation aligned with professional interests in widening access. The potential for increased student numbers in the wake of the Robbins reforms also helped consolidate law's place in the modern university. At the same time the idea of academic law was evolving, with greater substance being given to the idea of law as a 'contextual' and increasingly interdisciplinary subject.[45] A more autonomous and, in some respects, more vocationally orientated law degree system was also emerging in the college/polytechnic sector.[46]

Consequently, the Atkin recommendation for a new advisory committee was dusted off again,[47] and finally taken up by the Ormrod Report. The latter saw continuing co-ordination as critical to its objective of integrating an expanding legal education and training 'system' 'into a coherent whole'.[48] Its recommendation

41 See generally Twining, n. 19, 33.

42 See, eg, the statement of Lord Gardiner LC announcing the appointment of the Ormrod Committee: 'Committee to foster cooperation in legal education', *The Guardian*, 21 December 1967, p. 12.

43 See notably the influential text by Martin Andrew and Gerald Gardiner, *Law Reform Now!* (London, Gollancz, 1963); also Society of Labour Lawyers, *Legal Education: Society of Labour Lawyers Report*, Fabian Research Series No 276, April 1969.

44 W.H.G. Armytage, 'The Superseding of the Private Patron: Recent Developments in the English Civic Universities, 1930–1952' (1954) 13 *American Journal of Economics and Sociology* 305.

45 See, eg, Ralph Folsom and Neil Roberts, 'The Warwick Story: Being Led Down the Contextual Path of Law' (1979) 30 *Journal of Legal Education* 166; William Twining, 'Reflections on Law in Context' in Twining, *Law in Context: Enlarging a Discipline* (Oxford, Oxford University Press, 1997).

46 The Council for National Academic Awards (CNAA) established its Legal Studies Board in November 1965 with the first CNAA law degrees approved to begin in September 1966: S.B. Marsh, 'The CNAA Law Degree' (1983) 17 *Law Teacher* 73, 74.

47 Notably by Southampton's Professor John Wilson who was subsequently appointed to the Ormrod Committee: J.F. Wilson, 'A Survey of Legal Education in the United Kingdom' (1966) 9 *Journal of the Society of Public Teachers of Law (NS)* 1, 124; similarly I.H. Jacob, 'Legal Education – The Next Ten Years' (1967) 1(2) *Law Teacher* 4, 10–11.

48 Ormrod Report, n. 15, para. 85.

was followed through insofar as a new Lord Chancellor's Advisory Committee was created. However, the latter was denied government funding. Consequently, it fell to the professions to underwrite the exercise, a fact which enabled them in turn largely to dictate the direction of its work. The committee subsequently overrode a number of Ormrod's original recommendations regarding the extent of the academic core and the adoption of a (single rather than two-year) graduate conversion course, alienating its academic members in the process.[49]

Post-Ormrod, the fate of the advisory function has been subjected to the policy equivalent of a game of 'pass the parcel'. The Advisory Committee limped on, but was subsequently criticised by both Benson and Marre, the latter describing it as lacking in dynamism, and calling for its replacement by a more 'vigorous' body.[50] In response, a new, independent and centrally funded ACLEC was established by the Courts and Legal Services Act 1990, with both professional and lay membership. However, ACLEC proved to be too independent for its own good, and, following its criticism of government plans for reforms to criminal advocacy, the Committee's work was cut short by its dissolution in 1999. ACLEC in turn was replaced by a 'Legal Services Consultative Panel' with a narrower remit and significantly less resources.

This body too was ultimately scrapped by the Legal Services Act 2007. This brings us to the present situation, in which frontline accountability for education and training has devolved to the independent regulatory bodies (thus divorcing it somewhat from the traditional professional bodies) while responsibility to 'assist in the maintenance and development of standards' of education has passed to the oversight regulator, the Legal Services Board (LSB).[51] How well such consultative and advisory functions sit with the role of an oversight regulator is moot. Certainly the level of legal education expertise 'on tap' within the LSB appears to be less than that available to ACLEC. This leads to my next point.

Accountability and control (1): Who is in charge?

One other consequence of 'stages and fiefdoms' thinking has been to distribute and demarcate authority over legal education and training widely between different bodies. I suggest that, in this context, legal education review processes need to be seen as part of an increasingly complex politics of responsibility, control and accountability.

Professional control in the Anglo-Welsh system has been exercised largely through three mechanisms: professional exemptions for graduates; control over

49 Michael Zander, 'Lawyers reopen schism', *The Guardian*, 26 November 1973, p. 5; Thomas and Mungham, n. 22, at 95, 129–30; also Fiona Cownie and Ray Cocks, '"*A Great and Noble Occupation!" The History of the Society of Legal Scholars* (Oxford, Hart, 2009), 129–37.

50 Marre Committee, n. 17, paras 17.3–17.4.

51 Legal Services Act 2007, s. 4; this is equivalent to the statutory duty exercised by ACLEC under the 1990 Act.

vocational training, and a continuing 'apprenticeship' requirement. The majority in the Ormrod Committee sought to disrupt that model by weakening the profession's control over supply and by reducing the profession's role in providing the vocational stage of training; in both respects it experienced a degree of push-back from the profession, both in the Committee itself and subsequently, though not enough to undermine its reforms entirely. By carving out a space for university legal education, Ormrod did give greater responsibility to the universities. In the words of the Report, it put the degree 'in the hands of professional educationalists', rather than the 'enlightened amateurs' of the profession.[52] Yet it also thereby left control over the core, professional component of the degree and of the vocational stage very much in the hands of those same (hopefully) enlightened amateurs. That approach limited the ambitions of vocational education, at least until the reforms of the late 1980s, and perhaps beyond, and continues to dog debates about the academic 'foundations'.

If the separation of responsibility and control was a largely unresolved problem, then Ormrod said and did even less about accountability. In this respect Ormrod remained closer to the nineteenth- and early-twentieth-century approaches to legal education reform than to more recent reviews. The modalities of *post hoc* accountability simply did not fit with the legal world's assumptions about self-regulation, *propter hoc* responsibility and the narrow effectiveness of training outlook that has tended to shape the review agenda. Indeed, according to the logic of the time, insofar as such review processes provided a means for the professions to demonstrate their continuing control over their systems of education and training, they also provided justification for limiting the professions' (external) accountability.

However, as lawyers, law schools and their regulators have reacted to the increasing interests of government and lay bodies, the debates in the more modern reports have become more nuanced and professionalised. Discourses of regulation and accountability, quality assurance (QA) and the formalisation of standards have moved increasingly to the fore. The reforms to vocational training in the late 1980s and early 1990s can, in this context, be seen as the start of what has been a profession-led (and subsequently, in the LETR, regulator-led) response to precisely this new 'audit society' discourse.[53] Aside from any pedagogic virtues, these developments also served, for a time, as a means for the professions to retain control of their territory through an adoption of limited accountability mechanisms. ACLEC can be seen as part of the institutional adoption of this new discourse. Professional education and training systems for ACLEC had to be able demonstrably to assure quality, and the means of doing so was through competence-based education and enhanced QA.[54] The broad acceptance of an outcomes approach by respondents

52 Ormrod Report, n. 15, para. 47.
53 Michael Power, *The Audit Society* (Oxford, Oxford University Press, 1997).
54 See, eg, ACLEC Report, n. 18, para. 2.2.

to ACLEC, and subsequently by the Committee itself, set down a significant marker for future developments, including the work of the Law Society's Training Framework Review Group,[55] and the LETR itself. Competences, standards and QA mechanisms, in short, had become not just educational tools, but the new means of legitimation and techniques for maintaining an 'aura of professionalism and the independence of a professional cadre'.[56]

Accountability and control (2): In whose interest?

Thinking about accountability and control also invites us to consider in whose interests any given system should operate, and where, in the public interest, control should sit. Harry Arthurs argued, in his discussion of the Ormrod Report, that ultimately this boils down to one question of principle: 'is the public interest well served by ultimate professional control over legal education?'[57] His own answer to that question was a pretty unequivocal 'no':

> 'the public interest (and that of the profession) is best served by the existence of a vital centre of legal scholarship in which new ideas and skills and values will continuously be generated. In part, these ideas, skills and values will be disseminated through books and articles and professional "continuing education" programmes. In part they will result from the active participation by academics in law reform and professional affairs. Mostly, their adoption by the profession will occur by osmosis as the result of the absorption of new recruits who will act as change agents . . .[58]

This, Arthurs considered, was unlikely to occur in an environment in which 'there is something vaguely improper about teachers who undertake social engineering, students who question, lawyers who negotiate and manoeuvre, and judges who make law'.[59] Readers familiar with the international legal education literature will recognise that this forms a kernel of the vision Arthurs subsequently articulated in *Law and Learning*, a report which sought, with mixed success, to modernise Canadian legal education in the early 1980s.[60] Alongside the US MacCrate Report,[61] Arthurs' model of an education in

55 See Boon and Webb, n. 19.

56 LETR, *Literature Review*, Ch. 2, para. 2, available at http://letr.org.uk/wp-content/uploads/LR-chapter-2.pdf (accessed 18 September 2015).

57 H.W. Arthurs, 'The Ormrod Report: A Canadian Reaction' (1971) 34 *Modern Law Review* 642.

58 Ibid., 644.

59 Ibid., 654.

60 Humanities and Social Sciences Research Council of Canada, *Law and Learning* (Ottawa, HSSRC, 1982).

61 American Bar Association, *ABA Task Force on Law Schools and the Profession: Narrowing the Gap* (Chicago, ABA, 1992).

'humane professionalism' also influenced ACLEC's thinking. It is perhaps unsurprising therefore that, if Ormrod largely ignored the public interest, ACLEC sought from the outset to frame its work as 'fundamental to our commitment to constitutionalism and the maintenance and extension of the rule of law . . . [and] crucial to our country's commercial success in the face of global competition'.[62]

Of course, framing proposals for reform in the context of the public interest assumes that government, professions and the law schools (i) agree with your interpretation and (ii) are actually motivated and interested to act in a way that advances public interest objectives. The failure of ACLEC invites us to doubt those assumptions.[63] Marre and the TFR (for example) also suggest that, when under pressure, the profession has preferred, when possible, to manage reform from beneath its own protective carapace. The risk is, of course, that in such an environment there may be a temptation to ignore the public interest question entirely, or to adopt the old stratagem of assuming that public and professional interests are aligned, and that the profession may safely be relied upon to act as guardians of both. Arguments about the common training of solicitors and barristers have been a recurrent example of an issue where pragmatism and self-interest have, arguably at least, been allowed to override public interest considerations. Thus, while the Marre Committee's deliberations highlighted strong public interest arguments for the fusion of solicitors' and barristers' training, it pointedly made no recommendation to that effect, deferring the question to its proposed 'Joint Legal Education Committee'.[64] Similarly, the persistence of Bar and Law Society representatives on the Ormrod Committee in insisting on their own courses in their own independent law schools effectively killed any prospect of sustained public funding of the vocational stage, and set in train many of the subsequent cost and access problems that the professions have since struggled (unsuccessfully) to resolve.[65]

The obligation on the LSB and frontline regulators under the Legal Services Act to regulate in the public interest should, subject to the possibility of regulatory capture, substantially reduce that risk. At the same time, however, the creation of multiple and overlapping regulatory objectives under the 2007 Act also potentially complicates the 'in whose interest' question in any given scenario, a point to which we shall return.

62 ACLEC Report, n. 18, 3.

63 Cp also Harry W. Arthurs, 'Half a League Onward: The Report of the Lord Chancellor's Advisory Committee on Legal Education and Conduct' (1997) 31 *Law Teacher* 1, 2–4.

64 See Marre Report, n. 17, paras 14.5–14.23. The risk that such a move would constitute fusion 'by the back door' may well have motivated members to tread carefully. The Committee had decided early on in its deliberations that it would not enter the fusion debate, almost certainly because that would have left it divided along partisan lines.

65 Twining, n. 19, 35.

Implementation is (nearly) everything

The lessons of history suggest that achieving legal education reform is seldom straightforward. It requires goodwill, resources, structures and systems for implementation. If any of those are lacking, then the relevant reforms are likely to face a problem. Legal education reform must also battle against a mix of disinterest, complacency and conservatism. The attempts between 1872 and 1876 by the Legal Education Association to establish a scheme for a 'general school of law' are instructive in this regard. These were sunk ultimately by a combination of Parliamentary disinterest, opposition from the profession (both within and outside Parliament), and from the University of London, which feared the proposals would undermine its own law schools at University and King's College. Thereafter, despite extensive grassroots support, not only the scheme, but the Association itself faded rapidly into oblivion.[66] The Atkin, Ormrod and ACLEC Reports all recognised the importance of having a post-review structure in place capable not just of guiding and overseeing implementation, but actively promoting and managing change as change was required. The terms of reference of both the Atkin and Ormrod Committees required them to achieve closer co-ordination between the work of the law schools and the professional bodies. Ultimately, they both failed in this regard, largely blocked by stakeholder, and particularly professional, conservatism.

The results of all this have been mixed for both the academy and the profession, though at some level everyone has achieved at least some pragmatic gains. The academy has, particularly since ACLEC, negotiated itself into a position where it experiences relatively light touch regulation while benefiting (in terms of relatively strong demand for courses) from the advantages of professional recognition. Vocational course providers have, at least until recent reforms to the Bar Profession Training Course (BPTC), generally seen some increase in autonomy over course design and delivery, albeit subject to quite extensive programme specification and monitoring requirements. The professions have been spared a significant burden of quality assuring university courses, enabling them to focus their resources (in theory at least) on the vocational stage and post-qualification training.

Let us now consider where Lord Neuberger's contribution fits into this story.

Re-reading 'Reforming Legal Education'

In many respects Lord Neuberger's Lord Upjohn Lecture stands out from earlier judicial pronouncements, both in the depth and breadth of its engagement with the issues. It is, in my view, rightly critical of the 'fitness for purpose' discourse advanced by David Edmonds and the regulators at the start of the LETR,[67] and focuses on a number of central issues of legal education reform. It advances

66 See Abel-Smith and Stevens, n. 11, 72–4; Ormrod Report, n. 15, para. 23.
67 *RLE*, 6.

a moderate, if not downright cautious, call for reform to both the academic and vocational stages of training. It thus invites some rethinking of the academic core, with a view to both rationalising and possibly extending the same.[68] It calls for the development of a practical 'skills curriculum' at the initial stage,[69] and for the greater development of legal ethics and values on both undergraduate and vocational programmes.[70] It is distinctive in acknowledging the potential role of CILEX in opening up access to not just the solicitors' profession but also the Bar, [71] and sensitive (at least to a point) to the larger problem of diversity.[72] But at the same time there is a pervasive sense of *déjà vu*. Lord Neuberger's vision for reform can be seen as a direct descendant of the compromise positions adopted by the earlier reviews. And, in case you think I am being unduly harsh on his Lordship, I also acknowledge that a number of those same flaws are apparent in the LETR Report.

First, Lord Neuberger does nothing to question the conventional stage model. Though the paper cites, with qualified approval, the Carnegie Report's[73] framework of intellectual, practical and identity apprenticeships, it maps these largely onto the existing stages, thereby disregarding both the extent to which other professions adopt an *integrated* model of all three apprenticeships in the discipline, and Carnegie's own assumption that an integrated model should be adopted for law.

Second, it is particularly defensive of the status quo in respect of training for the Bar, despite the scale of cost, over-supply and diversity problems that have assailed the Bar's vocational course and pupillage. It would be easy, and unfair, to point rather cynically to an assumed judicial tendency to defend the Bar against all comers, because the problem is actually larger than that. History shows us more generally that legal education reform has repeatedly foundered when it has sought to challenge the traditions and liberties of the Bar, and the debate about common training tends to be a particular crunch point. My own view (strengthened and clarified by the LETR experience) is that it is a mistake to treat common training as the (only) alternative to the BPTC. There is much to support a move to post-initial qualification training for the Bar, as exists in Scotland and some Australian jurisdictions. This, in my view, is not really common training. Rather, it treats training for the Bar as a proper post-qualification specialisation. It provides an opportunity for would-be barristers to get a better

68 Ibid., 11–12.

69 Ibid., 12, though the manner in which skills are addressed raises the question whether Lord Neuberger is aware of (i) how much is already being done by many universities in this area and (ii) the concern in some parts of the profession that the emphasis on a good intellectual grounding in law is not diluted by an excessive focus on other things like professional skills – see *LETR Report*, n. 7, para. 2.104.

70 *RLE*, 13.

71 Ibid., 10–11.

72 Ibid., 13–14.

73 William M. Sullivan *et al*, *Educating Lawyers – Preparation for the Profession of Law* (New York, Wiley, 2007).

sense of their career interests, strengths and weaknesses, to develop potential client relationships and build their 'office' and litigation management skills before commencing more advanced litigation and advocacy training.

As ACLEC and the LETR have tended to show, this is not an easy debate to have in the midst of a wider educational review, where fusion as such is not on the agenda, and anything that looks like common training is likely to be considered the thin end of the fusion wedge and judged accordingly. It may be necessary to return once again to the larger debate about fusion, as Lord Neuberger suggests, if only to have space rationally to argue that it is possible to reimagine training for the Bar in a way that does not assume wholly or even predominantly common training. Such a transformation could ultimately strengthen the Bar's position as a quality referral advocacy profession, not weaken it.

Third, Lord Neuberger's analysis very much follows the tradition of earlier reviews in focusing on initial competence, through academic and vocational education and training, while disregarding or at best underplaying the importance of assuring continuing competence of legal services providers through continuing professional development and/or re-accreditation.[74] The English legal profession has largely failed to take continued professional development (CPD) seriously as a regulatory matter, and has certainly failed to keep pace with effective practice in other professions. This is of course a matter on which the LETR Report ultimately placed considerable emphasis,[75] and on which regulatory action has been promised.

Fourth, while Lord Neuberger acknowledges some need for collaboration between the professional bodies, the judiciary and consumers in phase two of the LETR,[76] his discussion of the future of legal education and training reform and the challenges of implementation might also be considered lacking. Even leaving aside the rather curious apprehension that, because the research phase has been led by academics, the academic community has somehow had its turn, it tends to overlook the complexity of co-ordination. The Legal Services Act (LSA) regulatory settlement has created a complicated network of authorised regulators with overlapping jurisdictions and often loosely defined or otherwise difficult to compare training standards. There is also a growing paralegal workforce intersecting in interesting ways with regulated and unregulated legal services. Legal education reform is no longer a matter confined to solicitors, barristers and (even) chartered legal executives. The segmentation of the market and the increasing focus on both entity- and activity-based regulation[77] are likely to increase the need

74 Although the Ormrod Committee briefly considered the need for a framework of continuing education (see n. 15, paras 170–7), ACLEC was the first review to give the subject any substantive attention, but its recommendations, in its *Second Report*, were underwhelming, largely endorsing the steps then being taken by the professional bodies.

75 *LETR Report*, n. 7, paras 5.82–5.117.

76 *RLE*, 5.

77 See *LETR Report*, n. 7, paras 3.47–3.53.

for mechanisms to assure quality and comparability of standards across the sector. Given the problematic history of co-ordination and collaboration highlighted in this chapter, and the extent to which it is the very lack of effective ongoing collaboration which keeps dragging the sector back into these not just recurrent, but repetitive review processes, this lacuna is troubling.

Last, neither Lord Neuberger nor the LETR process has adequately addressed the mounting access to justice challenge and, I suggest, neither could, whilst locked into traditional legal education thinking and structures. Lord Neuberger rightly highlights the 'fundamental' nature of two of the LSA regulatory objectives: the need to protect and promote the public interest, and the need to support the constitutional principle of the rule of law.[78] The cost of legal services in general and the increased cost and legislative constraints on access to the courts, are a direct threat to the public interest in the proper administration of justice and a challenge to the rule of law. As a senior Canadian practitioner has recently opined, access to justice is shaping up to be 'the legal profession's equivalent of global warming'.[79] As the latest legal aid reforms show, traditional practice models, and perhaps even innovations like alternative business structures, may not be adequate to narrow the justice gap.

What has this got to do with legal education reform? I suggest three things. First, there is a danger that, when thinking about legal education, too much of our attention is drawn to the needs of the corporate sector. This is the sector that employs the majority of trainees, and commercial litigation also tends to dominate the work of the senior courts. When Lord Neuberger expresses his fear that the harbour of English law will become, like the ancient commercial centre of Bruges, an 'estuaire inutile oubliépar la mer', a useless estuary abandoned by the sea,[80] it is tempting to assume from the metaphor that it is a decline in the inward flow of complex, high-value, international commercial litigation that is uppermost in his mind. Of course this is important, but it should not be allowed to distort our assessment of training needs *in the public interest*. Second, the cost, duration and level of training required for practitioners are part of the problem. The market for training, geared as it is to the expectations of commercial practice, actively distorts the supply of legal services, by creating an oversupply of trainees to corporate law firms, whilst leaving large areas of personal legal services unable to compete:[81] existing training costs are not just a significant transaction cost, but a direct barrier to participation in the training market. Moreover the current regulatory

78 *RLE*, 7.

79 David Scott, cited by Richard Devlin and Jocelyn Downie, 'Public Interest Vocationalism: A Way Forward for Legal Education in Canada' in Fiona Westwood and Karen Barton (eds), *The Calling of Law: The Pivotal Role of Vocational Legal Education* (Farnham, Ashgate, 2014), 85, 88.

80 From the poem 'Bruges' by Ernest Reynaud, first published in the collection *La Couronne des Jours* (Paris, 1887), available at https://archive.org/stream/lacouronnedesjo00rayngoog/lacouronnedesjo00rayngoog_djvu.txt (accessed 18 September 2015).

81 Gillian K. Hadfield, 'The Price of Law: How the Market for Lawyers Distorts the Justice System' (2000) 98 *Michigan Law Review* 953.

system makes no one accountable for creating a system of competent low-cost alternative provision, for example, through quality-assured independent paralegal practitioners. Third, legal education reform alone is unlikely to make much difference to the access to justice crisis. A focus on access to justice requires us to think more creatively and more broadly about the design of legal systems as *rule of law systems*, not just the design of legal education.[82] We need to identify a range of reforms to court organisation and the delivery of (alternative) dispute-resolution services, in the use of information technology, in who is able to provide legal advice, as well as to legal education and training, which will *together* make law more open and accessible.[83] In this context the practice of self-contained, time-limited, profession-centric legal education reviews, typified by the processes discussed in this chapter and by the LETR itself, is not the solution, but part of the problem.

Conclusion: A tale of two cities

As Lord Neuberger started with a city metaphor, I will finish with one. It will come as no surprise that I prefer another place to Bruges, an entirely imaginary place: the city of Fedora, as described in Calvino's novel, *Invisible Cities*.[84]

Invisible Cities comprises a set of 55 stories told by the explorer Marco Poloto the great Kublai Khan. Each story is a description of a city the explorer has visited, except that all are allegorical: cities of the imagination rather than real places. Fedora is Polo's allegory of unfulfilled potential and imagination. In the centre of the city there stands a museum with a crystal globe in every room. Within each globe is a model of a different Fedora, an imagined, ideal, realisation of what the city could have been if Fedora 'had not become what we see today'.[85]

The point is somewhat obvious; whatever our ability to imagine a different legal education, the present (shaped by the past) exerts a gravitational pull. To continue the design metaphor, as King observes:

> 'All architecture, for its part, is (mere) translation – from the chaotic, jumbled, forever unreadable text of the city . . . and from the architect's half-recalled memory of a million other texts (other labyrinths of time, the confusion of all things ever seen or imagined).'[86]

82 This is, of course, a large question in its own right. For interesting contributions to thinking about legal design and the rule of law, see, eg, Gillian K. Hadfield, 'The Levers of Legal Design: Institutional Determinants of the Quality of Law' (2008) 36 *Journal of Comparative Economics* 43; Gillian K. Hadfield and Barry R. Weingast, 'Microfoundations of the Rule of Law' (2014) 17 *Annual Review of Political Science* 21.

83 See the report of the (Australian) Productivity Commission, *Access to Justice Arrangements* (December 2014), available at http://www.pc.gov.au/inquiries/completed/access-justice/report for a recent attempt to take a more holistic, though arguably still limited, view of the kinds of reform necessary to enhance access.

84 Italo Calvino, *Invisible Cities*, trans. William Weaver (London, Vintage 1997) (first published 1974).

85 Ibid., 28.

86 Ross King, 'Labyrinths' in Steve Pile and Nigel Thrift (eds), *City A–Z* (London, Routledge, 2000).

Over the last 150 years, the architects of each new legal education reform process have each engaged in their 'mere translation' of the labyrinths of legal education, offering some breaks from, but more often continuities with, the past, closing down possibility and cementing the present (system) ever more firmly into place. Lord Neuberger's analysis, despite its merits, largely follows in the tradition of these successive reviews of legal education, which have focused heavily on defining (largely *a priori*) the content and fixed structures whilst paying insufficient attention to the interplay between educational and other systemic processes, and the need for ongoing research, co-ordination and review. Without this shift of focus, I argue that we are fated to be like the citizens of Fedora, revisiting dreams of what could have been in the glass spheres of the museum, while the realised city continues beyond its walls.

If we are to escape that pattern, we need to break from the past; the fear of silting up our own estuary of the Zwin remains a fundamental constraint on so doing. To reinvent legal education and training will take some boldness and creativity, a willingness to challenge assumptions, take risks, invest in experimentation and evidence-gathering, and create a design system that is no longer dependent on the 'one-shot' approach, and institutionally capable of moving beyond the constraints of history and traditional stakeholder inertia.

The LETR is a start, but in retrospect the first phase (at least) was, in my view, too institutionally constrained, too evidence-based (in the absence of much pre-existing evidence) and too close to the one-shot model to break away. The research team's call for a Legal Education Council to continue this work was, in part, a recognition of this fact,[87] and a plea:

> 'On the map of your Empire, O Great Khan, there must be room both for the big stone Fedora and the little Fedoras in glass globes. Not because they are all equally real, but because all are only assumptions. The one contains what is accepted as necessary when it is not yet so; the others, what is imagined as possible and, a moment later, is possible no longer.'[88]

87 See *LETR Report*, n. 7, Recommendation 25.
88 Calvino, n. 84, 28.

5 Fortieth Lord Upjohn Lecture 2011

Widening Participation in a Changing Educational Landscape

*Wes Streeting**

In 1997, the committee of inquiry on lifelong learning, chaired by Helena Kennedy Q.C., published its report that would, in many ways, set the tone for the widening participation agenda that would come to dominate higher education policy for much of New Labour's period in power. It exposed the harsh reality of Britain's education system: a system where "if at first you don't succeed, you don't succeed".

That report, *Learning Works*,[1] made the case that education is the key to economic prosperity and social cohesion. And that the expansion of post-16 education had not been inclusive of those who had experienced social and economic disadvantage. It concluded that all should have the opportunity to access education at level 3 – and should receive the funding to make that a reality.

The Dearing Report set out an equally compelling vision for the role of universities in expanding opportunity as a moral imperative. "The long struggle for equal opportunities" the report argued "will not be won until the elitist culture of many universities is changed."[2]

The widening participation agenda was an attempt to increase not simply the numbers of people benefiting from a higher education, but also the proportions of those entering the sector from "under-represented backgrounds": those on low incomes, disabled students, mature students, students from some black and minority ethnic communities to name but a few.

Under New Labour, significant progress was made: both in terms of widening participation in higher education for under-represented groups and in narrowing the gap between the opportunities enjoyed by the richest and the poorest.

In 2009/10, participation among 19- and 20-year-olds in higher education had increased by 20% since 1994/95.

* This text was delivered as the fortieth Lord Upjohn Lecture at City Law School on 11 November 2011.

1 H. Kennedy (1997). "Learning works: widening participation in further education." Coventry: Further Education Funding Council.

2 R. Dearing (1997). "Higher education in the learning society." Leeds: National Committee of Inquiry into Higher Education. Available at http://www.leeds.ac.uk/educol/ncihe/r5_019.htm (accessed 16 January 2012).

The proportion of young people from the most disadvantaged communities entering higher education has increased by over 50% in the last 15 years.

And since the mid part of the last decade, the gap in participation between those from the richest and poorest backgrounds has begun to narrow.

The words uttered by ministers can sometimes be as powerful as deeds. In spite of the long-running debate about the empirical basis for establishing a target of getting 50% of young people into higher education, there can be no doubt that when Tony Blair announced his commitment that half of all young people should enter university, the words of the prime minister prompted an unprecedented level of investment in, and activity by, higher education institutions.

Throughout the best part of 15 years we've seen a plethora of initiatives: outreach programmes, open days, summer schools, bursaries, websites and so on. But in spite of all that hard work, determination and public investment, much more remains to be done.

It remains the case that just one in five young people from the most disadvantaged neighbourhoods enter higher education, compared to the one in two from the most advantaged neighbourhoods.

Just 16% of pupils who are eligible for free school meals progress to university compared to 96% of those who are taught in independent schools.

And, perhaps most depressing of all, a recent survey of 2300 young people, conducted by the Prince's Trust, revealed that those from deprived backgrounds were three times more likely to say that they thought they would "end up on benefits".

Poverty of aspiration is a term sometimes used to describe young people with such low expectations. But it's not the poverty of aspiration *of* young people that worries me; it is the poverty of aspiration that some continue to hold *for* young people, that gives me the greatest cause for concern.

I don't want to dwell on past debates, but I never understood why the idea that 50% of all young people could and should benefit from higher education was so controversial, when in so many affluent communities across Britain this is already the reality.

As Lord Kinnock, a patron of the Helena Kennedy Foundation, once asked in one of his most famous speeches:

> "Why am I the first Kinnock in a thousand generations to be able to get to university? . . . Is it because our predecessors were thick? Does anybody really believe it was because they didn't have the talent or the strength or the endurance or commitment?"
>
> "Of course not," Kinnock replied, "It was because they had no platform upon which to stand."

Of course, the higher education sector doesn't have the sole – or even primary – responsibility for creating that platform.

Around 13.5 million people in Britain live below the poverty line, more than half of which are in families that include at least one child.

Children eligible for free school meals, by definition from the poorest families, are around half as likely as others to get five good GCSEs. And we know that prior attainment is the key determining factor in whether an individual progresses into higher education and where they end up.

So we can take it as a given that universities cannot be expected to fire a silver bullet to correct deep inequalities that are entrenched from early years.

But there are things that we can do, have done and should continue to do to create an education system in which every citizen can achieve his or her full potential. To succeed we need to get the framework right.

Since the formation of the Coalition government, there has been a subtle shift in the language of ministers, signalling a significant shift in the emphasis of government policy.

In the revised grant letter to the Higher Education Funding Council for England in June last year,[3] Vince Cable and David Willetts stated:

> "*Social mobility, fair access* and *widening participation* should be a key strategic objective and you should continue to require an annual Widening Participation Strategic Assessment (WPSA) from all institutions. This should cover not only young people from low income backgrounds but all those from groups under- represented in HE, taking into account issues facing disabled students, ethnic minorities, part-time and mature students." (Emphasis added)

Again, in their guidance letter to Sir Martin Harris[4] in February of this year, they wrote:

> "Increasing *social mobility, extending fair access to Higher Education (HE) and the professions*, and *attracting a higher proportion of under-represented groups*, particularly those most able but least likely to apply, are *priorities* for the Coalition government." (Emphasis added)

And in the government's strategy for social mobility,[5] Nick Clegg said:

> "The true test of fairness is the distribution of opportunities. That is why *improving social mobility is the principal goal of the Coalition Government's social policy*." (Emphasis added)

Fair access to selective universities, and widening participation more broadly, could and should be understood as two sides of the social mobility coin. But there are important distinctions to draw between each of these three priorities.

3 Available at http://www.bis.gov.uk/assets/biscore/higher-education/docs/h/10-1359-hefce-grant-letter-20-dec-2010.pdf, p. 2 (accessed 16 January 2012).

4 Available at http://www.bis.gov.uk/assets/biscore/higher-education/docs/g/11-728-guidance-to-director-fair-access, p. 2 (accessed 16 January 2012).

5 Cabinet Office (2011). "Opening Doors, Breaking Barriers: A Strategy for Social Mobility," p. 3.

There are a number of ways of defining social mobility. This government is primarily concerned with promoting intergenerational social mobility – defined in its strategy as "the extent to which people's success in life is determined by who their parents are"; and relative social mobility, defined as "the comparative chances of people with different backgrounds ending up in certain social or income groups".[6]

In practice, this had led to a White Paper far more concerned with ensuring fair access to selective universities, than it is about widening participation across higher education more generally.[7]

Of course we should be concerned about fair access to our most selective institutions. Over many years, the Sutton Trust has catalogued the extent to which those from more privileged backgrounds dominate those institutions characterised by many as our "best" institutions. For the sake of political correctness, we will call them the most "selective" universities. The most disadvantaged young people are seven times less likely than those with the most advantage to attend the most selective universities.

I have no problem with the concept of academic elitism within our higher education system, but too often our most academically selective universities appear to be socially selective. This has far-reaching consequences beyond the higher education system, when so many of the levers of social, political and economic power in Britain are wielded by those who wear the Oxbridge scarf and the old school tie.

But we should bear in mind the numbers involved in this game. When we talk about those who have the grades to secure a place on the most sought-after courses, but choose not to apply, we're talking about a few thousand. But when we think of those who have the ability to benefit more broadly from higher education, we're not talking a few thousand; we're talking hundreds of thousands if not millions.

There is a risk that too narrow minded a focus on a certain notion of social mobility could lead to a deeply individualistic approach that picks a few winners and leaves the rest behind, or that says that in order to ensure long-term social mobility, we must focus all of our investment and resources in early years, to the detriment of adult education and lifelong learning.

It's a vision in which we seek a means of escape for children living in poverty and deprivation, but leave their communities to be let down and left behind once more.

When the number of children living in absolute poverty is set to rise to 3 million by 2013, you will get no dissension from me that we must continue to invest in children, families and early years in particular. All the evidence suggests that this is the best way to ensure that every child can reach their potential. But just as we would wish that no child born in Britain today is left

6 Cabinet Office (2011). "Opening Doors, Breaking Barriers: A Strategy for Social Mobility", p. 15.

7 Department for Business, Innovation and Skills. (2011). "Higher Education: Students at the Heart of the System." No. CM8122.

behind, we should act to ensure that those failed in previous generations are given a second chance.

This government would not be the first to create false choices between investment in early years education and lifelong learning. We need to reframe the debate, making the case for investment in educational opportunities full stop.

Because if you invest in a mother on a council estate with high levels of unemployment and low levels of skills, you not only improve her lot in life: you inspire her children, her friends and her neighbours. The ripple effect of that investment not only transforms one life, it has the power to transform an entire community.

Some policy changes have been well publicised and heavily contested. For much of the past year, tuition fees and changes to the student finance system have barely been out of the public eye. Huge student demonstrations and the novelty of new Coalition politics kept the political debate alive in the media and as the system becomes a reality it is likely to remain so with every trend and pronouncement picked apart.

What the government is attempting is nothing less than the largest big bang reform of tuition fees and student finance ever attempted by any government, anywhere, ever.

There is a real risk that students could be deterred by myths and misconceptions about the new arrangements. A poll published to coincide with Universities Week 2011[8] revealed that 55% of people think the new system makes higher education less attractive. Worryingly, 40% of people still think that students will have to pay at least part of their tuition fees up front – with 26% thinking they will have to pay full tuition fees in advance.

Up-front tuition fees for full-time undergraduates haven't existed in England since 2006. We know that a lack of information, advice and guidance will not be a universal experience. Some will fare better than others, with lots of support at home from well-connected parents and dedicated support at school, which in some cases even extends to the provision of an Oxbridge tutor. For others, who lack the social and cultural capital available to those from more privileged backgrounds, the task of navigating an increasingly crowded and complex landscape of information will seem overwhelming.

In this context, the government's decision to abandon AimHigher seems absurd. AimHigher established strong, collaborative networks and an army of practitioners with knowledge, skills and experience that are desperately needed. At the same time, local authorities, facing front-loaded, swingeing cuts to their budgets, are passing on those cuts to local Connexions services.

The loss of AimHigher is not the only setback the widening participation agenda has suffered in the past 18 months. The abolition of the Education Maintenance Allowance (EMA) was widely reported in the media and is now being felt

8 Poll published by Universities UK and conducted by YouGov. Summarised at http://www.universitiesuk.ac.uk/Newsroom/Media-Releases/Pages/Thirdofparentshavelittleornounderstandingofnewuniversityfeessystem.aspx (accessed 16 January 2012).

in the pockets of many students who need it. All of the younger students we work with at the Helena Kennedy Foundation were recipients of the EMA and nothing about their experience of struggling to afford the costs associated with studying for courses in sixth forms and colleges leads me to believe that the EMA is a dead weight cost. Thirty pounds might not sound like a lot, but when you're from a family living below the poverty line, it's the difference between being able to afford your bus pass and not. The so-called EMA replacement pales in comparison.

Elsewhere in the pre-HE system, for students over 24, free access to level 3 is over. We will be inducting these students into fees and debt far earlier and at greater risk.

Some students may not make it to level 3 at all as access courses close across the country from September. Last year, I visited a college in South London and walked down a corridor where every classroom was filled with students on access courses. For the most part, they were over 24, black and possessed few if any formal qualifications. As we walked down the corridor the principal told me that from September none of these classes would be running. That's a devastating blow to an important pipeline of talent to our universities. The mantra of "if at first you don't succeed, you don't succeed" looks set to return.

There are some immediate steps the government could take to ensure that the progress that has been made to widen participation does not slip into reverse gear.

The first thing we need to do is to redouble our efforts to convey the facts about fees. It is clear that politicians have become incapable of communicating the detail of the new student finance arrangements – and not through want of trying. Such was the toxic nature of the debate and the recriminations around the politics of the decision to hike up fees, that whenever a minister takes to the airwaves to explain how the system works, they are ambushed by accusations of broken promises.

That's why Martin Lewis of moneysavingexpert.com and I agreed to lead an independent taskforce on student finance communications. We are both critics of the new arrangements, but we feel very strongly about the need to separate the communication of the facts behind the system from the political debate about its merits.

Perhaps it's all very Big Society, but we've put together a big tent involving UCAS, UUK, Guild HE, NUS, student money advisors, consumer groups – in fact anyone with a willingness to help – to use every means at our disposal to ensure that potential students and their families are able to make informed decisions about what to study, where to study or whether to even study at all. We're not interested in selling the fees model or sugar-coating the system.

We highlight some of the facts that may come as a more pleasant surprise to those terrified by the prospect of affording student life and life after graduation. Like the fact that you pay nothing up front and only if you're a new starter in 2012; that graduate repayments will be lower under the new system than under the existing system; and we point out that repayments are the same whether the sticker price on your degree was £9000 or £6000.

But we're clear that graduates *will* owe money for longer, *may* pay more than at present and will pay interest at a higher level than inflation (though not at the same level as a high street loan).

We've developed guides for students, parents and advisors, lesson plans for teachers in schools and a whole range of materials and resources.

If able students, particularly those from under-represented backgrounds, are deterred from higher education because of the student finance system, the government will need to think again. But if they are deterred through myths and misconceptions it will have been a tragedy that we might have avoided.

That's not to let government off the hook around the provision of information, advice and guidance. I've covered "slash and burn" so let me explore what they ought to put in its place.

There is a clear emphasis in the provision of greater amounts of information in the White Paper, but there is a real lack of attention to addressing advice and guidance. This was a particular failure under the last government and the present government is in danger of repeating past mistakes.

I'm not calling for more demands to be placed on schools, colleges or universities, although there will be more information from institutions through the new key information sets (KIS). Schools are already laden with vested interests and a preoccupation with league tables at the expense of their students. Universities have an inherent self-interest in promoting higher education as the key route to success in life and their institution in particular as the best possible choice. So more of the same from the vested interests will not do.

Instead, we need a radical overhaul that places advice and guidance at the top of the agenda: independent, personalised and targeted on the most disadvantaged communities. This is not simply Connexions mark II. It's about harnessing the purchasing power of central government, local government, schools and colleges to create a rich landscape – and competitive market – of providers that can deliver timely, appropriate and customised support to different individuals and communities. I'm not convinced that the all age careers service making its way through Whitehall machinery will cut the mustard, or emerge as anything else besides yet another website.

On student finance – the money available to students' pockets to help them afford the maintenance costs associated with studying – the government is at risk of serious complacency. We say that anyone who wants to go to university can afford to do so, but the reality is that some are more able to afford it than others. In spite of grants, loans and bursaries, some students still struggle to meet the costs. Some are forced to work longer hours in paid work to the detriment of their studies and participation in extra-curricular activities. Those from low income backgrounds have more difficult decisions to make about what to study and where to study, sometimes finding themselves forced to study locally or part time because they simply can't make ends meet.

I can understand why the Treasury might want universities to offer fee waivers instead of bursaries, but from a consumer finance point of view it makes no sense whatsoever. The sticker price of the course will often bear no relation to the amount that a student will pay, because of the income contingent repayment system and debt write-off period after 30 years. It is shameful that universities have been pressured by the government – through the Office for Fair Access – to cut back on financial support in favour of fee waivers. The sector should abandon fee waivers altogether and give students the support they need, when they need it: up front and for those who need it most.

While we wait for the government to act, there is plenty we can do ourselves. Throughout the lifetime of AimHigher we have accumulated a huge amount of knowledge and experience about raising aspirations and promoting participation that need to be harnessed. The huge amount of intellectual property sitting in AimHigher research and practice, not to mention the valuable human resources we have, needs to be deployed.

There is a risk that collaboration on this kind of activity will be lost in a new climate of tough competition. There is also a risk that a sharper focus on participation data and results leads to universities focusing their energies on schools and colleges (though mainly schools) where they are likely to get the greatest return on investment when the admissions round is completed.

Either scenario would be a terrible mistake. Universities should enter this new era with a renewed commitment to collaboration: with each other, with schools and colleges, with business and big society. We all have a valuable role to play and a united front will strengthen our approach.

If universities complain that their success at widening access is hampered by problems earlier in the education system, then they should seek to play a greater role.

We also need to see progress on admissions reform. There are many impressive things about our higher educations system in the UK, but I never cease to be amazed by the ability of this sector to draw reform to a grinding halt through a succession of reviews about the same thing. We had the Wilson Review, the Schwartz Review, the Delivery Partnership Steering Group (more a partnership preventing delivery steering group) and now UCAS is looking at the issue of post-qualification applications.

Our current admissions arrangements, involving an eccentric combination of good choices, guesswork and pot luck in making choices based on what you'd like to get at A-level or equivalent and what you worry you might end up with, are bizarre and certainly not in the interests of the applicant. Perhaps some of the 3000 students who achieved the grades necessary to enter one of the Sutton Trust's 13 selective universities may have applied if they'd possessed the confidence of knowing that they would meet the entry requirements. And perhaps retention rates would be higher if we didn't have the anarchy of the clearing bargain basement forcing distressed students to make choices that will determine the rest of their lives within a matter of hours.

It's common sense. It's in the student's interest. And it's a reform long overdue.

But if we're serious about creating opportunity for all, the wider philosophy of widening participation is in need of reassertion and reinvention.

When the late Ron Dearing spoke of widening participation in higher education, he was referring not simply to the point of entry, but to ensuring a full and active part in the broader student experience.

I think the sector has been negligent in this regard: complacent about participation in the wider student experience and insufficiently focused on making a range of opportunities open to the most disadvantaged.

At the Helena Kennedy Foundation, we work with some of the most disadvantaged students entering higher education – specifically those from Further Education colleges, which have a tradition of providing second chances to adult learners and where 56% of learners are from the lowest three socio-economic groups, compared to just 22% in maintained school sixth forms. They are living proof that learning works and that education is a route into active citizenship. They include care leavers, carers, asylum seekers, disabled students and students who have experienced violence and abuse. Most importantly, they are students who are triumphing against the odds.

We seek to give our students access to three key ingredients for success: access to the money, the networks and the know-how that so many others are able to take for granted.

Since the Foundation's creation we have provided financial support through bursaries. These bursaries are now at £1500, and we know from our student surveys that they have a real impact: 49% of students tell us that without it, they're not sure they would have stayed at university and 96% said it had made a real difference to their ability to afford their studies.

But increasingly, we're focusing on their personal development. We run courses and sessions around areas like debating and business writing. We run insight days in some of the top professions. We provide mentoring and coaching and we seek opportunities for our students to undertake paid work placements in professions and industries of interest to them.

We have a retention rate of about 96%. Why is this? And what might the sector learn from our experience?

Our service is personalised. We know our students and they know us. Often they ring us first if they have a problem with paying their accommodation fees, or if a family situation has left them behind with their deadlines.

We care about their ambitions and aspirations and we try to match them with people in their chosen careers so that they have the know-how necessary to navigate their options and the confidence to know that they'd fit in.

And we highlight the importance of building their CVs, recognising the skills they have and seizing opportunities to give them sharper elbows in an increasingly competitive market.

This personalised approach to personal development is most important when working with students who lack the cultural and social capital enjoyed by those from better connected families. For many students, it's not what you know.

Some students have the financial freedom to spend their time on the rugby pitch, on the stage or in the students' union during term time, and the ability to spend a summer working for free in an unpaid internship.

Some students have the connections to get a placement in chambers, in an exclusive London bank or on a national newspaper. And some students have parents behind them that have imparted good careers guidance and high expectations from the outset. But for the student who spends their spare time stacking shelves and pulling pints to make ends meet, the conventional student experience can seem like something that other people enjoy.

It should be of no surprise to us that 70% of High Court judges and 68% of top barristers are privately educated, even though the privately educated account for just 7% of the population. The legal profession is one where money, networks and know-how make all the difference.

Simply gaining the professional qualifications necessary to qualify comes at great costs. Networks and connections mean professional currency. Many students reading law at university, with ambitions of becoming Kavanagh Q.C. have no idea how to do it and even if they already have their sights on a training contract, they may have no idea how to secure one and how competitive the market is in the current economic climate.

Even in these financially straitened times, universities need to think about the kind of student experience they foster and who is able to participate.

In the last week alone I've met HE staff who are developing innovative new schemes around paid internships, opportunity bursaries to help students play a more active part in sports clubs and societies and personal tutor systems that provide friendly faces and timely interventions for those most at risk of dropping out.

But there is some way to go to narrow the opportunity gap between the "haves" and the "have nots". There is also a business case and a moral case for doing so and partnerships between business and big society have their part to play too.

So these are testing times for the sector. And while things are not as we may have wished them to be, I believe we need to focus on the things we can do and keep our eyes on the prize of what success might look like.

Alan Milburn, the government's social mobility advisor contends that "it is not ability that is unevenly distributed in our society, it is opportunity".[9]

To redistribute opportunity in our society we must never lose sight of the inherent value of widening participation in education in the broadest terms and we should celebrate and value the transformational power of higher education in its various manifestations and wish it for more than simply our own children.

I want to end by talking about two universities that I love and whose diverse missions deserve to be valued: the University of Cambridge and the University of East London.

I love the University of Cambridge, because I spent four happy years there. They took a boy from Stepney, in Tower Hamlets – one of the few at the university who had received free school meals – made me feel welcome, gave me an outstanding education and a platform to develop new skills and the chance to seize opportunities that changed my life. Thanks to student politics, I found myself on the university's governing council before becoming a professional student in NUS. I certainly wouldn't be speaking to you today without that opportunity. And I am truly grateful.

It was social mobility in action. And I saw first hand the immense commitment of so many individuals in that university to the widening access agenda.

9 See http://www.guardian.co.uk/society/2009/jul/19/alan-milburn-uk-unequal-society.

I also love the University of East London (UEL). I love it for two reasons. First, it's my local university and it has had a huge impact on the East End of London, where I have spent my entire life. It has over 23,000 students, from over 120 nationalities, at the heart of one of Europe's largest regeneration areas. It has brought inward investment and a huge economic impact on the entire Thames Gateway.

But there's a second reason. And it is the most important reason. Unlike the towering buildings of the Docklands nearby, it doesn't sit as an ivory tower of bright lights and opportunities surrounded by a sea of relative darkness and poverty. It reaches out into the local community. It is part of the local community.

When I was part of the London Education Partnership Awards, I met two women who had benefited from a partnership between UEL and the London Borough of Barking and Dagenham. Both had left school with no qualifications. They felt they had failed. When they got jobs as classroom assistants they were encouraged by their head to do a Foundation course. They did it. They enjoyed it. And before long they were hooked and are now fully qualified teachers. One of them even planned to do a masters. They spoke with real passion about the impact it had made on their lives, but with even greater conviction about the impact it had made on their own children.

And I would argue that UEL has had a more transformational impact on those women, and their children, and the children that they are now teaching, than my university had on me.

That's what the widening participation agenda and the culture of lifelong learning is about. It is up to each of us to build a nation that can identify talent in unusual places, open doors, broaden horizons and set people free. A nation of education participation in which everyone can realise their potential.

6 Response: Transformation by Education

Graeme Broadbent

The choice of Wes Streeting to give the 2011 Lord Upjohn Lecture[1] was both bold and inspired. At the time of the lecture he was working in the voluntary sector, having previously been a president of the National Union of Students. He was recently elected as the Labour Member of Parliament for Ilford North in the 2015 General Election. Of all the Lord Upjohn Lecturers represented in this volume, he is the youngest and most closely attuned with the student perspective. He is also the most overtly political. His theme of widening participation was linked to a broader policy goal of social mobility which was embraced by the Labour Government of 1997–2010 and its Coalition successor (2010–2015). Under Labour, this found expression in ideas of social inclusion,[2] with economic activity as a key indicator, to be achieved through a variety of measures of which education was only one piece of the jigsaw. The power of education to transform lives has a long pedigree. In policy terms, the role of higher education as part of greater inclusivity rests on two particular tenets. First, that going to university is a desirable objective. This raises the question of the place of education in general and higher education in particular as priorities in the overall polices of government. The second is the link between higher education and enhanced economic benefit, made quite explicit in the Labour White Papers of 2003[3] and the Coalition

1 (2012) 'Widening participation in a changing educational landscape' 46(1) *Law Teacher* 3–14. On widening participation generally, see also, for example, Catherine Macdonald and Erica Stratta (2001) 'From Access to Widening Participation: responses to the changing population in Higher Education in the UK' *Journal of Further and Higher Education* 25(2) 249–258; Louise Archer, Merryn Hutchings and Alistair Ross (2003) *Higher Education and Social Class* (London: Routledge Falmer); Lois S. Bibbings (2006) 'Widening Participation and Higher Education' *Journal of Law and Society* 33(1) 74–91; Paul Greenbank (2006) 'The Evolution of Government Policy on Widening Participation' *Higher Education Quarterly* 60(2) 141–166; Penny Jane Burke (2012) *The Right to Higher Education* (Abingdon: Routledge); and ARC Network (2013) *Literature review of research into widening participation to higher education* (Bristol: HEFCE).

2 Ruth Levitas (2005) *The Inclusive Society? Social Exclusion and New Labour* 2nd ed. (Basingstoke: Macmillan).

3 Department for Education and Skills (DfES) (2003) *The future of higher education* Cm 5735 (London: TSO); Department for Education and Skills (DfES) (2003) *Widening participation in higher education* (London: TSO).

White Paper of 2011,[4] to both the individual and the country. Put shortly, there are individual benefits arising from higher levels of pay in graduate occupations, while the country benefits from an educated and skilled workforce in terms of greater economic performance.[5]

There are many examples of social mobility over the course of history, with the law providing its fair share of high achievers from modest backgrounds. Some of them have been spectacular. A draper's son became the longest serving Master of the Rolls in the 20th century.[6] A grocer's daughter became prime minister.[7] Wes Streeting himself is an example, having recently entered the House of Commons from a working class background in Tower Hamlets. In all three cases, higher education played a part on their way to high office: Lord Denning and Margaret Thatcher studied at Oxford University while Wes Streeting read history at Cambridge University. Many other individual examples can be identified. But Streeting's concern is, quite rightly, not with these individual instances of transformation but rather with the structural inequalities and attitudes that prevent such examples being multiplied more widely.[8]

Streeting is not against elitism per se and declares himself in favour of academic elitism, but not the social elitism that often accompanies it in educational provision.[9] It is, of course, entirely possible to have widening participation within an elite system of higher education. That is what the Robbins Committee[10] had in mind when proposing that higher education should be available to all those who could benefit from it. Robbins had in mind the removal of barriers, in particular financial, to participating in higher education. The impact of other factors, such as the cultural and social barriers, which have assumed more significance in more recent discussions, were largely absent from the Committee's thinking. Once there, the Robbins notion of student life (what would now be called 'the student experience') was an all embracing one: students would not only study together but would also share accommodation in halls of residence and engage not just in course-related

4 Department for Business, Innovation and Skills (BIS) (2011) *Higher Education: Students at the Heart of the System* Cm 8122 (London: TSO).

5 This argument is not universally accepted: see, for example, Alison Wolf (2002) *Does Education Matter? Myths about education and economic growth* (Harmondsworth: Penguin) and (2004) 'Education and Economic Performance: Simplistic Theories and their Policy Consequences' *Oxford Review of Economic Policy* 20(2) 315–333.

6 Lord Denning (1981) *The Family Story* (London: Butterworths). The Dennings were a remarkable family: one of Lord Denning's brothers was a general; another was an admiral.

7 Hugo Young (1990) *One of Us* (London: Pan).

8 Denial of the opportunity to benefit from higher education is a theme that runs through his lecture: 'But we should bear in mind the numbers involved in this game. When we talk about those who have the grades to secure a place on the most sought after courses, but choose not to apply, we're talking about a few thousand. But when we think of those who have the ability to benefit more broadly from higher education, we're not talking a few thousand; we're talking hundreds of thousands if not millions': Streeting, n. 1, at p. 6.

9 Ibid.

10 Lord Robbins (chairman) (1963) *Higher Education* Cmnd 2154 (London: HMSO).

activities but in a range of recreational and social activities. In other words, being a student would be all that a person did throughout the duration of a university degree course. As far as social mobility was concerned, Robbins had in mind mobility in social class rather than the economic mobility emphasised more recently. University was seen, as Halsey observes,[11] as a form of finishing school, essentially socialising students into middle class values by activities such as dining together and engaging in culturally uplifting activities rather than as a vehicle for economic growth. The context of Robbins was, however, rather different. There were post-war shortages across a range of disciplines; there was a greater demand as the expanding population of children of the 1940s and 1950s were to reach university age; the position of women was radically different – this was still an era where women gave up work to get married and where careers ended on the birth of children; and most significantly it was an era where graduates were all but guaranteed employment in higher paid jobs.[12] The context remained, however, that this should operate within an elite system of higher education with limited participation, even though the committee recognised that some expansion of the sector was necessary in the national interest, and where the maintenance of standards was essential to secure the status of degrees as high level qualifications. Nor was Robbins advocating a consumer model whereby anyone who wanted to go to university should be able to do so: the notion of benefit implied a threshold standard for entry. The Robbins recommendations were adopted and a raft of new universities came into being,[13] accompanied, as is almost inevitable when any expansion of higher education occurs, with doom-laden protests about the threat to standards.[14]

Much has happened in the intervening years with many of Robbins' goals achieved, to a greater or lesser degree, in terms of widening participation. Most notable has been the increase in female students to the point at which there is now something of a moral panic about encouraging male students to attend university.[15] Numbers of black, minority ethnic (BME) and disabled students have

11 A.H. Halsey (1992) *Decline of Donnish Dominion* (Oxford: Clarendon Press) at p. 5.

12 See generally on the post-war years Arthur Marwick (2003) *British Society since 1945* 4th ed. (London: Penguin Books).

13 See John Gledhill, (2001) 'The Modern English Universities' in David Warner and David Palfreyman (eds) *The State of UK Higher Education* (Buckingham: SRHE/OU) 95–102. The term 'new university' now tends to refer to the post-1992 universities.

14 For example, Kingsley Amis (1971) 'Pernicious Participation' in C.B. Cox and A.E. Dyson (eds) *The Black Papers on Education* (London: Davis-Poynter Limited).

15 Statistics from HESA show that, for all full-time study in 2013–2014, there were 924,530 female students and 771,340 male students; the figures for law are quite striking, with 6,940 female as against 5,565 male postgraduates and 36,765 female and 21,885 male undergraduates: https://www.hesa.ac.uk/free-statistics (accessed 3 July 2015). Despite the predominance of female students in law schools, the curriculum and pedagogy do not reflect this: see, for example, Rosemary Auchmuty (2010) 'Feminists as Stakeholders in the Law School' in Fiona Cownie (ed) *Stakeholders in the Law School* (Oxford: Hart) 35–63. See also, on attracting men into higher education, Penny Jane Burke (2006) 'Men accessing education: gendered aspirations' *British Educational Research Journal* 32(5) 719–733 and (2007) 'Men accessing education: masculinities, identifications and widening participation' *British Journal of Sociology of Education* 28(4) 411–424.

also increased,[16] although not so dramatically and, in any event, unevenly across the sector. The position of mature students has also changed. The abolition of national service, with the last conscripts leaving in 1963, the year of the Robbins Report, reduced the average age of undergraduates, many of whom would previously have undertaken their national service before starting their degree course. Those who, in more recent times, entered higher education other than following A levels were thus more noticeably different from the majority of their peers, and again they are distributed unevenly across the sector. The major failure, as Streeting highlights, has been among lower income groups who, as he amply exemplifies, are still significantly under-represented in higher education.

Most discussions of participation in higher education are of a generalised nature, and Streeting's is no exception, though he nods in the direction of his audience by occasional references to law. They also tend to focus on the point of entry: the establishment of the Office of Fair Access,[17] as its name suggests, is part of the agenda that sees securing the entry of a more diverse student body to institutions of higher education as a key objective. However, as the work of Mantz Yorke[18] and others has indicated, merely securing entry to a university is only the starting point. In his work on retention, Yorke identifies four factors that are especially significant in successful completion of university courses. The student should be on the right course for that individual student, at the right university for that individual student, in the right location for that individual student, and the student should not have been admitted through clearing.

Whilst successive governments have encouraged entry to university, they have been less forthcoming about the subject studied. The balance between subjects in universities has been largely left to market forces, subject only to entry requirements, as both the Browne Review[19] and the 2011 White Paper[20] have been keen to encourage student choice, and as such have not sought to interfere to correct imbalances. Law has been attractive to university managements and students alike for a variety of reasons. It is attractive to university managements in that law schools are relatively cheap to run and attract significant numbers

16 For full-time law students in 2013–2014, there were 630 postgraduates and 4,750 undergraduates who declared a disability; and, of those who declared ethnicity, 1,430 non-white (using HESA classifications) postgraduates and 15525 non white undergraduates.

17 See http://www.offa.org.uk/ (accessed 3 July 2015).

18 See, for example, Mantz Yorke (1999) *Leaving Early: Undergraduate Non-completion in Higher Education* (London: Falmer Press) and (2000) 'The Quality of the Student Experience: what can institutions learn from data relating to non–completion?' *Quality in Higher Education* 6(1) 61–75; (with Liz Thomas) (2003) 'Improving the Retention of Students from Lower Socio-economic Groups' *Journal of Higher Education Policy and Management* 25(1) 63–74.

19 Browne Review (2010) *Securing a sustainable future for higher education* archived at http://webarchive.nationalarchives.gov.uk/+/hereview.independent.gov.uk/hereview/ (accessed 3 July 2015).

20 BIS, n. 4.

of students.[21] For students, law is perceived as a valuable degree which leads to well-paid and attractive employment.[22] As such, demand for law continues to grow with latest UCAS figures showing a 4% increase in full-time enrolments on the previous year.[23] New law schools continue to be established,[24] so that forecasts that demand would exceed supply have not been realised. Contrast this with the position of other disciplines such as natural sciences and languages. Language departments in universities have seen declining demand to the point of closure or shrinkage.[25] Despite a plea for more scientists to sustain the needs of the economy and some initiatives to support this,[26] there has been no significant growth here. Studies of non-traditional students suggest[27] that such students incline more to courses in the caring professions such as nursing and social work or to social sciences, so, for certain types of student at least, there appear to be imbalances in the subject to which they gravitate.

There are many variables in the nature of universities and these will affect how individuals experience them, whether positively or negatively. For example, a university may consist of a number of buildings spread across a city or may be in one location on an out-of-town campus. Accommodation may be on site or scattered

21 Richard Abel (2003) *English Lawyers between Market and State* (Oxford: Oxford University Press) at p. 476 and Bob Hepple (1994) 'Some concluding reflections' in P. Birks (ed) *Reviewing Legal Education* (Oxford: Oxford University Press) at p. 110. Despite suggestions (see Phil Harris and Sarah Beinart (2005) 'A Survey of Law Schools in the United Kingdom 2004' *The Law Teacher* 39(3) 299–366) that the demand for places for law degrees may exceed supply, the growth of new law schools and consequently places for students, has ensured that this has not happened.

22 See Alison Bone (2009) 'The twenty-first century law student' 43(3) *Law Teacher* 222–245, esp. at 226–231.

23 See UCAS *End of Cycle Report 2014* (December 2014) available at http://ucascomstg.prod.acquia-sites.com/sites/default/files/2014-end-of-cycle-report-dec-14.pdf (accessed 3 July 2015).

24 Recent years have seen the establishment of law schools at York and Roehampton Universities as well as a growth in private providers, both new and established, satellite campuses and franchised provision together with developments in distance learning.

25 Reports by both Ofsted, in January 2011 and the House of Lords EU Select Committee in March 2012, for example, have highlighted concerns about the study of languages in schools leading to reductions in the numbers studying languages at university: see Ofsted, *Modern languages: achievement and challenge 2007–2010* available at http://www.ofsted.gov.uk/resources/modern-languages-achievement-and-challenge-2007–2010 (accessed 3 July 2015) and House of Lords, European Union Committee, *The Modernisation of Higher Education in Europe*, 22 March 2012 (HL 2010–12, 275) available at http://www.publications.parliament.uk/pa/ld201012/ldselect/ldeucom/275/275.pdf (accessed 3 July 2015). See also Michael Worton (2009) *Review of modern Foreign Languages provision in higher education in England* (Bristol: HEFCE); Jocelyn Wyburd 'Seeking Commitment' *Times Higher Education* 4 September 2014 p. 34; Sally Weale 'University modern languages courses easier to get on than five years ago' *the Guardian* 15 May 2015 available at http://www.theguardian.com/education/2015/may/08/university-modern-language-courses-easier-to-get-on-than-five-years-ago (accessed 3 July 2015).

26 House of Commons Science and Technology Committee (2006) *Strategic Science Provision in English Universities: A Follow-up* (HC1011) (London: TSO).

27 See, for example, Marion Bowl (2003) *Non-traditional entrants to higher education* (Stoke-on-Trent: Trentham Books); Penny Jane Burke (2002) *Accessing Education* (Stoke-on-Trent: Trentham Books).

around a town. The university may be near to where students live, encouraging students to stay at home rather than in university or other accommodation, which can affect their experience and engagement with the university. Apart from its type or geographical location, the culture of a university can be distinctive. The relationship between research and teaching is a key factor which can have a profound impact on the student experience, with research often privileged and prioritised over teaching especially in the more selective and research-intensive universities,[28] despite attempts by the government to encourage a greater focus on teaching.[29] Matters such as timetabling, library facilities or student support services can also be significant. While these are issues directly affecting students, their experience of university will also be affected by matters not directly linked to their course such as campus security or the quality of catering. When considering barriers to participation in higher education, Robbins tended to focus on financial barriers without giving full weight to social or cultural barriers, which have been appreciated and explored in more recent studies. Universities also have distinctive cultures in the type of student they attract and studies suggest that the question of whether they will 'fit in' is an important facet of university life.[30] Universities

28 See, for example, Angela Brew and David Boud (1995) 'Teaching and research: Establishing the vital link with learning' *Higher Education* 29(3) 261–273; Sue G. Burroughs-Lange (1996) 'University Lecturers' Concept of their Role' *Higher Education Research and Development* 15(1) 29–49; Lewis Elton (2000) 'The UK Research Assessment Exercise: Unintended Consequences' *Higher Education Quarterly* 54(3) 274–283; Kelly Coate, Ronald Barnett and Gareth Williams (2001) 'Relationships Between Teaching and Research in Higher Education in England' *Higher Education Quarterly* 55(2) 158–174; David D. Dill (2005) 'The Degradation of the Academic Ethic: Teaching, Research and the Renewal of Professional Self-Regulation' in Ronald Barnett (ed) *Reshaping the University* (Maidenhead: SRHE/OU) 178–191; Rosemary Deem and Lisa Lucas (2006) 'Learning about research: exploring the learning and teaching/research relationship amongst educational practitioners studying in higher education' *Teaching in Higher Education* 11(1) 1–18; Pat Young (2006) 'Out of balance: lecturers' perceptions of differential status and rewards in relation to teaching and research' *Teaching in Higher Education* 11(2) 191–202; Christine Halse, Elizabeth Deane, Jane Hobson and Gar Jones (2007) 'The research–teaching nexus: what do national teaching awards tell us?' *Studies in Higher Education* 32(6) 727–746; Jonathan Parker (2008) 'Comparing Research and Teaching in University Promotion Criteria' *Higher Education Quarterly* 62(3) 237–251; Angela Brew (2010) 'Imperatives and challenges in integrating teaching and research' *Higher Education Research & Development* 29(2) 139–150.

29 See BIS, n. 4.

30 See, for example, the studies by Bowl and Burke, n. 27 and Lyn Tett (2000) '"I'm Working Class and Proud of It" – gendered experiences of non-traditional participants in higher education' *Gender and Education* 12(2) 183–194; Richard Cooke, Michael Barkham, Kerry Audin, Margaret Bradley and John Davy (2004) 'How Social Class Differences Affect Students' Experience of University' *Journal of Further and Higher Education* 28(4) 407–421; Mary Stuart (2006) '"My friends made all the difference": Getting into and succeeding at university for first generation entrants' *Journal of Access Policy & Practice* 3(2) 162–184; Louise Archer and Carole Leathwood (2003) 'Challenging cultures? Student Conceptions of "Belonging" and "Isolation" at a Post-1992 University' *Studies in Higher Education* 28(3) 261–277; Paula Wilcox, Sandra Winn and Marylynn Fyvie-Gauld (2005) '"It was nothing to do with the university, it was just the people": the role of social support in the first-year experience of higher education' *Studies in Higher Education* 30(6) 707–722; Rachel Brooks (2007) 'Friends, peers and higher education' *British Journal of Sociology of Education* 28(6) 693–707.

may tend towards homogeneity or heterogeneity in their student body, and the ideal university is one where students feel they belong: feelings of isolation or not belonging can colour students' whole experience of university and may cause them to drop out.

The location of the university can also affect the experience students have of it, again both positively or negatively. Visiting somewhere for an interview or open day is not the same as living there.[31] The relationship between 'town and gown' may be significant, with local residents' responses ranging from open-armed welcome to outright hostility. The cost of living varies considerably across the country. This may present problems for less affluent students who want to go to a particular university and are qualified to do so where that university is located in a particularly expensive part of the country. The impact of finance and fear of debt should not be underestimated as a deterrent to undertaking a course in higher education.[32]

The facilities available in the town or city – cultural, social, sporting etc. can enhance or detract from the enjoyment of living in a particular location. Travelling to and from university also impacts on student engagement. The availability of public transport, journey times and the distance involved can all affect engagement. Some universities recognise the importance of transport to their students and have dedicated bus services, sometimes free, which recognise the need to travel between campuses or to get to a remotely located site and also the impact a large student population can have on the regular public transport services in a particular location. Car parking can become an issue causing tension with local residents if adequate parking facilities are not available on campus. Being able to take a car may be important to some, not to others.

One of the key components of the higher education policy of the coalition government was the idea of student choice.[33] For students entering through clearing this choice is limited, which is why they are often at risk of not completing. Such students often have to make decisions about course and university in a very short space of time without the careful thought that might go into a decision taken in a more measured way. They may not have visited the institution they are about

31 The point is neatly captured by a student quoted in *The Guardian* guide to things students wish they had known: 'you really learn what university is like when the weather turns crap. In the prospectus, it looks brilliant. Even when you visit, the uni is somehow bathed in sunshine, and the people smiling. As soon as you live in the place, it becomes grey and miserable – as do the people', 17 May 2011 available at http://www.guardian.co.uk/education/2011/may/17/university-guide-student-advice (accessed 3 July 2015).

32 This was an issue for some students even before the recent rise in tuition fees: see, for example, Merryn Hutchings (2003) 'Financial barriers to participation' in Louise Archer, Merryn Hutchings and Alistair Ross, *Higher Education and Social Class* (London: Routledge Falmer) 155–173; Claire Callender and Jonathan Jackson (2008) 'Does the fear of debt constrain choice of university and subject of study?' *Studies in Higher Education* 33(4) 405–429; Alison Bone (2009) 'The twenty-first century law student' 43(3) *Law Teacher* 222–245.

33 See BIS, n. 4.

to attend, nor the town or city in which it is located, nor even, in some extreme cases, know where it is. In one sense, this step into the unknown is a characteristic of many law students who are embarking on a degree course in a subject they have never studied previously. The availability of information about law, law courses, universities and their locations becomes important in allowing prospective students to make decisions about what to study and where to go but is just as vital in any other subject and, as it is a significant theme of Streeting's lecture, it is worth dwelling on.[34] Once students have embarked on a course they are basing their decisions much more on experience, but this initial decision depends on the information that is available to the person seeking to undertake a course in a higher education institution before and at the time of the application. This operates at a number of levels, primarily divided between official and informal sources of information.

The provision of information by universities was one of the key components in the recommendations of the Browne Review of Higher Education.[35] The Review was an unashamedly free market proposal for higher education which would allow students to exercise choice in a market in which universities competed with each other and, by implication, subjects competed with subjects. It accepted that there was much official information available, but argued that as it existed in different formats and was distributed across various webpages and publications it was not easily comparable. The Review therefore commissioned some research from Oakleigh Consulting and Staffordshire University to find out what information students would find most useful when making decisions about where and what to study at university. This recommendation was accepted by the government and led to the production of Key Information Sets (KIS) which contain information provided by universities in specific categories which may then be compared across universities and subjects.[36] One of the Browne Review recommendations was that students should be given a pot of money which they could then take to the university of their choice. Universities should be able to charge what they think is appropriate and allow market forces to determine the validity of this: part of the decision-making process would involve students deciding whether they thought that universities were providing value for money in relation to what they were charging as against what they said they were providing. The government, in deciding to place a cap, currently standing at £9000, on the

34 On the information available to prospective law students, see Graeme Broadbent and Pamela Sellman (2013) 'Images of Law and Legal Education: Law School websites and the provision of information' 4(1) *European Journal of Law and Technology* available at http://ejlt.org//article/view/180/280 (accessed 3 July 2015); (2013) 'Great Expectations? Law Schools, Web Sites and "the Student Experience"' 47 *Law Teacher* 44–63; (2013) 'KIS and tell' 47 *Law Teacher* 97–101; (2014) 'Information, information, information . . . overload?' 48 *Law Teacher* 359–366.

35 Browne Review, n. 19.

36 The Oakleigh/Staffordshire research and KIS are discussed in detail in 'Images' and 'KIS and tell', n. 34.

fees that universities can charge, eroded any notion of differentiation on price, as nearly all universities charge the full £9,000.[37]

The debate about information, however, continues.[38] The basic problem with the provision of formal information remains: what can be provided is necessarily of a generalised nature, whereas individuals want information about the things that matter to them as part of their individual decision-making. The Oakleigh/Staffordshire research almost inevitably produced information that was most commonly mentioned as being of importance by its respondents. Whilst this may be helpful to significant numbers of prospective students, it does not necessarily assist the widening participation agenda. For example, there is nothing in KIS about what it is like to study at a particular university other than data from the National Student Survey (NSS). This is of limited value as it reflects the experiences of final year students who have studied on a particular course at a particular university. It does not follow that because the students who are ending their course have had a good or bad experience that will be the experience of the prospective student reading this information. As the recent Office of Fair Trading (OFT) report points out,[39] the quality of provision at a particular institution is not known until the student has experienced it. The OFT goes on to say that the quality of information about it becomes important but that gives rise to questions of what 'quality' means for the person reading the information and how, if at all, it can be measured. The report goes on to list other items of information that it thinks would be useful to prospective students in addition to that already provided by KIS. It is worth bearing in mind that the KIS data are only a fraction of the vast amounts of information that exist on university websites and other official sources of information.

Readers do not lack for information. It is also worth bearing in mind that the KIS data only provide factual information: interpretation of that information opens up a whole range of other questions, some of which may be answered elsewhere.[40] One of the features of KIS was the provision of purely factual information without any marketing spin. Law school and university websites contain a mixture of verifiable information as well as opinion, hype and material

37 On the market in higher education and fees, see Vida Allen and Graeme Broadbent (2011) 'A Handful of Dust? Some thoughts on the future funding of legal education and allied matters' 45 *Law Teacher* 231–240 and (2012) 'Plus ça change, plus c'est la même chose' 46 *Law Teacher* 179–189. On the fee cap and the response of universities to it, see Jack Grove '£9K Fees: Now It's Exceptional Not To Charge Them' *Times Higher Education* 24 July 2014 available at http://www.timeshighereducation.co.uk/news/9k-fees-now-its-exceptional-not-to-charge-them/2014710.article (accessed 3 July 2015).

38 See 'Information, information, information . . . overload?', n. 34.

39 Office of Fair Trading (2014) *Higher Education in England* OFT 1529 (London: Office of Fair Trading) at p. 23.

40 See 'KIS and tell', n. 34 for further discussion.

generally designed to show the institution in a good light.[41] Herein lies the problem: a recent report commissioned by the Higher Education Funding Council for England (HEFCE)[42] argued that too much information actually inhibits effective decision-making by overwhelming the decision-maker. There seems to be no way through this conundrum: prospective students need information on which to base their decisions about higher education, yet there is no agreement as to what is too much or too little. Self-evidently there is no one-size-fits-all solution. One possible avenue of assistance is the availability of good quality careers advice tailored to the needs of particular individuals. While this exists in some parts of the country and at some schools, a recent report from the National Careers Council[43] suggested that careers advice is patchy and that there needed to be uniformly good quality advice available to all. Outside the formal careers service, organisations such as the Helena Kennedy Foundation, for which Wes Streeting was working at the time of his Lord Upjohn Lecture, do provide advice for some of those who most need it as they do not have access to good quality advice elsewhere; the Foundation was especially helpful in providing advice tailored to the particular needs of the individual.[44] One area Streeting highlighted in his lecture where information was not having the impact that it should have was in relation to the new arrangements for student finance which were due to come into force in 2012.[45] At the time of his lecture, it seems that the system was not universally understood and that various myths were circulating about how the scheme would operate. This has now hopefully been corrected and students entering higher education under the new scheme, which is in its third academic year of operation, are aware of how it works. But this episode illustrates the importance of having ready access to accurate and understandable information, something just as significant with regard to any other information about higher education. Streeting rightly emphasises that widening participation is not just a matter for universities alone, but that they should work in partnership with schools and other organisations, particularly those involved in adult education.[46]

Official advice is, however, only one source of information about higher education. There are no official league tables for universities or subjects, but there exists a plethora of unofficial ones, each constructed in a different way, which

41 See 'Great Expectations' and 'Images of Law', n. 34 on the nature of law school websites.

42 Abigail Diamond, Jennifer Roberts, Tim Vorley, Guy Birkin, James Evans, Jonathan Sheen and Tej Nathwani (2014) *UK Review of the provision of information about higher education: Advisory Study and Literature Review* (Report to the UK higher education funding bodies by CFE Research, April) (Bristol: HEFCE).

43 *Taking action: Achieving a culture change in careers provision* (NCC 2014). See also BIS, n. 4, at pp. 56–58.

44 Streeting, n. 1, at pp. 11–12.

45 Ibid., at pp. 7–8.

46 Ibid., at p. 9. He gives an example of such interaction at pp. 13–14.

makes them difficult to interpret.[47] For students and their families, who may be used to the official school league tables, the absence of something comparable for higher education may be puzzling. There is evidence that, notwithstanding their unofficial nature, there is, nevertheless, reliance on them.[48] Universities certainly take them seriously and will often advertise their position in those league tables in which they are towards, or at, the top. There are also various sites and books providing all manner of information about universities. Social media also provides a rich source of information of varying quality. There are also individual contacts, such as family or friends, who can provide information from their perspectives and can influence decisions.[49] There is some evidence to suggest that this informal information may be regarded as being of greater value in certain respects than official information in relation to school choice: Ball and Vincent[50] found that informal knowledge was particularly valued in relation to the unmeasurable aspects of schools such as reputation or happiness. It is likely that this is also true of decisions about where and what to study at university. Reputation is, however, a dangerous concept, despite the value attaching to it: good reputations can last longer than is justified while bad reputations can stay too long. These informal sources of information are, of course, outside the control of either universities or any official agency and thus need careful interpretation, particularly when set against more official sources.

Widening participation is, however, about much more than just getting people into higher education, as Streeting recognises. It is also about their experience during their course. University practices may conflict with the expectations of students, some of which are generated by the university itself. The notion, now firmly embedded in both official and everyday discourse, sees the student as a consumer

47 See, for example, Mantz Yorke (1997) 'A good league table guide?' *Quality Assurance in Education* 5(2) 61–72; Colin Berry (1999) 'University league tables: artefacts and inconsistencies in individual rankings' *Higher Education Review* 31(2) 3–10; Malcolm Tight (2000) 'Do League Tables Contribute to the Development of a Quality Culture? Football and Higher Education Compared' *Higher Education Quarterly* 54(1) 22–42; Rachel Bowden (2000) 'Fantasy higher education: university and college league tables' *Quality in Higher Education* 6(1) 41–60; David Turner (2005) 'Benchmarking in universities: league tables revisited' *Oxford Review of Education* 31(3) 353–371; Roger Brown (2006) 'League tables – do we have to live with them?' *Perspectives* 10(2) 33–38; Rod Gunn and Steve Hill (2008) 'The Impact of League Tables on University Application Rates' *Higher Education Quarterly* 62(3) 273–296.

48 See particularly Gunn and Hill, n. 47.

49 Rachel Brooks (2004) '"My mum would be as pleased as punch if I actually went, but my dad seems a bit more particular about it": paternal involvement in young people's higher education choices' *British Educational Research Journal* 30(4) 495–514.

50 Stephen J. Ball and Carol Vincent (1998) '"I Heard It on the Grapevine": "hot" knowledge and school choice' *British Journal of Sociology of Education* 19(3) 377–400.

of university 'products' and services.[51] It is a powerful force in terms of the way universities are regarded by students, especially under the new fees regime. Applying consumerist notions to university performance is increasingly visible, with universities coming under scrutiny from consumer organisations such as the Competition and Markets Authority,[52] the Advertising Standards Authority (ASA)[53] and *Which?*.[54] As we have seen, one of the aims of the Browne Review was to make universities competitive in the student market and, even in the watered-down version created by the government, elements of competition are still present. An interesting question, yet to be answered, posed by the recent report of the now defunct OFT,[55] was whether the regulatory regime imposed on universities by the various regulatory bodies, particularly in those areas where uniformity is required, makes them anti-competitive. Other consumerist devices such as the NSS,[56] which features prominently in KIS,[57] may be seen as essentially measures of customer satisfaction. Student evaluation of teaching or teaching awards of various kinds may also be seen as part of the same agenda.[58] Echoing the title of the 2011 White Paper,[59]

51 For discussions of students as consumers, see, for example, Mete Sirvanci (1999) 'Are Students the True Customers of Higher Education?' 29(10) *Quality Progress* 99–102; S.V. Scott (1999) 'The Academic as Service Provider: is the customer "always right"?' *Journal of Higher Education Policy and Management* 21(2) 193–202; Geoff Sharrock (2000) 'Why Students are not (Just) Customers (and other reflections on Life After George)' 22(2) *Journal of Higher Education Policy and Management* 149–164; Louise Morley (2003) 'Reconstructing students as consumers: power and assimilation?' in Maria Slowey and David Watson (eds) *Higher Education and the Lifecourse* (Maidenhead: SRHE/Open University Press) 79–92; Tim Kaye, Robert D. Bickel and Tim Birtwistle (2006) 'Criticizing the image of the student as consumer: examining legal trends and administrative responses in the US and UK' 18(2–3) *Education and the Law* 85–129; Lynne Eagle and Ross Brennan (2007) 'Are students customers? TQM and marketing perspectives' 15(1) *Quality Assurance in Education* 44–59; Tony Woodall, Alex Hiller and Sheilagh Resnick (2014) 'Making sense of higher education: students as consumers and the value of the university experience' 39(1) *Studies in Higher Education* 48–67.

52 The Competition and Markets Authority replaced the OFT with effect from 1 April 2014.

53 The ASA has oversight of advertisements in all media, and has dealt with complaints about advertising by universities: see generally http://www.asa.org.uk/ (accessed 3 July 2015).

54 See, for example, the *Which? Guide* to universities available at http://university.which.co.uk/search/institution (accessed 3 July 2015).

55 Office of Fair Trading, n. 39, Ch. 6.

56 On the NSS, see John T.E Richardson, John B. Slater and Jane Wilson (2007) 'The National Student Survey: development, findings and implications' *Studies in Higher Education* 32(5) 557–580; Paula Surridge (2009) *The National Student Survey three years on: What have we learned?* (York: HEA); Jacqueline H.S. Cheng and Herbert W. Marsh (2010) 'National Student Survey: are differences between universities and courses reliable and meaningful?' *Oxford Review of Education* 36(6) 693–712; Claire Callender, Paul Ramsden and Julia Griggs (2014) *Review of the National Student Survey* (Bristol: HEFCE); HEFCE (2014) *National Student Survey results and trends analysis 2005–2013* (Bristol: HEFCE). In relation to legal education, see Graeme Broadbent (2007) 'The National Student Survey' 41 *Law Teacher* 330–334.

57 See 'KIS and tell', n. 34.

58 See Graeme Broadbent (2007) 'Student evaluation and the quality of legal education' 5 *Journal of Commonwealth Law and Legal Education* 3–17.

59 BIS, n. 4.

such devices put students at the heart of the system. Clearly, in the modern era, students, as active participants in the university or in the law school,[60] do and should play an active role in the way the institution functions.

Tensions may, however, be created by this consumerist approach. Given the variety of students in any cohort, not every individual wish can be catered for. As with the Oakleigh/Staffordshire approach to identifying the most important information students wanted, the views of the majority will tend to prevail.[61] The university has to cater for all its students. Matters such as timetabling can cause unhappiness if individual wishes are not realised; individualised timetables may be beyond the capacity of the university. Some of the respondents in Marion Bowl's study wanted classes to be scheduled at times that would allow them to fit with their childcare responsibilities;[62] others might want classes to be scheduled so as to allow for religious observance;[63] while yet others might want classes that fit in with their part-time work commitments,[64] the last of these a reality for many students and especially for those from poorer backgrounds. Assumptions that students know how to study at degree level, which may be radically different from what they have experienced at school or college, may lead to dislocation or anxiety and inhibit effective study if they are not shared, as may a lack of familiarity with the conventions of language used in higher education, for example by way of feedback on written work.[65] Fellow students

60 See Andrew Boon and Avis Whyte (2010) 'Will there be Blood? Students as Stakeholders in the Legal Academy' in Fiona Cownie, n. 15, at pp. 185–224.

61 See 'Images of Law', n. 34 for discussion of the Oakleigh/Staffordshire methodology.

62 Bowl, n. 27 at p. 67.

63 Tariq Modood (2006) 'Ethnicity, Muslims and higher education entry in Britain' *Teaching in Higher Education* 11(2) 247–250.

64 See, for example, Susan Curtis and Najah Shani (2002) 'The Effect of Taking Paid Employment During Term-time on Students' Academic Studies' 26(2) *Journal of Further and Higher Education* 129–138; Andrew Hunt, Ian Lincoln and Arthur Walker (2004) 'Term-time Employment and Academic Attainment: evidence from a large-scale survey of undergraduates at Northumbria University' 28(1) *Journal of Further and Higher Education* 3–18; Claire Callender (2008) 'The impact of term-time employment on higher education students' academic attainment and achievement' 23(4) *Journal of Education Policy* 359–377.

65 See, for example, the studies by Bowl and Burke (n. 27) and Kate Chanock (2000) 'Comments on Essays: do students understand what tutors write?' *Teaching in Higher Education* 5(1) 95–105; Paul Sander, Keith Stevenson, Malcolm King and David Coates (2000) 'University Students' Expectations of Teaching' *Studies in Higher Education* 25(3) 309–323; Richard Higgins, Peter Hartley and Alan Skelton (2001) 'Getting the Message Across: the problem of communicating assessment feedback' *Teaching in Higher Education* 6(2) 269–274; Houston Lowe and Anthony Cook (2003) 'Mind the Gap: are students prepared for higher education?' *Journal of Further and Higher Education* 27(1) 53–76; Berry O'Donovan, Margaret Price and Chris Rust (2004) 'Know what I mean? Enhancing student understanding of assessment criteria' *Teaching in Higher Education* 9(3) 326–335; Karen Clegg (2004) *Playing safe: learning and teaching in undergraduate law* (Coventry: UKCLE); Kevin Williams (2005) 'Lecturer and first year student (mis)understandings of assessment task verbs: "Mind the gap"' *Teaching in Higher Education* 10(2) 157–173; Melanie R. Weaver (2006) 'Do students value feedback? Student perceptions of tutors' written responses' *Assessment and Evaluation in Higher Education* 31(3) 379–394; Vera Bermingham and John Hodgson (2006) 'Feedback on Assessment: Can We Provide a Better Student Experience by Working Smarter than by Working Harder?' *The Law Teacher* 40(2) 151–172.

can have an impact: this may be positive or may cause feelings of alienation and isolation.[66] The subject chosen, particularly if it is one such as law which has not been studied previously, can prove more challenging than anticipated. Once enrolled onto a course, with all the commitments, not least of which are the financial and emotional, it is a brave decision to withdraw and some students struggle on in circumstances where it is hardly in their best interests. Negative attitudes from university staff do not help. Some studies suggest that staff see 'non-traditional' and part-time students as likely to be higher risk, more demanding, needing greater support, taking up time that could be spent on other aspects of the job, especially research, and, generally, posing a threat to the university's standards, standing and reputation.[67] This is often attributed to widening participation, which is thus seen in negative terms. It is, however, worth disentangling two threads that are often conflated, namely widening participation and mass higher education. Widening participation does not necessarily depend on expanding numbers, though for Robbins the two went hand in hand given the conditions of the 1960s: there were more people meeting the Robbins criteria than there were university places available. A further factor, post-dating Robbins, was the creation of polytechnics from 1965 onwards,[68] which led, amongst other things, to an expansion in law teaching both on academic and vocational courses. Mass higher education is conceptually different and envisages a different type of expansion. As Peter Scott has pointed out,[69] it involves both a quantitative and a qualitative change: the sector is bigger in size and different in character. Much of the expansion envisaged under the 2003 White Papers[70] was anticipated to take place by means of foundation degrees, though this has not happened to the extent anticipated by the government. Instead, more students have undertaken the traditional degrees offered by universities, creating the paradox that students in a mass system are undertaking elite qualifications. In arguing for greater participation in higher education, Streeting does not address the question of the type of qualifications students might obtain.

66 See the works cited in n. 30.

67 See, for example, Heather Rolfe (2002) 'Students' Demands and Expectations in an Age of Reduced Financial Support: the perspectives of lecturers in four English universities' *Journal of Higher Education Policy and Management* 24(2) 171–182; Onora O'Neill (2002) *A Question of Trust* (Cambridge: Cambridge University Press); Laurie Lomas (2002) 'Does the Development of Mass Education Necessarily Mean the End of Quality?' *Quality in Higher Education* 8(1) 71–79; Tamsin Haggis (2006) 'Pedagogies for diversity: retaining critical challenge amidst fears of "dumbing down"' *Studies in Higher Education* 31(5) 521–535; Universities UK (2010) *The supply of part-time higher education in the UK* available at http://www.universitiesuk.ac.uk/highereducation/Documents/2010/TheSupplyOfPartTimeHigherEducationInTheUK.pdf (accessed 3 July 2015).

68 On the contribution of polytechnics to higher education, see John Pratt (1997) *The Polytechnic Experiment 1965–1992* (Buckingham: SRHE/OU).

69 (1995) *The Meanings of Mass Higher Education* (Buckingham: SRHE/OU); and also Peter Scott (2005) 'Mass higher education – ten years on' *Perspectives* 9(3) 68–73.

70 DfES, n. 3.

It is worth reflecting here on institutional differences with regard to widening participation. The name, the Office for Fair Access, would suggest that its remit runs only to enabling entry to higher education, but it is also concerned that students are appropriately supported during their course. It makes access agreements with universities that are designed to ensure that students have equal opportunities to succeed on a course and at an institution appropriate to their needs and wishes. Yet widening participation has not been felt evenly across the sector.[71] It seems that, despite the abolition of the binary divide in 1992, there are still distinctions between pre-1992 and post-1992 universities in practice.[72] The division in focus between them, with pre-1992 universities focusing on research while post-1992 universities focus on teaching, is breaking down as the unified sector grows, but there remains a perception that some, largely post-1992, universities are 'widening participation' institutions,[73] though some of the more selective and prestigious universities are making efforts to accommodate a broader range of students, in particular recognising that academic considerations are not the only factors that affect the decision of which university to apply for and which subject to study.[74] This has an effect on non-traditional and part-time students who usually have geographical limitations which means that they are confined to their local university.[75]

While there have been efforts across the sector to address the widening participation agenda there are other factors that may yet inhibit the advancement of students drawn from a wider range than has hitherto been the case. As increasing numbers of students graduate, and graduate with a good degree, the pressure for students is to do something extra to make them stand out. Work experience, internships and placements are also commonplace, and, Streeting points out, much more easily come by for those from wealthier backgrounds with business or family connections.[76] Another option is to undertake a higher degree, but this

71 See generally http://www.offa.org.uk/ (accessed 3 July 2015); also HEFCE (2005) *Higher education admissions: assessment of bias* (Issues paper 2005/47) (Bristol: HEFCE); Tariq Tahir, 'For Some, Campus is Still Another Country' *Times Higher Education* 31 August 2007.

72 See John Pratt (1992) 'Unification of Higher Education in the United Kingdom' *European Journal of Education* 27(1/2) 29–44; Mary Henkel (2000) *Academic Identities and Policy Change in Higher Education* (London: Jessica Kingsley); Louise Morley (2001) 'Subjected to review: engendering quality and power in higher education' *Journal of Education Policy* 16(5) 465–478; Fiona Cownie (2004) *Legal Academics: Culture and Identities* (Oxford: Hart); Malcolm Tight (2009) *Higher Education in the United Kingdom since 1945: an oral history* (Maidenhead: Open University Press).

73 See, for example, Burke, nn. 1 and 27.

74 Joan M. Whitehead, John Raffan and Rosemary Deaney (2006) 'University Choice: What Influences the Decisions of Academically Successful Post-16 Students?' *Higher Education Quarterly* 60(1) 4–26.

75 See Bowl and Burke, n. 27; also Andrew Marks (2000) 'In Search of the "Local" University: considering issues of access for mature learners' *Journal of Further and Higher Education* 24(3) 363–371; HEFCE (2014) *Pressure from all sides: Economic and policy influences on part-time higher education* (8 April) (hereafter '*Pressure*') available at http://www.hefce.ac.uk/media/hefce/content/pubs/2014/201408d/HEFE2014_08d.pdf (accessed 3 July 2013).

76 Streeting, n. 1, at p. 12.

then delays the possibility of earning for a further year or so and involves the accumulation of greater debt when added to the undergraduate debt. This is not something that the widening participation debate has really addressed in any meaningful way.[77] For law students, undertaking the LPC or BPTC adds considerably to their undergraduate debt.

Much emphasis is placed on the employability of graduates and their ability to contribute to the growth of the national economy as well as the personal benefit they may enjoy.[78] Universities are encouraged, in line with the emphasis the government places on the contribution of higher education to the economy, to ensure that graduates are equipped for the world of work, whatever that may mean. Higher paid employment, such as that which law is perceived to offer,[79] has been a motivation for students to undertake degree courses, a line of thinking encouraged by the government. It also harks back to notions of social mobility which have economic benefit as a key indicator. As a force to encourage people to undertake a course in higher education, this only works if the supply of graduate jobs matches the demand for them. If it does, then graduates enjoy the benefits of working in graduate level employment and the remuneration that accompanies it. The attractiveness of higher education diminishes if supply exceeds demand and graduates have to take non-graduate jobs. They may then question why they have incurred significant amounts of debt only to be in a job that they could have taken years earlier, earning during those years and without the attendant debt. For those thinking of applying to university, if the perception is that they will not get a well-paid graduate job at the end of it, university ceases to be an attractive proposition. Also, the whole notion of 'graduate' levels of pay may be threatened in an age of mass higher education. One of the factors keeping graduate levels of pay at higher levels than non-graduate occupations has been the relatively small numbers of graduates performing high level and specialist tasks that command those higher rates of pay.[80] One consequence may be to redefine the notion of graduate occupations so that premium pay rates no longer attach to jobs where graduates are recruited, thus again undermining that reason for going to university. It also has consequential effects for those with lower level qualifications. If jobs that they would normally expect to take are taken by graduates then a form of qualification inflation occurs which may eventually bear down on the least qualified. There are also possible consequences in terms of job satisfaction if people are doing jobs below their capabilities.

77 Though see Burke, n. 27.
78 See BIS, n. 4.
79 See Bone, n. 22; Wolf, n. 5; Louise Archer (2003) 'The "value" of higher education' in Louise Archer, Merryn Hutchings and Alistair Ross *Higher Education and Social Class* (London: Routledge Falmer) 119–136.
80 See Wolf, n. 5.

Law is a particularly acute example of supply and demand. The bottleneck in pursuing a legal career comes in relation to obtaining a training contract or pupillage. It is relatively easy to get a place on an undergraduate law course for those with appropriate qualifications. The supply of courses is still not exceeded by the demand from suitably qualified applicants. Equally, it is relatively straightforward for graduates to obtain a place on the BPTC and, especially, the LPC if they want to undertake the professional qualifications. The problem is progressing beyond this point, and there is evidence of students with LPC and BPTC qualifications taking jobs as paralegals or outside the law, which was not what they set out to do.[81] Two factors are significant here. One is that the information about the supply and demand for places in the traditional branches of the legal profession is not readily available. This is national information and is not available via KIS or university material – no law school is going to advertise that students have limited chances of becoming solicitors or barristers: indeed the image of the barrister is one commonly featured on law school webpages.[82] Second, perception is important. If prospective applicants believe that they can qualify as solicitors or barristers then it does not matter whether their chances are slim as long as this is what they believe. It is, however, at the point of applying for a training contract or pupillage that inequalities surface again.[83] Whilst the traditional branches of the legal profession have made efforts to ensure equality of opportunity,[84] students from non-traditional backgrounds face even greater barriers to those they faced in trying to get a place at university.

The general tenor of Streeting's argument – that there should be much greater participation in higher education, not just wider participation in the existing system and especially entry to the more selective universities – is not one that would be universally endorsed. His approach is generalised and lacks discussion of some key issues that would be consequential on an expansion of higher education that he envisages, though he provides some striking examples of the inequalities he seeks to eliminate. As ever, the devil is in the detail. For example, what type of qualifications would be undertaken? What are the implications for employment?

81 See Boon and Whyte, n. 60, at p. 189ff. Note also the consequences of the Legal Services Act 2007, the growing commodification of legal service provision and the consequent growth of the paralegal sector. This is addressed by a number of the other contributors to this volume.

82 See 'Great Expectations', n. 4.

83 It is interesting to note that the accountancy firm PricewaterhouseCoopers has recently decided to stop using A level results as a requirement for its graduate programme as it found this privileged those who had attended private schools. The firm believed the change would enable recruits to be selected on merit rather than background: see 'PwC recruiters say A level results unfairly aid private school pupils', *Guardian*, 3 May 2015 accessible at http://www.theguardian.com/education/2015/may/03/pwc-recruiters-say-a-level-results-unfairly-aid-private-school-pupils (accessed 3 July 2015). Law firms may also be engaged in similar initiatives.

84 See the Lord Upjohn Lecture by Geoffrey Vos (2008) 'An Accessible Legal Profession Working in the Public Interest: Dream or Reality?' 42(1) *Law Teacher* 1–8. Also Alan Milburn (2012) *Fair Access to Professional Careers* (London: TSO) Ch. 3.

Widening participation in higher education by those who have traditionally not gone to university has been one of the failures in the system of higher education which is systemic and will not easily be corrected. All manner of initiatives over the last 50 years have not produced any significant change and there are no short-term solutions. It will be interesting to see if Wes Streeting can use his position as a Member of Parliament to bring about any changes.[85]

85 We should perhaps not expect too much too soon: 'Fresh from the triumph and elation of victory at the polls where he is the pivot of activity, the M.P. finds himself a very small fish lost in the goldfish bowl of Parliament . . . Members are so often regarded by their constituents as "those who run the country" that many of them actually believe it. The truth is that, while Members have a direct line to decision-makers on a host of minor matters affecting individual constituents, it is a rare occasion when a Member is able to influence serious departmental policies': Paul Rose (1981) *Backbencher's Dilemma* (London: Frederick Muller) at p. 51.

7 Thirty-ninth Lord Upjohn Lecture 2010

Training the Lawyers of the Future – A Regulator's View

*David Edmonds**

Why should a regulator be invited to talk about education and training? The Legal Services Board, of which I am the Chairman, has now been in existence for just over two years. We were created by the massive piece of legislation called the Legal Services Act 2007. This followed a period of enquiry and then a Parliamentary process that lasted for four or five years. The basic purpose of the Act was to bring about a new system of regulation for legal services – a system of regulation by which the consumer – in all forms – was recognised as the essential beneficiary and which provided for the first time that self-regulation was both given objectives relating to those who received legal services and a new degree of oversight to ensure that this happened. In essence existing legal regulators were forced to recognise that regulation needed to be separated from representation of the interests of the providers. And the legislation further provided that new forms of business models could be created – within a clear regulatory framework – enabling external investment to be made, reducing barriers to entry, and widening consumer choice. Interestingly, the legislation set statutory objectives for the new regulator – my Board – which was created to sit over the existing regulators.

We share those objectives with those frontline regulators. And one of those underpinning statutory objectives is to encourage an independent, strong, diverse and effective legal profession. That is my locus for taking a deep interest in the education and training of lawyers. How can that legal profession be created without an education and training framework that is founded on the principles of independence and diversity? On an understanding of effectiveness and the ability to deliver for the consumers good advice and workable solutions? So I do not bring to this lecture the degree of specialist knowledge to the subject that the distinguished previous speakers have. But as a still relatively new face on the scene, I can share my emerging thoughts on the possible implications for legal education and training of the changing legal landscape – commercial and regulatory – as well as the changing educational context post the Browne Review.

* This lecture was delivered as the thirty-ninth Lord Upjohn Lecture at Inner Temple on 19 November 2010.

I have more questions than answers. But I am struck by the questioning that seems prevalent throughout many parts of the legal services landscape as to where what we now see as the route into the law – whether as a solicitor or a barrister or a legal executive – is fit for purpose. Whether the system that we now see is too unrelated to the needs of working lawyers? Whether the costs of legal training are making demands that are simply too much? Whether the right numbers of lawyers are being trained? And so on.

A changing environment

The legal services market in England and Wales is in a state of transition – or rather, one of rapid evolution. That change only partly stems from the establishment of the new regulatory regime and the work of my Board to implement the Legal Services Act 2007. But, of course, regulation is only one of the factors in play. Let me list some of the others:

- Consumerism – a word that is controversial in some quarters, but one for which I don't apologise. The consumer isn't always right – and indeed lawyers are never more loyal to their professional responsibilities than when they have to tell demanding clients that they are wrong. But consumers are right to expect quality, value and respect – and the pressures on lawyers to deliver that kind of service, rather than the paternalistic model of old, will only increase.
- Technology – the head of the American Bar Association, Steve Zack, said at a recent Harvard Conference that he only kept law books in his office to try and convince clients that he could read. He could not recall the last time that he had opened one to find a fact, rather than finding it online. And, of course, technology doesn't just change the way lawyers access case law and information. It alters the speed and manner in which they interact with clients. Perhaps even more importantly, it alters the way clients interact with the law – increasingly cutting out the legal middle man in the process all together.
- Broader social change – the population of Britain looks very different to how it looked at the time of the Ormrod Report in 1971. Or the Benson Royal Commission at the end of the seventies. Or even the Clementi Report in 2004. And that change is about need – the ever-increasing number of questions which can be addressed by the law, the increasing volume of legislation and the need for consistent vigilance to ensure that the relationship between individual and state remains healthy – quite as much as about diversity per se.

A changing regulatory landscape

My Board's role is essentially to free up the regulatory framework to enable lawyers to react as flexibly as possible to this ever-changing landscape, whilst maintaining and improving consumer protections. I would contend that, with our partners in the frontline regulators – the Solicitors Regulation Authority (SRA), the Bar Standards Board (BSB), ILEX Professional Standards and others – we have made a strong start.

The initial phase of reforms has focused on institutional change. We are embedding independence across the frontline regulators. We are driving a new outcomes-focused approach to regulation, backed by better risk management and enforcement. I believe that this is essential to give the right incentives for ethical practice.

We are liberalising the market to stimulate innovation – by new entrants and existing firms and chambers alike. That innovation is already underway. The new regulatory framework for Alternative Business Structures (ABS) which will be in place in just under a year will enable that change to accelerate by allowing an even greater diversity of partnerships and business models. Clearly it is practitioners and businesses, rather than consumers, who innovate – but consumers decide whether innovation succeeds and this drives the future.

Above all, we have been working to address the regulatory objectives that we share with the front line regulators in the round. So, for example, meeting the regulatory objective of improving access to justice is, for me, ultimately what ABS should be judged on. A more accessible service for those whom legal aid will never reach, even in the most favourable of economic conditions. Likewise, we are rigorous in testing all our work against its impact on our objectives about the rule of law and the wider public interest, as well as that of consumer benefit more narrowly.

Regulation and education

In addition to that regulatory objective to 'encourage an independent, strong, diverse and effective legal profession', we also have a specific duty to assist in the maintenance and development of standards in relation to the education and training of authorised persons. Those are important issues and they underpin our wider agenda. That's why we will be giving workforce development increasing weight in the coming year.

If the law is ever more effectively to serve the public, then the profession – or rather the entire legal *workforce* – needs to have the right skills and knowledge. That includes the capability to constantly update both skills and knowledge. In other words, meeting the objective isn't just about making sure that people jump the right hurdles in their early twenties. It is about achieving a constant interplay between practice and education, with the two spheres in constant dialogue, each driving improvement and innovation in the other to the broader public good.

The hypothesis that I would like to see tested is that that dialogue and interplay is not happening at the level that it should. If the current framework is simply not fit for purpose – and it is what I hear consistently from educationalists and practitioners alike – then there is a clear need for the current education and training arrangements to develop at a much quicker pace to keep up to date with the challenges lawyers will face day in, day out in the future.

Our partners in the frontline regulators have already started to act, with a range of solid initiatives to which I will return. But my questions for this evening are these: 'Can we be doing more and faster? And how can we ensure a consistent strategic framework in which these initiatives take place?'

Changes in legal education - numbers and requirements

Let me return to changes in the market – the legal education market as well as the legal services market. Much good work was done in the 1990s by ACLEC (the Lord Chancellor's Advisory Committee on Legal Education and Conduct). But the last fundamental analysis of education and training in the legal services sector as a whole was the Ormrod Review in 1971. It took more than three years and produced a 250-page report. The members of that Committee would believe that they had returned to a different world entirely, were they to resume their work today, just at the level of sheer numbers.

We currently have almost 14,000 students annually graduating with a Qualifying Law Degree, and around 5,000 enrolled on the Graduate Diploma in Law. Of those, over 11,000 enrolled last year on either the Legal Practice Course or the Bar Professional Training Course. Following the postgraduate stage, 6,271 commenced either a training contract or a pupillage. And the size of the profession has grown dramatically. Between 2000 and 2009 the number of practising barristers rose by 20%. In 2000 there were 83,000 practising solicitors and 105,000 on the roll. Last year there were 121,000 practising solicitors and 154,000 on the roll. This growth of over 40% follows a growth in numbers of 50% between 1990 and 2000. So the field of education has widened and expanded: but are the needs of participants in terms of preparedness to practise still being properly met?

Any attempt to answer that question must be made against an understanding of wider changes. As the market changes, as the needs of clients change, as the body of law changes, so must the disciplines and competencies covered at all stages of education and training.

Clearly one major issue is the impact of globalised markets. Many larger firms are transnational entities, operating across a number of jurisdictions. The transnational barrister is a growing phenomenon, as indeed is the international mediator, using English law to resolve disputes on the other side of the world. The development of European Union trading and commercial laws has run alongside economic integration. And, of course, it's not just the law itself but the needs of clients. The scale of inter-dependencies between nation states, and between multi-national companies is considerable, with changed technologies underpinning commercial relationships across the world. So many American Law Schools are now arguing that international and comparative law needs to be taught more rigorously and at an earlier stage of professional formation. Is that right for England and Wales as well?

In that globalised market – but also on the High Street – we are increasingly seeing legal services being delivered in partnership with other professional services – tax advice, property services, accounting. As I implied earlier, external ownership via ABS is, in a real sense, taking changes that are already taking place in the market to the next logical level – rather than being some radical experiment. ABS will clearly trigger specific education and training requirements, around governance issues for example. But I would argue that it will trigger wider needs as well, with more employers thinking more broadly about the development needs of their entire workforce.

Lawyers are already working in more diverse business models. The problem is that the pre-ABS regulatory regime finds it difficult to manage risk of consumer detriment from abuse without causing potentially greater detriment by restraining innovative practitioners. The SRA and BSB's latest proposals have set the ball rolling in moving beyond this tension by seeking to bring regulation up to date. The impact will be that we begin to see more – and more diverse – relationships between lawyers, providers of other professional services and investors.

The market is now characterised by increasing plurality, but a rather unique plurality in which there is BOTH more commoditisation AND more specialisation. The spectrum of services is widening – ranging from large corporate firms with 400 or more partners to near industrial scale personal injury firms to small specialist 'boutique' practices and new 'virtual law firms'. In parts of this world at least, commercial and management skills are as important as legal skills for the senior leadership of firms – and indeed for many in the centre of organisations as well. So are general management skills and commercial awareness no longer discretionary, but something that is needed at an earlier stage of education – to meet the needs of employers as well as their commercial clients? I will add here that this is about the skills of all those who work in businesses supplying legal services – not just the lawyers. They, the lawyers, need to decide what skills they are best placed to deliver – leaving officers in other divisions to deliver the remainder, for example IT, financial and HR leadership.

In this world, only a minority of practising solicitors and their other qualified staff do 'a bit of everything' in the way that traditional high street practices commonly offered in the past. Even fewer barristers would claim to be legal general practitioners. Arguably it was relatively easy to devise an education and training framework for a world where all lawyers ran their business in broadly the same way. It was relatively easy to teach regulatory obligations against a set regulatory rulebook. But how do we ensure that the framework evolves – and continues to evolve – against the changes to the market and the more sophisticated outcome-focused approach to regulation that I have described?

As a minimum, I think that we will be looking at a changed and earlier emphasis on the teaching of professional ethics and wider responsibilities to the client, a point I hear repeatedly from practitioners. I will return to this in looking at the balance between innovation and maintaining core professional principles.

Changing conditions do not simply have an impact on ancillary skills. We need to look again at the very nature of what it means to be a lawyer – and then evaluate what skills we need, how we develop them and how we test for them.

One feature of modern life, for example, is the increasing amount of legislation being passed onto the statute book: 14,580 pages per year in 2005 compared with 8,270 pages in 1975.[1] This has brought increasing complexity to the function of

1 http://www.parliament.uk/documents/commons/lib/research/notes/snsg-02911.pdf.

the individual lawyer. So the key legal skill is increasingly about how to find the legal principles and apply them to the circumstances of the case rather than about accumulating knowledge per se. There is, of course, still great value in historical understanding of the evolution of law, but practitioner skills are increasingly about the application, rather than simply the academic knowledge, of those principles.

Alongside this, we are increasingly seeing collapsing boundaries between different types of lawyer. The extension of higher court rights of audience to solicitors and the emergence of Legal Disciplinary Partnerships are illustrations of this phenomenon. There will be others. Baroness Ruth Deech, the Chairman of the BSB, commented earlier this year that it was odd to force students into specialisation decisions at the age of 20 or 21, before they really understand the demands of different branches of the profession and have the maturity to understand their own fitness for them. I agree with that questioning.

I am tempted to go further and say that it is even odder to force an early decision in a world where the decision may be becoming ever more irrelevant in the medium-term. In the past, there was greater uniformity in the skills and knowledge needed to practice successfully. There was greater predictability in the setting in which lawyers applied those skills. But we are now in a paradoxical time: a time in which we see both ever greater specialisation and complexity within the profession, but ever more fluid boundaries between the traditional branches of the profession and between that legal services sector and other areas of the economy. What does that mean for how we train people – and when and how we ask them to decide to make major decisions about their future career direction and degree of specialisation?

The demands of modern practice have changed and will continue to do so. This can be seen in the breadth of business acumen required, in the level of commercial understanding required from practitioners, and in terms of the essence of 'lawyering' itself. Educational practice and the regulatory requirements in relation to education and training are evolving in the light of that. But regulators, educators and practitioners alike must not see that process as a one-off 'modernisation', but need to rise to the challenge of keeping requirements moving at the pace of a 21st century, wired (or rather, wireless) world.

Priorities for education and training

Clearly, identifying ways of meeting a challenge of this scale is far from easy. Identifying the way forward is going to take a period of deliberation and dialogue, potentially with competing priorities across the workforce. An important starting point is to acknowledge that there are almost certainly going to be a number of approaches that meet that challenge. A single solution for education and training is no more credible than a single business model for firms or chambers.

In fact, we are already seeing plurality through different and equally effective ways of delivering the same outcomes – for example academic study versus so called 'clinical legal education' versus on-the-job experience for those entering the profession via further rather than higher education.

One crucial yardstick is that the outcomes of all those diverse routes must deliver the important professional attributes demanded by the regulatory objective – independence, strength, effectiveness and diversity – and must also ensure that the professional principles are lived out in practice. The key issue is what works. The models might be – must be – diverse, but in all cases they must deliver the full range of skills that consumers need to see from practitioners. Multiplicity can never be a synonym for dumbing down.

Let me, as a layman, suggest some areas that education and training needs to cover:

- *Ethics – first and foremost*
- Navigating the law
- Professional skills – particularly in applying legal principles to the facts of the case, but also the procedural knowledge applicable to different areas of law
- Functional skills, such as drafting and advocacy
- Client-handling and other wrongly termed soft skills – every other part of the economy regards those as professional and rightly so
- Management skills and commercial awareness

I hope that there would not be much dissent from that as a high level list – the challenge is about precisely what should be taught at what stage and how. And that is what I, as a layman, would invite the profession and educators alike to consider – but with the final suggestion that there is unlikely to be a single answer. The boundaries between different levels of education and training in other words may need to be as fluid as those increasingly porous divisions I have already described.

The place of CPD

Nobody has all the answers. Genuine and effective enquiry into these issues relies on regulators working with academics, educators and practitioners to tell us what capacity-building steps are necessary in the system for education and training. We need to ask firms and chambers what skills they need amongst the next generation of pupils and trainees.

As part of that discussion, we need to get their views on the extent to which the current framework prepares lawyers for practice, as well as what steps are needed to develop fledgling practitioners once in the job.

Continual professional development (CPD) is a critical part of ensuring that the workforce can react to change, but the early period of practice is a uniquely sensitive one in which competencies are framed. Is there a case for an accountancy style model of initial training? In that model professional training takes place during full-time employment. It must be worth considering whether such a model could be developed for law, to address the issue of students completing the vocational stage (and accumulating significant debts in the process) without the offer of a training contract or pupillage on completion. Indeed, do we need to assume that the training contract and pupillage need to be inviolable parts of *everybody's* career progression or should they be one route among others? We also need to consider how we approach post-initial qualification training to ensure competence is maintained and developed into specialist skills.

What is unequivocal, however, is that we are seeing a premium placed on those lawyers who offer more than just technical expertise. Alongside aptitude to be a lawyer, practitioners need to demonstrate professional service skills and the ability to relate to clients' needs responsively. General legal knowledge needs to be supplemented by specialist knowledge and skills – fortified by programmes of CPD that are respected as both worthwhile and reflective of changed practice.

Ethics and professionalism

I mentioned professional ethics earlier. Let me return to that theme.

The strategic objective is clear: to equip the workforce to deliver for consumers at a time of heightened change and expectations, whilst also maintaining the intellectual integrity, the ethical strength and the global competitiveness of our legal qualifications. I don't apologise for mixing morality and economics in that sentence. The strength of the legal profession and the legal services sector relies on precisely that admixture – and I'd argue that the strength of legal education ought to lie in precisely the same mix.

The teams around lawyers are changing: the ABS framework envisages a Head of Legal Practice taking on a key role in governance and accountability, for example, and the SRA's proposals see a similar arrangement in mainstream firms. Already many lawyers work in new business models, supervising unregulated – but not unskilled – paralegals. The emerging plurality of provision and education to which I have referred challenges old orthodoxies, but has the potential to stimulate partnerships and new ways of working that can both serve consumers better and enhance the reputation of the profession.

Notwithstanding this, there are enduring values for legal professionals, values at the centre of the rule of law. The core elements are independence and integrity, a commitment to the best interests of the client and the overriding duty to the court. All of these are, of course, in the professional principles spelled out in the Legal Services Act 2007. When I say the interests of consumers are at the core of professional service, there is sometimes perceived to be a disconnect with those principles. But the best interest of the client is at the heart of that list.

Whilst ethics teaching cannot instil integrity in and of itself, the education stage needs to expose students to some of the complex ethical scenarios they are likely to encounter in practice. Of course, maintaining the collective sense of identity across the profession is a key part of incentivising professional conduct. The challenge is to retain and enhance that but without sustaining unnecessary barriers to entry and restricting competition. Competition can have a positive effect on consumer choice, but can also help import new working practices into the profession and challenge orthodoxies in a positive way. Legal ethics has a lot to teach general business ethics – but exclusion and misplaced moral superiority aren't among the relevant lessons.

Importantly, we should always remember that lawyers are in a special position of trust – with consumers engaging lawyers at particularly sensitive times in their lives and in the course of their business dealings. Research shows that clients struggle to evaluate the quality of service they receive, meaning they need to trust and rely on the provider. Regulation needs to ensure that this trust is well placed. These twin duties to the client and to the court (and, through that, public service) form the pillars of professionalism in the industry.

With all the talk of change – and the volume of real and pressing change – we must not forget that the real challenge is how we educate in a way that both reflects changed consumer expectations and ensures the maintenance of these fundamental values. My Board's statutory duty in relation to education is rightly framed. 'Maintenance and development of standards' – it's both, not a choice.

Reserved activities – A wider issue

Let me raise two wider issues. Legal services regulators can set the terms of debate only for the range of activities over which we have responsibility. A crucial part of the next stage of our work is to examine the scope of regulation and the appropriateness of the areas over which we have oversight. This is why my Board is looking again at the extent of reserved legal activities, the regulatory landscape and the impact this has on education and training. The recent work from the College of Law's Policy Institute carried out by Stephen Mayson demonstrates that the definition and scope of reserved legal activities, which has evolved over time, is arbitrary – laughably arbitrary in fact. It bears only the slightest relationship to the interests of consumers now and probably not enough for the consumers of the future.

But the powers that Parliament has consciously given my Board enable us to address the question of the appropriateness of that landscape and how best to protect those future consumers. The evolution of that regulatory framework, by essence, has an impact on how we resolve to reshape education and training. The purpose of that system is to produce lawyers who are theoretically competent for practice across the range of reserved activities. To some extent, it is that range of activities which drives the scope of the current curriculum, particularly at the vocational stage of training. Broader questions, therefore, surround whether regulation in general (and education and training in particular) ought to be so focused on the reserved activities, to the exclusion of other elements of legal work. The fundamental question of risk of consumer detriment needs to be the starting point, with regulatory requirements being tailored appropriately.

Diversity and social mobility

Second, workforce diversity is a crucial driver for education and training policy. Both the current and former governments have kept alive a debate on the role of the professions in promoting diversity and social mobility – with access and progression amongst practitioners from non-traditional backgrounds being a key measure of success. Achieving that step-change at senior levels of the profession – and I should acknowledge right away the excellent progress made at entry level – is a complex challenge, with drivers running right the way back to early years of education. But there is great commitment in the profession and we need to develop that momentum.

It is not just a moral cause. It's also in the pragmatic interests of the profession itself, of the legal system and of the rule of law that we widen participation to the best and most able lawyers regardless of background. There are some difficult trade-offs. I understand the worries of those who feel that we are in danger of training people who have little or no chance of making a successful professional career in the current environment. The danger is that initiatives to protect the over-optimistic educational consumer may inadvertently have the effect of reinforcing stereotypes about the exclusivity of the profession. We should make sure that managing unrealistic expectation doesn't lead to legitimate aspiration being dampened.

Regulators and educationalists alike need to contribute to the public policy debates that determine priorities for spending and support. We need to be alive to the impact of the government's proposals on higher education funding, whilst creating a sharper focus on the postgraduate stage and what changes will mean for students who wish to enter the profession later in life. An emerging opportunity for the sector is the increasing number of non-graduate entry routes to access – and I would like to see regulators do more to consider what this means for improving the 'gene pool' of talent in the market. There are perhaps lessons from past apprenticeship models, which are worthy of being revisited.

There used to be the old five-year route from school to professional qualification – the market place has delivered a contemporary version of that today. Technology has liberated legal education so that students can now do an online law degree/Graduate Diploma in Law and the LPC with just four weekends of face to face. That can be studied from home or better still the workplace – combining study with work-based learning and new forms of apprenticeship. Across the sector we can already see examples of initiatives aimed at widening access to the legal profession, led by educators and regulators. One impact of these programmes has been the acceptance of greater flexibility at the postgraduate stage. Alongside this, integrated courses have been developed that enable students to complete the various stages of qualification as part of a single course. And we should surely be able to make transitions easier – I understand why people argue for aptitude testing, but shouldn't any qualifying degree worth its name give people the necessary aptitude?

Over time, we have seen the development of delivery methods that more closely align teaching to the demands of legal practice. As student finance becomes ever more difficult, I really hope that we see this type of initiative being taken even further. For those leaving school and aiming for a legal career, we need to see the total length of time spent in education – and so the total amount of debt – shrink.

This is linked to ensuring that students do not need to make crucial, and costly, investment decisions too early on, before getting a real 'feel' for the area of practice and all that it will involve. For those already in the sector, we need to see multiple routes to progression. I refuse to believe that it's not in the wit of those in this room tonight to find ways of doing that without reducing standards in any way.

A good base on which to build

Reforms led by the regulators are already playing a major role in modernising education and training. For example, the SRA has introduced much less prescriptive requirements for the LPC that are designed to enable educators to be more flexible on course design and delivery. Alongside this, they are looking ahead to help students bridge the gap between the postgraduate stage and the demands of the first year of training. New work-based learning pilots are providing 'on the job' training that, whilst not requiring a formal training contract, enables students to be assessed against 'day one outcomes'.

I also welcome progress at the Bar. Lord Neuberger's report on entry generated many new initiatives. Their implementation has been overseen by the Bar Council but also embraced by Derek Wood Q.C., who has also taken on other onerous responsibilities in reviewing the BVC, pupillage and now CPD requirements. Looking slightly further back, we have seen a stronger emphasis on practical training events, particularly in relation to advocacy skills. This is supplemented by the work of other bodies on supporting preparedness to practise, particularly the Inns of Court notably in the field of advocacy through the development of the Advocacy Training Council, a resource to which I hope all sections of the profession with rights of audience will have access.

That level of rigour, imagination and sheer hard work represents an excellent base on which to build. And I am delighted to say that there is agreement on the broad shape of those next steps.

The Regulators' Review

The Legal Services Board (LSB) has been discussing how to make further progress with the SRA, the BSB and ILEX Professional Standards. There is consensus on the need for a more overarching strategic review to complement and frame existing initiatives.

We have agreed what the main questions are – although I am sure that these will develop further as the dialogue broadens in the coming months.

Let me just run through them:

- First, what should be the contribution of legal education and training to the delivery of the Regulatory Objectives set out in the Legal Services Act 2007, taking account of the factors I have discussed today?:
    - The likely shape of and demands on legal services by 2020 in the light of changing consumer/client demand, technological change and other factors

- The effects that the shape of legal services may have upon the legal and other skills demanded from different kinds of lawyers and others employed in legal services in the future. This is about a fundamental re-evaluation to meet the needs of the workforce of 2020
- The need for high quality, competitive legal services and education and training providers and high ethical standards for lawyers and legal services entities
- The need to promote social mobility and diversity
- Forthcoming changes to the education sector and how these may affect legal education and training

- Second, what might be the specific consequences of the implementation of the Legal Services Act 2007 for the system of legal education and training?
- Third, to what extent (if any) should the formal regulation of legal education and training be extended to include groups other than those regulated by the SRA, BSB, ILEX Professional Standards and other Approved Regulators (e.g. paralegals, other providers of legal services and those employed in entities)?
- Fourth, what measures can or should be taken to address the issue of career development and mobility between branches of the legal profession at all stages of the student experience and legal careers?
- And finally, what recommendations arise for the LSB, Approved Regulators and other bodies from these questions? None of us are interested in this being an academic exercise in the pejorative sense of the term.

The answers to these questions need to be considered in the context of the complex domestic and international changes to the landscape which I described earlier.

Making the Review work

This is very much an exercise in the spirit of oversight regulation. We have developed the thinking jointly with the frontline regulators. It is our agreed agenda and their Review. I am now looking forward to their practical proposals on how they will address it. But let me say a little more about what needs to be done if this is to be a genuine watershed.

First, we all agree strongly that joint consideration of the issues that span the entire workforce is necessary if we are to reach a set of conclusions that have cross-sector application. It's not about one regulator going alone or one part of the profession being looked at independently. Nor is it about any part of the student journey being considered off limits.

Second, this needs to be genuinely ambitious and forward-looking in scope. There will need to be new evidence-gathering, with original research being funded and commissioned where deeper insights are needed to fill gaps in our shared knowledge. Part of that process of collecting evidence needs to look beyond the boundaries of the legal profession, outside the sector and beyond the UK to the experience of other jurisdictions, to learn from wider experiences.

Third, the Joint Review needs to complement existing initiatives rather than duplicate the detail of them. Collective endeavour mustn't lead to individual planning blight.

Fourth, the Joint Review will need to engage the widest range of stakeholders – including students and firms – not just the usual regulatory and educational suspects. And, as I have already said, but make no apologies for reiterating, most importantly of all, the Review needs to generate concrete recommendations that can be agreed and implemented by all relevant parties. If this produces papers for learned journals alone, it will have failed. Work needs to begin this year and we will expect to see conclusions begin to emerge during 2011. What this Joint Review absolutely cannot represent is any kicking-into-the-long-grass of these crucial issues.

These are the yardsticks against which my Board will assess the credibility and effectiveness of its outcomes. They are the essential characteristics needed to demonstrate that this initiative is capable of living up to the scale of the challenge on workforce development. We need a blueprint for action to give society the legal workforce it needs for the future. I am confident that our partners can and will deliver this. We will offer constructive challenge throughout the process, filling any gaps that emerge that would benefit from support at oversight regulator level.

Conclusion

That is a daunting agenda, but I believe that it is challenging and stimulating, rather than worrying. Above all, it is a necessary agenda, one which cannot be delayed if we are to give students, employers and, above all, the public the certainty they need – the certainty that the building blocks are in place to ensure that the lawyers of the future and the legal services market of the future are going to be ever more able to meet the changing needs of justice in an increasingly demanding future.

8 Response: Of Competence, Confidence and the Last Chance Saloon

Stephen Mayson

Introduction

In his Lord Upjohn Lecture 2010, David Edmonds anticipated the Legal Education and Training Review and set out his expectations of what such a review should address. From a regulator's perspective, he was clear about the underpinning objectives that the framework of legal education and training must support, as well as the environmental and other challenges then facing practitioners and regulators.

In this chapter, I summarise the objectives, questions and concerns raised by Mr Edmonds in his lecture, and then assess whether he identified all the key issues of the time. I next address whether the Review and subsequent developments have met the objectives and expectations set out by Mr Edmonds.

Mr Edmonds's lecture was considered radical at the time. The conclusions explored in this chapter are that the Review was not radical enough in addressing its remit, and that we still have a long way to go in tackling the challenges of assuring competence and consumer confidence in legal services, and avoiding regulatory arbitrage.

The LSB concerns

In his Lord Upjohn Lecture 2010, David Edmonds, the then chairman of the Legal Services Board, set out what he saw as the potential shortcomings of legal education and training in 2010, and his expectations of what became the Legal Education and Training Review (LETR). The concerns he expressed were:

(1) that the entire legal workforce, not just the legal profession, needs to have the right skills and knowledge;
(2) that meeting the regulatory objectives in the Legal Services Act 'isn't just about making sure that people jump the right hurdles in their early 20s'[1] but

1 'Thirty-ninth Lord Upjohn Lecture 2010: Training the Lawyers of the Future – a Regulator's View', p. 74.

about a constant interplay between practice and education with 'each driving improvement and innovation in the other to the broader public good';[2]

(3) the challenge of 'collapsing boundaries between different types of lawyer',[3] as well as the impact of globalised markets and more competitive approaches to qualification in other jurisdictions;
(4) the need to construct education, training and governance requirements for a liberalised market with more diverse business models – specifically in relation to alternative business structures (ABSs) and external ownership; and
(5) the challenges of a market offering both more commoditisation and more specialisation.

In a telling passage, he also said:

> 'Arguably it was relatively easy to devise an education and training framework for a world where all lawyers ran their business in broadly the same way. It was relatively easy to teach regulatory obligations against a set regulatory rulebook. . . . We need to look again at the very nature of what it means to be a lawyer – and then evaluate what skills we need, how we develop them and how we test for them.'[4]

This strongly suggested that a 'business as usual' conclusion with some minor, incremental changes was not going to be enough. Mr Edmonds's expectations of the LETR were therefore ambitious:

(1) a set of conclusions that had cross-sector application, acknowledging that a 'single solution for education and training is no more credible than a single business model for firms and chambers', while ensuring that 'diverse routes must deliver the important professional attributes demanded by the regulatory objectives – independence, strength, effectiveness and diversity';
(2) a forward-looking review that looked beyond the boundaries of the legal profession, outside the sector and beyond the United Kingdom;
(3) engagement of the widest range of stakeholders; and
(4) concrete recommendations that can be agreed and implemented by all relevant parties – 'a blueprint for action to give society the legal workforce it needs for the future'.[5]

Mr Edmonds's lecture was considered radical at the time. Disappointingly, the LETR Report has not risen to that challenge and consequently we have not yet gone far enough in tackling the challenges of assuring competence and consumer confidence in legal services, and avoiding regulatory arbitrage.

2 Ibid.
3 Ibid., p. 86.
4 Ibid., p. 76.
5 Ibid., p. 84.

The LETR and its Report

The LETR was established in June 2011 by the Solicitors Regulation Authority (SRA), the Bar Standards Board (BSB) and ILEX Professional Standards (IPS). The LETR website states:

> 'The primary objective of the Review was to ensure that England and Wales has a legal education and training system that advances the regulatory objectives contained in the Legal Services Act 2007, and particularly the need to protect and promote the interests of consumers and to ensure an independent, strong, diverse and effective legal profession. It examined regulated and non-regulated legal services. The Review explored all stages of legal education and training, including the academic stage(s) of qualification, professional training and continuing professional development of the regulated professions. It identified both the scope for deregulation of existing training requirements and whether there was a case for bringing aspects of the non-regulated sector within a scheme of regulation.'[6]

The LETR final Report was issued, after some considerable delay, in June 2013.[7] It is a long Report, and unfortunately not the easiest read. Most disappointingly – given David Edmonds's explicit expectations – the Review rejected radical reform and recommended incremental enhancements. It focused mainly on the requirements for professional qualification and continuing competence (perhaps not surprising, given that it had been funded by solicitors, barristers and chartered legal executives).

The Review's principal conclusions can be summarised as:

- the current training regime has done a reasonable job;
- there has been too much reliance on initial qualification and needs to be a shift to assuring continuing competence;
- there should be prescribed learning outcomes, including 'Day 1' learning outcomes for authority to practise, and appropriate assessment of those outcomes;
- there needs to be more emphasis in learning and assessment on legal research, writing, critical thinking and professional ethics;
- enhanced common training for barristers and solicitors should be explored
- vocational study should be blended with on-the-job experience – which would mean changes to training contracts and pupillage, as well as the development of apprenticeship schemes to encourage more non-graduate routes into the legal profession;
- a Legal Education Council should be created.

6 See http://letr.org.uk/background/what-is-letr/index.html (accessed 10 September 2015).
7 See http://letr.org.uk/the-report/index.html (accessed 10 September 2015).

To my mind, the Review needed to look at the scope, reach and proportionality of the regulation of legal education and training for the emerging and future legal services market. The starting point should not have been, 'How can we tweak the current framework to meet the needs of the future?'. The market of 2010 was already fundamentally different to that prevailing when the pre-LETR structure of education and training was put in place (and the future market will surely be even more so). It seems inherently problematic then to surmise that the education and training that underpinned it would *not* need fundamental reform.

It could not be right (and Mr Edmonds said as much) to proceed on a premise that the only issue that needed exploring was that of regulating the education and training of 'the legal profession' (or, on more enlightened days, 'the legal professions'). The Legal Services Act 2007 certainly does not start with the assumption that legal services will only be delivered by those who are legally qualified and hold a professional title. On the contrary: it heralded a mix of the concurrent regulation of individuals, activities and entities.

Unfortunately, the present framework for the regulation of education and training very definitely starts with the regulated professions and individual practitioners, so it is perhaps not surprising that a review that was sponsored by the main professions should assumptively start from the same, historically embedded, point.

One of the darker consequences of such a starting point, though, is the insidious and invidious proposition that legal services delivered by those who do not hold a professional title must necessarily be of low or poorer quality, or even incompetent. The assumption that competence and ethics can only be demonstrated by those who are legally qualified is arrogant and unjustifiable. Indeed, the falseness of this view is written into the very core of the Act.

Parliament has already decided that legal services do not need to be delivered only by those individuals who hold a protected title, but can be offered by individuals who are authorised, or entities that are licensed, in relation to one or more of the reserved activities. To suggest that any such authorisation should only be founded on the same breadth of education and training as those who hold a professional title is to seek to achieve by the back door what Parliament has opened the front door to avoid.

In terms of the expectations that Mr Edmonds set for the LETR, it missed its mark. The Review was not in the end a cross-sector review (it focused too much on solicitors and barristers); it was not sufficiently forward-looking for a legal services market that will be fundamentally different and in which legal services provided by those who hold a professional title will be a declining proportion of the overall services supplied for reward; it did not achieve wide engagement; and it did not produce a blueprint for action to give society the legal workforce it needs for the future.

The future market

The market for legal services in the future will therefore not be one where only qualified lawyers deliver legal services. We already know this – even if we do not yet appreciate the full variety of those who will, in time, be authorised or licensed. Lawyers will become a subset of the total number and type of providers. The task for the LETR should not have been self-limited to how to adopt or adapt the route to professional qualification for broader purposes (and, to be fair, its terms of reference did not suggest that it was).

The future will also have reserved activity specialists and non-lawyers engaged in the delivery of legal services, as well as in the ownership, financing, governance, compliance and management of the entities providing those and other services. To assume that their education and training needs can (or, worse still, should) somehow be carved out of a legal qualification process geared towards the award and retention of professional titles to me presented the greatest threat – and perhaps even delivers the fatal blow – to the credibility of any proposals for future education and training.

Even if we accepted that the current process of education and training for those who seek or hold a professional title is not broken and is entirely fit for purpose, the nature and breadth of the future market must surely mean that the same process cannot possibly be adequate for the new market in its totality. A system designed for one purpose (even assuming that it is fit for that purpose) is not necessarily or inevitably fit for a different purpose.

One only needs to consider the imperative to address the unmet needs in society for legal services and access to justice, accompanied by changes being driven by technology and innovation, multidisciplinary practice and globalisation, to realise that the world of professional protection and constrained competition for which the pre-LETR framework was devised no longer exists and is not coming back.

Barely a whisper was heard through the review process about the training needs of those employed in the broader market. Although the expectations and needs of clients are assumed and mentioned throughout the Report, their views and perspectives are not well represented: the wide engagement that Mr Edmonds wished for was dashed by the limited input from consumers and consumer organisations.

Not surprisingly, then, the discourse of the LETR was dominated by justification and defence of the current framework for training those who seek or hold a professional title. However, until we disconnect the award and retention of a title from the quality and standards of competence and ethics required of those authorised to deliver a regulated activity, we cannot even be on the starting blocks of a proper debate about the future scope, reach and proportionality of regulation for legal education and training.

Let me be clear: the pre-LETR system was not totally unfit for purpose. There are some examples of stunningly high-quality lawyers and law firms emerging from that system. My point is that it is not fit *enough* for its new purpose. This is a purpose that must apply not just to qualified lawyers, but that needs to encompass support staff and multidisciplinary practice. It is not just about legal expertise, but must include client service, management and ownership. It is not just about practitioners, but needs to extend to managers, owners and investors. It is not just about England

and Wales, but must address the global influence of English law and the English courts, as well as the needs of UK plc. And it is not just about individuals, because we must also think about regulating and training within entities.

The missed opportunities

What we are facing in the future, therefore, is a fundamental separation of the regulated legal professions and the legal services market. We are moving from a world where these have been coterminous to one where they are co-existent and possibly concentric.

We are also continuing to move from a world where technical expertise alone was once regarded as sufficient to be competitive, through a more recent one where there has been increasing recognition of the need also to deliver excellent client service, to a completely new world where value creation (both for clients and legal 'businesses'), project management and business skills are necessary components. The requisite knowledge and skill-set, as well as the market, are now very different from those for which the pre-LETR regime was designed.

There are also some challenges at the heart of the current regulatory framework that have implications for the need for and scope of education and training. They include:

- the distinction between reserved legal activities and non-reserved activities;
- the difference between protected titles and authorisation to practise;
- the need to regulate both individuals and entities;
- the different roles of the practising lawyer and of those in positions of ownership, management or control; and
- the regulatory gap between those within the jurisdiction of the Legal Ombudsman and 'the untouchables' (by which I mean those who do not deliver reserved activities and are not authorised to do so, but who can deliver non-reserved services without any regulatory oversight).

We therefore needed to address a broader question first: what is the proper scope, reach and proportionality for the regulation of the (not simply legal) education and training of all those who are or will be authorised or licensed to deliver regulated services, or who work within regulated entities? Only then could we move on to consider whether the pre-LETR framework for regulating the education and training of those who presently hold professional titles had the proper scope, reach and proportionality consistent with those broader needs and objectives. To do otherwise is to start at the wrong end of the telescope: we should be looking from the outside (market) back in, not from the inside (professions) out.

Where the outcomes are not good enough

We are now in an era of outcomes focused regulation (OFR). While in favour of OFR in principle (I welcome the idea of principled others being trusted to do the right thing), there are still some practical challenges to be overcome – in particular being able to identify what the right outcome is. Be that as it may, my starting point on education and training is about the outcome: does the system of legal education and training produce lawyers who are fit for practice?

My view on that, regrettably, is that although we produce more than enough 'lawyers', we do not produce enough who are truly fit for twenty-first century practice. We are also not producing enough who can communicate effectively with consumers so that they are encouraged to seek legal advice and representation; nor is enough *affordable* and effective legal advice and representation available to satisfy the significant unmet need for legal services and access to justice (which can only increase as public funding for legal aid is reduced). We must question the efficacy and credibility of a framework for education and training that leads to such shortcomings.

In summary, there are five critical areas where I think practitioners too often fall short:

(1) *Basic legal underpinnings of their work.* We cannot reasonably expect practising lawyers to know all the technical law they will ever use. But they should be able to carry out the necessary research to find it when they need it (and too many law firms report deficiencies in this). More critically, we should also expect practising lawyers to know the fundamentals (which is why I am shocked when some senior litigators apparently rush to negligence actions without considering duty of care, breach or causation). Even at these basic levels, the legal education and training process often fails – despite prescription in the qualifying law degree (QLD).
(2) *The ability to apply their technical advice.* Too often, we hear from clients and other sources of feedback that a lawyer's advice, while technically correct, has not been applied in a contextualised, meaningful and valuable way that helps the client address their underlying personal or business problem. 'Here's my legal advice: make up your own mind what to do with it' will hardly endear lawyers to clients or justify the fees that many lawyers seek to charge for their 'help'. If we are training lawyers to give advice that is technically correct but of no practical utility, the combination of QLD, Legal Practice Course (LPC) or Bar Professional Training Course (BPTC), and work-based learning is failing.
(3) *Project management skills.* There is also little point in training lawyers to give accurate – and even useful – advice and assistance if they are unable to scope, price and deliver their services in an effective and efficient way, at a fee that clients regard as value for money, and that the firm regards as a fair return on the resources used. A large part of the costs debate and Lord Justice Jackson's search for better proportionality of costs to the issues and value at stake derived from an often deep-seated unwillingness of lawyers to manage and be managed, even (or especially) at the case level. This is a matter of professional and organisational culture as well as education and training.
(4) *The ethical and regulatory framework of legal practice.* Integrity and fair dealing are promoted as major selling points of legal practice. Regrettably, the level of

complaints (formal and otherwise) suggests that too many lawyers just do not deliver on this. Or perhaps we simply have too many lawyers to be able to maintain quality and ethics? I fully endorse the LETR's conclusion that greater attention is needed here.

(5) *Law as a business.* Despite many moves in the right direction, we still do not have enough lawyers with the ability to build and manage sustainable and valuable business entities that are effectively structured and governed, efficiently run, and capable of surviving beyond the current generation of owners. This is often characterised as a dichotomy between law as a profession and law as a business. This is an old, tiresome and futile argument. Modern legal practice is both: if lawyers charge people for the advice they give, they are in business. There is no reason why this cannot be done professionally and ethically while at the same time being efficient and making a profit.

Of course, there are many exceptions to each of the five criticisms made above. There are some for whom the education and training framework of legal practice has worked superbly. However, that is no consolation to the clients who are subjected to the worst examples of each criticism, and any number of combinations of them: for these people, the legal education and training system has failed them utterly.

If the incumbent legal professions are going to sit on a high horse of exceptional quality and ethical integrity, then they have set a very high standard for judgement. Based on the standards and expectations that are set – by the market, regulators and clients – there are far too many manifestations of incompetence, poor service or unethical behaviour. So, judged on this outcome, my conclusion – despite the assertion of the LETR – is that the pre-LETR framework was not sufficiently fit for purpose.

It would seem that the SRA, at least, agrees. In a response to the LETR Report, the then chief executive, Antony Townsend, said in October 2013:

> 'Put simply, the regulation of legal education and training has failed to keep pace both with changes in the sector and with modern regulatory practice. We are doing too little to assure appropriate standards, and too much in fiddling with detailed educational designs and inputs. We need to get out of prescribing the educational "how" others are much better placed to do that; and we need to get a grip on assuring standards of competence against a framework fit for modern legal practice.'[8]

The missing links

Starting with the outcome, then, the pre-LETR chain of educational development was not reliably strong enough to produce the breadth and depth of competence and skill that twenty-first-century legal practice now demands. If one adopts the

8 In a Speech to The Westminster Legal Policy Forum in London on 8 October 2013.

LETR's premise of preparation for professional titles, it seems to me that each of the academic, vocational, training contract and continuing professional development stages has a role to play, and forms a link in that chain. Unfortunately, each has *to some extent* (i.e. not totally or universally) been broken in its contribution to the next stage, resulting in the systemic shortcomings described earlier.

Against this backdrop, these are the propositions and questions which I believe the LETR should have addressed about the links in the chain:

(1) There has been too much prescription in the QLD; why is *any* regulatory prescription of this nature in otherwise regulated university degrees required? Admittedly, the Report does not encourage any greater regulatory intervention, but equally still considers that some prescription by legal regulators is appropriate.

(2) The LPC is not preparing students adequately for practice (see the five critical areas already mentioned), and the burdens of cost and expectation are not fairly placed (by requiring students without training contracts already in place to fund and undertake the course in the hope that they will nevertheless at some point be able to practise).
The Report offers little in the way of firm recommendations for improving competence in the reserved activities (though acknowledging that this is needed, especially for advocacy – and suggests, wrongly, that will-writing is a reserved activity and as such also requires further attention to quality within the LPC). Recommendations for the LPC are therefore confined to modifications to increase flexibility of delivery of the course and the development of specialist pathways.

(3) The training contract and pupillage are barriers to entry (by limiting the number of entry points to qualification and practice).
Here there are some welcome recommendations in the Report suggesting more flexibility for periods of supervised practice, combined with apprenticeship and other non-graduate pathways – albeit still aimed at entry to a regulated profession rather than authorisation to carry out specific legal activities.

(4) Clients are no longer willing to bear the cost of post-LPC training (through being charged by law firms for trainees' time on matters).
In maintaining its focus on entry to regulated professions, the Report does not take a rounded view on where the costs of education and training for practice should properly fall (as between employers, individuals and clients).

(5) Continual professional development (CPD) is discredited and ineffective in assuring continuing competence (largely because it requires only physical presence for a prescribed minimum period of CPD activity, which needs bear no relevance to the practitioner's daily client engagements and does not need to result in any change of learning, attitude or behaviour): it provides no guarantee of continuing competence.
In its conclusions (paragraph 7.38) and recommendations (16 to 19), the Report still adopts a primarily input-based viewpoint to CPD. Greater links to the assurance of ongoing competence and relevance are not pursued.

Although there are welcome suggestions that different regulators should co-operate more with each other and co-ordinate their approach to education and training, this necessarily perpetuates a focus on regulated professions rather than regulation and authorisation for specific legal activities or of regulated entities carrying out a variety of such activities.

Into the future

The future world of legal practice will not support a one-size-fits-all approach to the structure and delivery of legal services. It will not, therefore, support a similar approach to education and training.

We need to be clear about the core knowledge and skills that are necessary in the twenty-first century to justify the award of any protected title and the privilege of practising in one or more of the reserved activities, as well as how much of that outcome and process needs to be prescribed by regulation. At the same time, that entry point also has to provide a robust enough foundation for supporting a practitioner's diversification into any of the near-infinite possibilities and opportunities that the new world might offer.

Regrettably, the LETR did not adequately address such a cross-sector, forward-looking structure for the future, or the regulation necessary to support it.

Perhaps just a little paradoxically, given their funding of the LETR, the main regulators seem to have been developing their own parallel thoughts. In their responses to the LETR, therefore, some of them have been able to outline plans for progress that go beyond the LETR recommendations.

For barristers, the BSB had already introduced centralised assessments for the BPTC, and an aptitude test to ensure that students who undertook the BPTC were likely to have the ability to complete it.

It also announced that six programmes will be developed:[9]

- developing a competency framework for barristers;
- aligning the Bar's training regulations to modern regulatory standards;
- establishing an outcomes-focused approach to continuing professional development;
- sharing data to support our regulatory objectives in education and training;
- improving access routes to the profession;
- collaborative development of academic stage regulation.

However, the most radical response has come from the SRA, which has adopted the most open-minded and speedy response to reviewing and changing the future framework for the education and training of solicitors (see, for example, the chief executive's early response to the LETR Report[10]).

9 See https://www.barstandardsboard.org.uk/qualifying-as-a-barrister/letr-next-steps/.
10 In a Speech to The Westminster Legal Policy Forum in London on 8 October 2013.

As a result, new SRA regulations were introduced with effect from 1 July 2014 as a result of which:

- new law students no longer need to register with the SRA (saving them an £80 registration fee) or get a certificate of academic standing from the SRA;
- the SRA no longer stipulates the employment terms of the training contract;
- trainees' salaries are subject to national minimum wage regulations; and
- a new 'equivalent means' application is introduced under which candidates who can demonstrate that they have met the training requirements through equivalent experience or qualifications can seek admission as a solicitor.

The SRA is also reforming the CPD framework to adopt a new approach to continuing competence so that regulated entities and individuals have the freedom and flexibility to determine their own training and development needs to ensure continuing competence and the delivery of competent legal services. The SRA intends to remove the annual 16 hours CPD requirement with effect from November 2016, and then to allow individuals and regulated entities to determine for themselves how they best ensure continuing competence.

The SRA is also developing a new competence statement for solicitors that will accurately reflect what solicitors do and will need to do in the future. This will also allow solicitors to reflect on their competence and help providers who develop courses leading to qualification. Finally, in a similar vein, the SRA is working on articulating the level that a 'day one' solicitor should be able to achieve.

Conclusions

David Edmonds sparked a long-overdue review of legal education and training and set out some clear expectations for it. The LETR was therefore a much-needed investigation, and rightly confirmed a number of issues and challenges with the pre-LETR structure and regulation of legal education and training. Where the LETR fell short in meeting Mr Edmonds's objectives was in not taking a cross-sector view, in not being sufficiently forward-looking, in not securing wide engagement in its work, and in not producing a blueprint for action.

The response to the LETR Report from those regulators who sponsored it has been encouraging and, at least in the case of the SRA, is demonstrating a willingness to be much more radical than the LETR recommended.

Unfortunately, the LETR also fell short of its potential in merely perpetuating a framework and regulatory approach that focuses predominantly on entry to the regulated professions rather than competence in specific legal activities and employment in regulated entities providing a range of such activities. Although the regulators' early responses have been encouraging, this distorted focus sadly remains.

If competence cannot be sufficiently assured, the public generally, and consumers more specifically, will not have the confidence in legal services that they deserve. Developments in the legal marketplace are now moving at a rapid pace, and combine with reductions in legal aid and the consequences for access to justice. An approach to legal education and training that is focused on and driven by regulated professions will fail to rise to the challenges faced across the legal sector, now and into the future. If the academy and regulators also fail to grasp this nettle, the LETR may well prove to have been the last chance saloon for targeted, proportionate and effective legal education and training truly fit for its future purposes.

9 Twenty-ninth Lord Upjohn Lecture 2000

The Education, the Justice System Requires Today*

Lord Woolf C.J.

It is a pleasure to give this lecture at the invitation of Lord Templeman. When you become a Law Lord you move from the Strand to Westminster. You feel very much like a new boy who has changed school. A warm welcome by the senior boys is very much appreciated. On my arrival the second most senior boy was Sydney Templeman. Not only was he very kind at the time I arrived, but he continued to be a marvellous mentor until he retired. I particularly admired the manner in which he could distil the essence of what took me 20 pages to express into half a page of elegant prose. There are, no doubt, many reasons for the Association of Law Teachers selecting Lord Templeman to be their President, but I am sure one of the reasons was his qualities as a lawyer. The Association made a wise choice.

This lecture is of course named after the first President of the Association, Lord Upjohn. The fact that I received my invitation from Lord Templeman and that the lecture is in memory of Lord Upjohn meant that Lord Templeman's invitation was not one that I could refuse.

I have previously been the Lord Upjohn Lecturer. It was back in 1986 when I had just become your President. My previous lecture was my first engagement in public as your President. By coincidence this is my first public engagement as Chief Justice. I suppose I should offer you an apology. You were expecting to be addressed by the Master of the Rolls but instead you have a mere Chief Justice. Certainly while I was MR (my opinion may be changing) I always regarded the office of MR as much more distinguished than that of Chief Justice. Almost all jurisdictions have a Chief Justice. Even Gibraltar, where there are only two judges, has a Chief Justice and a Deputy Chief Justice. Furthermore it is much simpler to make jokes about the office of MR than that of Chief Justice. In Paris I was described as the 'maitre de petit-pains' and in Japan, recalling a famous letter that Lord Denning received from someone in India, who wished to be employed at the Rolls Royce factory, I introduced myself as Master of the Honda.

* This lecture was delivered as the Twenty-ninth Lord Upjohn Lecture by the Lord Chief Justice at the Inns of Court School of Law on 14 June 2000.

Prior to coming here this evening I looked up my previous Lord Upjohn Lecture given 14 years ago. I had completely forgotten about the subject of my talk. Because of the anecdotes of which I have been told concerning Lord Upjohn I took as my title Civil Procedure – Time for Changes. As this was over a decade prior to my Access to Justice Report, it is interesting to speculate whether Lord Mackay, who launched me on that project, was in the habit of reading *The Law Teacher* in which the lecture was published.

If there is a connection, this is ironic because I commenced the earlier lecture by referring to the fact that Lord Upjohn was the only person of whom I have heard who regularly slept with a copy of the *Supreme Court Practice* by his bedside. It is interesting to speculate as to whether, if Lord Upjohn were still alive, he would now sleep with a copy of the Civil Procedure Rules (CPR) by his bedside. If he would, I would like to know which is the better antidote for insomnia.

The changes to civil procedure are part of the explanation for my title. I do believe that civil procedure is a subject the importance of which has been grossly under-estimated in the past by both academics and practitioners. With a modest number of distinguished exceptions, the input to the subject from the universities has been modest. This probably explains why I have not heard of many students who picketed Parliament or even the Royal Courts of Justice protesting about the lamentable state of our civil procedure. The Overriding Objectives in Part 1 of the CPR have fundamentally changed what is involved in deciding cases justly. The law of evidence has been dramatically transformed by the CPR. Full advantage has been taken of an apparently modest provision in the First Schedule to the Civil Procedure Act of 1997. The provision allows the new Rules to '*modify the rules of evidence as they apply to proceedings in any court within the scope of the Rules*'. Relying on this provision, the CPR virtually abolish the old technical rules of evidence.

Let me remind you of the terms of Part 32.1 of the CPR. Rule 1 states:

> '(1) The court may control the evidence by giving directions as to –
>
> (a) the issues on which it requires evidence;
> (b) the nature of the evidence which it requires to decide those issues;
> (c) the way in which the evidence is to be placed before the court.
>
> (2) The court may use its power under this Rule to exclude evidence that would otherwise be admissible.
> (3) The court may limit cross-examination.'

The changes are ones which I regard as being beneficial. (I would do so wouldn't I?) They release evidence from the bondage to which it has been subjected because of the supposed inability of the jury properly to evaluate evidence and their supposed inability to recognise the prejudicial as well as probative qualities of evidence. Except in limited circumstances, we no longer have any juries, but as Professor Jolowicz points out, the ghost of the jury system was still controlling what evidence could be placed before a court prior to the introduction of the CPR.

The Rules of Evidence, together with Rules of Procedure, play at least as important a role as the substantive law in the justice system. However, if some of the anecdotal information which I am given is correct, both subjects are at best given a minimal role during the academic stage of the training of the would-be lawyer. The new culture of the CPR in redefining, as it does, what is involved in achieving justice, is not being given the scrutiny it deserves, in the academic as well as the vocational stage of training. It is after all quite fundamental to have jettisoned our traditional view that the public has no interest in how private law litigation is conducted. In addition, young lawyers have to appreciate that case management, by lawyers, including a full appreciation of the contribution which can be made, is no longer an optional extra for specialist lawyers. Dispute resolution is now a pre-litigation process.

Public law is recognised as being one of the foundations of legal knowledge by the Bar Council. It is a required part of the academic stage of training for the Bar. However, both procedure and remedies have played a fundamental role in the development of our public law. The new procedure leading to the harmonisation of public and private law is likely to have as great an influence on the development of public law in the future as Order 53 had in the past. But I am not confident that the young are being taught the importance of this. The young lawyer needs to be aware that procedural law and the availability of remedies can have significant effects on substantive law.

The changes in civil procedure are only one of the fundamental changes which are taking place in our law and constitutional arrangements at the present time. We may not have a federal system which is equivalent to that in the United States, but devolution has fundamentally changed our constitutional arrangements.

Lord Justice Sedley is not only one of our most distinguished administrative law jurists, he is responsible for overseeing the judicial education which the Judicial Studies Board is providing prior to the Human Rights Act 1998 coming into force. His invitation to this lecture provoked him to send me a letter he had written a year earlier to Professor Paterson, who was about to chair a meeting of the heads of UK law schools. The letter was copied to the heads of the law schools. In the letter to Professor Paterson, Lord Justice Sedley, in my view correctly, commented that if lawyers simply use the Act and Convention as a fall-back where no other argument is available 'they will rapidly lose credibility and the Act will become a dead letter. If, on the other hand, lawyers make intelligent and creative use of the new law, we can hope to develop a true judicial Human Rights culture'. Lord Justice Sedley went on to say that it is to 'the generation which now and in the coming years passes through law schools that we are going to have to look for educated help in making the Act and Convention work. This requires a re-casting of much of the law school curriculum. It is no good treating Human Rights as an optional extra to existing courses. The need is to rethink pretty well every area of law in a way which will make human rights an integral part of it. Lord Justice Sedley in his letter to me said that the enquiries which he had made a year later suggested that relatively few teachers are changing what they teach. Human rights is typically still being offered as a bolt-on extra in university law courses, taught by a specialist lecturer. He speculated as to whether perhaps it was not the judiciary who needed a shake-up but the academics.

Like Lord Justice Sedley, I can only speculate as to the position within the law schools. If, however, Lord Justice Sedley's fears are justified this would be unfortunate because if the Act and the Convention are to be the force for good that they should be, it is essential that the change of culture which they are intended to bring about is given a central role in the education of the next generation of lawyers.

Why it is so important that the Human Rights Act and Convention should be given a central platform in the academic training of our lawyers is because of the value judgments which are required. Our substantive law has hitherto consisted of a spectrum of relatively sharply defined concepts. The Convention is couched in general terms subject to broad qualifications. Ascertaining the law requires lawyers to be involved in a critically important task so far as society is concerned. That task is the making of value judgments between conflicting fundamental rights and values. In almost any situation, before you can ascertain the impact of the Act and Convention, a complex value judgment has to be made. The facts of a dispute have to be carefully assessed against the conflicting human social rights and human values before the law can be ascertained. This is a task which is fundamentally different to that involved in seeking to make sense of badly drafted contracts or legislation.

The new approach is not confined to human rights. It applies across the whole tapestry of the law. In order to resolve legal issues, especially where the law is unclear, a more broadly based approach is required than hitherto. Greater emphasis has to be placed on the social and economic consequences of developing the law. This is already apparent when deciding whether a duty of care exists to provide protection from economic loss. The threefold test laid down in *Caparo Industries Plc v Dickman* [1990] 2 AC 605 involves as one of its requirements that it should be just and reasonable to impose the duty. The economic and social consequences of imposing a duty are highly relevant in determining what is just and reasonable. The considerations which are relevant are complex and the process involves new skills on the part of the lawyer. The European Court of Human Rights has been criticised for the decision in *Osman v UK* (2000) 29 EHRR 245. It has been suggested that they should not have become involved in a question which was an issue of substantive law within this jurisdiction. However, the European Court saw the situation differently. They saw the issue as having a procedural dimension. The European Court considered, in my view not without justification, that this was the type of issue which could not be determined as a preliminary issue on an application to strike out. The process of ascertaining substantive law has become much more policy-based than was the position hitherto.

Another illustration is provided by the recent decision of the Court of Appeal as to what is the appropriate level of damages for non-pecuniary loss (*Heil v Rankin* [2000] 34 ER 138). Injuries, pain and suffering cannot be simply converted into currency terms. The Law Commission made a report suggesting a substantial adjustment was required. In coming to a conclusion that a more modest adjustment was required, the Court saw it as its task to ascertain a figure which reflected what was fair, just and reasonable to the different interests involved. The interests of the injured person, the interests of the defendant and the interests of the wider community had to be taken into account. The wider community interests had to be considered because it is the public which will ultimately have to bear the burden of the additional expense. This would be either in the form of higher insurance premiums or reduced health care in the case of claims against the health service.

Even the task of interpreting documents is now broader than hitherto. The matrix of relevant surrounding circumstances is continuing to expand. The process which plays such an important part in determining whether a liability exists under a contract is evolving. I do not know whether these developments are influencing the teaching of the law to the extent they should if the content of the law is to be understood properly. The approach is becoming ever broader.

Lord Bingham, when a Lord Justice, gave something of the flavour of the change. He said: 'Just as equity remedied the inadequacies of the common law, so has the law of torts filled gaps left by other causes of action where the interests of justice so required' (see *Simaan General Contracting Company v Pilkington Glass Limited (No.2)* [1988] 1 QB 758 at 782).

I appreciate that the universities today have a much broader role than merely to provide a vocational course to lawyers wishing to move directly into practice. I understand that something like 10,000 law graduates are produced by universities each year and more than half are not moving directly into practice. Instead they move into post-graduate law courses and use their legal education in multifarious fields of endeavour, including insurance, banking, public service, welfare advice and so on. (See 'Innovation in a Conservative Community: Teaching Law Off Campus in the UK' by G. Slapper, Director of the Law Programme, the Open University, delivered at the University of Adelaide 12 April 2000). The interests of the non-practitioners must not be neglected. However, the broadening of the approach to education in the law, which I am suggesting may be necessary, is very much in the interests of both those who do and do not intend to practise. The universities must prepare lawyers to enter the profession and the wider world to which they are making an ever growing contribution.

A few years ago Judge Harry Edwards of the United States Court of Appeal for the District of Columbia Circuit delivered a damning indictment of the law schools in the United States. Under the title 'The growing disjunction between legal education and legal profession' (1992) 91 *Michigan Law Review* 34–70 he first referred to the statement of Felix Frankfurter that 'in the last analysis, the law is what the lawyers are. And the law and the lawyers are what the law schools make them'. Judge Edwards expressed the fear that American law schools and law firms were moving in opposite directions. He said:

> 'The schools should be training ethical practitioners and producing scholarship that judges, legislators, and practitioners can use. The Firm should be ensuring that associates and partners practice law in an ethical manner. But

> many law schools – especially in so called "elite" ones – have abandoned their proper place by emphasising abstract theory at the expense of practical scholarship and pedagogy. Many law firms have abandoned *their* place, by pursing profit above all else. While schools are moving towards pure theory, the firms are moving towards pure commerce, and the middle ground – ethical practice – has been deserted by both. This disjunction calls into question our status as an honourable profession.'

Judge Edwards' criticisms of the American scene must be seen in the context of a system where there is not our division between the academic and vocational stage of legal education. However, even making that allowance, I would certainly not make the same criticisms as the judge makes of the law schools in our universities. I suspect that most members of our judiciary would regard the quality of contribution to academic journals as being extremely high and of significant relevance to the practice and development of the law. Our problem is finding the time to keep abreast of the massive volume of extremely valuable academic writing which is available. Whereas at one time it could have been said that the divide between the academic and the practitioner was too broad and too deep, numerous bridges have since been built between those who are engaged in the teaching and the practice of the law. My concern, like that of Lord Justice Sedley, is whether law courses in the universities are aware just how rapidly developments in the law are taking place. Those developments have to be taken into account in teaching the law. While the universities have to be responsive to the needs of those who will not be practising law, both future practitioners and non-practitioners have to develop, during their academic training, the hallmarks of the good lawyer. They must be able to analyse problems and, having done so, find the correct solutions. That requires not only the skills of a traditional black letter lawyer but also the ability to identify the broad principles which are involved in creating a just society subject to the rule of law.

Judge Edwards also expresses concern about the need to inculcate the lawyer of the future with the correct ethical standards. Here he sees a very serious conflict between increasing commercialism and the maintenance of professional standards.

The same conflict exists in this jurisdiction. The pressures on the young lawyer today, whether an academic, a solicitor or a barrister, are growing continuously more intense. Commercial activities, including arranging conferences and billable hours, are becoming as important on this side of the Atlantic as they are in the States. Competition is intensifying. The profession is having to adjust to conditional fees and the fact that lawyers have a stake in the outcome of the litigation and have to assess risk. Fresh temptations are being placed in the way of the lawyer to serve his own interests rather than those of the client's. The profession is becoming increasingly polarised according to the work which it does. Some types of work are generously, perhaps even over-generously, rewarded, while other work which is equally important to society is inadequately rewarded. It is regrettable but understandable that there should be talk by some lawyers of withdrawing their services because of the inadequacy of the rewards provided out of the public funds. The university law schools now have the heavy responsibility of empathising with the importance of our professional standards. An understanding of the responsibilities which lawyers owe to the courts has to be inculcated.

Fortunately there is considerable evidence of young lawyers on both sides of the profession developing a greater recognition of their obligation to provide pro bono legal services and to provide part time assistance at law centres and citizens' advice bureaux. Splendid evidence of the value of their contribution is provided by the support which they are providing to the Citizens' Advice Bureau in the Royal Courts of Justice. The assistance is, however, far from confined to London.

A danger, however, remains because of the contrasts in the fortunes of different parts of the profession. We are fortunate that in London the big city firms have provided exemplary support for pro bono schemes and law student activities.

However, a recent development which causes me concern is the decision of eight of the most important city firms to establish their own legal practice course. It must be for these firms to decide for themselves whether the existing training is satisfactory or not. However, it would certainly have been preferable if they could have influenced the existing providers to improve their standards rather than singling out three providers. I appreciate that the selected providers will not restrict their intake to the nominees of these large city firms. However, what is proposed will inevitably result in two standards. This is implicit in what is proposed. The consortium is seeking to create a more demanding course which will provide trainees for the city firms with the enhanced qualities for which they are looking.

The distorting effect of what is proposed should not be ignored. The same city firms already recruit from the most able graduates of the universities. Their recruits are an elite. For the elite to go to a small percentage of the provider colleges is bound to influence adversely the other providers. In any educational institution the less able students benefit from the contribution made by the more able. It is important that the lawyers emerging into practice regard themselves as one profession. If the vocational training is divided, this is more difficult to achieve.

The city firms depend on recruiting the brightest lawyers to maintain their competitiveness within a global legal community. However, with candidates of the quality they attract, it should be possible to provide any enhanced training which they require after an LPC which is common to the profession as a whole.

Having identified the challenge it only remains for me to acknowledge what I believe to the case. The quality of our young lawyers today is higher than it has ever been during my time in the law. The law teachers must be on the whole providing the education the lawyer of today requires. Nonetheless, it is always possible to do even better.

10 Response: Education in Times of Developing Law and Civil Procedure

Hon. Sir Vivian Ramsey

Introduction

At the time when Lord Woolf gave his lecture in 2000, the Civil Procedure Rules 1999 (CPR)[1] had recently been introduced and the Human Rights Act 1998 was to come into force in October 2000. He identified these developments as evidencing fundamental changes and introducing a new approach which applied across 'the whole tapestry of the law'. He said that, in order to resolve legal issues, especially where the law was unclear, a more broadly based approach was required. In this new approach he indicated that greater emphasis had to be placed on the social and economic consequences of developing the law. He also pointed out that the task of interpreting documents to determine liability in contract was now broader, as was the task of the law of torts to fill gaps left by other causes of action where the interests of justice so required.

In relation to legal education, he identified a number of areas in which the changes in approach raised particular issues of education and training for lawyers. He thought that the new culture of achieving justice under the CPR was not being given the scrutiny it deserved in the academic and vocational stages of training. This included case management and the pre-litigation stage of dispute resolution. Another area which required training was the value judgments between conflicting rights and values required under the Human Rights Act. He contrasted this with the spectrum of relatively sharply defined concepts in other areas of substantive law.

He identified changes in the role of legal education. Vocational training at university had to cater not only for those lawyers intending to practise but also for the majority of law graduates who did not practise but who use their legal training in such fields as insurance, banking, public service and welfare advice. In doing so he said that this would also prepare practising lawyers for the wider world in which they were making an ever growing contribution. He referred to criticism in the United States that American law schools were moving towards pure legal theory and law firms were moving towards pure commerce, leaving

1 Civil Procedure Rules 1998, SI 1998/3132.

a deserted middle ground of ethical practice. He said that such criticism did not apply here. There were, however, concerns arising from the conflict between increasing commercialism and the maintenance of professional standards, where the profession was having to adjust to conditional fees and the fact that lawyers had a stake in the outcome of the litigation. There was, he thought, a need for training in the importance of professional standards but he was encouraged by the fact that both sides of the profession were developing a greater recognition of their obligation to provide pro bono legal services and assistance at law centres.

In this chapter I shall pick up the themes which Lord Woolf mentioned in terms of civil procedure, development of the law and trends in legal training and consider how things have changed, if at all, in the 15 years since he gave his lecture. Given the central role of Lord Woolf in the development of civil procedure, I have concentrated on civil procedure and how it has developed since 2000.

The development of the CPR under the Woolf Reforms

The Woolf Reforms heralded a new era. Civil procedure under the new CPR sought to introduce a fresh approach from that which existed under the Rules of the Supreme Court (RSC). Whilst any change in the way in which litigation is conducted necessarily faces both reluctance and opposition from the legal profession, the overall result has been beneficial, although some areas, particularly costs, have required further changes.

In his report, *Access to Justice*,[2] Lord Woolf concluded that the existing system of civil justice was too slow, too expensive, too complex and too inaccessible. One of the main features of the reforms was a statement, in the form of the overriding objective, that the CPR was a new procedural code with the overriding objective of enabling the court to deal with cases justly.[3] What 'justly' meant in that context was then the subject of a number of non-exclusive further objectives: ensuring that the parties are on an equal footing; saving expense; dealing with a case in ways which are proportionate to the case; ensuring that a case is dealt with expeditiously and fairly; and allotting to it an appropriate share of the court's resources, while taking into account the need to allot resources to other cases.[4]

The overriding objective was to be given effect when the court exercised any power under the new CPR or interpreted any of those rules.[5] There followed a period of uncertainty as to how the overriding objective should be applied in the context of particular rules and how, if at all, the principles applied in the previous procedure under the RSC should be applied to the CPR.

As part of the new approach to justice, Lord Woolf promoted a system where the courts were responsible for the management of cases.[6] In applying case

2 *Access to Justice, Final Report.* HMSO July 1996 ('Access to Justice').
3 CPR, r 1.1(1).
4 CPR, r 1.1(2).
5 CPR, r 1.2.
6 Access to Justice, Ch. 1.

management he said that the courts should decide what procedure is suitable for each case, set realistic timetables, and ensure that the procedures and timetables are complied with.[7] Under the previous system the same procedures were applied to all cases regardless of financial weight, complexity or importance. In the new system cases were allocated to appropriate tracks for case management and trial. For the heavier cases dealt with under multi-track the CPR introduced a case management conference shortly after the defence was filed, and a pre-trial review a few weeks before the trial.[8]

The Woolf Reforms were successful in changing the culture of litigation through the overriding objective and the introduction of case management. There have, however, been concerns that certain aims of the reforms have not been achieved. Foremost among these concerns was the control of costs.

The costs of civil litigation and the Jackson Reforms

One of the principles of the Woolf Reforms was that the civil justice system should offer appropriate procedures at reasonable cost whereas the previous system was seen as being too expensive, with costs often exceeding the value of the claim.[9] This aim was not achieved, in large part because the availability of Legal Aid was much reduced and, in its place, the Courts and Legal Services Act 1990, as amended by the Access to Justice Act 1999, introduced the principle that success fees on conditional agreements and after-the-event (ATE) insurance premiums were recoverable as part of the costs of litigation.

The justified perception that the costs of litigation continued to be a problem led to the then Master of the Rolls asking Lord Justice Jackson to review the costs of civil litigation. The terms of reference given to Sir Rupert Jackson required him to review the rules and principles governing the costs of civil litigation and to make recommendations in order to promote access to justice at proportionate cost. He was also required to review case management procedures; to have regard to research into costs and funding; to consult widely; to compare the costs regime in the English courts with those of other jurisdictions; and to prepare a report setting out recommendations with supporting evidence. Sir Rupert produced his Preliminary Report in May 2009 and his Final Report in December 2009.

He found that conditional fee agreements had been the major contributor to disproportionate costs in civil litigation, particularly in relation to person injury claims. He recommended that the two key drivers of cost under such agreements, the success fee and the ATE insurance premium, should cease to be recoverable from unsuccessful opponents in civil litigation. To mitigate the fact that a party

7 The importance of these concepts was emphasised by Sir Rupert Jackson, *Final Report on Civil Litigation Costs*, December 2009, and reiterated in *Mitchell v News Group Newspapers Ltd* [2013] EWCA Civ 1537, [2014] 1 WLR 795. See also Stuart Sime, 'Sanctions after Mitchell' [2014] CJQ 133.

8 CPR, rr 29.3 and 29.7.

9 Access to Justice, Ch. 7.

would have to pay the success fee and ATE insurance premium from sums awarded as damages, he recommended that general damages for pain and suffering and loss of amenity should be increased by 10%, that referral fees by which solicitors brought cases should be abolished and that qualified one-way cost shifting[10] should be introduced so that unsuccessful claimants were no longer liable for the other party's costs and therefore did not need to take out ATE insurance.

His other major recommendations included a proposal that costs should be fixed for personal injury fast track cases and ultimately in all fast track cases, with a new Costs Council being introduced to review such costs on a regular basis. Another major recommendation was that lawyers should be able to enter into contingency fee agreements with clients for contentious business, now known as damages-based agreements (DBAs).[11] He recommended that such DBAs should be subject to two important provisos: first, that the unsuccessful party, if ordered to pay the successful party's costs, should only be required to pay an amount for costs reflecting what would be a conventional amount and, secondly, that the terms on which contingency fee agreements might be entered into should be regulated.

In addition to those major recommendations, Sir Rupert also looked at ways in which the costs of litigation could be controlled. In this area he reviewed provisions of the CPR which had been introduced as part of the Woolf Reforms. He recommended that substantial parts of *Practice Direction – Pre-Action Conduct*[12] should be repealed. In relation to ADR he found that it played a vital role in reducing the costs of civil disputes, by fomenting the early settlement of cases but was under-used and should be the subject of a serious campaign to promote it with the assistance of an ADR Handbook.[13]

In the area of case management, he proposed changes to disclosure, witness statements and expert evidence as well as steps to make sure that judges took a more robust approach to case management, so that realistic timetables were observed and that costs were kept proportionate. In addition to these changes he also proposed a wholly new approach to controlling recoverable costs by way of costs management. Costs are managed by the parties providing budgets of their proportionate costs and the court formulating directions and orders which it makes with a view to ensuring that costs do not become disproportionate by, for example, limiting disclosure, or limiting the number of witnesses.

By primary and secondary legislation and changes to the CPR the Jackson Reforms were implemented from April 2013. Whilst the focus of the Jackson

10 This is a process whereby the traditional costs shifting rule (that the loser pays the winner's costs) will not apply to an unsuccessful claimant. It only applies in personal injuries claims, and is 'qualified' because it does not apply in cases of misbehaviour.

11 Damages Based Agreements Regulations 2013, SI 2013/609.

12 For the current text, see http://www.justice.gov.uk/courts/procedure-rules/civil/rules/pd_pre-action_conduct (accessed 17 March 2015).

13 This Handbook has now been published: Susan Blake, Julie Browne and Stuart Sime, *The Jackson ADR Handbook* (Oxford University Press, 2013).

Reforms was on controlling costs, it can be seen that the proposals to do so were a development of the principles which had formed part of the Woolf Reforms.

The changes to disclosure, witness statements and expert evidence all refine the procedure introduced under the CPR and give the courts the necessary discretion to minimise expenditure in these areas to make the costs of the proceedings proportionate.

In relation to costs management Lord Woolf had proposed case management conferences and pre-trial reviews at which the parties would have to give an estimate of the costs they had incurred to date and the likely further cost if the case proceeded to trial. Those estimates had become formulaic, with reference being made to broad figures, although through amendment of the costs practice direction they had an increasing importance in relation to assessment of costs. The new approach to costs management has led to a detailed procedure by which the costs budgets of the parties are agreed or, if not agreed, the court decides on the proportionate figures and approves the budget. That then becomes the basis for standard assessment.[14]

The importance of proportionality

At the heart of the Jackson Reforms was the principle of proportionality. Sir Rupert's terms of reference included making recommendations in order to promote access to justice at proportionate cost. As he observed, the concept of proportionality came to the fore in the Woolf Reforms. The third of the eight basic principles, which Lord Woolf considered should be met by the civil justice system, was that 'Procedures and cost should be *proportionate* to the nature of the issues involved'. Lord Woolf explained in Chapter 2 of his final report that the new rules which he proposed would require the court to deal with cases in ways proportionate to the amount involved, the importance or complexity of the issues and the parties' financial position. He considered that a system of litigation which usually paid those who litigated cases as much as, and sometimes more than, the victims received in compensation failed to command public confidence. The concept of proportionality therefore extended to costs and Lord Woolf sought to secure a regime in which costs would be proportionate and he stated that the aim of the new procedural rules was to 'ensure that litigation is conducted less expensively than at present and to achieve greater certainty as to costs'.

As a result, a requirement of proportionality was incorporated into the test for assessing costs on the standard basis. The concept of proportionality was also incorporated in the overriding objective, which as originally formulated in CPR rule 1.1(2) provided:

> 'Dealing with a case justly includes, so far as is practicable . . .
> (c) dealing with the case in ways which are proportionate –
> to the amount of money involved;

14 CPR, rr 3.12–3.18.

to the importance of the case;
to the complexity of the issues; and
to the financial position of each party . . .'

By the time Sir Rupert came to consider costs, the judgment of the court by Lord Woolf in *Lownds v Home Office*[15] had provided further guidance on the meaning of proportionality but had raised concerns arising from an approach illustrated in this passage in paragraph 38:

> 'Giving appropriate weight to the requirements of proportionality and reasonableness will not make the conduct of litigation uneconomic if on the assessment there is allowed a reasonable sum for the work carried out which was necessary.'

The judgment in *Lownds* had been seen as reintroducing the concept of necessity which, as Sir Rupert observed, had been embodied in rules of court for over a century before being dropped in 1986. The relationship between proportionality, reasonableness and necessity formed a crucial part of his exegesis of proportionality. He pointed out that disproportionate costs do not become proportionate because they are necessary so that if the level of costs incurred is out of proportion to the circumstances of the case, they cannot become proportionate simply because they were 'necessary' in order to bring or defend the claim.[16] In relation to *Lownds*, Sir Rupert observed that the two-stage test had been thought to be a neat way of applying the proportionality test and one which would bring costs under proper control. However, experience had taught otherwise. This led him to conclude that the time had come to say that the guidance given by the Court of Appeal in *Lownds* was not satisfactory as it had the effect of inserting the Victorian test of necessity into the modern concept of proportionality.

Instead he considered that, on an assessment of costs on the standard basis, if it was concluded that the total figure, or some element within that total figure, was disproportionate, the disproportionate element of costs should be disallowed. His view was that disproportionate elements of costs could not be saved, even if the individual items within it were both reasonable and necessary. On this basis he proposed a change in the rules so that on an assessment of costs on the standard basis, proportionality should prevail over reasonableness and the proportionality test should be applied on a global basis. He advocated an approach by which the court should first make an assessment of reasonable costs, having regard to the individual items in the bill, the time reasonably spent on those items and the other factors listed in what was then CPR rule 44.5(3). At that stage the court should

15 *Lownds v Home Office* [2002] EWCA Civ 365, [2002] 1 WLR 2450. See also Stuart Sime and Derek French, *Blackstone's Guide to the Civil Justice Reforms 2013* (Oxford University Press, 2013) at paras 10.71–10.82.

16 Jackson, *Final Report* (n. 7) at Ch 3, para 5.10; Sime and French (n 15) at para 10.75.

stand back and consider whether the total figure was proportionate. If the total figure was not proportionate, the court should make an appropriate reduction.

He proposed that the CPR should be amended to include a definition of proportionate costs by reference to the sums at stake, the value of any non-monetary remedies claimed and any rights in issue, the complexity of the litigation, conduct and any wider factors, such as reputational issues or public importance. That led to the implementation of what is now CPR rule 44.3(5) and to the amendment of the overriding objective to add a reference to proportionate cost so that CPR rule 1.1(1) states the overriding objective as being to enable the court 'to deal with cases justly and at proportionate cost'.

On one level it could be said that these changes to the CPR were not necessary because proportionality had been fully dealt with already. This would ignore the fact that the decision in *Lownds* had eroded the place of proportionality in the assessment of costs and it was necessary to reaffirm the importance of proportionality which lay at the core of Sir Rupert's terms of reference. The concept of proportionality has been one of the developments in the law where, as Lord Woolf said, a new approach has been adopted and where a more broadly based approach was required.

Development of the law

One of the main areas of development of the law has been the assimilation of the Human Rights Act into English law. A full analysis of the impact of the Act on English public law is beyond the scope of this chapter, which merely seeks to comment more broadly on developments in the law. However, the Act has perhaps had two major effects. First, it has provided the judiciary with standards by which to ensure that, in broad terms, the rule of law is complied with by the executive. This has meant that, as Lord Woolf said, the courts have had to take a new approach, with a greater emphasis being placed on the social and economic consequences of the developing law.

A second impact of the Human Rights Act has been the introduction of a new principle of interpretation of legislation. The courts have had to interpret legislation so as to be compatible with the Convention. This, combined with the possibility of a declaration of incompatibility, has meant that decisions of the courts under sections 3 and 4 of the Act have been seen as impinging on the sovereignty of Parliament.

The court's decisions have therefore, in certain areas, led to judgments which have conflicted with political priorities in a way which has brought criticisms of the judiciary, which at one stage, either by legislation or by convention, would have been impossible to contemplate.[17]

17 A well-publicised example is *Hirst v United Kingdom (No. 2)* (2006) 42 EHRR 41 in which the UK Government initially appealed an ECtHR decision that the Representation of the People Act 1983, s. 3, which prevents prisoners from voting, was incompatible with Art. 3 of Protocol No. 1. The Government subsequently sought to introduce legislation to remove the incompatibility but this was rejected by Parliament (*Hansard*, Commons Debates, 10 February 2011, cols 493–584) in a debate which made reference to the Woolf reforms amongst many other issues. At the time of writing, the incompatibility remains.

Lord Woolf also foresaw developments in contractual interpretation and the law of tort. Whilst there have been plenty of judgments dealing with the topic of contractual interpretation, there has been refinement rather than major development since Lord Woolf gave his Lecture. The decision in *ICS v West Bromwich BS*[18] has stood the test of time despite the number of decisions. In relation to the law of tort, the relationship between negligence and the right of claimants under the Human Rights Convention has seen significant developments, as has the area of economic torts. As Lord Woolf observed, the law of torts has continued to fill gaps left by other causes of action where the interests of justice so require.

Education for the justice system

As Lord Woolf stated, the new culture of achieving justice under the CPR required training, as did the difficult value judgments required under the Human Rights Act. The topics of civil procedure and Human Rights are now well-embedded parts of the curriculum both at the academic and vocational stages of legal training.

There is also a continuing need for training at university to cater not only for those intending to practise law but also for those who use their legal training in other fields. Recent statistics show that only some 33% of those who take a qualifying law degree or a graduate diploma in law proceed to practise law. This emphasises the importance of broadening the training for law degrees or diplomas so that it caters for lawyers who take on a broader role outside the world of legal practice. Equally, the disciplines which are needed nowadays as part of a legal practice are much broader than they were even in 2000.

Lord Woolf contrasted the difference of approach in the United States and here. Since he wrote his article there has been a change in the size, scale and composition of international law firms. With mergers between English firms and American, European and Australian firms, the challenges in the area of legal ethics have increased. This has been met by ethics forming an essential part of the legal training. Lord Woolf identified the difficulties of conflicts arising where lawyers were paid on a conditional fee basis so that they had a stake in the outcome of the litigation. The methods of funding arising from the Jackson Reforms, including DBAs and Third Party Litigation Funding, emphasise the need for well-defined and clear ethical standards.

Since Lord Woolf delivered his paper, the number of litigants in person has increased, partly by the absence of legal aid and partly because of the cost of litigation. Whilst the Jackson Reforms are aimed at providing access to justice at proportionate cost, there will continue to be a substantial number of litigants for whom the cost of legal representation is beyond their means and who cannot or do not wish to fund that litigation. Fortunately, there has been a very large rise in pro bono legal services and assistance at law centres, given by those in the legal professions. For many this pro bono work starts at the stage of legal training and

18 *Investors Compensation Scheme v West Bromwich Building Society* [1997] UKHL 28, [1998] 1 WLR 896.

continues as part of their legal practice. As Lord Woolf observed, law firms have provided exemplary support for such pro bono activities.

Conclusion

Lord Woolf's paper identified major developments which would have an impact on the law. The introduction of the CPR changed the procedural landscape of the courts and has changed the approach of lawyers to litigation. Those changes have now been given new impetus through the Jackson Reforms and their emphasis on access to justice at proportionate cost. The Human Rights Act has similarly introduced new approaches and new areas of legal development. Both of these areas of legal development have been shown to have had the effect predicted by Lord Woolf.

The challenges to legal training have been taken up both at academic and at vocational stages. Civil procedure is now seen as an important subject in its own right. Human rights law is now a core subject. Legal ethics is also now treated with the importance it deserves. The perception is that, today, the justice system is provided with the education which it requires.

11 Fourth Lord Upjohn Lecture 1974

Fact-finding: Art or Science?[1]

Lord Justice Ormrod

The Law is rather short on eponymous lectures; at least compared with Medicine, in which they proliferate freely. The Lord Upjohn Lectures are a fairly new addition to the list and I am both honoured and pleased to have been asked to be this year's lecturer. Lectures of this kind serve many useful purposes, especially in the Law, in which they provide another plank in the bridge which is still being built, much too slowly, between the academic and practising members of the profession. They also give judges an occasional chance to express views out of court; few people realise just how silenced a minority we are! They serve another purpose too, which is good for the lecturer if not for the audience; they concentrate the mind wonderfully and force him to think out and formulate ideas which would otherwise float about in his mind in an inchoate, if not chaotic, form.

I chose fact-finding as my subject, first because, as a topic, it has received little, if any, study. Some work has been published about juries both here and in the United States, but fact-finding by judges is, as far as I know, a virgin field. Second, and consequentially, students receive no instruction on it at any stage of their training until they enter pupillage where they pick up their masters' and other members of chambers' hunches about judges. Like old wives' remedies for chronic ailments, these contain a kernel of truth, much obscured by cobwebs of gossip and what would technically be called barristers' stereotypes of judges. Yet, today, it is the dominant issue at first instance in every civil suit; in daily practice, 'points of law' have acquired a scarcity value which makes them quite exciting. Third, there was a more personal reason. Your President's invitation arrived soon after my days as a fact-finder had been brought to an end by my appointment to the Court of Appeal. The moment seemed especially opportune; I had not yet forgotten what it is like to be a fact-finder but was free to talk about it without embarrassing revelations of my personal idiosyncrasies which the more astute practitioners so assiduously study. Like skilled fishermen, they know, or think they know, the flies which the fish, before whom they are appearing, is most likely to swallow, and it is embarrassing for the fish to expose his taste in public, always supposing that he has enough insight to know what it is!

1 This lecture was delivered as the fourth Lord Upjohn Lecture at the Connaught Rooms on 5 February 1975.

[Sir Roger then presented the major changes in civil procedure over the previous 30 to 40 years. This included discussions of the shift away from jury trials, leaving the judge as finder of fact and changes in the burden of proof.]

Evidence and procedure

As I mentioned earlier, practice and the Civil Evidence Act 1968 have at last eliminated from civil litigation most of the exclusionary rules of evidence. Nothing could be less 'scientific' than the exclusion of relevant data for fear that it might be 'prejudicial' or overvalued. In jury trials this may still be a wise precaution but it cannot be justified in civil matters where the trial is conducted by a judge. Since the 1968 Act came into force, judges are not often handicapped by rules of this kind but there is still one restriction which the lay public cannot understand at all and which can deprive the judge of valuable and even essential data. This is the rule that precludes a party from cross-examining his 'own witness'. This phrase, which is invariably used in this context, is significant. The adversary system tends inevitably to the identification of witnesses with the party calling them. The theory is that a party vouches for the credibility of his witnesses, so that it is logical that he should be bound by the evidence which they give in the witness box. But this rule means in practice that unless the party has a statement or proof from the witness, he must take the risk, usually unacceptable and unreasonable, of calling him 'blind' and being obliged to accept his answers. Consequently, by simply declining to make a statement to the solicitors for both parties, a valuable, even an essential, witness can avoid appearing in court, and the judge is deprived of what may be a crucial part of the data.

I have been placed by this rule in the absurd position of having to decide whether a man who injured a fellow employee by kicking over a brazier, did it as a 'prank', or by carelessness or, more accurately, whether the plaintiff had proved that he was negligent, neither side daring to call the man himself who sat in the front row of the public gallery, watching me wrestling with this conundrum. The public simply cannot understand why a reluctant but relevant witness cannot be called into the witness box and 'questioned'. I believe that this rule is the most serious surviving defect in the forensic process, forcing the court to make a decision on evidence which is known to be incomplete, and visibly failing to make full enquiry into the facts. There is no good reason, except slavish adherence to the theory of the adversary process, why either side should not, subject to the judge's discretion, be permitted to call and interrogate such a witness, or, if the word is preferred, cross-examine him. The power of a judge in a criminal case to call a witness of his motion (which is an unsatisfactory proceeding anyway because, inevitably, it brings the judge into the arena) is not available in civil cases.[2] Nor does the practice relating to hostile witnesses meet the case. 'Hostile' has acquired a technical and restrictive meaning which so limits the operation of the rule as

2 *Re Enoch and Zaretsky* [1910] 1 KB 327.

to render it virtually ineffective. The Civil Evidence Act has gone some way to improve the position by providing that a previous statement, oral or in writing, of such a witness shall be admissible in evidence, although it is not easy to assess its value. But at least it is admissible and can be considered, in contrast to the position in crime where the prosecution is usually totally defeated if a witness goes back on his statement or deposition. The logic of this strikes me as simplistic. What would be valuable would be to have some idea of the circumstances in which the first statement was made and to hear the witness's explanation for the change. This actually happens when a witness is confronted in cross-examination with an earlier inconsistent statement: and it can be very illuminating, particularly if the first statement was made to an enquiry agent!

Fact-finding techniques

I must now turn to the process of fact-finding itself and must say at once that this part of my address is, unavoidably, highly subjective. It may not even be true but it is the best that my introspection can do! I begin with two main objectives in mind – to define as quickly as possible the area of common ground, and to get the feel of the personalities of the parties and their witnesses. The common ground usually turns out to be much wider than one would expect and the area of conflict correspondingly narrower: there will be much conflict on detail but most of it can be eliminated fairly easy because it does not in fact affect the issue one way or the other. So I always look carefully for admissions on both sides. Then I look for what might loosely be called the objective facts, or the data which cannot be disputed: for example, the position of vehicles after the accident, point of impact and other findings of independent observers, including sometimes the views of expert witnesses. This provides a frame of reference against which the conflicting stories can be compared. A preliminary estimate of probabilities can be made at this stage either by comparing what I suppose a reasonable person's reactions would have been in the circumstances with the evidence of each party as to what he actually did, or, safer, by considering how each account fits the frame of reference. One version may fit fairly easily, the other may require quite an elaborate hypothesis to reconcile it and make it fit. Probability is not a good word in this context: I am really asking myself 'Is this story a likely one in the circumstances?'

Questions like this, of course, presuppose that the parties will have acted predictably, that is, as I would predict. This is the point where the assessment of personality and the ability to see the situation, however dimly, through the witness's eyes becomes of vital importance. The psychologists call this quality 'empathy'. Some people have it or can develop it, some find it difficult to acquire but, undoubtedly, experience of similar situations as an advocate or as a judge, or in real life outside the courts, is of the greatest value. This is what I mean by getting the 'feel' of a witness or, in more formal language, 'seeing, hearing and observing the demeanour of the witness'. It means much more than 'honest' or 'shifty' or 'evasive' or 'over-confident'. Some reliable witnesses appear shifty and others over-confident, but the best liars, by definition, appear 'honest.' In matrimonial cases in particular, the range of variation in individual responses to stress of different kinds is very wide and can only be learnt by experience. The disappearance of contested cruelty cases, otherwise to be welcomed, has removed the finest training ground for the fact-finder. Only by arguing, or trying cases of this kind, can a lawyer learn about the extraordinary ways of fantasy and the extent to which two people, both under stress, can see the same facts in totally different ways. Under such conditions wish-fulfilment can operate on the conscious mind much as it does in dreams. It is, perhaps, as well that the contested divorce suit has virtually disappeared because it was becoming increasingly obvious that the forensic process could not accommodate such subtle assessments. There is no doubt that Freud, whether we have ever read a word of his work or not, created what Lionel Trilling has called 'a new mode of judgment'.[3] I believe that outside the criminal courts, lying in the witness box is as rare as malingering in the consulting room. They have much in common; not least that both involve a high degree of careful planning, without which exposure is inevitable. Few people are sufficiently strongly motivated to attempt to overcome the difficulties which lie in their way.

Cross-examination

To enable a judge to work through this kind of process to a reasonably reliable conclusion, cross-examination is essential. However, I suspect that all but the most skilled cross-examiners see it differently from judges. The advocate thinks of it as 'discrediting' the witness, which all too often means attacking his credibility, by, as language implies, an aggressive or hostile approach. The judge sees it as a means of revealing another side of the witness's personality. Examination-in-chief and cross-examination provide, as it were, cross-bearings on the personality. The most experienced advocates use it in this way, often with devastating results. The late Sir Geoffrey Lawrence was the most superb exponent of this style of cross-examination I have ever heard. It is another powerful and sensitive instrument which can be dangerous when misused. Sometimes it converts an unconfident, hesitant witness into a forthright one, almost radiating the truth, but more often, when conducted in a rude, offensive, or bullying manner, it achieves nothing except to cause the witness to leave the box, vowing that if he is going to be treated in such a way he will never give evidence again. Such cross-examinations should, in my opinion, be stopped by the judge at an early stage, in the interests of justice generally. Answers to questions put in this manner, or to questions framed as catch questions, involving either two questions in one, or an incomplete question, should be discarded by the judge as quite valueless.

3 See his introduction to the abridged edition of Ernest Jones, *The Life and Work of Sigmund Freud* (New York, Basic Books, 1974).

Recollection and observation

There are, of course, many other indications which help to test a witness's reliability. Of these, consistency always appeals to me, so I attach great weight to contemporary descriptions of events. Letters can provide a valuable cross-check on the account given in the witness box or may reveal inconsistent attitudes. Diaries, especially if kept on legal advice, always reveal much more about the diarist than anybody else: the obsessional or paranoid features of the personality always emerge. Ordinary diaries are usually dangerous documents. They may enable the witness to fix an important date, or the sequence of events, but, if carefully studied, they nearly always also reveal illuminating facts about the author. The importance of a more or less contemporary account of the accident is always great, although allowance must be made, but not too much, for the shock, pain or confusion of mind which is always relied on to explain away inconvenient statements. When I was a junior, judges always attached weight to the contents of the 'letter before action', and we were often instructed to settle it. Today, solicitors who habitually act for plaintiffs have a simpler and cheaper technique: they give no account of the accident at all, merely 'intimating a claim' for damages arising out of an accident on a given date. The statement of claim which used to contain some more or less specific details of the accident has become of little value. It had become completely stereotyped in road accident cases many years ago: the same allegations of negligence appear in the same order in every case. Divorce petitions are a little more informative, although one need scarcely read the opening allegations of unreasonable behaviour so general and so universal have they become. The principle of throwing in everything in industrial accident cases usually obscures the issue, while demonstrating the knowledge of the pleader of the more obscure regulations made under the Factories Act. In case after case the plaintiff's counsel in his opening abandons most of the allegations pleaded so laboriously. Defences are as bad or worse, but briefer.

This determination not to commit oneself in advance is a recognition of the importance of the contemporary or near-contemporary account. It also tends to obscure the truth. The evidential rules do not help. Contemporary statements could always be used in cross-examination, if the other side could get hold of them, but they were rigorously excluded from examination-in-chief under the hearsay rule in favour of the oral evidence of the witness given from recollection, not so much of the events as of the contents of his proof. He is entitled to sit outside the court reading it but must leave it behind him when he enters the witness box. If he forgets an important item, his counsel, with varying degrees of ingenuity, will try to remind him of it without committing the sin of 'leading'. The judge may well guess what is missing, from these efforts, or, if it is a defence witness, he will know what has been forgotten from the questions put at an earlier stage in cross-examination. But the witness's proof remains inviolate. The Civil Evidence Act 1968 has slightly improved the situation. The proof can now be put in after the witness has given his oral evidence but, of course, it will not be if it is inconsistent with it.

This insistence on what Professor Cross has called 'orality' reflects, I think, two things: first, the value of actually hearing the witness describing the events;

and second, mistrust of documents prepared by lawyers for the purpose of the litigation. There is no doubt about the value of hearing and watching the witness give his evidence-in-chief but the mistrust of the documentary material is exaggerated. It is very difficult to settle an affidavit, upon which the deponent is liable to be cross-examined, which conceals material facts, or puts a gloss on them, which is resistant to cross-examination, although one can improve the 'tone' of a deponent. I think that the witness should give his evidence orally but his proof should be available to the other side on request and that either side should be entitled to put it in evidence if it thinks fit.

Similarly, any document which can now be used to 'refresh' the witness's memory should be part of the evidence in the case. The present rule is a farce which is compounded by the current practice of asking the wrong question. Everyone asks 'Did you make these notes at the time?' and absurd decisions are made about the meaning of the phrase 'at the time', with the result that sometimes the witness is not allowed to look at them in the box, although he may have been reading them five minutes earlier in the corridor. The proper question is 'Did you make the notes while the events were fresh in your memory?', a much more practical and realistic test.[4] I am sometimes amazed at the capacity of police officers for 'total recall' of conversations with the accused and at the generally uncritical acceptance of such evidence in spite of the usual attacks on it; in fact the crudity of these attacks often enhances the credibility of the evidence whereas a more subtle approach might throw doubt on it.

The unreliability of evidence of observation is often commented on by theoretical writers. Certainly psychologists have no difficulty in demonstrating experimentally gross errors of perception. The optical illusion has been a source of amusement for centuries and all kinds of geometrical figures and photographs can be devised to illustrate it. But, in practice, courts are not concerned with perceptual errors of this kind except when identity is in issue. Normally, the issues in the case are fairly broad and the conflicts of observation are gross. Moreover, there is nearly always a certain amount of objective data available such as the findings at the scene after an accident or other material against which to check the observations. It is often possible to argue that if witness A's observation is accurate other reliable evidence can only be explained on some elaborate and improbable hypothesis while B's fits well with the other facts. Evidence of identification by recognition can sometimes be checked in this way, but if quite uncorroborated it is undoubtedly dangerous.

Expert evidence

Expert evidence in civil litigation is, generally speaking, the victim of the adversary system. The temptation to 'shop around' for an expert who is willing and able to support one's case is hard to resist, with the inevitable result that standards tend to fall. The conventional attitude of the courts towards experts is one of scepticism, or rather they pretend it is, because in practice considerable weight is usually attached to such evidence. As a rule it is difficult to brush aside

4 *Archbold*, 38th edn, para. 515(c); citing *R v Richardson* (1971) 55 Cr App R 244.

and often very helpful. But in civil litigation, in contrast to criminal cases, it is not used to the best advantage. Forensic science has become a highly developed speciality which can provide invaluable data to the courts in many different kinds of case, and it is widely used in the criminal sphere. In civil litigation, engineers are called to describe defects in the machine and doctors give evidence, usually in the form of medical reports, about the injuries and the resulting disability, but little attempt is made to use medical evidence to throw light on the accident itself. Sometimes the nature of the injuries sustained does not fit at all easily with the description given of the accident, and much can often be deduced about the accident from the injuries. This has been demonstrated very clearly in the investigation of air crashes. By correlating the post-mortem findings with the place where each passenger in the plane was sitting, it has proved possible to deduce a great deal about the nature of the accident and its probable cause. Road accidents and industrial injuries, of course, are on a relatively miniscule scale, but in some cases at least, medical evidence, if properly used, could be a valuable check on the conflicting accounts of the accident. Similarly, competent engineers can deduce much valuable information about road accidents from the damage to the vehicles and their movements after the collision. Unfortunately, this kind of evidence has been devalued by indifferent experts to such an extent that it is now rarely used. I have nearly always found expert evidence very helpful, mainly because it limits the area of conflict by demonstrating that one side's version of the facts involves the acceptance of a highly improbable hypothesis whereas the alternative version is consistent with a much simpler explanation of the events in question. Expert witnesses are always supposed to disagree with one another and produce conflicts of evidence which are difficult to resolve. Sometimes this does happen but the most efficacious way of stopping it is by an exchange of reports before trial as is now provided for under the Civil Evidence Act 1972. Advocates hate to be forced to 'show their hand' in advance (which means when they are not present) and have a deep-seated love of surprise (which rarely happens anyway). But disclosure of his report to a peer beforehand has a very salutary effect on the expert. Since the practice of exchanging medical reports became general there have been significantly fewer disagreements between doctors in the courts, mainly because each can see where the difference between them lies, which often leads to agreement or, at worst, to a narrowing of the disagreement. There is another way in which the value of expert evidence might be increased. Just as counsel have a duty to the court to call attention to authorities which are against them, so experts should owe a duty to the court to explain the limitations of their evidence. Scientists are accustomed to drawing attention in their papers to the limits of accuracy of their experiments, so they should help the court to place the proper weight on their evidence.

The judge

Finally, the fact-finder himself must be looked at rather closely. Observer error is a well-known phenomenon in many of the sciences and has been studied quite intensively. It is not a chance phenomenon; each observer turns out to have a characteristic pattern of error which, when he is made aware of it, he can correct to some extent, but not completely. For example, in reading blood pressures, most observers read to a round number, but some habitually take the higher and others the lower, introducing quite an appreciable difference between them. The analogue to the observer for present purposes is, of course, the judge, whose personal equation is an unavoidable factor in the fact-finding process. This includes his taste in flies which I mentioned earlier but there are many other aspects of it. Norman Mailer has called it 'that core of psychological substance out of which one concocts one's life's judgments'.[5] One tries to correct for such of these propensities as one knows about but can do nothing about those which one does not recognise. Juries, of course, have their personas too, only there are 12 of them and nothing is known of any of them. Presumably it is hoped that, by averaging, the margin of error will be reduced. But in human affairs we must accept human limitations. There is an astonishing and rather flattering assumption that 'the judge' will get it right and in most cases they probably do reach the right conclusion *on the evidence before them.* That is their function. But if a judge begins to worry about whether his conclusions are right absolutely, whether other evidence might have been put forward which would have altered his decision and so on, he is on the road to an anxiety state and ultimate breakdown. Sometimes I comfort myself by reflecting on the words we use for various activities or ideas. 'Judge' is an interesting word. When we use it as a verb it means the antithesis of measurement or precision. 'I judged the distance to be 100 yards', 'judging by experience', 'a good judge of men'. These usages all indicate that we are talking about an estimate or an approximation made with all the care and skill we possess and that is all that any forensic process can hope to achieve. Art or science? Let me read an extract from a recent paper by the Regius Professor of Medicine at Oxford, Sir Richard Doll, a very distinguished, and properly so-called medical scientist.

> 'It is, of course, axiomatic that observation alone cannot prove that any particular agent is the cause of disease in man. In this respect epidemiology in no way differs from animal experiment. In both types of study conclusions about the cause of human disease derive from reasoned arguments; based on the one hand, on knowledge of the metabolism of different species and the experience of extrapolation from one species to another; and on the other hand, on the likelihood of alternative explanations and the compatibility of the preferred explanation with other evidence.'[6]

Mutatis mutandis, that sounds like a succinct and accurate description of the fact-finding process; but judges have no animal houses in which to check their conclusions!

5 *Marilyn* (London, Grosset and Dunlap, 1973).
6 *Oxford Medical School Gazette* (1974), Vol. XXVI, No. 3, p. 10.

12 Response: Preparation for Practice

Developing Effective Advocates in a Changing World of Adversarial Civil Justice

Nigel Duncan

> 'It was easy to be called, but it was difficult to practise at the bar. I had read the laws, but not learnt how to practise law. I had read with interest "Legal Maxims", but did not know how to apply them in my profession. "Sic uteretu-outalienum non laedas" (Use your property in such a way as not to damage that of others) was one of them, but I was at a loss to know how one could employ this maxim for the benefit of one's client. I had read all the leading cases on this maxim, but they gave me no confidence in the application of it in the practice of law.'[1]

Gandhi was an alumnus of the City Law School, in whom it feels great pride. He studied at the Inns of Court School of Law in the late 1800s. As you can see, his experience there prepared him little for the practice of law. He says:

> 'The curriculum of study was easy, barristers being humorously known as "dinner barristers". Everyone knew that the examinations had practically no value. In my time there were two, one in Roman Law and the other in Common Law. There were regular text-books prescribed for these examinations which could be taken in compartments, but scarcely any one read them. I have known many to pass the Roman Law examination by scrambling through notes on Roman Law in a couple of weeks, and the Common Law examination by reading notes on the subject in two or three months. Question papers were easy and examiners were generous. The percentage of passes in the Roman Law examination used to be 95 to 99 and of those in the final examination 75 or even more. There was thus little fear of being plucked, and examinations were held not once but four times in the year. They could not be felt as a difficulty.'[2]

Gandhi's description of how his personal commitments led him to make a difficulty of that easy process and the other requirement, the eating of dinners, makes

1 Gandhi, Mohandas, 1927, 2001, *An Autobiography: The Story of My Experiments with Truth*, London, Penguin Modern Classics 88, Part 1, p. 25.

2 Ibid., 87.

entertaining reading. However, for our purposes we will focus on the programme of learning offered to aspirant barristers and how it has developed over the years in an attempt to prepare its graduates for the demands of practice.

Over 80 years had passed by the time Sir Roger Ormrod came to his Lord Upjohn Lecture. Two developments were in the forefront of his mind. One was his work on the Committee on Legal Education, the report of which[3] was the fullest and most wide-ranging report on legal education in England and Wales until the recent Legal Education and Training Review.[4] It had required widespread consultation and a thorough analysis of the complex of demands that faced legal educators. It had sought to establish the relationship between legal education and legal practice. It identified the need for legal education and training to prepare lawyers with 'the ability to handle fact, both analytically and synthetically', and also to 'acquire the professional skills and techniques which are essential to practice, and a grasp of the ethos of the profession'.[5]

The other development was the then relatively new change of the judge's role from umpire to decision-maker.[6] Judges, not juries, were the deciders of fact in virtually all civil proceedings. This made a profound change in the way in which advocates prepared and presented their cases. In his Lord Upjohn Lecture he drew attention to the significance of this development and went on to criticise a number of factors in the ways in which civil litigation operated at that time. These criticisms extend to the approach towards drafting, the use of written statements, examination-in-chief, cross-examination and the use of expert witnesses. This chapter will explore the developments in the rules and practice of civil litigation in the context of those criticisms and the impact that this has had on the vocational education of advocates in recent years. It will do so by identifying each of the main criticisms he makes and, providing examples, show how students on a modern Bar Professional Training Course are shown how to use the new procedural rules and to develop their written and oral communication skills to clarify factual situations in the interests of justice. This will encompass not only the ways in which the expectations of adversarial courtroom practice have changed but also the growing expectations to explore settlement and alternative dispute resolution. It will focus on the courses provided by the Inns of Court School of Law, subsequently City Law School, in order to present a coherent line of development at the School which historically held a monopoly in Bar training.

By the time Sir Roger Ormrod came to deliver his Lord Upjohn Lecture things had changed considerably at the Inns of Court School of Law since Gandhi's day.

3 Ormrod Report (1971), *Report of the Committee on Legal Education*, Cmnd. No. 4595. London: HMSO.

4 LETR, 2013, *Setting Standards: The future of legal services education and training in England and Wales*, http://letr.org.uk/, v (accessed April 2015).

5 Ormrod, n. 3, Ch. 3.

6 In *Williams v Beesley* [1973] 3 All ER 144, 146, Lord Diplock had said, 'The fact that a case involves issues of credibility is not a ground for departing from the usual rule that cases, other than those in which a prima facie right to trial by jury is conferred by statute, should be tried by judge alone'.

It still held a monopoly on training for the Bar.[7] The Vocational Stage was then known as Part II of the Examination for Call to the Bar. There were six unseen examinations with three compulsory sections:

I. General Paper 1: Common Law and Criminal Law;
II. General Paper 2: Equity and a special topic (Remedies for Breach of Contract in that year);
III. Civil and Criminal Procedure and Evidence.

In addition students undertook three from a choice of options including: Revenue Law, Family Law (and Procedure), Law of Landlord and Tenant, Sale of Goods and Hire-Purchase, Local Government and Planning Law, Practical Conveyancing, Conflict of Laws, Law of International Trade, and Public International Law.[8]

These represented a real shift towards addressing the exigencies of practice. The General Papers each required the writing of two Opinions[9] with associated drafting tasks. Civil and Criminal Procedure and Evidence required five answers, spread between the three sections. Thus the General Papers, although covering substantive law already addressed at the undergraduate stage, required students to adopt a client perspective and to undertake practical tasks. Section III required an understanding and application of the rules of procedure and evidence, the questions being mostly problem-based, although a few were more of an essay form.[10]

Students who wished to practise at the Bar (as opposed to merely being called and becoming a non-practising barrister) had to take the Revenue Law option and were also required to undergo Practical Exercises. These included 'Forensic Exercises in Advocacy' alternating weekly with 'Chambers Exercises' plus six day-long court visits. The advocacy exercises involved students observing advocacy demonstrations and then practising submissions, examination-in-chief or cross-examination in front of practitioners. The Chambers exercises involved drafting tasks under the supervision of a practitioner and usually in chambers. These activities were marked, but did not contribute towards the final assessment.

The problems in the final examinations had the characteristic of most problem questions in that they were relatively shortly-stated and assumed the accuracy of the facts contained in them. In this, they will have been familiar to students coming from the academic stage but significantly different from the reality of a set of papers that a newly-qualified barrister would be likely to meet in practice. This provides a context for Sir Roger Ormrod's lecture.

Nearly 40 years later the rules of procedure and evidence have changed radically, as has the education and training undergone by lawyers.

7 A monopoly that was retained until the opening of the Bar Vocational Course to other providers in 1997.
8 Council of Legal Education, *Calendar 1975–76*, Part III, 18.
9 Written advice commissioned by a solicitor for the lay client.
10 Council of Legal Education, *Trinity Examination 1975*, filed with author.

Developments in civil procedure

Civil procedure is now regulated by the Civil Procedure Rules 1998 (SI 1998/3132) ('the CPR'), regularly updated by the Civil Procedure Rule Committee established by the Civil Procedure Act 1997, s. 2. This is comprised of 80 Parts, most of which are supported by Practice Directions which give more detailed guidance on the application of each rule. Amendments have implemented two major reforms, the Woolf reforms[11] and the Jackson reforms.[12] The thrust of these reforms has been to address many of the criticisms of the civil justice system identified by Sir Roger. The modern approach is to encourage parties to abandon the practice of holding as many cards as possible close to their chests and to get their case down on the table as early as possible. This is designed to encourage settlement if possible and is in the interest of proportionality. How is this achieved?

The overriding objective

CPR rule 1.1 establishes an overriding objective which is to enable 'the court to deal with cases justly and at proportionate cost'.[13] Dealing with cases justly is explained as follows:

> 'Dealing with a case justly and at proportionate cost includes, so far as is practicable
>
> (a) ensuring that the parties are on an equal footing;
> (b) saving expense;
> (c) dealing with the case in ways which are proportionate –
>
> (i) to the amount of money involved;
> (ii) to the importance of the case;
> (iii) to the complexity of the issues; and
> (iv) to the financial position of each party;
>
> (d) ensuring that it is dealt with expeditiously and fairly;
> (e) allotting to it an appropriate share of the court's resources, while taking into account the need to allot resources to other cases; and
> (f) enforcing compliance with rules, practice directions and orders.'[14]

It is noteworthy that the concept of justice includes 'ensuring that the parties are on an equal footing' and refers to dealing with the case 'fairly'. However, every

11 Woolf, H, 1996, *Access to Justice – Final Report*, London, Lord Chancellor's Department, http://webarchive.nationalarchives.gov.uk/+/http:/www.dca.gov.uk/civil/final/contents.htm (accessed 3 July 2015).

12 Jackson, R, 2010, *Review of Civil Litigation Costs*, London, Ministry of Justice.

13 CPR, r. 1.1(1), http://www.justice.gov.uk/courts/procedure-rules/civil/rules (accessed 3 July 2015).

14 Ibid., r. 1.1 (2).

other element of the concept addresses proportionality and cost-saving. The one possible exception is (f), newly introduced in 2013, the effect of which depends very much on the rule, practice direction or order to be enforced. It authorises considerable judicial case management.

Pre-Action protocols

Twelve pre-action protocols have been published to guide pre-action behaviour in a number of specific types of case, including personal injury, low-value road traffic accidents, rent arrears and judicial review.[15] The object is to give best practice guidance and the courts are empowered to impose sanctions for breaches.[16] This will not be done for minor infringements, but where a party's behaviour leads to proceedings being commenced unnecessarily, or otherwise causes unnecessary costs to be incurred, the court may order that party to pay all those costs.

Track allocation

Once a claim has been issued and the defence submitted, parties will have had to declare the extent to which they have complied with any pre-action protocols. The judge will then allocate the case to one of three tracks:

(a) Claims up to £10,000 are generally allocated to the small claims track. This provides for a simplified procedure, parties to serve the documents they intend to rely on at least 14 days before the hearing, no expert evidence and a hearing before a district judge. This will be informal, often in the district judge's room, with the expectation that the parties will represent themselves. The strict rules of evidence will not apply and the district judge has considerable discretion to proceed in a fair way.[17]

(b) Claims between £10,000 and £25,000 which are unlikely to involve more than a day's hearing are generally allocated to the fast track, with standard directions[18] and an expectation that all procedures before trial will be completed within 30 weeks. Since April 2013 cases are assigned to a specific judge to achieve continuity of judicial case management.

(c) Claims over £25,000 are generally allocated to the multi-track. As some of these will be relatively simple and others enormously complicated or valuable, judicial directions will vary appropriately, with simple, low-value cases being directed much as fast-track cases.[19]

15 For the full list and texts see Jackson, Sir Rupert (ed), 2013, *The White Book*, London, Sweet & Maxwell, section C.

16 CPR, r. 3.1(4) and (5).

17 Sime, Stuart, 2013, *A Practical Approach to Civil Procedure*, Oxford, Oxford University Press, 27.01–16.

18 Ibid., 28.03–11.

19 For details of the variety of directions available see ibid., 29.01–36.

Active case management

CPR, r. 1.4(1) requires the court to further the overriding objective by active case management. This includes (r. 1.4(2)):

(a) encouraging the parties to co-operate with each other in the conduct of the proceedings;
(c) deciding promptly which issues need full investigation and trial and accordingly disposing summarily of the others;
(e) encouraging the parties to use an alternative dispute resolution procedure if the court considers that appropriate and facilitating the use of such procedure;
(f) helping the parties to settle the whole or part of the case;
(h) considering whether the likely benefits of taking a particular step justify the cost of taking it;
(j) dealing with the case without the parties needing to attend at court;
(l) giving directions to ensure that the trial of a case proceeds quickly and efficiently.

I have chosen those provisions which most directly address the shift to encouraging settlement, avoiding unnecessary cost and ensuring proportionality.

Active case management occurs at several stages. When a case is allocated to a particular track the judge will set a timetable for such matters as exchange of documents and witness statements, and if necessary, a case management conference at which more detailed directions can be given. These may include rejecting the need for expert witnesses (or requiring the parties to agree an expert), controlling the evidence which will be admitted at trial, restricting oral evidence, limiting the length of the trial and reducing costs which are not proportionate to the value of the case.[20]

Thus parties may be directed to exchange witness statements by a specific date and to collaborate in the preparation of bundles. The nature of bundles has changed in the light of technological changes. For example, the availability of a printout of an email string often provides hard evidence of the negotiation of a contract and can limit the genuine issues that need to be decided by the court in comparison with those cases where evidence is based on the uncertain memories of the contracting parties. Counsel for each party should prepare a skeleton argument identifying the basis of their case and any legal issues which are relevant, together with their submissions on factual and legal issues. Thus, before the trial itself, each party should have a clear idea of the case they oppose. Given the cost of hearings, this itself is designed to encourage settlement without trial.

20 For the extent to which the courts are now willing to exercise control over costs, see the litigation arising from the 'Plebgate' affair, especially *Mitchell v News Group Newspapers Ltd* [2013] EWCA Civ 1537, [2013] 6 Costs LR 1008.

Educators' response

Learning

The Bar Standards Board currently lays down detailed requirements for the teaching and assessment on the Bar Professional Training Course (BPTC).[21] Each provider has a certain latitude to design a course which they think best meets those requirements. What follows represents the approach of City Law School, the originator of Bar training.[22]

The BPTC requires students to learn and to be assessed in the skills of Conference Skills, Drafting, Opinion Writing and Advocacy (including submissions to the judge, examination-in-chief and cross-examination); and also in knowledge areas: Civil Litigation, Evidence and Remedies; Criminal Litigation, Evidence and Sentencing; Resolution of Disputes out of Court and Professional Ethics. Also, not discretely assessed, but essential learning in order to perform the skills competently is Case Preparation, incorporating the ability to analyse a factual dispute in order to identify the factual and legal issues, and the consequent Legal Research. The goal is to develop in students a shift in perspective, from approaching law as a subject for academic study as in their undergraduate or postgraduate academic studies to one where it is a tool to be used, where possible, to meet the optimal outcome for their client. City Law School approaches this task through a course that, to a considerable degree, integrates the learning across these skills and knowledge subjects.

In a typical week, students will have three or four large groups plus up to six streams of small group classes. In addition they will have regular activities on the university's virtual learning environment, Moodle. Three of the small group streams address criminal practice; three address civil practice. Classes last 80 minutes and small groups take place with 12 students at a time (or six for most advocacy and some conference skills classes). All classes expect students to have prepared and to be willing, where appropriate, to perform. In written skills classes they will be required to come to the class with a fully-drafted opinion or statement of case which the tutor will project for discussion and peer and tutor feedback. In oral skills classes they must come prepared to conduct advocacy or a client conference. In knowledge subjects they must have undertaken research in order to be able to answer questions and enter into discussion about the concepts addressed. Failure to prepare will be recorded and students' attention drawn to how they are missing opportunities to learn from feedback. Most of these classes will be based on realistic sets of case papers in which facts are contested and uncertain and which are used in sequence to address different skills and concepts.

21 Bar Standards Board, 2013, *Bar Professional Training Course: Course specification requirements and guidance, 2013–14*, https://www.barstandardsboard.org.uk/media/1542061/bptc_handbook_2013-14.pdf (accessed 3 July 2015).

22 Other providers of the BPTC may, for example, have different degrees of integration or have replaced some Large Group classes with online lectures.

Key to understanding how students' learning is directed to the developments since Sir Roger Ormrod wrote is the detail of the tasks that they undertake. I will present these through one case (*Pemberton*) with which they work over a series of classes.[23] The claimant is a house-owner who has engaged a specialist firm to fit new windows and doors to a substantial property. The written contract is basic and many of the terms arise from discussions between the parties that are contested and only partially evidenced. The claimant regards the performance of the contract as seriously defective in a number of ways and refuses to pay the second half of the contract price. Students work on this case, undertaking different activities, and are required to represent different parties, over a number of small group classes.

The first class is a case analysis class for which they prepare by writing a chronology and completing blank grids designed to help them to analyse the issues in the case and to identify the legal principles that will apply. This sets them up for the second class, in which they arrive with a fully-drafted opinion (their first of many on the BPTC). Tutors project student opinions to discuss how to structure effective advice and encourage peer feedback on the quality of the analysis and the clarity of the advice given. Opinions are required not merely to address the facts and law but also to identify where evidence is uncertain or lacking and to suggest how such gaps might be filled. Advice is required to be supported by reasoning, to explain the chances of success and to indicate necessary procedural steps. Students are expected to advise on the prospects for alternative dispute resolution and to indicate which methods might be most appropriate to this particular case.

This case is one in which mediation might be helpful and the third class involves the role-play of a mediation. Students, who were representing the claimant in the first two classes, are now divided between claimant and defendant and are given specific roles: counsel, client or mediator. They have all been given appropriate guidance for these tasks and receive further guidance during the class to improve the realism of their role-play. While the mediation is being conducted students receive a phone message from their instructing solicitor giving details of costs incurred to date and the likely cost of pursuing the matter to litigation. In this way the availability and desirability of settlement and the dominance of costs to the litigation process is made clear.

In fact the case does not settle and the next task for students, representing the claimant once again, is to draft particulars of claim. Drafting is an activity that has changed markedly from the approach that Sir Roger complained about. He said, in the context of accident claims: 'solicitors . . . give no account of the accident at all . . . The statement of claim which used to contain some more or

23 A fuller explanation of the workings of this case may be found in Duncan, NJ, 2015, 'Representation: Objectivity and Artistry for Trainee Lawyers', in Courtney, N, Poulsen, C and Stylios, C (eds), *Case Based Teaching and Learning for the 21st Century*, Faringdon, Oxfordshire, Libri Publishing, pp. 171–197. The case papers and integrative design presented here are the work of Julie Browne, Deputy Director of the BPTC at City Law School.

less specific details of the accident has become of little value'.[24] This approach has been completely changed in the light of the Woolf reforms, and teaching on the BPTC reflects this. Students are taught to draft in such a way that all the details of the claim plus the reasons for them are laid out clearly. Evidence is not included, but the factual basis of the claim is. Thus, while at this stage there is still some scope for withholding the evidential strength (or weakness) of a claim, there should be no doubt about what exactly forms the basis of the claim. The small group class in which this is addressed, like the opinion writing class earlier, requires students to bring a full draft to the class for peer and tutor feedback.

At this point, when court proceedings are just commencing, students have already undertaken a variety of tasks that integrate the development of their analytical, writing and communication skills with a growing understanding of the costs and consequences of litigation. A recurring theme is the centrality of evidence. Although they need to provide a cogent and detailed legal structure within which to pursue the claim, relying on both statutory and common law principles, they discover that, like most real cases at first instance, this case turns on what can be proven, and thus on the evidence available. As Sir Roger Ormrod argued, fact-finding is key.

The next two small group classes require students to develop their advocacy skills by making submissions to the judge. Here they work in groups of six and come with two copies of a skeleton argument, prepared to address the judge. They work opposed, with those who represented the claimant in the mediation now representing the defendant. They come with a flash drive on which their performance, peer feedback from other students and tutor feedback are video-recorded.

The first of these advocacy classes addresses a problem for the defendant. As a result of health difficulties he has failed to submit a defence and the claimant has been given judgment in default. The defendant is seeking to have this judgment set aside and the claimant is resisting that application. The second advocacy class (after the first application has been successful) flows from a dispute over disclosure of documents. The defendant resists an application by the claimant for three different classes of document. Once again, students are required to represent a different client. They will be expected to use their skeleton argument to take the judge to relevant provisions in the White Book and the evidence bundle. As they make their submissions the judge will intervene so as to force them to respond rather than simply reproduce what they have prepared. The choice of issue in these hearings illustrates three things:

(a) the importance of procedural law and practice in litigation;
(b) the importance of costs at every stage;
(c) the crucial significance of evidence in establishing the facts on which the judge will take a decision on the merits.

These two advocacy classes form part of a series of 24 advocacy small groups in total, in which students develop their skills at addressing the court,

24 Ormrod, R, 1975, 'Fact finding: art or science?', 9, 2 *The Law Teacher*, 70–83, 79. And See p. 117, above.

examination-in-chief and cross-examination. Each class requires them to perform and receive instant oral feedback, which focuses on the key issue they need to address at that point in their development as an advocate. Tutors will explain why that is an issue for improvement, suggest a remedy, perhaps demonstrate how it might be done better and give the student an opportunity to try it again. Students are encouraged to take their flash drive and record further performances (acting as judges and witnesses for each other). They are provided with a pro-forma designed to encourage a reflective approach to this reiterative process. In this way the sequence of classes and further practice operates as a progressive spiral curriculum,[25] a reiterative learning cycle[26] through which students practise, reflect and prepare for a further more challenging task. This represents a major shift in approach to an integrated curriculum design with reflective practice[27] built into it, when compared with the Bar curriculum of 1975.

Assessment

The assessment regime on the Bar course at the time of Sir Roger Ormrod's Lord Upjohn Lecture has been described earlier. The six unseen exams did require some opinion writing or drafting, but were based on set facts and separated the substantive from the adjectival law. Today the assessments are much more focused on the practical demands of practice. Thus while students used to have to write two drafts and two opinions in three hours, they now focus on one task in a three-and-a-half-hour exam, based on a much more realistic set of papers. Current assessments also achieve a considerable degree of constructive alignment[28] with the learning methods used. The value of constructive alignment includes consistency between what students have to do in class and in the assessment, thus preparing students for assessment. It does, of course, require careful assessment design so that students genuinely demonstrate the skills, knowledge and understanding they need to move to the next stage of their legal education.

Maximum alignment is achieved in the advocacy assessments, where students are given papers in advance, required to submit a skeleton argument a week before the assessment date, and then come before an assessor acting as judge to record their submission. As in the classes the judge will make interventions and the assessment criteria are the same as the criteria that inform tutor feedback in classes. Drafting and opinion writing achieve a degree of alignment in that the task is the same as that which students practise in class and is based on an analogous set of papers. Just as in opinion-writing classes, the papers will contain gaps and ambiguities, so that students should advise on how this impacts on strengths and

25 Bruner, Jerome, 1976, *The Process of Education*, 2nd edn, Cambridge, Mass., Harvard University Press, 13, 52–54.

26 Kolb, David, 1984, *Experiential Learning: Experience as the Source of Learning and Development*, Englewood Cliffs, Prentice Hall.

27 Schön, Donald, 1987, *Educating the Reflective Practitioner*, San Francisco, Jossey-Bass.

28 Biggs, JB and Tang, C, 2007, *Teaching for quality learning at university*, Open University Press/ Mc Graw-Hill, 95–110.

weaknesses of the case and what further evidence is required. The one difference is the regulator's requirement that these be sat as unseen three-and-a-half-hour exams.[29] To maintain as much realism as possible, students are given a note in advance as to the areas of law that will be covered in the assessment, are able to conduct their legal research and bring the results to the examination hall.

The other areas of the curriculum that are addressed by this series of classes are the knowledge areas: Civil Litigation, Evidence and Remedies; Criminal Litigation, Evidence and Sentencing; and Professional Ethics. Students have a series of classes running alongside the ones described which are much more focused on the sort of learning necessary for passing the assessments here. These take the form of unseen exams comprised of multiple choice questions and short answer questions. These are far from simplistic but may face the criticism that they tend to encourage shallow rather than deep learning.[30] The level of integration on the programme should minimise this, but it is inevitable that a high proportion of student energy goes to rote learning of the rules and codes as opposed to learning how to use them effectively and ethically.

Recent research on students' attitudes towards these classes[31] has revealed a high degree of satisfaction. For example:

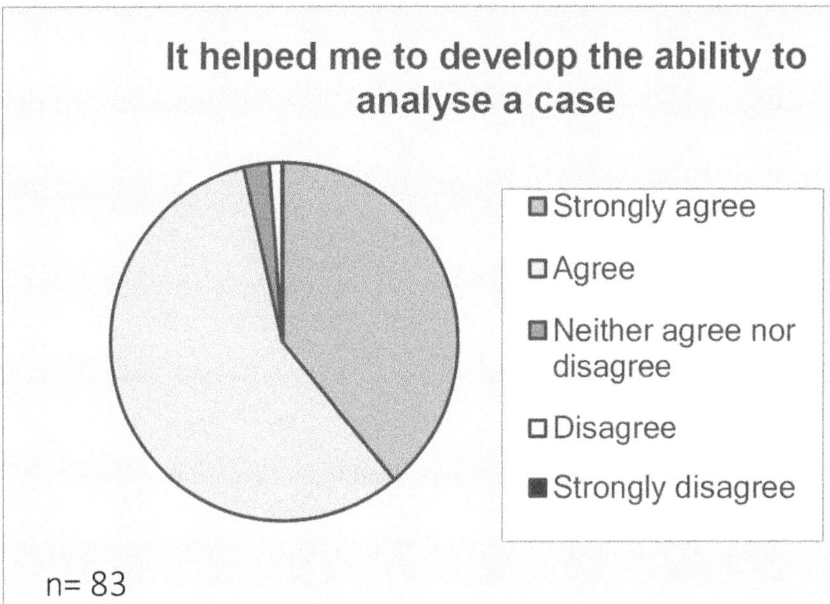

29 Bar Standards Board, n. 21, A 2.1.3.

30 Biggs, JB, 1987, *Student Approaches to Learning and Studying*, Hawthorne, Australian Council for Educational Research.

31 Duncan, n. 23.

Students' developing understanding of the facts, and their need to approach them proactively, is clear. Comments include:

> 'My work from the first classes on Pemberton and the last ones we've had could be like the work of two different people.'
>
> 'The addition of new material over the weeks was good because it made you return at times to re-evaluate all the evidence available.'

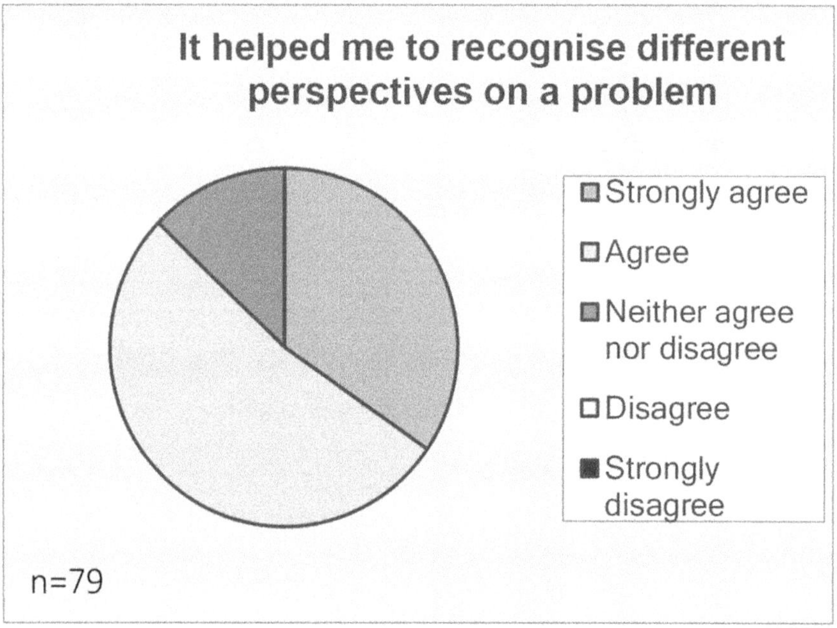

The change in perspective was clearly significant. Comments included:

> 'Changing what side you were on helped to view the case from all perspectives.'
>
> 'It helpfully brought together lots of different areas of the course, such as opinion writing, ADR, advocacy and civil litigation. It was useful to see a practical illustration of how these inter-relate.'

This is evidence of a level of preparedness for practice which far exceeds that in the 1975 Bar Finals course.

Clinical developments

A significant part of the BPTC curriculum is, as can be seen from the description earlier, delivered through simulated clinical activity.[32] To understand the extent of the development since 1975, the introduction of real-client clinical learning[33] should also be addressed.

City Law School encourages its students to undertake pro bono work advising and representing real clients. We offer a range of internal advice clinics and external opportunities with many different organisations, mostly in the United Kingdom, but also in South Africa.[34] However, we also pioneered introducing students' work with real clients into the Bar curriculum[35] with an option whereby, instead of attending classes and undertaking a simulated written assessment (usually involving opinion writing and/or drafting) a small group of students become accredited representatives with the Free Representation Unit (FRU) and represent clients in real employment tribunal cases. This has become recognised by the regulator as a proper basis for a BPTC Option[36] and has been developed at City, where we now offer three such options. As well as taking Employment Tribunal cases, students may represent clients in Social Security Tribunal cases, also with the support of FRU, or, through the National Centre for Domestic Violence, act as McKenzie Friends supporting victims of domestic violence in seeking protective injunctions.

These options provide for profound experience. Student reflections on their work include statements like:

> 'The BPTC year is all about doing practical things, writing an opinion, drafting, conducting a cross examination, largely in a theoretical or role-playing scenario. Doing [this] case made sense of the year. It was for real. It involved real civil litigation – the test for strike out for example being crucial in the [ ] case. It involved advocacy, persuading the judge. It involved ADR, mainly in the form of negotiation. It involved conference skills, fact management and legal research, all for a real person, whose life was being deeply affected by the situation at play. It meant that some of the Civil Litigation which we had to learn for the BPTC exam made much more sense. It gave me a lot of confidence for my advocacy and conference assessments.'[37]

32 Brayne, Hugh, Duncan, Nigel and Grimes, Richard, 1998, *Clinical Legal Education: Active Learning in your Law School*, London, Blackstone, 173–208.

33 For a recent analysis of the value of this, see Giddings, Jeff, 2013, *Promoting Justice through Clinical Legal Education*, Melbourne, Justice Press, Part 1.

34 City Law School 2014, *Pro bono*, http://www.city.ac.uk/law/careers/pro-bono-professional (accessed 3 July 2015).

35 Nigel Duncan, 1997, 'On Your Feet in the Industrial Tribunal', 14 *Journal of Professional Legal Education* 169.

36 BSB, n. 21, 2.3.13.

37 Student reflective report, on file with author.

As such, this real experience of representation acts as a capstone for effective integration of the overall BPTC curriculum.

The external examiner's report on these options in 2014 said: 'An absolutely excellent set of files, I was blown away with the quality of research and documentation that the students had prepared.'[38] It is, of course, not surprising that students put extra effort into their work when they are representing a real client, compared with undertaking simulated activities. The reason for presenting this here, however, is to identify further the extent to which modern Bar training has developed since 1975. Although the examples presented are from one BPTC provider, the serious application of educational theory is widespread. Changes in civil practice, with its judicial case management, control of costs and encouragement of settlement has gone a long way to address Sir Roger's concerns. Educators' response has been no less radical and I like to think that both Sir Roger Ormrod and Gandhi would have approved.

38 On file with author.

13 Thirty-eighth Lord Upjohn Lecture 2009

The Student Contract*

Baroness Ruth Deech D.B.E.

I am pleased to have this opportunity to pay tribute to Lord Upjohn, a name to conjure with for students of law, and synonymous with many of the most discussed, most intellectually challenging and welcomed decisions made in my time as a law student. In the year that I took my final law examinations, we were all overwhelmed by the last-minute decision on 13 May of *National Provincial Bank v Ainsworth* [1965] AC 1175, HL and the judgment of Lord Upjohn reversing the law we had painfully mastered only a few months before in *NPB v Hastings Car Mart* [1964] Ch 128. It was in part due to Lord Upjohn's realisation that the law was not coming to the aid of the deserted wife and the pressure he exerted that the law was changed in the act of 1967, a case study to delight any law teacher. Unsurprisingly, his judgments are still cited today in English and foreign courts.

I remember him with respect because of the teaching I had; and all the more appropriate that his name bedecks the annual lecture sponsored by the Association of Law Teachers (ALT). We have heard much in recent times about the true function of higher education – to prepare students for the real world of industry, or of commerce; to supply the nation with the economic manpower that it needs; to foster research and development. All of these things are true, but there is one overriding purpose and that is to teach, to hand on the lessons learned in earlier generations and the wisdom of the faculty to a new generation. To prepare them for citizenship, to give them ambition, to help them develop a purpose in life, a sense of their place in society, the ability to contribute to the betterment of all our conditions by the use of the law with which they are involved; intelligibility and articulacy; a sense of responsibility and awareness of the value received in higher education and an awakening and stretching of the mind; the chance to discover what they *love* in higher education (HE), and I use the word advisedly, for to pursue a course because it will earn you a living or because your parents want you to, is more likely to end in failure and frustration than the pursuit of a topic that is compatible, for on that topic you may spend the rest of your life. And you can readily see that much of the unease expressed by today's students comes from a misunderstanding of the purposes of HE. We teachers hold the

* This lecture was delivered as the thirty-eighth Lord Upjohn Lecture at City Law School on 24 October 2008.

remedy in our hands by remembering and insisting on its true purposes: education not training; knowledge not skills; teaching not rote learning. You have all, I am sure, like me encountered former students who greet you with a recollection of something you once said or an observation made during teaching; but I have never yet met a student who remembered me, or anybody else, for their research or administrative gifts, valuable though they may be in other contexts.

The purpose of the student contract

I would therefore like to look at the student contract in the context of university development today, and put it to you that the current interest in the student contract is a symptom of changes taking place in the relationship between the university and the student. I would also like to speculate on what Lord Upjohn would have thought about student contracts. The student contract, existing or in contemplation, reflects the public understanding of the availability and function of HE, of the personal relationship between each student and his or her lecturer, between parents and universities, teaching staff and universities, and between employers, government and HE providers. The benefit of the device of the contract is that it may be used to express the values and aspirations of the parties in a form which had never crystallised before; it may express their respective rights and responsibilities in relation to the studying and teaching experience, and give clarity in a competitive market enabling comparisons to be made about the university offer and the hopes of the student. The less favourable view of the contract is that it represents the increasing commercialisation of HE in the sense that students, their parents or the government are paying considerable sums for it and see it as a benefit that is bought. Now that access to HE has widened, there will be many parents who have had no university experience themselves, and are anxious about what to expect and whether they will get value for money. Commercialisation is reinforced by the fact that as participation in HE has grown to encompass a very large proportion of school leavers, the degree is the prerequisite to any worthwhile career, and a good degree is highly sought in order to differentiate the many graduates from one another. In any such situation the parties involved will want their rights, duties and enforcement measures set out. The contract also brings home to universities the importance of fulfilling the attractive promises they make in their prospectuses.

There was a time when the university was described as one's *alma mater*, responsible for raising certain young people to adulthood and civic responsibility. The satisfaction for lecturers lay in power (the ability to direct), lifestyle, research and scholarship. Complaints, which were rare, tended to relate to admission and exclusivity, and sometimes discipline. The rules reflected the society of the time (or an earlier one, in the case of women's colleges!). Today the student sometimes seems to want only a good degree result as a passport to the next step in life. As the economic climate deteriorates, this feeling may intensify. On the part of the university, it still wants success for its students: the lecturers have chosen them, have invested effort in them, and the success of the students in future life is the success of their teachers. The university makes a little money from its students, but not much; more, proportionately, from research and outside relationships. There is no longer a good salary for lecturers or an exceptional lifestyle and respect; research has been mutated by the demands of the Research Assessment Exercise (RAE), and university professors do not seem to be so highly regarded by society any more. Consequently, complaints tend to relate to the paper qualifications that the student will receive on leaving, for that is the one focus.

Sometimes students assert that, having paid for the course, there is a legitimate expectation of a good result, and maybe that is what corporations demand when they invest in university research. Universities cannot help but reflect a society where there is a culture of complaint and litigation, an emphasis on confrontational demands, and resolution by conciliation or alternative dispute resolution. Diversity is a major issue because of the presence of so many international and ethnic minority students. Even the bullying and violence that are found in society at large manifest themselves on campus; and some of the staff have adopted the attitudes of other trade unionists in their attitudes to pay, conditions and general politics. University and College Union (UCU) has forfeited respect as a professional body by promoting an academic boycott. Hence, as elsewhere in society, a document setting out rights and duties seems logical.

Many universities believe the student contract is a good idea. But students tend to resist the idea. Much may be said about the point of origin of the contract, its disadvantages and difficulties, its enforceability, the clauses that may be desirable and the form that it should take, but I will confine myself only to its place in the culture of universities today.

The formation of the contract

Any law student will know that it is clear that there has *always* been a contract, albeit informal and sometimes unwritten, between the student and the university, going back several centuries. Just as there is an implied contract in law when a passenger gets on a bus, or a patient goes to hospital, or one makes a bid on eBay, so a *de facto* contract arises by the mere fact that the university offers to admit the student and the student takes up his or her place there. Some lawyers would maintain that the contract is formed at the point of offer, others that it is formed when the student registers; yet others would say that a preliminary contract is formed on admission and is augmented at the point of registration by incorporating the rules of the university. Therefore what is new now is that universities feel the need to gather together in one formal and public document the implicit and explicit terms that already exist, and some new ones, so that the attention of the student is drawn to them, and they sign up to an express arrangement that is intended to have full legal consequences and to be legally binding on both sides. After all, a significant amount of resources turn on the certified presence of the student and the universities are also aware of the amount of general law that governs the situation and needs to be taken into account.

Current British university contracts range in length from 3 pages to 10, and other relevant documentation may run to hundreds of pages, that is, the examination regulations, student union rules and accommodation terms etc. About 9 British universities (Oxford, Chester, Christ Church Canterbury, Kent, Bristol, Robert Gordon, Aberdeen, Arts and Napier) now have a formal contract, 17 are considering it, more than half of all British universities are not considering it, and about 20 (including Newcastle and St George's) have a more informal broad declaration of expectations, sometimes called a 'Charter'. [The word 'charter' is sometimes used to dignify a contract that has Royal approval: some old universities are based on Royal or religious charters, so is the BBC. A 'charter' is also used to give expression to a set of aspirations which may not be met: passengers on the railways have a passengers' charter of expectations about a punctual and efficient service, which are not fulfilled in practice and may prove to be unenforceable. The same is true of promises to patients in the NHS.] Already the issue of a standard contract for all British universities has been lost, because they are going their different ways and students cannot argue that the same level of provision is to be expected at each university.

So far, the idea of a new formal contract in one document is not popular with British students. The reasons are many. Some students think that the new contracts have been designed to give more legal protection to the university against claims that the students might make against it for failure of provisions. Some students say that their claims relating to, for example, poor teaching will be defeated by the university's assertion that the student did not take up all that was on offer to help him or her and that therefore the student did not fulfil his or her side of the bargain by full participation. Students say that there was no consultation about the drafting of the contract, so that the resulting terms favour the university, not the students, by placing heavier and more specific responsibilities on the students than on the university. Students particularly dislike detailed contract terms about attendance at lectures and the handing in of coursework (terms that were implicitly dominant in universities 50 or more years ago). They say that this inflexibility does not allow for the pressures on the modern student, who has to pay higher fees, and who may have to work to earn money and who may have childcare responsibilities, and thus finds university schedules almost impossible to comply with. Recent findings showed that 38% of students who have jobs miss lectures, and 21% of them fail to hand in coursework on time. Hence the increased reliance on the handout and the powerpoint slides, so readily transmissible. Nevertheless, the first set of proposals to emerge from the new National Students Forum in October 2008 called for universities to publish the contact hours and assessment styles that students can expect on their courses. In general the students in this project wanted more information, and they wanted it in a formal style. It could therefore be asserted that, unsurprisingly, students are not averse to contracts containing their rights, if not their duties.

Students complain that contracts are one-sided. *'Students are not slaves. Universities still operate a master-servant relationship with their students'* (from a student letter to the newspapers). For example, universities in general do not bind themselves to provide a minimum level of teaching or accommodation (*'The content of programmes varies widely and the university therefore does not specify any minimum amount of teaching which you will receive on the programme'* (Chester 2.2)). At the same time the contracts may make attendance at lectures and classes compulsory and force the students to accept accommodation and finance terms, and to agree to the jurisdiction of the English courts even if they are overseas students who may have returned home before starting to enforce the contract. *'Breach of any of these conditions may give rise to disciplinary action being taken against you under the disciplinary procedures of the university and/or termination of this Agreement'* (Chester 1.5). The contracts are not, in my view, as one sided as they seem, for students acquire the right to complain if they do not get the promised facilities, and as has been said they do not see themselves as bound to attend all the lectures if the schedule is unreasonable in their view.

General law applying to the university-student relationship

There is a general background and context of English legal principles which will apply to any contract, written or unwritten, and which serve to put a different interpretation and effect on the words that students sign up to. For example, a child under 18 is not bound by a contract unless it is for his or her benefit. Students are deemed to be consumers for the purposes of the Unfair Contract Terms Act 1977 and the Unfair Terms in Consumer Contracts Regulations 1999, and some terms of the student contract might be unlawful and unenforceable under these laws. The 1999 Regulations focus on terms that are not individually negotiated or where there is an imbalance between the parties, which will fit the university-student situation. This means that there is an element of uncertainty about some parts of the student contract, because one will not know whether it is 'unfair' until there has been a declaration by a court, or possibly the Office of Fair Trading, and the courts might imply some terms or flesh out others. Everyone is subject to the law of tort, and the universities' duty of care is of an unknown extent and not likely to be embedded in the contract. It is likely that there is a duty of care to provide tuition to generally acceptable standards and to ensure that placements and years abroad are adequately safeguarded, that welfare issues are attended to, for example, obvious distress or mental ill health, that steps are taken to avoid sports injuries and that health and safety regulations are observed. Universities need insurance to protect against health and safety claims; indeed universities need general extensive insurance cover to protect against all sorts of legal claims. Insurance brings with it its own complexities in that insurers may seek to determine the university's behaviour where there is a student claim against it, or may interfere too much, from a natural justice point of view, in a panel hearing about a student.

There are many other general laws which universities and students are subject to and I can touch on only a limited number. I wonder whether universities realise quite how much legislation affects that relationship. Some modern legislation specifically targets universities; other legislation affects them unintentionally. Universities were singled out for freedom of speech guarantees after a number of incidents in the 1980s where right wing speakers were heckled and jostled on campus visits. The Education (No. 2) Act 1986 places a special duty on universities to afford a platform for all speakers on campus, regardless of their views, *provided that they are within the law*, and universities have to have a Code of Practice relating to Freedom of Speech. By provisions of the Education Act 1994 the university has to draw the attention of the students' union to that Code annually, and fresh responsibilities are imposed on universities in relation to students' unions and on unions towards their members. My experience at the Office of the Independent Adjudicator for Higher Education (OIA) gave me the impression that universities may not realise that the scope of freedom of speech *within the law* has been narrowed in recent years by for example the Terrorism Acts of 2000 and 2006, the Racial and Religious Hatred Act 2006 and the Protection from Harassment Act 1997, so that it is now a sensitive job to pick out an avenue for free speech between left and right.

Universities and students have special relationships in relation to discrimination. The Race Relations (Amendment) Act 2000 places a positive duty on universities – although possibly not on students' unions – to foster good relations between different race groups on campus. This is reinforced by the Racial and Religious Hatred Act 2006 and the Equality Act of the same year, with the effect that the very strong ethnic and religious minority representation on campus is a fruitful ground for complaint and dissatisfaction, whereas in truth campus should be the best place in which to commence and continue dialogue between dissonant groups. Disability is strongly protected by the Disability Discrimination Acts 1995 and 2005 and the Special Educational Needs and Disability Act 2001. The requirements made of university are complex and proactive and present a sensitive area of dissatisfaction and the need for interpretation. For while the visible handicaps of sight and mobility are relatively easy to cope with in the academic context, the invisible ones such as dyslexia and mental ill health are not, and the question of how to truly assess and report the academic abilities of the students with special needs has yet to be satisfactorily, consistently and honestly addressed.

Other Acts inadvertently have significant effect on the student-university relationship: the Protection from Eviction Act 1977 as it affects the student room; the Data Protection Act 1998 (DPA) and the Freedom of Information Act 2000 (FOIA). The consequences of the enforcement of the last two on universities can hardly have been considered when they were passed. The DPA enables students to obtain from the university copies of the documentation relating to them personally, including references and the comments of examiners on their scripts. Under the same law students' and alumni consent must be obtained before the university processes and obtains sensitive personal data. The provisions of the DPA have ended the practice of publishing complete lists of degree results in Oxford (quite unnecessarily in my view, as it is not personal information) and have rendered written references next to otiose as well as legally sensitive. The FOIA has opened up university records and files to students and brought to light much general and statistical information about examination and general policy that informs the student's view of whether he or she has been fairly treated.

From this very limited survey of some of the general laws that affect universities, it can be seen that quite apart from any student contract and its terms, there is an ever increasing burden on universities of compliance with the law, and the disclosure enactments help students to get the information they need to file a claim. Only a few years ago, university committee minutes and references were written in the belief that they would be confidential; now virtually nothing can be kept from the light of day. Consider too, new laws and regulations about fees and bursaries and the impact of the Human Rights Act, always unforeseeable, on any of these statutory matters.

Judicial review

The area of education law is one of rapid development (Farrington and Palfreyman's book *The Law of Higher Education* (Oxford: Oxford University Press, 2006) is one of the thickest tomes around); it is also a subject of judicial investigation by way of judicial review. Judges may revisit a decision by a body within the university to check whether it is unreasonable or unfair or outside its powers. This means that the universities must operate all their powers and procedures according to the principles of natural justice (some of the gateposts are always on the move), which are unlikely to be well known to university staff. Universities, understandably, are sometimes not fully aware of the requirements of public law and anti-discrimination law, and their expenditure on legal advice and litigation is considerable. It may well be that the court throws out the request for judicial review with scant support, holding that academic judgment is outside its scope and that judicial review will be exercised only in the most narrow of circumstances. But until the parties to the litigation get to that point, much valuable time, limited resources and stress have been expended, because the belief is around that judges will judicially review anything and everything, a view for which the judges must bear some responsibility.

Contracts and the OIA/ombudsman jurisdiction

The effect of the formal contract such as described earlier may be that there is too much legalism and too little trust, too much inflexibility and too much exercise of power. But in England and Wales, the OIA has a separate and, I believe, more humane jurisdiction over the student experience. No matter how difficult or demanding the contract terms, under legislation (the Higher Education Act 2004) the OIA has a remit over every 'act or omission' of a university; and under the OIA Rules the OIA may make a decision whether the university's actions were fair and reasonable in all the circumstances. The contract terms may be less generous than the OIA's approach and powers: there may be a conflict between what is 'fair and reasonable' in the eyes of the OIA, and the terms the student has signed up to in the formal university contract, but the OIA's powers will prevail, if it is resorted to, because they are based on statute. We may see a new phenomenon, however: the university suing a student in contract for a breach by him or her, for example fraud. This is an area where the OIA's determination might come into conflict with a court action if the student who was sued simultaneously pursued a complaint against the university. It is to be hoped that a court would expect student problems to be considered in the first instance by the OIA, because the English courts and the government are committed to alternative dispute resolution. This causes one to consider again whether the contract is (a) useful and (b) good for students and universities.

Conclusions

I would conclude that the contract is useful as a general indication that the relationship between students and universities is a special and complicated one and above all one where each side must make a contribution. The contract that spells out the contribution to be expected from students is useful to dispel the notion that university education can be 'delivered' in a passive one-sided fashion. It is also uniquely a contract with no fixed outcome, because the quality of the experience in the end is determined not only by the facilities and teaching offered by the university but also by the aptitude and hard work of the student. In this it is like a contract between a doctor and a patient, because no matter how well the doctor performs his services, the patient may not get better. It is like the analogy I frequently resort to, the contract between the member and the sports club: there is no guarantee that the member will become fit and lean even if he or she uses the facilities properly and even less so if no effort is made by the member. The formal written student contract may be blamed for entrenching a more commercial attitude, although it is more likely to be the result of the attitude that already exists. There is no avoiding an increase of legalism because, as my brief exploration of all the other laws that apply to the situation will have shown, there already exists a wealth of detailed law applying to the student-university relationship in any case, arising simply from the application and effect of the general law of the land.

My conclusion is that education may be one of a class of some major events in life which do not readily lend themselves to incorporation and control in a contract drawn up by individuals. This is because the situations are too emotional in origin, or because their progress is towards an unknown and unquantifiable outcome; or because there is an imbalance of power between the two sides which can be corrected only by state intervention; or because the issue is too important for the nation as a whole to be left to the wishes of the individual parties.

Consider by way of analogy the contracts of marriage, transport, hospitalisation, parental involvement in schooling, and property. The marriage contract is made in church or in the registry office by the vows taken by the couple in relation to each other. Yet these vows of lifelong fidelity, parenthood and sharing are not enforceable; in Western society marriage is no longer for life but may be ended easily by divorce; neither husbands nor wives may be forced to become parents or to take care of each other in illness and old age, as promised on the wedding day. Human nature has made these vows impossible to enforce and the state has had to step in with its own inescapable provisions.

Transport is a necessity, and a contract is formed every time the passenger steps into the railway carriage or onto the bus. But the passenger is largely unaware of the terms and conditions imposed on him or her by the transport company, and the state and the general law have to intervene to protect the passenger. This is also true of medical treatment. The patient may consider that he or she has a contract with the doctor or the hospital for certain procedures, but if they go wrong, the general law has to intervene. There can be no contracting for a definite outcome in medical treatment because of the uncertainties in our physical response and healing properties. The state has control over the facilities involved, such as drugs and hospital services, which take the matter out of the control of the two parties to the contract.

It has sometimes been suggested in England that parents should make a contract with the school about encouraging their children's education and making sure that the children do the homework required by the school. On the whole, this has proved impractical because there is no real way to enforce it, and those parents who are most likely to offend are the ones least likely to accept the contract and abide by it. Finally, property law also falls in this important category. In England, more so than in most countries, landlord and tenant are not left to make their own contract because it has been accepted for decades that the power is unbalanced and the need for a roof over one's head is very great and capable of opening the tenant to exploitation. So the law provides for general standards and some element of security, no matter what contract terms in the lease have been signed. Contracts for credit and hire purchase are controlled because of the opportunities for exploitation. Indeed, we now know that every aspect of our relationship with our banks, our creditors and our mortgagees may be abruptly displaced by the state!

Higher education has every claim to fall in this category. It is of the utmost importance to the individual and to the nation that the student has the fullest opportunity to learn and to demonstrate that he or she has met the requisite standards. The formal written contract for education puts much power in the hands of the university, and to impose it when making an offer of higher education may be an occasion involving emotion and difficult choices by a very young person, sometimes under the age of majority. There is no guaranteed learning outcome and the personal chemistry between any student and lecturer may be variable. The contract is useful but it is not the answer to all the questions. It is unlikely that a university wishes to see the contract terms enforced by law; it is much more likely that mediation or some form of settlement is the preferable outcome. The contract is also not necessarily protective or fair towards a young person, possibly from a family with no experience of higher education and maybe with no older person to give advice at the crucial moment. That is why the jurisdiction of the OIA and other similar ombudsman-type schemes in higher education is preferable. The OIA may determine what is fair and reasonable in all the circumstances; give a remedy that is tailored to the needs of the student (not just damages, as arise from breach of contract), but possibly the opportunity to re-take an examination or repeat a year, to have an appeal re-heard or to rejoin a course.

This is surely of more value than contract remedies to the student, because it is intended to give him or her an opportunity to prove himself or herself. The specialised jurisdiction of the OIA is more valuable to the university, giving it the opportunity to provide the promised teaching or correct procedural errors and retake decisions, which is better than requiring the payment of a sum of money with no corrective action. Flexibility, fairness and equality of opportunity need to be considered, and whether they are better achieved in a contract, or in a charter of less detail, or by national complaints-handling coupled with contract, remains to be seen.

A final general point about the use of contracts and the provision of public services, if a university education can be seen as such. The use of the contract model changes the emphasis of the student-university relationship to a market-based one as distinct from public accountability. (Cane, *Administrative Law*, 4th edn (Oxford: Oxford University Press, 2004)). Instead of, or in addition to, holding universities answerable (for their public funding) to Parliament and the public interest, the contract focuses on consumer choice, price and competition. Its use assumes that satisfying the customer-student is the most important element. Enforcing individual contracts is a way of holding universities accountable for the *way* in which education and educational services are made available but it does not add to accountability for decisions about *what* type of education is being provided. The contract emphasises choice and giving good value and satisfaction to the individual student, but it has nothing to contribute in the debate about what sort of education should be available or how it can be made affordable and resourced and what happens if unwise decisions are made by the consumer. Moreover, if certain university services are contracted out to third parties, for example, accommodation, the student has no contractual relationship with the provider, and devices have to be found to link together the university, the student and his or her housing. Overall, the emphasis on the new formal contract may lead to more micro-management, box-ticking, checking and inspection but not necessarily to greater quality or public benefit. Lord Upjohn might well have said that a student has a special status vis-à-vis the university, not one that creates firm legal rights, but one of status, mirroring his view of Mrs Ainsworth and her right to be housed.

14 Response: Changing Terms

A Response to Professor Deech

Rebecca Huxley-Binns

Professor Baroness Ruth Deech's Annual Lord Upjohn Lecture in 2009 positioned the function and role of the university through the lens of the student contract. Her thesis included the assertion that the 'one over-riding purpose' of higher education is 'to hand on the lessons learned in earlier generations and the wisdom of the faculty to a new generation'[1] and that the remedy to student unease is to insist on 'education not training, knowledge not skills'.[2] Professor Deech's assertion about knowledge strikes at the core of modern higher legal education. Ultimately, her thesis can be accepted or rejected according to an appreciation of the terms of the contract between the student and her higher education institution, the validity of the distinction Professor Deech makes between skills and knowledge, and an analysis of the 'true' purpose of higher legal undergraduate education in the 21st century.

The law student of the future (today)

Let us try to visualise the law student experience from the perspective of the law student.[3] A first year full-time law undergraduate starting her degree in the autumn of 2015, after taking A levels in May and June 2015, was born in 1996. I appreciate she is not the only model of the undergraduate student population, but for the purposes of exploring present and future student expectations, she will be my exemplar. The point is that she was born in *1996*. Of course, how you remember 1996 will depend on how old you, dear reader, are, and thus how old you were then. Feel free to take a moment to reflect.

1996; a sobering thought. This was the year I got my first mobile phone and was appointed to my first full-time teaching job. It was the year Charles and Diana were divorced and the year of the Atlanta nail bombing. It was the year of *Jerry Maguire* and *Independence Day* in the cinemas. Some further context; it was

1 Ruth Deech, 'The student contract' (2009) 43:1 *The Law Teacher* 3, 3.

2 Ibid., 4.

3 Rebecca Huxley-Binns, 'Do you remember what it was like to be 18?' (Nottingham Trent University Annual Learning and Teaching Conference, Nottingham, 2013, <http://www.ntu.ac.uk/adq/document_uploads/events/143571.pdf> accessed 28 July 2014).

seven years *after* the fall of the Berlin Wall, five years *after* the USSR ceased to exist, and two years *after* the end of South African apartheid. At the start of the 2007 financial crisis, my law student to-be had only just started secondary school. Even today, she may never have heard of the Northern Rock Building Society, but if she needs to know about it, she can Google it. For, you see, the average undergraduate student has lived all her life with Google (which started as a research tool in, you guessed it, 1996) and Wikipedia (which launched in 2001). She is also able to access a MOOC (Massive Open Online Course) whenever she wants to or needs to know something new.

This should not, I hope, come as news to anyone teaching in higher education in 2015. These changes clearly did not start in or after 2009 and Professor Deech's lecture did not reflect the fact that this 'now' had already arrived. For, in the same year as her lecture, Martin Bean, Vice Chancellor of the Open University, delivering a keynote speech,[4] showed how the position of universities had already undergone unprecedented change brought about by technology.[5] It is the thesis of the response that technology has impacted, and will further impact on, the educational expectations of my undergraduate law student; expectations which we must heed.

The psychological contract

Professor Deech's Lord Upjohn Lecture focused almost entirely on the nature and terms of the legal contract between the student and the university. It is my contention, however, that of far more importance is the *psychological* contract which students enter with the university.[6] Organisational theory posits the existence in the employment field of a psychological contract which runs parallel to the legal contract and which represents the beliefs, perceptions, informal obligations and expectations between an employer and employee.[7] Although not yet recognised as extending to the higher education field, it is my assertion that the psychological contract applies equally to higher education. Because the psychological contract sets the affective dynamic for the relationship from the outset, expectations are built from the start (the recruitment process in employment and the prospectus and Open Days in higher education). If I am right, drawing a further parallel from the psychological employment contract, the first year is critical to the subsequent success of the relationship (the parallel to student retention is, I hope, obvious).

4 Martin Bean, 'A journey in innovation' (Association for Learning Technology Annual Conference, 2009, <http://www.youtube.com/watch?v=HJSRkhx4T3k>, accessed 14 July 2014).

5 At 16 minutes and 35 seconds, he calls on the audience to reflect on classic education and the skills needed to succeed in the 21st century. He follows this train of thought for the next 20 minutes or so.

6 It is more important because it is of more day-to-day relevance, and legal contracts tend to be ignored unless terms are breached.

7 D M Rousseau, 'Psychological and implied contracts in organizations' (1989) 2 *Employee Responsibilities and Rights Journal* 121. See also Jacqueline A-M Coyle-Shapiro and M Parzefall, 'Psychological contracts' in Gary Cooper and Julian Barling (eds), *The SAGE handbook of organizational behavior* (SAGE, 2008) 17; Chris Aigyris, *Understanding Organizational Behavior* (Homewood, IU Dorsey Press, 1960).

Feldheim, an organisational scholar, further suggests that the psychological employment contract is divided into two strands.[8] The first is transactional and represents the economic or monetary base of the relationship. The era of full fees and loans in higher education bears this out; the oft-cited assertion is that students are paying now and therefore make more demands (have higher expectations). The second strand is relational. This represents the socio-emotional base that underlies expectations of shared ideals and values, and respect and support. The importance of this to the law student is well documented elsewhere.[9] On reflection, perhaps the reason why MOOCs are having better success with students who already completed tertiary education[10] is because those students have clearer expectations about the nature of learning than students without. It is this aspect, student expectation, which I intend to discuss further, in the context of what my exemplar student, DOB 1996, *expects* from her undergraduate legal education.

Student expectations in 2015

Expectations are determined by a combination of experience, cognitive processes, communication with others, and cultural norms.[11] Therefore, my exemplar student's expectations will be the norm for her generation.

Various labels have been used to describe the characteristics or norms of modern generations. These labels are most commonly used in the fields of education, technology, sociology and marketing. The first generational term, 'Gen X', was coined in the early 1950s by a photographer, Robert Capa, in a photo essay which first appeared in *Picture Post* (UK) and *Holiday* (US) in 1953:

> 'We named this unknown generation, The Generation X, and even in our first enthusiasm we realised that we had something far bigger than our talents and pockets could cope with.'[12]

Since, there has been no universally agreed set of dates for generational boundaries, but it is broadly accepted that 'Gen X' was born between the early 1960s and the early 1980s (after the Western post-World War II 'baby boomers'). Gen X was followed by Gen Y (also called the Millennials) born between the early 1980s and the early 2000s; and now we have a new generation, the title of which

8 Mary Feldheim, 'Downsizing' (Southeastern Conference of Public Administration, St. Petersburg, FL, 6–9 October 1999).

9 'Affect and Learning' in Caroline Maughan and Paul Maharg (eds), *Affect and Legal Education* (Ashgate, 2011), Pt III. See also A Damasio, *Descartes' Error* (Vintage Books, 2006).

10 Gayle Christensen, Andrew Steinmetz, Brandon Alcorn, Amy Bennett, Deirdre Woods and Ezekiel J Emanuel, 'The MOOC Phenomenon: Who Takes Massive Open Online Courses and Why?' (6 November 2013), http://dx.doi.org/10.2139/ssrn.2350964> accessed 28 July 2014.

11 Anon, <http://www.goodtherapy.org/blog/psychpedia/expectation> accessed 15 July 2014.

12 John M Ulrich, 'Generation X: A (Sub)Cultural Genealogy' in John M Ulrich and Andrea L Harris (eds), *GenXegesis: Essays on Alternative Youth (Sub)Culture* (Popular Press, 2003).

has not (yet) settled comfortably into place. From the educational perspective, this labeling can be very informative in curriculum design, because research appears to show that the younger generations think and process information in fundamentally different ways compared with previous generations[13] and, if true, this has profound implications for education. Prensky's assertion has not been universally supported; Bennett et al suggest that young people are not radically different, and they question the validity of some of the generational characteristics, especially in respect of technological know-how.[14] However, if societies are seeing generational changes in access to and ease with technology, including exposure to, experience of and developing technological expertise,[15] then we in higher legal education need fully to grasp these points or we will fail to engage students in how they do, and want to, learn,[16] and we will do them a disservice in their potential to graduate as knowledgeable and skilled citizens.

So, what are the possible new labels mooted for my exemplar student? She is a member of the generation variously labeled Generation Z, the Zeds, the iGeneration, the Internet Generation, the gamers generation, or the Homeland generation. North American online news reports seem to think the term 'the plurals' has won the labeling competition. This term was coined by Frank N Magid Associates, but is of limited applicability outside the United States[17] because it refers to the fact that this will be that last generation of North Americans with a Caucasian majority. The label may have limited geographical use, but the characteristics it encompasses are interesting: the plurals are ethnically diverse and positive about it, but they are risk averse. They are more likely to reject 'traditional' gender roles having experienced both parents involved in both careers and families. Another label is the 'Multi-Gen'. Coined by Twenge,[18] it captures the generation most likely to be multi-cultural, multi-racial and *multimedia*. My exemplar Multi-Gen student will therefore expect flexible working, telecommuting, child-friendly working and seamless access to technology.[19]

13 Marc Prensky, 'Digital Natives, Digital Immigrants: Part 1' (2001a) 9(5) *On the Horizon* 1; Marc Prensky, 'Digital Natives, Digital Immigrants: Part 2: Do they really think differently?' (2001b) 9(6) *On the Horizon* 1.

14 S Bennett, M Maton and L Kervin, 'The "digital natives" debate: A critical review of the evidence' (2008) 39(5) *British Journal of Educational Technology* 775.

15 Ellen Helsper and Rebecca Eynon, 'Digital Natives: where is the evidence?' (2009) *British Educational Research Journal* 1, 12.

16 G Kennedy, T Judd, A Churchward, K Gray and K Krause, 'First year students' experiences with technology: Are they really digital natives?' (2008) 24(1) *Australasian Journal of Educational Technology* 108.

17 Professor Jean Twenge, quoted in <http://usatoday30.usatoday.com/money/advertising/story/2012-05-03/naming-the-next-generation/54737518/1> accessed 10 July 2014.

18 Ibid.

19 The first thing I check when booking a hotel is whether there is free wifi in the rooms. I will not book if I have to pay. I am not quite at the level of insisting that it is a human right, but I saw a funny cartoon online; picture an unhappy child, with a few tears on his cheeks, clearly responding to an adult's question, 'No I did not have a good first day at school. They didn't even have free wifi!'

Professor Deech recognised some of these issues, especially in respect of the need for flexibility, acknowledging the pressures on the modern student;[20] and there is a strong link between lifestyle flexibility and expectations about use of and access to technology. In November 2013, 18 per cent of the share of 18–34-year-olds (and this is the generation *older* than my exemplar; these are the Millennials) are mobile *only* internet users.[21] That is, nearly one in five Millennials do all of their internet browsing, shopping, emailing, Google searching, social networking on a smartphone or a tablet. They do not have, and do not need, desktop computers (or landline telephones).

As educators, I am not sure how many of us have recognised, never mind welcomed, these changes, and nor do we necessarily grasp that these behaviours have evolved and continue to evolve, and where we are now is simply a snapshot on a continuum. Whilst we continue to ignore this, we will be dissatisfied with our teaching because students will be dissatisfied with their learning. Therefore we have to be prepared to build a curriculum better to engage students, and better to equip them for their ability to understand and use law. We should build on their experiences and expectations, recognising the influence and importance technology has in their lives. This applies not only to future lawyers and future legal professionals, and future professionals who will work outside law, but are currently under our tutelage; it applies equally to *their* future customers and clients. The Multi-Gens will always start by checking Google, YouTube, or TedX, to find a legal answer to a problem.[22] So, what will the expectations be about the *value* added to the legal services by a lawyer or other professional service provider in person in 2030?, in 2040? And, in the context of this thesis, what are the expectations that feed backwards from that to our Multi-Gen's expectations now?

I am happy to admit that my Multi-Gen's motivations and my own differ, and her expectations and mine are *necessarily* different because of the different experiences we have had in our lives to the start date of our undergraduate experiences, due in no small part to the fact that the dates are 25 years apart. I am not asserting, indeed I reject any assertion that my Multi-Gen behaves worse than I did when I was younger simply because we are a generation apart. And I do think it is wrong if I were to treat my Multi-Gen student's expectations as the same as mine (or, worse, to *force* her to behave as if her motivations and expectations mirror my own 25 years ago). Her, and my, expectations form the terms of the

20 Deech (n 1) 6.

21 Adam Lella, 'Why are millenials So Mobile?', <https://www.comscore.com/Insights/Blog/Why-Are-Millennials-So-Mobile> accessed 14 July 2014.

22 I have just received an email revealing that the internet has overtaken personal referrals when people need to find a solicitor: <http://www.legalfutures.co.uk/latest-news/internet-overtakes-friends-family-main-way-find-solicitor> accessed 18 July 2014.

psychological contract and hence are directly and psychologically linked to her likely well-being,[23] motivation[24] and resilience.

So what does she expect of higher education after having completed her primary and secondary stages in the second millennium AD? What does she *expect* in particular about, say, attendance at lectures (an issue raised by Professor Deech). Students can and do expect to learn on a digital platform. Why are we channelling information in a half-filled lecture hall at 9am when our student wants to be (and perhaps is) asleep? Why, when we can easily migrate this information-channelling online so she can learn at midnight when she is wide awake?[25] My exemplar student retrieves digital information with ease. She is confident about learning online. The law school she needs, now, for her future, recognises that students can get high quality, freely available and easily accessible knowledge online 24/7/365:

> 'The analytical and doctrinal training law schools have emphasized for more than a century is precisely the legal training that *is most amenable to being taught over the Internet.*'[26]

Therefore the assertion that the university is best placed 'to hand on the lessons learned in earlier generations and the wisdom of the faculty to a new generation'[27] in an era of democratised, online, freely available knowledge in fact renders the university obsolete, if it were true. It is, I am delighted to report, not. What the university is best placed to provide is the forum for the development of high-level intellectual academic skills and that is what the Multi-Gen student expects.

The knowledge vs. skills distinction

There is a common complaint among my peers that young people do not know as much as we did when we were young. I disagree; it is not about quantity of knowledge but quality. Young people certainly do know lots of stuff, and they know lots of stuff that I do not know, and what worries me is whether all the stuff that I know, and that they do not know, they can learn online. I would be

23 To access a very detailed reference list for this, see <http://www.tjmf.org.au/wellness-network/wellness-network-resources/> accessed 30 July 2014.

24 Graham Ferris and Rebecca Huxley-Binns, 'What students care about and why we should care' in Caroline Maughan and Paul Maharg (eds), *Affect and Legal Education* (Ashgate, 2011); Rebecca Huxley-Binns and Graham Ferris, 'Putting theory into practice: designing a curriculum according to self-determination theory' (2013) 19(3) *International Journal of Pedagogy and Curriculum* 1; Graham Ferris and Rebecca Huxley-Binns, 'Escaping the wasteland: the multiple needs for explicit incorporation of values into the core curriculum of contemporary legal education' (2010) 3(1) *World Universities Journal* 63.

25 Professor Robert Beichner features in the University of Portsmouth video, now at <https://www.youtube.com/watch?v=jeLV6ZSwAGk#t=402> accessed 18 July 2014.

26 Michael R Pistone and John J Hoeffner, 'No Path but One: Law School Survival in an Age of Disruptive Technology' (2013) 2014–1007 Villanova University School of Law Public Law and Legal Theory Working Paper 195, 200. Emphasis added.

27 Deech (n 1).

right to be worried if all that I know is just *knowledge*, which is reasonably easy to learn.[28] It is a great comfort to see that the *Oxford English Dictionary*'s definition of knowledge includes a reference to skills and practical understanding:

> 'Facts, information, *and skills* acquired through experience or education; the theoretical or *practical understanding* of a subject' (emphasis added)

I have an opportunity to clarify here what might cause you, my reader, some concerns. What do I mean by 'skills' or 'practice' of law? Undergraduate law students in England and Wales may not become professionally qualified or regulated to provide legal services; they may in fact intend never to become so qualified from the start of their undergraduate studies, but what they do want is to read *law* as a discipline. To distinguish legal knowledge from legal skills seems, at best, an exercise in futility. Law exists both in the textbooks and in the world. Law is neither purely theoretical nor purely practical; it is intellectual and analytical, and it is knowledge-based and it has unique and subject-specific skills and practices, involving socio- and politico-legal concepts, as well as the allocation and exercise of power, and the use of language. Knowledge is more meaningful when contextualised, and the context of the law is legal practice, so there is nothing wrong in enhancing the law student experience by making legal doctrine applicable to legal practice. Undergraduate legal learning must be supportive of student expectations, so it needs to be dynamic because the law is; it needs to be active and not passive to make for a better experience for all, and embed skills *as much as* doctrinal knowledge. The purpose of higher legal education is to produce graduates who can think at a very high level, solve complex problems with legal solutions and make a full contribution to society. And because 'the future belongs to those who can work best with machines, not to those who can work best without them'[29] we, as providers, need 'enormous effort and creativity',[30] imagination[31] and a commitment to change because we need to blend technology into the legal learning processes of our multi-generational students to equip them with life-long legal skills and knowledge.

I do not deny that there *are* different levels and types of skills, as there are different levels and types of knowledge. Aristotle distinguished theory from action from practice[32] and it might be said that valid parallels can be drawn from theory

28 I am making an assumption here about abilities to learn legal information, even complex information, and I am comfortable in that assumption given that the context is higher legal education and students will have been admitted based on their ability to date to learn.

29 Pistone and Hoeffner (n 26) 264. See also David Thomson, *Law School 2.0, Legal education for the Digital Age* (LexisNexis2009)

30 Pistone and Hoeffner (n 26) 204.

31 Sarah Glassmeyer, 'Changing the Law School Curriculum' (2014), <http://sarahglassmeyer.com/?p=1255> (accessed 18 September 2015), cited in Paul Maharg, 'Research Skills: a failure of imagination' (2014), <http://paulmaharg.com/2014/03/01/research-skills-a-failure-of-imagination/> (accessed 18 September 2015).

32 Aristotle, *The Nicomachean Ethics of Aristotle* (David Ross trans, CreateSpace Independent Publishing Platform, 2009).

to knowledge, and from action to application and thence practice to skill. This article need not rehearse the debates[33] but the context is well known:

> 'It has long been common in academia to look down on "practice", carrying forward the Aristotelian preference for the intellectual life (and associated forms of declarative, written knowledge) to which academics commit themselves. Much like the blind men and the elephant, however, some academics have been blind to the multiple dimensions of these concepts or assumed in error that the terms employed refer to similar things.'[34]

Therefore, it is neither accepted nor supported that the true purpose of a university is to transmit knowledge *as distinct from* skills.[35] Knowledge as distinct from skills is a false and unhelpful dichotomy which cannot, I suggest, reflect law student expectations. That said, it is true to say there *are* valid concerns across the legal academy that the undergraduate law degree, with which this article is concerned, could indeed be 'dumbed down' if the 'wrong sorts' of skills are taught. For example if the undergraduate law degree included instruction on how to complete conveyancing forms, or box-ticking exercises linked to some of the more mundane transactional bureaucracy, which may certainly be associated with some 'law jobs',[36] these evidently and emphatically do not have a place on any undergraduate degree which is, and has to be seen internationally to be, a *intellectual* qualification.[37]

And even if the law degree is to a larger extent about legal knowledge and to a lesser extent about skills, *the way we regard, and handle, knowledge has evolved since 2009*:

> 'Traditionally, universities held the key to knowledge, in both a physical and philosophical sense . . . Now knowledge is open to anyone globally with a device and connectivity – not just facts and figures, but also analysis, interpretation and curation of knowledge.'[38]

33 Paul Maharg, *Transforming legal education: learning and teaching the law in the early twenty-first century* (Ashgate, 2007), 153.

34 Judith Welch-Wegner, 'Symposium 2009: A legal education prospectus: law schools & emerging frontiers. Reframing legal education's "wicked problems"' (2009) 61:4 *Rutgers Law Review* 868, <http://lawreview.newark.rutgers.edu/vol61n4/Wegner_v61n4.pdf> accessed 29 July 2014. In her context the theory/practice distinction could be said to have a similar lexicon as on this side of the pond re the knowledge/skills distinction.

35 Julian Webb, Jane Ching, Paul Maharg and Avrom Sherr, 'Setting Standards, The Future of Legal Services Education and Training Regulation in England and Wales' (2013) *The Legal Education and Training Review*. See also Rebecca Huxley-Binns, 'Teaching in the disciplines: Law' in Marshall et al (eds), *Handbook on Teaching and Learning in Higher Education* (Routledge, 2014).

36 Richard Susskind, *The End of Lawyers? Rethinking the Nature of Legal Services* (Oxford University Press, 2009).

37 Jessica Guth and Chris Ashford, 'The Legal Education and Training Review: regulating socio-legal and liberal legal education?' (2014) 48:1 *The Law Teacher* 5.

38 Ernst and Young Australia, 'University of the future. A thousand year old industry on the cusp of profound change' (2012), <http://www.ey.com/Publication/vwLUAssets/University_of_the_future/$FILE/University_of_the_Future_2012.pdf> 7 accessed 29 July 2014.

Technology has disrupted knowledge delivery entirely,[39] but will not, it is asserted, 'cause the disappearance of the campus-based university'.[40] Indeed, those universities that seize the day today are 'uniquely positioned to bring credibility'[41] to that content. How? Contact time needs to be fully utilised so that it adds a unique dimension to the student experience. Given my exemplar student's ability to retrieve online information, what she needs, and gains great value from, are face-to-face classes which (at least) show her how critically to assess that information[42] and discern its credibility and provenance.[43] Should this comment be taken out of context, I am not asserting that face-to-face classes should be no more than a forum for students to develop critical thinking, but that should certainly be *part* of our teaching. Once as much material as possible for the content delivery is online (not all centres will create their own; it will be freely available and global and high quality; and we should use each others), value will be created above and beyond pure knowledge:

> 'In brief . . . law school must move the regulated norm . . . to a place where online schools cannot follow, by mandating the extensive teaching of skills that require, to be taught effectively, face-to-face, in-person interactions.'[44]

The law school's priority, both to survive the technological revolution and to provide law students with the education they deserve, and expect, must therefore involve increasing the amount, availability and value of experiential legal learning.[45] This can be, for example, though flipped learning,[46] clinic,[47] simulation[48]

39 Pistone and Hoeffner (n 26) 195.
40 Ernst and Young (n 38) 9.
41 Ibid., 21.
42 S Livingstone, 'Taking Risky Opportunities on youthful content creation. Teenagers' use of social networking sites for intimacy, privacy and self-expression'(2008) 10(3) *New Media and Society* 383.
43 Be honest, would you despair if a student cited Wikipedia? Yes? What if a Justice of the Supreme Court did? How about the President of the Supreme Court? See <http://www.supremecourt.uk/docs/speech-140212.pdf> accessed 20 July 2014, fn 28.
44 Pistone and Hoeffner (n 26) 202.
45 D A Kolb, *Experiential Learning* (Prentice Hall, 1984); D A Kolb and R Fry, 'Toward an applied theory of experiential learning' in C. Cooper (ed.), *Theories of Group Process* (Wiley, 1975); Sally Kift, 'Lawyering skills: Finding their place in legal education' (1997) 8 *Legal Education Review*, 43.
46 Jonathan Bergmann and Aaron Sams, *Flipped Learning: Gateway to Student Engagement* (International Society for Technology in Education, 2014); Isabella Wallace and Leah Kirkman, *Talk-Less Teaching: Practice, Participation and Progress* (Crown House Publishing, 2014).
47 Hugh Brayne, Nigel Duncan and Richard H Grimes, *Clinical Legal Education: Active Learning in Your Law School* (Blackstone Press, 1998); Kevin Kerrigan and Victoria Murray (eds), *A Student Guide to Clinical Legal Education and Pro Bono* (Palgrave Macmillan, 2011).
48 Caroline Strevens, Richard Grimes and Edward Phillips, *Legal Education: Simulation in Theory and Practice* (Ashgate, 2014).

and/or problem-based learning opportunities.[49] It is unhelpful to continue to regard these as fringe, or extra curricular activities. We must employ our legal educational expertise to design curricular activities to facilitate student development of law-specific and general transferable graduate skills and knowledge, so that students can show that they are able to think critically, work collaboratively, and be independent and true global citizens. Moving knowledge content online gives us the opportunity I suggest we need to enhance the face-to-face, contact time, to build these activities into the classroom more effectively to make for a better learning experience. This is what makes the university unique in the 21st century and as we survive the democratisation of knowledge. This is our new raison d'être.

Conclusion

It is a time of unsettled higher education but that unsettling provides unprecedented opportunities;[50] opportunities to design legal curricula in light of the psychological contract with a new generation of students with a new set of experiences and expectations, and one in which we recognise and respect student expectations, experiences and choices. Professor Deech rightly placed the student in the centre of the university experience,[51] and also in the broader context of society, parents, other students, the university teachers, employers, the government and so on, and discussed student expectations in terms of value for money, as well as rights and responsibilities. My focus on the purpose of legal education for the Multi-Gen student has not, I hope, suggested that we can or should ignore the *role* of the law student in her learning process; but rather, with genuine respect, recast the student as an active party, contributing to her own educational experience.

Professor Deech explained that higher education is unique – its experience, its parties, the nature of the events contained therein, its unpredictability, its outcomes, its importance, individually and for the public good.[52] She acknowledged the limitations of the legal contract, noting that contracts do not add accountability for decisions about *what* type of education is provided.[53] I hope that in some way I have been able to add to the debate by broadening the discussion to encompass the psychological contract and by casting a wider net on what our students' expectations might be. We teach better if we understand, appreciate and empathise with the fact that students learn differently to how we did (and perhaps still do).

49 Cath Sylvester, Jonny Hall and Elaine Hall, 'Problem-based learning and clinical legal education: What can clinical educators learn from PBL?' [2004] *Journal of Clinical Legal Education* 39; F Martin, 'Using a modified problem based learning approach to motivate and enhance student learning of taxation law' (2003) 37(1) *The Law Teacher* 55; G A Moens, 'The Mysteries of Problem-Based Learning: Combining Enthusiasm and Excellence' (2007) 38(2) *The University of Toledo Law Review* 623–32; Karen Barton, Patricia McKellar and Paul Maharg, 'Authentic Fictions: Simulation, Professionalism, and Legal Learning' (2007) 14 *Clinical Law Review* 143.

50 Ibid.

51 Deech (n 1) 4.

52 Ibid., 10.

53 Ibid., 12.

15 Sixth Lord Upjohn Lecture 1977

The Law as Taught and the Law as Practised*

Hon. Sir Robert Goff

Every age is given a label – the age of reason or enlightenment, the age of darkness or the age of revolution. For those of us interested in the training of lawyers – this is the age of the law graduate.

My researches lead me to believe that in 1939 there were law faculties in not more than 17 universities in England and Wales. There are now 58 faculties of law at the universities and polytechnics in this country. The Society of Public Teachers of Law has now 970 members, and the Association of Law Teachers has a membership of 720. You thrust into the world, polished and labelled, some 3,300 law graduates each year. There is no sign yet of this flood abating. Many of these young men and women come to the legal profession. I cannot speak for the solicitors; but there come to the Bar's vocational course each year about 650 intending practitioners, of whom at present 550 (let us say 85%) are graduates, and over 400 (let us say 65%) are law graduates.

The system of local education authority grants encourages them to read law; if they choose first to read some other subject, they are unlikely to obtain a grant then to read law. Is it a bad thing, this preponderance of law graduates now entering the legal profession? Many of the older generation believe it to be so. How often have we all suffered from the distinguished practitioner – judge, Queen's Counsel, or senior partner in some prosperous firm of solicitors – who visits the law faculty and who, after judging a moot and delivering a witty judgment in flat contradiction of what we have taught our pupils, or giving a talk in which he explains, with equal wit, that everything they are learning is quite useless – then chats in a fatherly way to the students and tells them that they should not be reading law at all, they should be doing what he did – immersing themselves in some liberal subject such as philosophy, history or English literature, or even studying those languages long since dead whose study is itself now perhaps dying.

They tend to regard only what is lost, and to overlook what is gained, by the academic study of the law. Moreover, when they make any comparison, it is usually a comparison between, on the one hand, three or four years' rich grazing in the lush pastures of academe, and on the other a few months' rapid and arduous

* This lecture was delivered as the sixth Lord Upjohn Lecture at King's College, University of London on 14 January 1977.

cramming for a professional examination. Even so, what is a university? What is a liberal subject? Is mathematics or any one of the sciences a liberal subject? If they are not, is the study of a liberal subject a necessary diet for great lawyers? The most famous lawyer of our age read mathematics, one of our most distinguished law lords read chemistry, and our principal judge never darkened the doors of a university. Yet law is the very skeleton of civilisation. Without laws there would be no civilisation at all; without laws, there would be no visual arts, only anarchy and darkness.

I do not wish it to be thought for one moment that I am decrying other studies than law. In an ideal world, where time did not press, money was no object, and education could be pursued at leisure, it would no doubt be desirable for all lawyers to treat the academic study of the law as a second degree study. This is not possible nowadays; but the Bar at least will always welcome non-law graduates, even as a comparatively small proportion of their new recruits. As a matter of history, few of our greatest lawyers studied law academically. What is so interesting about their achievement is not only their astonishing skill as lawyers, but their awareness of the desirability to adapt the law, as a living institution, to the needs of their times. It was not unusual for the judges of that generation to have been members of Parliament. Men like these did not study law academically, though when Richard Bethell, later Lord Westbury, founded the Council of Legal Education in 1852, when the study of common law in our universities was still in its infancy, he was seeing to it that others should begin to do so. My suggestion is that a law degree is an excellent, but certainly not the sole, academic qualification for the profession of the law.

Properly taught, law can be one of the most admirable of all subjects. Borrowing Jane Austen's phrase from a very different context, I do not consider that the contrary opinion deserves the compliment of rational opposition. Students of the law can, and should, work with the primary sources of their subject, the statutes and reported judgments of the Courts. Another basic virtue is that law is in itself a discipline. Sloppiness of thought is incompatible with true lawyerly qualities. No case can be properly understood without knowledge of the precise facts, and identification of the true basis of the decision reached on those facts; and no written work is acceptable which attempts to cloak inadequate study or slipshod reasoning with the exercise of the essayist's literary skill. They can develop a style more concise and appropriate for a lawyer's written work – an invaluable attribute, not only in the profession of the law, but also in industry, commerce and government. The law is the most disputatious of all subjects, and what better place for the study of an argumentative subject than an academic institution?

However, the study of the law is, or should be, not merely concerned with knowledge of the statutes and cases, important though this is; it is concerned with the identification and critical study of the principles which underlie the primary sources, and of the concepts employed in the formulation of those principles. It therefore encourages abstract reasoning, but always stimulated by actual decisions based upon events which have occurred in real life. This type of study involves both analysis and the making of value judgments which in time, with knowledge and experience, will enable the student of the law to learn how to practise the craft which Lord Coke, in his celebrated answer to King James I, described as the 'artificial reasoning of the common law'.

Last but not least, the student should be encouraged to study the principles of the law in their context, and to consider critically whether they are apt to meet the needs of society today. It is in this last element that, I think you may agree, the most striking and fundamental change has taken place in the teaching of law in this country over the past few years. In my day, as student and teacher, the emphasis was all on analysis; law was not regarded as a social science. Nowadays, in many law schools the emphasis is very much the other way. This is undoubtedly a healthy and overdue development.

In the end, those who are responsible for schools of law have to decide how to find a balance between these three elements – knowledge, analysis and the social context. The true identity of the law school will to a large extent depend upon the syllabus, not only on the choice of subjects, but upon their content and the chosen method of teaching. Knowledge there must always be; but the pendulum of fashion seems to swing between analytical and sociological jurisprudence. Each has its value, and I trust that the pendulum will not be allowed to swing too far either way. We must not forget that the techniques of analysis form an essential part of every lawyer's equipment. But this raises the whole question of the relationship between law as taught and law as practised. One of the most fundamental points is that whereas in the law schools it is the law which is all important, in practice it is the facts.

First, the substance of the law is studied through the medium of actual decided cases or hypothetical factual situations. This has the result that, in our law schools, the facts are never in doubt; they are conveniently summarised. The discussion is about the application of the law to those facts. How should the statute be interpreted? What do the cases decide? The merits of alternative solutions are weighed and tested, analytically and sociologically. The law is nearly always in doubt; even if it is not in doubt, it is usually subjected to criticism.

How different it is in practice. There, in most cases, the law is reasonably clear, or at least is believed to be so. The real dispute – in the solicitor's office, in counsel's chambers, even in court – is about the facts. The work itself is largely about facts – collating documents, taking statements, advising on and gathering evidence, sifting material, examination and cross-examination of witnesses, and so on.

At law schools facts are studied in a given legal context. In the broadest sense, the student knows that he is faced with a problem, say, in the law of tort; in the narrowest sense, he knows that he is concerned with the effect of a particular legal decision, or of a particular statutory provision. The parameters are defined. In practice, of course, it is quite different. The court, still more the barrister, and still more even the solicitor, is presented with an undigested and often incomplete mass of facts and documents in which the relevant and irrelevant are intertwined. Indeed, until the legal context has been identified, it is impossible to begin to judge what is relevant; and one case can raise more than one legal problem, so may have more than one legal context.

In most cases in practice, as I have said, the law is reasonably clear. But when it is not clear, what are the techniques to be applied? Here, I believe that there are subtle differences between the law schools and the profession. The law schools are at the same time both more and less venturesome than the profession. They are more venturesome in that, rightly, they spread their net more widely and more speculatively than do those in practice. The law teacher is at liberty to reject and sweep aside as unsatisfactory the decisions of even appellate courts. The practitioner seldom does this; the decisions of the appellate courts are his navigating lights, and moreover he knows from experience that they are seldom extinguished even by those who have the power to pull the switch. The interrelation between law and fact is something which is widely understood by the legal profession. The degree of consensus is remarkably high; the existence of a small Bar, whom all solicitors may consult, has perhaps something to do with this. Indeed, it can be argued that, in matters of doubt, the law is quite simply what the profession at any particular time believes it to be.

Let me turn to another fundamental distinction between law as taught and law as practised. In practice, the lawyer's vision and understanding of the law is controlled by the needs of his clients. In the law schools there is no such limit: the controlling factors are far wider – the length of the course, the nature of the syllabus, the skill and imagination of the teacher, the ethos of the particular school of law. The difference is profound. Practising lawyers frequently acquire a very high standard of expertise in the areas of the law with which they are familiar. Their knowledge and grasp of the law within their own specialisations is often of a very high calibre indeed; in this sense, the standards of scholarship in the Temple and Lincoln's Inn are often higher than in the academic world. Second, through constant contact with their clients and their clients' problems, they acquire a very real understanding of the factual context within which they work, and of the way the law operates within that factual context.

It is remarkable how much the views of practising lawyers are coloured by their own work – by the nature of their own practices. It is remarkable, too, how little those who work in one field of expertise know about what goes on in other fields. In the case of barristers, the Chancery barrister for example knows little or nothing about one of the most important areas of the law – the criminal jurisdiction. The specialists all work in worlds of their own. In the law schools, it is exactly the opposite – and, may I hasten to add, this is as it should be. It is at his law school that a student can look at a topic as a whole, and learn how the various pieces of the jigsaw puzzle fit together to build up the whole picture. Looking at the picture not from the limited view of the practitioner, but as a whole, the student can be encouraged to ask more fundamental questions about the law. Viewed from that position, the institutions of the law themselves can be critically examined, and questions asked whether they are sufficient or effective in modern society, and whether the old techniques are capable of adapting themselves in a period of rapid change. In an age when anarchy is becoming almost respectable, and when stories of corruption in high places leap from the pages of our newspapers, the study of the very nature and function of law assumes a particular relevance. The two greatest influences which the teachers of law can exercise over the practising lawyer are in the writing of textbooks, and in the teaching of future practitioners. In both, the standard since the war has been, at its best, remarkably high. Other modes of influence can be overestimated; for example, I do not think that many practitioners read the law reviews.

One question I find myself being asked, by teachers and students alike, is this: do I think that law as taught in academic institutions is sufficiently practical? I respect the independence of law faculties. Every law school has to find its own identity, just as every human being has to discover his or her own personality. Of course, at the heart of all law teaching there has to be certain fundamental knowledge which, as is said in the Ormrod Report, every lawyer has to possess before he can call himself a lawyer. If law degrees are to provide the academic stage for professional training, that fundamental knowledge has to be identified, though it may be changed from time to time as society changes. But there has to be a selection, and although I realise that the present selection of core subjects has been criticised, I believe that it commands at this point of time a reasonable degree of consensus. But, subject to providing that basic fundamental knowledge, every law school should be free to design its syllabus as it believes to be best.

What is meant by the word practical? You, who teach at polytechnics, must have a fundamental belief that your teaching should be practical in its purpose. But it does not follow that you should burden your academic courses with teaching the techniques of a practising lawyer. If law as taught in our universities and polytechnics is to be regarded as an admirable academic subject, then the study of law at our academic institutions must surely not be allowed to develop into a study of professional techniques. In this context, may I remind you that the Bar already has its own vocational course, now nearly eight years old and going very strong: and that the Law Society is preparing to set up its own vocational course, which it hopes to bring into being in 1980. The very existence of these courses enables the teaching institutions, who provide the academic stage for lawyers' training, to exclude from the academic stage the training which can safely be left to the vocational stage.

What I would like to share with you is the experience of the Inns of Court School of Law in running the vocational courses for Bar students in this country. There is no question of the vocational course being in any way a substitute for pupillage – it is pre-pupillage training. The Inns of Court School of Law is in fact the main pioneer of vocational training in this country. In the first year of our course, 1970–71, which occurred shortly before the publication of the Ormrod Report, we provided practical exercises for about 50 students. In the next year, the number was 550. Since then we have provided practical exercises for about 600–50 intending practitioners each year, sharing the straight teaching with the College of Law. Our experience in providing practical training has been made freely available to enquirers from overseas, as have copies of the materials used in our training programme. The School has enjoyed particularly fruitful relations with Osgoode Hall, the Nigerian Law School and the profession in Australia; visits have been paid to the School by teachers, officials and judges from

Nigeria, Ceylon, West Indies, Bangladesh, New Zealand, South Africa, Scotland and Northern Ireland to learn about our programme. Over the last six or seven years, there has been a large number of visits by American lawyers and teachers, either as personally interested individuals, or on research missions, to encourage interest in similar forms of practical training there.

We are very conscious that there is room for improvement in our course. Indeed we regard it as being in a continuous state of development. But you must forgive our pride in what has been achieved so far. This is the work, not only of the Dean and his staff, but of distinguished academic lawyers and of hundreds of practitioners who have assisted in the work of the School. I would like, therefore, to take this opportunity to share our experience with you.

The first lesson is that we have become increasingly convinced of the desirability of involving practitioners in the course. We have received very strong indications that the students greatly appreciate contact with practitioners in the more practical parts of the course. First, they conduct the forensic exercises in advocacy (both the demonstrations and the individual practices), and the chambers exercises in drafting; second, they provide lectures on the more practical subjects – such as procedure.

The second lesson is, however, that, if you employ practitioners on your course, this throws a great burden on the administration. Obviously they cannot be continuously involved in the work of the School; on those who run the School falls the burden of preparation of teaching materials (which, in a practical course, is very considerable), and of developing teaching methods. You will appreciate that there are as yet no books available for use in teaching practical techniques. Moreover, there is a built-in risk of a practitioner failing to materialise on the day, due to sudden professional commitments or pressure of work, but we believe that the risk is a price worth paying for the benefit which we receive from the involvement of practitioners in the work of the School.

The third lesson is that there is every difference in the world between running a course for 50 students, and running a course for 650 students. The difference is not merely one of degree, but of kind, because the scale of the operation is so large.

The fourth lesson is that the length and style of the course is inevitably controlled by financial considerations. Not all our students are in receipt of grants, and we are very cost-conscious. The present fee for the vocational course at the School is £395, the course running from October to May. You may wish to compare that figure with the average cost of tuition at a polytechnic, which on the latest official information is £1,750 per student per annum. In view of the threat to discretionary grants we are thankful that we have kept our fees so low, though they are bound to rise. I would like to point out that if one wants to indulge in more elaborate forms of vocational training, such as intensive exercises or 'war games' in small groups, the teacher/student ratio can rapidly rise to such an extent that, quite apart from the problem of recruitment of teachers, the cost can easily become excessively high.

The fifth lesson is that, if you are running a vocational course which leads to a qualification to practise, it is impossible to limit the course to pure training in professional techniques. We believe it necessary to include in our vocational course not merely training in advocacy and drafting, but also problem classes in which student participation is encouraged and which introduce students to matters such as relevance and the identification of legal problems. We try to make the examinations as much orientated to practice as possible; it enables students to acquire a practical knowledge of certain subjects which may be of use to them in the early years of practice.

The sixth lesson is that, if a course is to be limited (as ours at present is) to a period from October to May, it is very intensive, both for students and teachers. It is certainly possible that it will be lengthened – possibly by further practical training after the examination has been taken.

The seventh lesson is that I cannot see how it would be practicable to run combined vocational courses for barrister and solicitor students. Their practical work is so very different that, on a combined course, both groups of students would be subjected to much extra useless teaching with a corresponding waste of time and increase in cost. Obviously, it is desirable that each should learn about the other's profession; but to train them all in the professional techniques of both professions would be absurdly wasteful.

There is much more to be said about vocational training. The existence of these courses should provide not merely valuable training for future practitioners, but a liberating factor for the academic stage. The academic stage and the vocational stage can become truly complementary, each deriving benefit from the different type of training which the other provides. With vocational training providing a bridge between learning law at the law school and practising law in the profession, the differences between law as taught and law as practised become not merely facts we must live with, but desirable in themselves. The students that are coming forward to us now are of a very high calibre indeed. We look forward in the future to close and harmonious co-operation with you in this most rewarding field of legal education.

16 Response: How Well Are We Moving Forward in the Teaching v Practice Debate in Law?

Susan Blake

In 1977 Lord Goff provided a very interesting overview of key issues in how the academic study of law and training for legal professional practice were developing, and how they inter-related. He was well placed to do this, being a senior judge with wide experience of practice, but also having some experience of teaching law, and being at that time the Chairman of the Council of Legal Education. He was speaking at an interesting time, when the Ormrod Report (1971)[1] was being implemented. This Report had recommended the law degree as the standard mode of entry to the legal profession, with a one-year Common Professional Examination (CPE) (now the Graduate Diploma in Law (GDL)) for non-law graduates. It also recommended that a separate stage of vocational training be provided by The Law Society and the Council of Legal Education (now the Solicitors' Regulation Authority and the Bar Standards Board), with those bodies playing a role in the co-ordination of training and of qualifying examinations. The Council of Legal Education had at the time taken early steps in developing legal professional training for barristers.

Lord Goff was talking at a key time of change for both academic and vocational training in the light of the Ormrod Report. As that Report has formed the basis for legal education and training for the last generation his views on the situation as it began to be implemented are valuable, but he also put his observations into a wider context, looking back over 30 years to 1940, and looking forward with comments on areas of legal professional education and training that required further development.

This is an excellent time to review Lord Goff's comments, as we are now over 30 years on, with another generation of experience to reflect on. We are also at the point of another major reconsideration with the Legal Education and Training Review (LETR).[2] The wide canvas he took for his comments also enables us to compare legal education and training in the generation up to the 1970s, in the generation since then, and potentially for the generation to come. Has the

1 Ormrod Report, 1971, *Report of the Committee on Legal Education*, Cmnd. 4595, London: HMSO.
2 LETR, 2013, *Setting Standards: The future of legal services education and training in England and Wales*, http://letr.org.uk/ (accessed April 2015).

situation developed as Lord Goff envisaged? How far have issues he raised been addressed? What issues remain for the next generation? Are there new issues, or are the core issues for legal education and training in essence the same?

Some of Lord Goff's comments on the legal world in 1977 show strong signs of time passing, and perhaps cause a quick intake of breath – he refers to some 3,300 students graduating in law each year 'with no sign of the flood abating', and a Bar Professional Training Course costing £395, while a law degree cost £1,750 a year. In a generation the flood of law graduates each year has risen to exceed 20,000 a year, with Bar Professional Training Course fees reaching £17,000 in London, following the cost of a law degree at £9,000 a year.

In looking back to 1940, he provides an interesting insight into the level of change a generation can bring. Before the Second World War there were only 17 law faculties in England and Wales, and there were questions about the value of law as an academic discipline. Many of those who became successful lawyers and judges had not studied law, and indeed had not necessarily been to university, bringing experience of life and perhaps of politics to practice rather than structured academic study of law. There was no professional training save for pupillage for barristers or articles for solicitors. In 1977 Lord Goff notes ongoing debates about the value of a law degree, with arguments that the study of classics or history at undergraduate level was to be preferred, and doubts as to whether a science degree provided an appropriate liberal arts background. Nonetheless he sees 1977 as being part of the age of the law graduate as the study of law becomes generally respected.

Lord Goff provides a range of facts and figures, and it is interesting to note some of the changes from 1977 to now. The 58 law faculties he noted has risen to about 100, with the total of law degree providers nearing 140.[3] The 650 he noted as entering training for the Bar annually has risen to about 1,700 in 2011–12.[4] The membership of 970 in the Society of Public Teachers of Law (SPTL) has grown to about 2,900 in the Society of Legal Scholars.[5] Putting the figures into a more general context, within the last generation the number of law faculties has doubled while the number of undergraduate students starting a law degree has grown by a factor of 6 to over 20,000 a year.[6] The number of barristers practising in 2010 was over 15,000 (having grown by a factor of about 4)[7] and the number of solicitors with a practising certificate is now over 150,000 (having grown by a factor of over 6).[8] In 1977 about 65% of those training as barristers were law graduates, a figure which has, if anything, decreased, but which is not radically different.

3 See http://www.ucas.com (accessed 21 April 2015).

4 See https://www.barstandardsboard.org.uk/media-centre/research-and-statistics/statistics/bptc-statistics/ (accessed 21 April 2015).

5 See http://www.legalscholars.ac.uk/ (accessed 21 April 2015).

6 See http://www.hesa.ac.uk/ (accessed 21 April 2015).

7 See http://www.barcouncil.org.uk/about-the-bar/facts-and-figures/statistics/ (accessed 21 April 2015).

8 See http://www.lawsociety.org.uk/representation/research-trends/annual-statistical-reports/ (accessed 21 April 2015).

To some extent these figures suggest an apparently overall positive and relatively stable environment. Most figures have at least doubled, with the number of barristers and solicitors in practice growing substantially. In a very broad sense the size of the practising profession has grown proportionately in line with the number of law undergraduates, though of course in terms of actual numbers more individuals are completing a law degree and not entering the profession. The proportion of law graduates going on to qualify as lawyers is probably very broadly similar to what it was in the 1970s, with the majority choosing other careers for a range of positive reasons and with the range of potential careers following a law degree widening.

Lord Goff identifies a number of issues that have been a matter of ongoing development and debate. He strongly defends the value of a law degree, and of liberal arts study, and potentially of scientific study, which would continue to get widespread support today. He raises the interesting question of the overall focus of legal study, suggesting that in the generation up to 1977 it had moved from analytical to sociological. In the last generation it is arguable that the overall focus has shifted from sociological to business.

A further core matter is the overall relative roles of academic and practising lawyers. Lord Goff clearly draws the distinction, which would probably still get strong support, that academics tend to focus on the nature and content of law, whereas practitioners tend to focus on facts and real life situations. He views these two different approaches as complementary, but perhaps does not really unpack the issues this can present to a student moving from academic to practice-focused study, where the difference of approach is perhaps still not as well articulated or managed as it might be.

The role of professional training, which was in its early stages of development at the time Lord Goff was speaking, is examined as a third core issue. He provides a very constructive defence of the value of professional training as being separate from but complementary to academic training, providing a transition from study to practice. Lord Goff identifies issues in professional training that have remained matters of debate ever since, through the years of successful development of professional training for barristers and solicitors: the role of practitioners; the cost, length and style of courses; administrative complexities; and the size of cohorts. Since he spoke, more work on practical training for the Bar led to the development of the Bar Vocational Course in 1989, with practical training for solicitors following a few years later with the launch of the Legal Practice Course. He sees joint training as unrealistic, but that debate has rumbled on. He makes interesting comments on the extent to which legal professional training in this jurisdiction has been developed with some international collaboration, and has provided a model for other jurisdictions.

Having considered Lord Goff's main themes, it is interesting to consider how far developments over the last generation have been successful in the light of what he foresaw. Probably it can be said that he was right to label this as the age of the law graduate. The law degree has gone from strength to strength to become one of the more popular undergraduate subjects, and the quality of the study of and research into academic law within law faculties has flowered. The development of legal professional training has also been successful. The initial experiments with practical classes at the Inns of Court School of Law developed to become the Bar Vocational Course in 1989. A quarter of a century later that has been reviewed and modified, but the basic model proved robust. The Legal Practice Course followed, proving generally similarly successful. Interest from other jurisdictions, noted by Lord Goff, has continued. It is interesting to note that the Ormrod Report[9] included discussion of whether vocational training might be best placed within universities, and this has to a significant extent come to pass, with many universities offering Bar Professional Training Course and Legal Practice Course qualifications, the Inns of Court School of Law being incorporated in City University, London, and the College of Law becoming the University of Law with degree-awarding powers.

However, the clear division between the academic study of law and training for professional practice is different from the approach taken in some other jurisdictions, and it is not without tensions and some drawbacks. While the ideal is that academic and vocational study of law be complementary, the reality is that goals conflict. Just to give some examples, the need for academic lawyers to carry out research that meets research excellence framework (REF) requirements means that academics need to build an international reputation. This can pull them away from focusing on law within a single jurisdiction, with less research focusing on core law topics and common law. In contrast, as practitioners face funding difficulties and are having to develop ever more commercial business models, practice is if anything moving further from the study of academic law.

Despite these different pressures, shared interests between legal academics and legal practitioners could be more fully developed. Lord Goff makes the rather controversial statement that standards of scholarship in the Inns are often higher than in the academic world. Perhaps it would be more politic, and accurate, to say that standards are as high, but the approach to the detail of law is often different. Academic lawyers focus on writing for peer-reviewed journals, whereas a practitioner or judge will often use similar in-depth reading and analysis to develop an argument for the Court of Appeal or write a judgment. The need for accuracy and peer respect simply takes a slightly different form. The gulf between practitioners and academics is being bridged in various ways, and this is much to be welcomed and developed. Academic lawyers have become members of several sets of barristers' chambers, and significant use is being made of academic expertise to advance practice, for example in the background work to the Review of Civil Litigation Costs carried out by Lord Justice Jackson.[10]

However, some of the key issues touched on by Lord Goff have not been fully addressed, and others have arisen from the developments he foresaw. He touched

9 Ormrod (n. 1).

10 Lord Justice Jackson, *Review of Civil Litigation Costs: Final Report 2010*, http://www.judiciary.gov.uk/publications/review-of-civil-litigation-costs/ (accessed 3 July 2015).

on the swing in the 1970s to a sociological approach to law. He did not expand on this point, but it is undoubtedly right that there was a trend to courses looking at law in the context of its value to society, including areas like human rights.[11] The pendulum has now swung away with the focus now arguably on commercial law, with a financial rather than sociological focus. But Lord Goff also stressed the need for balance, and that can partly be seen in the growth of interest in pro bono work.

The question of funding for legal education and training, and problems with access to grants, was touched on by Lord Goff. This issue has proved to be timeless. Public funding is still only normally available for a first degree, and has moved from grant to loan based, which has implications for career development that have yet to be seen. Firms and Inns make significant sums available for vocational training but many students still need to fund professional training privately or borrow from a bank. There is growing concern that real access to the profession for students from a wide range of backgrounds is being limited, with decreasing numbers of pupillages and training contracts that tend to go to those with good degrees from Oxbridge and Russell Group universities. While academic excellence is important for practice, this has the effect of homogenising the range of legal practitioners, with many areas of society not being able to find legal representatives who have real insight into their lives. This remains an issue for another generation to wrestle with.

There are also questions round the role of 'core law' that must be studied in a qualifying law degree or a Graduate Diploma in Law. Lord Goff stressed the importance of law faculties developing various models and identities, but query how far this has really happened. With the majority of the syllabus prescribed there is a limited role for the study of a wide range of options. Current proposals from the Solicitors Regulation Authority (SRA)[12] maintain detailed prescription of content that should be studied, but link this simply to the outcomes that entrants to the profession need to demonstrate at the point of qualification. They do not need to be a specific element of the qualifying LLB degree. There may be an argument that law faculties could in fact do rather more to create stronger independent identities for themselves, and hopefully this will happen over coming years.

Having considered the last generation of legal education and training in the light of Lord Goff's remarks, the next step is to look forward for another generation, to about 2040. Will progress be as coherent as it has been over the last 30 years? Will the issues remain largely the same? Whereas the base for Lord Goff's remarks was the Ormrod Report,[13] the base to work from now is the LETR.[14] We do not yet know what the outcome of that will be, but the Legal

11 This development is exemplified by the growth of the Socio-Legal Studies Association and its journal, *Law and Society*, http://www.slsa.ac.uk/ (accessed 17 April 2015).

12 The SRA response to its recent consultation is at http://www.sra.org.uk/sra/consultations/competence-statement.page (accessed 3 July 2015).

13 Ormrod (n. 1).

14 LETR (n. 2).

Services Board has prescribed a shift to an outcomes approach[15] rather than tight prescription for professional training. This will probably reduce the extent of prescription of law degree coverage, and some shift, for example, to include training in ethics. As implementation will be largely in the hands of the Bar Standards Board and the SRA it seems that the model of separate academic education and vocational training will remain as a base, with separate training for barristers and solicitors. That said, the work of barristers and solicitors is much closer than it was, with higher rights of audience allowing solicitors to advocate cases in court, and direct access to barristers available to clients in appropriate circumstances (with about a third of barristers now offering direct access services).[16] From January 2014 properly qualified barristers have been able to conduct litigation (though there are still limitations on them holding client funds).[17]

On the face of it, this could mean another generation with legal education and training developing on existing lines with relatively little real change. However, there are a number of 'buts'. While an outcomes approach may lessen prescription, there may be tighter and more centralised assessment to see if outcomes have been met. While the model may remain largely the same in outline, the demand for fully qualified barristers and solicitors may not grow any further, with access to the legal profession therefore quite restricted. While the model for education and training might still be roughly familiar in 2040, much may have changed in terms of numbers. The last generation has seen massive rises in the number of law faculties, undergraduate law students, the number of students seeking to train as barristers and solicitors, and in the size of the Bar and solicitor professions. Query if the size and number of law faculties has reached a high water mark. It is strongly arguable that limitations in funding for both civil and criminal work will at the very least halt the expansion in the number of qualified barristers and solicitors because, over the years to come, the money will not be there to fund chambers and firms in the way it has been over the last few decades, which will limit professional training. The rise in numbers over the last 30 years may at best stabilise, and potentially decrease.

However, it is necessary to look beyond the core topics that Lord Goff analysed so ably. The wider context within which the legal profession operates is likely to see far more change over the next generation than it has seen in the last generation. In 2040 there are still likely to be very successful chambers of specialist barristers, and some very successful firms of solicitors, but these may well form a much smaller part of the delivery of legal services than they do now. This will make the

15 Legal Services Board, 2013, *Increasing flexibility in legal education and training*, http://www.legalservicesboard.org.uk/what_we_do/consultations/open/pdf/20130918_consultation_paper_on_guidance_for_education_and_training_FINAL_for_publication.pdf (accessed 3 July 2015).

16 For the rules on direct access see *The Bar Standards Board Handbook 2015*, https://www.barstandardsboard.org.uk/regulatory-requirements/bsb-handbook/the-handbook-publication/ (accessed 21 April 2015).

17 See https://www.barstandardsboard.org.uk/regulatory-requirements/for-barristers/authorisation-to-conduct-litigation/ (accessed 21 April 2015).

demands on legal education and training very different. We have already seen the growth of the paralegal, focusing on a particular area of legal service rather than being generally professionally qualified,[18] and this is likely to be a trend that develops. Change is likely to be driven to a significant extent by forces beyond the universities and the traditional roles of the legal professional bodies, albeit that they have major opportunities for influencing and shaping development.

In a relatively short article one can only identify briefly the forces that are most likely to influence developments in legal education and training over the next generation. All the following are likely to impact substantially on the jobs that professional lawyers are doing, and what education and training therefore need to prepare them for.

1. The categories of 'reserved activities' that can only be done by qualified lawyers are actually very limited. Indeed, it is estimated that about 80% of the work done by lawyers does not fall within these categories. The categories are: rights of audience in court, the conduct of litigation, activities associated with probate, the administration of oaths, and dealing with certain reserved instruments (that is formal documents). Other activities like managing legal knowledge, dealing with processes like disclosure of evidence, and dealing with legal costs are already done by companies and by individuals who are not fully qualified as barristers or solicitors. In making legal processes more cost effective it is likely that more tasks traditionally done by fully qualified lawyers may be done in other ways, though there are also arguments that new areas of reserved activity should be identified.
2. The growing use of technology is automating many legal processes, changing the sort of work that providers of legal services do. Professor Richard Susskind covers this well in his book *Tomorrow's Lawyers*.[19] The use of e-disclosure has grown substantially, and court processes are increasingly being supported by technology, with developments such as online filing for court papers. Lord Justice Jackson called for more investment in this area to improve court processes in his Report, and this has been backed by other senior judges such as Lord Thomas.[20] An online portal has been expanded to conduct the early stages of most small accident claims online.[21] While the underlying principles of law and procedure will be traditional, people with a wider range of skills including IT, management etc. will be required to deal with such processes.
3. Since the Legal Services Act 2007 was implemented to allow the use of alternative business structures, legal services are being offered in new ways. At one end of the market, large insurance companies are setting up their own legal

18 See, for example, Amanda Hamilton, 2014, 'In an ever-changing legal landscape, paralegals are the way forward', 48(1) *Law Teacher* 104–13.

19 Richard Susskind, 2013, *Tomorrow's Lawyers*, Oxford, Oxford University Press.

20 'IT for the courts – creating a digital future', http://www.judiciary.gov.uk/announcements/it-for-the-courts-creating-a-digital-future/ (accessed 21 April 2015).

21 See http://www.claimsportal.org.uk/en/ (accessed 21 April 2015).

arms, for example the AA (AA Law Ltd) and Direct Line (DLG Legal Services Ltd).[22] At the other end of the market, an increasing range of barristers and solicitors are offering fixed price services direct to potential clients. The possibility of lawyers working directly with other professionals is also changing the range of services that can be offered. These are all changing the model for traditional legal services, with implications for the education and training for those interested in a career related to law. Business management and entrepreneurship will be important alongside academic legal knowledge.

4. Many concerns have been expressed with regard to the cuts in legal aid and the fact that public funding has been largely removed from civil cases. However strong the concerns in this area are, it is unlikely that any government will in future be able to invest the level of funds in litigation services there has been in the past. Indeed, it is clear that government policy favours the use of more cost-effective alternative dispute resolution (ADR) options and more standardisation for lower value cases with fixed costs. Higher value cases are increasingly being funded through conditional fee agreements, third party funding and damages-based agreements, where early assessment of the legal position and the potential chances of success is important. Again, while the basic traditional principles of law and models for procedure will continue to underlie what happens, the types of jobs there are in the legal services and what those doing the tasks will need to know will shift.
5. In civil practice, most cases have always settled before trial, usually through negotiation. There is now a growing focus on the use of ADR methods, such as mediation, which offer a number of potential benefits in terms of meeting client objectives and saving time and cost. Indeed, courts now expect parties to make reasonable use of ADR with a potential costs penalty where this is not done. Lord Neuberger has called ADR the sister of litigation, reflecting the fact that ADR should now be considered alongside litigation at all stages.[23] Traditional litigation will remain important, but many disputes will be settled in other ways.
6. While legal systems form separate jurisdictions, globalisation increasingly means that lawyers need to work beyond the education and training they have received in a specific jurisdiction. This used to be most important for high value commercial cases, but now it is often the case in family disputes, concerns over transactions completed online, and so on. Ways have to be found to work practically where the laws of different jurisdictions may be relevant to a relatively low value case. Principles of conflicts of laws remain important, but in practice they cannot necessarily be applied wherever they might be relevant.

22 See http://www.sra.org.uk/abs/ for examples (accessed 21 April 2015).

23 See http://www.innertemplelibrary.com/2010/05/equity-adr-arbitration-and-the-law-different-dimensions-of-justice-speech-by-lord-neuberger-of-abbotsbury/ (accessed 3 July 2015).

These points are not separate but cumulative. For example, disputes over goods bought online from someone based in another jurisdiction are increasingly resolved online using ADR – it is simply not cost effective to consider all the relevant legal and procedural details in more than one jurisdiction.

In conclusion, Lord Goff's speech provided a good analysis of where legal education and training was in 1977, with an interesting glance back over developments in the previous 30 years, useful insights into what was likely to happen, and identification of relevant issues. In looking back from 2015, much of what he says seems familiar and good progress has been made. Both legal education and research in universities, and legal professional training have developed substantially and strongly, albeit with a range of ongoing issues. However, some issues he identified have not yet been fully addressed and tensions remain, not least as regards access to the legal profession, and achieving the most productive relationships between academics and practitioners.

In looking forward to what is likely to happen within the next generation, the crystal ball is far from crystal clear. While the underlying structure for legal education and training is likely to remain broadly similar to what it is now for another generation, the context within which it operates is changing substantially. Many students will need knowledge and training appropriate for different ways of providing legal services, with different roles for those with legal expertise. The picture is not negative – there are many opportunities for universities, legal professional trainers and qualified lawyers to seize – but there are challenges, and future needs remain to be more fully identified and articulated.

What will this be the age of? We are moving on from the age of the law graduate . . . possibly to the age of the legal service provider?

17 Tenth Lord Upjohn Lecture 1980

Legal Education and the Needs of the Legal Profession*

Sir Frederick Lawton P.C.

As some of you may have inferred from my reported judgments, I had no legal education as these words are understood today. I started to read Law at Cambridge for Part II of the Law Tripos in October 1932, having in the previous two years read History. I took my examination in May 1933. Passing gave me no exemptions from the Bar examinations so I had to get up three new subjects, Roman Law, Criminal Law and Constitutional Law, for Part I of the Bar examinations. I had covered enough contract and tort in the Law Tripos to get me through these subjects without much extra work. I completed Part I by December 1933 and started on Part II in January 1934. I took and passed my Bar finals in May 1934, that is in about twenty months after starting the study of the law. Save whilst at Cambridge, I had had no tutorials and no opportunity of discussing legal problems with any knowledgeable person. Had I not overlooked the then essential qualification for call to the Bar, namely a digestion which could cope with 36 Inn dinners spread over three years, I could have been called in Trinity term 1934 and have accepted briefs the next day. The omission delayed my call for sixteen months. I spent part of that time working as a schoolmaster and part doing my Bar pupillage. Looking back, the time I spent as a schoolmaster was probably of more help to me than most of the lectures I attended at Cambridge. Trying to teach fourteen-year-old boys in the bottom stream is an excellent preparation for making submissions to a difficult judge who does not want to understand.

That I could have become a practising barrister after twenty months' study of the law and without any practical training was, of course, a scandal which had to be, and now has been, brought to an end. But the fact that I, and many others, were able to establish ourselves in practice without doing too much harm to our clients has led me to wonder whether the present system of legal education is not over-elaborate and a wasteful of time and money, nowadays mostly public money. In my early days I may have been a menace in the Courts – I shall never know. My first client, whom I unsuccessfully defended over three weeks for a long-firm fraud,

* This lecture was delivered as the tenth Lord Upjohn Lecture at the London School of Economics and Political Science on 7 November 1980.

stopped me in the Strand shortly after my appointment to the High Court Bench and said, 'I'm proud to have been your first client: I boast about it to my friends.' It must have been only too obvious to him that he was my first client. His assessment may, of course, have been made with hindsight; but I, and many like me, must have had something more than legal learning which satisfied the legal market. Was it a sound general education? Is this more important than legal learning?

You may be asking what would have become of me had I had a proper modern legal education. I can answer that question unhesitatingly – I would have become a law don.

Looking back over nearly fifty years I think I can see what the legal profession can reasonably expect of those wanting to join it. It claims to be a learned profession. Those who enter it should surely be men and women of learning, and not solely learned in the law. Its beginners should be able to write and speak good, clear English. They should be able to understand the true meaning of the written word. They should be able to untangle complicated and confusing facts; and when they have done so they should be able to identify and apply the relevant principles of law. Finally those who intend to practise in the worlds of finance and commerce, and probably of industry too, should be able to speak fluently at least one European language besides English. I doubt whether the law schools are doing as much as they could to meet these needs.

I will start, if I may, with the basic need of ensuring that candidates for entry into the legal profession have had a sound education. By a sound education I mean that their minds have been so trained and developed that they can assimilate new knowledge and appreciate the significance of facts and theories which are brought to their attention. Lawyers in practice have to do this every working day. A young barrister or solicitor who cannot cope in this way is of little use; he can be a menace. In my opinion school, not law school, is where the young should receive the basis of a sound education. Attempts at law school to remedy possible defects in school teaching by introducing into the syllabus such subjects as international relations, criminology and, dare I say it, public international law, are, in my opinion, a waste of time and energy. If a student has been well taught at school and has sufficient intelligence to practise the law, by the time he gets to law school he should have enough interest in what is happening around him to find out for himself what is going on. He will soon learn that public international law is what prominent politicians on the world's stage think it is, not what professors claim it is. In saying this, I have not overlooked that some who are keen on public international law as a subject in law courses consider that it puts before students an ideal of law which they may find inspiring. They are likely to find ideals for themselves without professorial help. What most of them will not find in practice are problems of public international law, so why take up time teaching it? I met my first problem after 42 years in the law, and when I did it was not difficult to solve, even though I had never been taught the beginning of that subject.

What concern me are the ways in which the law schools try to identify those who have had a sound education. I understand that most of you have a fixed standard of attainment in 'A' levels, say two Bs and a C in any subjects in the 'A' level examinations, which you supplement with head teachers' reports. Because of the great numbers involved you do not, because you cannot, interview prospective candidates for places. This kind of system assumes that all passes at 'A' level are of equal worth when choosing prospective practising lawyers. Are they? I doubt it.

You will probably all agree that being able to write and speak good, clear English is an essential working tool for a practising lawyer. Who is the more likely to have this tool, a candidate with passes at the requisite levels in English, French and Latin or one with passes in Economics, Geography and Music? In my opinion it is regrettable that law schools no longer regard a knowledge of Latin as part of a lawyer's essential intellectual equipment. Those who have had a good grounding in that language have an appreciation of the structure of language which English grammar does not give. Since much of a lawyer's work is concerned with the use of words and finding out what they mean when they have been used, the mental discipline which comes from learning Latin is invaluable in practice. Of all the school subjects which I was taught as a boy, Latin is by far the one I put to most use in my work as a judge.

I appreciate that we cannot change the English education system for the specific benefit of lawyers. It is probably too late now to get more children taught Latin in school; but what, I think, those who control admission to law schools could do is to give preference to candidates who have shown by their 'A' level results that they can use language.

Those of you who have to deal with admissions have to cope with the inadequacies of the English education system, the principal one being, from the practising lawyer's standpoint, over-specialisation at too early an age. In my opinion it is unsatisfactory that in most schools the brighter children have to decide at about fifteen – and if they are very bright when they are even younger – whether they are going to study the humanities or the sciences. After the choice has been made, contact is usually lost with the other disciplines. This may not have mattered much to the old-style solicitor whose work was mostly concerned with conveyancing and probate or with circuiteers in bygone times. Nowadays, however, most barristers and many solicitors have to deal with cases involving an understanding of scientific and technological problems. In solicitors' offices of any size office machinery based on the silicon chip has to be used. Those practitioners who do not understand how these machines work will probably be wasting time and money – and understanding how they work requires a knowledge of electricity and mechanics. The practitioners who are involved in litigation are likely to meet the need for some scientific and technological knowledge early in their careers. Those, for example, who practise in the criminal courts are likely to be faced by scientific evidence relating to trace elements, staining and blood-grouping which will have to be tested. Personal injury litigation requires the practitioner to have an elementary knowledge of anatomy and physiology. Law schools cannot be expected to give courses in forensic science and medicine; but what they could do would be to give preference to those candidates for admission who have acquired good 'O' level grades in at least two of the basic sciences.

So far I have commented upon requisites for practice over which the law schools have little direct control. I turn now to aspects of legal education which they do control and in respect of which there is a gap between what the student is taught and what the young practitioner needs. I have three criticisms to make: first, too much attention is paid to the finer points of law; second, teaching emphasis is placed on the wrong parts of the law; and third, too much stress is put upon case law and not enough upon principles. I will illustrate my first criticism by an example taken from the teaching of criminal law. It is a common practice, so I understand, to introduce students to substantive law by teaching criminal law. In the past it was thought that this subject was easy to grasp and likely to arouse interest. I have been told that present-day students find difficulty with it and that in some law schools there is a high failure rate.

Why should this be so? The reason lies, so it seems to me, in trying to spell out principles from a few cases, such as *Feely*, *Majewski*, *Hyam*, *Nock*, *Husseyn* and *Haughton v Smith*. With the exception of *Feely's* case all dealt with unusual circumstances. For example, save for *Majewski's* case, which I dealt with on appeal, I have never come across a case in which an accused was so drunk that he did not know what he was doing. I have had to deal with the *Nock* and *Husseyn* problems on appeal but never in practice or at first instance. I appreciate that as a matter of theory the criminal law should spell out in clear terms which acts are dishonest and which are not; but attempting to do so would produce a definition which would be difficult to explain to juries or to be grasped by magistrates. The *Feely* direction works in practice. I question the wisdom of risking confusing students by overemphasis on the half-dozen borderline cases about which opinions might differ as to what was and what was not dishonest.

My second criticism of teaching emphasis being placed upon the parts of the law which are seldom met in practice is illustrated by the way two subjects are taught – contract and the 'core' subject of constitutional and administrative law. Students always seem to spend a lot of time on the formation of contract, consideration and mistake but little on the discharge of contract and remedies, with which the practitioner is usually concerned. Occasionally problems arise as to whether there has been a contract and whether the parties were thinking of the same subject-matter; but in all my time in the law I have never met a problem about consideration. What matters in practice is whether the defaulting party was entitled to do, or omitted to do, what he did, or should have done, and if he was not, what remedies are available to the wronged party. I accept that the student should be given, and the practitioner should have, some knowledge of our Constitution – but not much more is required than any educated man should have. Constitutional points seldom arise in practice. I have met them twice, which was in the *Laker* and *Gouriet* cases. One retired Lord Justice told me after the latter case that he had never had a constitutional problem to solve. The young solicitor, however, is likely to meet administrative law problems soon after qualifying. The occupier of a semi-detached house or the owner of a small business may be having trouble with the local planning authority over a desired development. He will want advice about what can be done to get what he wants. A parent may be at odds with a local education authority about the choice of school for an eleven-year-old child. Familiarity with the theory of Cabinet responsibility, or even with the decision in *Stockdale v Hansard* will not be of much help to the young solicitor when advising his client in cases of this kind. It has been the experience of both the Council of Legal Education and the Law Society that many students starting their professional training lack sufficient knowledge of the fundamental principles of administrative law to deal with simple problems.

My last of these criticisms is the most fundamental of the three. I base it upon my experience, which is fairly wide, of judging moots. Those taking part always start their submissions with references to cases, not with the exposition of principles illustrated by cases. Many young barristers, and some not so young who ought to know better, do the same. I spend a lot of my judicial time discouraging the over-citation of cases, and so do many of my brethren. This forensic vice, which wastes court time and increases the cost of litigation, seems to be acquired in the law schools, probably as a result of lecturers trying to reconcile cases by pointing to subtle differences and failing to emphasise that cases have no use save as illustrating the existence and development of principle. The young practitioner appearing at first instance has to be able to apply principle to the facts which the judge is likely to find – and these facts may be very different from what he was instructed they were. If he cannot apply principle to changing circumstances he will not be helping his client – and the cases which he has looked at on the assumption that the facts would be found as he was instructed they were, will not help him.

During the past twenty-five years I have had the pleasurable and rewarding benefit of friendship and acquaintance with many law dons. One fact, however, has struck me. Most dons seem to be something like ten years out of date about what is going on in the legal profession. In the 1950s, for example, there was a tendency to discourage young men, and particularly young women, from coming to the Bar. Had they read the signs rightly they would have appreciated that young barristers were about to have a period of prosperity, the like of which had never been experienced before. This was due to the coming of legal aid in criminal cases. By the late 1960s news of this reached the law schools. Recruiting for the Bar increased but, alas, the good times were coming to an end and the problems of the young were greatly increased by the difficulty of finding chambers.

Something of the same kind is happening today. The world of the practitioner is no longer bounded by the Royal Courts of Justice and the Crown and County Courts. For both solicitors and barristers it has become the world. They are engaged in courts in the Far East, Africa and Luxembourg and in arbitrations in many countries – and not always where English is the language of communication. Ease of travel brings clients of all nationalities to solicitors' offices. In my opinion if British lawyers are to take advantage of the prestige which they enjoy they must be able to talk to their foreign clients in their own languages, which means that a knowledge of languages is likely to be an essential tool for lawyers practising in the worlds of commerce and finance and probably of industry too. How is this tool to be acquired? A start must be made in schools. The finishing touches must be given in law schools. In my opinion those students who have some aptitude for languages as evidenced by good grades in 'A' levels should be encouraged to further their knowledge of languages by being offered the kind of courses which are available at King's College, Strand, and Birmingham University. Further, arrangements should be made for them to have access to language laboratories. A student who has not acquired a working knowledge of languages before he leaves law school is unlikely to acquire it afterwards. Once in practice there will not be time.

You may have found my criticisms unjustified and my comments unfair. My intention has been to be constructive, not denigratory. From my own observations I am satisfied that law schools nowadays no longer try to equip their students to be trainee clerks in the Chancery of Edward I, as one don who taught me did. Nor do they spend their time expounding theories of law which were unsound anyway and of no practical use to anyone, as another of my mentors did. Most of your students who come into practice are a credit to their law schools. All I want to see is an even higher standard. The practice of the law is highly competitive. There is little room for the incompetent.

18 Response: The Needs of the Legal Profession and the Liberal Law School

(Re)negotiating Boundaries

Chris Ashford

Sir Frederick Lawton was a celebrated judge whose judgments continue to occupy contemporary law students. In delivering his 1980 Lord Upjohn Lecture, Lawton was to focus on what he regarded as the needs of the legal profession, and thus what was required from providers of legal education.

His criticisms – that some A-levels are 'worth' less than others, the deficiency in adequate written and oral skills amongst students and a lack of focus on foreign languages by the education system – remain familiar to contemporary observers of education debates. Similarly, his criticism of an 'out-of-touch' academia that needs to better connect with the legal profession goes to the heart of an ongoing debate about the role of the law school in education and training for the legal profession.[1]

His own story inevitably shaped not only his judgments but his perspective on legal education. He was the son of a prison governor, a grammar school boy, a Cambridge graduate and a former political activist.[2] He also served in the Second World War.

Called to the Bar in 1935, he went on to be appointed a Lord Justice of Appeal in 1972 and found himself in conflict with the Director of Public Prosecutions (DPP) over a bargain over the first so-called 'super grass', Bertie Smalls, as to whether he should be allowed to go free in return for evidence provided against his former colleagues. The DPP thought he could; Lawton thought otherwise. He took a similarly 'conservative' approach to criminal law when, as Chairman of the Criminal Law Revision Committee, he recommended the abolition of the right to silence.[3]

The *Telegraph* obituary of Lawton described him as a man who 'often acted as if he believed civilisation could not survive without the slap of firm justice'.[4] His

1 Oliver has argued that 'the true opposites are education and training. Training is no substitute for a liberal law degree': see: Oliver, D, 'Teaching and Learning Law: Pressures on the Liberal Law Degree', in Birks, P (ed.), *Reviewing Legal Education* (Oxford: Oxford University Press, 1994) 86.

2 In 1936 he was adopted as the British Union of Fascists' candidate for Hammersmith North.

3 Morton, J, 'Obituary: Lord Justice Lawton', *Guardian*, 5 February 2001, http://www.theguardian.com/news/2001/feb/05/guardianobituaries1 (accessed 26 May 2015).

4 'Sir Frederick Lawton', *Telegraph*, 6 February 2001, http://www.telegraph.co.uk/news/obituaries/1321260/Sir-Frederick-Lawton.html (accessed 26 May 2015).

pupils included the future British Prime Minister, Margaret Thatcher,[5] Conservative MP Airey Neave and BBC journalist, Sir Robin Day.

Perhaps he could not therefore be described as one of the more liberal speakers in the history of the Lord Upjohn Lectures.

In such a context, one might approach Lawton's lecture with some expectation that his approach to legal education would be similarly conservative, reflecting the symbiotic nature of culture and Lawton's identity. His own cultural capital, and his own identity inevitably constructs his vision of legal education[6] as it does for anyone else. To understand this is crucial if we are to understand the stories that are told about both contemporary and historic legal education and the complex role that the legal profession plays within it.

The identity of being a legal professional, a judge or a barrister in Lawton's narrative is his central focus; the person who 'does' or 'performs' law. Perhaps one would not be surprised that a judge and a barrister, a legal practitioner, would see the law through the prism of practising it. Yet, we too often forget this when considering contemporary debates. If we ask practitioners what legal education should look like, they will inevitably view the question through their own lived experience and through the prism of practice. So, when legal education reviews ask legal professionals what legal education ought to look like, such answers must be viewed as merely reflecting their own unique perspectives. Of course, this does not even begin to consider the differences within the perspectives of the diverse legal profession, from high street firms to the 'Magic Circle' of elite commercial/City firms; from the paralegal in an insurance company through to the paralegal in a large international commoditised firm; from the regional chambers-based barrister to the corporate barrister based in London; from the judge with public and national profile, to the reader at a provincial court. As much as this might seem to be stating the utterly obvious, recent reviews such as the 2013 UK Legal Education and Training Review (LETR) suggest that voice is as much the exercise of power rather than a result of representative consultation.[7] Our stories of legal education are told and retold according to the character telling the story and place of its telling.

The tension at the heart of UK legal education has long been observed. Twining described a 'tug of war' between three aspirations:

> 'to be accepted as full members of the community of higher learning; to be relatively detached, but nonetheless engaged, critics and censors of law in

5 Thatcher described Lawton as 'witty, with no illusions about human nature or his own profession': Thatcher, M, *The Path to Power* (London: Harper Collins, 1995) 83.

6 See more generally Hall, S, 'Introduction: Who Needs Identity?', in Hall, S and Du Gay, P (eds), *Questions of Cultural Identity* (London: Sage, 1996). Also see Jenkins, R, *Social Identity* (London: Routledge, 1996).

7 See more generally Guth, J and Ashford, C, 'The Legal Education and Training Review: Regulating Socio-Legal and Liberal Legal Education?' (2014) 48(1) *The Law Teacher* 5–19.

> society; and to be service-institutions for a profession which is itself caught between noble ideals, lucrative service of powerful interests and unromantic cleaning up of society's messes.'[8]

Whilst this tension might take place within a law school, it is also a debate between law schools. Whilst there is tendency to talk of 'The Law School', there are many both in number and in culture. Twining's 'tug of war' might represent the desires of academics in the midst of this 'war' but it is one in which the marketplace is also a factor, pressurising law schools into a particular strategy to service – or in the hope to service – a perceived market of customers. Thus, if a law school believes its only market is to be 'service-institutions' for the legal profession, that is what they will be. For some law schools, there is nobody on the other end of the rope in their 'tug of war', with a stratification of legal education inevitably following.

For those law schools that are able to more fully engage in Twining's 'tug of war', we know, as Boon and Webb have previously noted, that the relationship between legal practice and academia is often problematic.[9] Yet whilst we have traditionally referred to 'practice' to include the bodies and characters that make up this amorphous form, we now have regulation hived off into a separate structure, separate to academia, and training and education providers, and also separate to the providers of legal services.

Nor, as Bradney has noted, is there one definition of the liberal law school,[10] itself a contested space, arguably witness to its own 'tug of war' of values and form.[11] This debate is, however, a reflection of the contemporary regulatory framework. The 'tug of war' has existed only as long as the various characters have had power. Up until the middle of the twentieth century, English legal education was essentially about an apprenticeship model[12] and there has never been an end point since that time, rather a period of continuous flux. The actors in Twining's 'tug of war' are themselves worthy of further examination.

Diversity and the legal profession

It is unclear whether Lawton was live to the issue of class, but he did demonstrate some awareness of gender. Towards the end of her twelve months (pupillage) with Lawton, Margaret Thatcher came to him and – according to Lawton – said that she needed to leave his Chambers because 'as a young married woman with young children I just could not lead the life you lead'.[13]

8 Twining, W, *Blackstone's Tower: The English Law School* (London: Sweet & Maxwell, 1994) 2.

9 Boon, A and Webb, J, 'The Legal professions as Stakeholders in the Academy in England and Wales', in Cownie, F (ed.), *Stakeholders in the Law School* (Oxford: Hart Publishing, 2010) 65.

10 Bradney, A, *Conversations, Choices and Chances* (Oxford: Hart Publishing, 2003).

11 See more generally Sarat, A (ed.), *Law in the Liberal Arts* (New York: Cornell University Press, 2005).

12 Boon and Webb, n. 9, 67.

13 Moore, C, *Margaret Thatcher: The Authorized Biography: Volume One* (London: Penguin, 2014) 127–28.

Margaret Thatcher – who became renowned for functioning as British Prime Minister on a minimum of sleep – could not hope to manage a legal career. British political, social and economic history might have been profoundly different if the Bar had a more enlightened approach to gender and family life. As others, notably Sommerlad, have commented, we continue to have a legal profession whose voice is more likely to be male than female, whose world-view is similarly gender privileged.[14]

There is a surprising lack of literature within legal education on the economics of access to legal education.[15] Andrew Francis' recent work has highlighted the desire of firms for candidates to display the so-called 'X-factor', a quality which inevitably aligns with cultural (and economic) capital.[16]

Illustrative of this is a further study conducted by Turner and Manderson[17] in which they explored the ways in which students 'perform' in a variety of university 'Coffee Houses' in Canada. These spaces take place every Thursday afternoon as between 100 and 300 law students start to crowd into a space sponsored by Montreal and Toronto law firms, which send their 'youngest and best dressed' lawyers to mingle with and meet the students. Their aim is to convince the best students to come to their firm. Alcohol, live music and pristine table linens are provided. The students may come in suits, the girls with jewellery. A performance of normativity and privilege ensures that the $5000 to $10,000 a firm may spend on each event is an investment in their future. One male student respondent commented:

> 'No, it's totally irrational, it's like I could see an attractive, beautiful woman and associate that with the firm. Like last week there was a lawyer serving wine who was really [good-looking], and a lot of people commented on it. A lot of people. . . . So people are thinking "This firm has hot women". . . . I was looking at the lawyers last week and thinking about why they send who they send . . . the guys seemed to be wearing really smart suits.'

14 See more generally Sommerlad, H, 'Let History judge? Gender, race, class and performative identity: a study of women judges in England and Wales', in Schultz, U and Shaw, G (eds), *Gender and Judging* (Oxford: Hart Publishing, 2013); and Sommerlad, H, 'That obscure object of desire: sex equality and the legal profession', in Hunter, R (ed.), *Rethinking Equality Projects in Law: Feminist Challenges* (Oxford: Hart Publishing, 2008).

15 A notable exception: Thomas, P A and Rees, A, 'Law Students – Getting In and Getting On', in Thomas, P, *Discriminating Lawyers* (London: Cavendish Publishing, 2000). See, more recently, Sommerlad, H, Webley, L, Muzio, D, Tomlinson, J and Duff, L, *Diversity in the legal profession in England and Wales: a qualitative study of barriers and individual choices* (London: Legal Services Board, 2010).

16 Francis, A, *At the Edge of Law: Emergent and Divergent Models of Legal Professionalism* (Farnham: Ashgate, 2011).

17 Turner, S and Manderson, D, 'Socialisation in a Space of Law: Student performativity at "Coffee House" in a University Law Faculty' (2007) 25 *Environment and Planning D: Society and Space* 761–782.

Beauty and style, glamour and youth are the dominant forces at these gatherings of the brightest law students and young practitioners of law in Canada. Future success is reduced to how 'hot' the women are, and how stylishly dressed the men might be.

Turner and Manderson's empirical study found that rather than seek to catch the eyes of would-be employers, or to spend time with them, there was an additional performance of appearing disinterested. It was a *faux pas* to appear as if one actually wanted to work for a particular firm.

Such performances, such presentations of self, inevitably raise questions as to the extent that the profession is 'diverse' and more broadly, how higher education and the law school operate to preserve or challenge these truths.

In the recent 2014 Milburn Report, former British Prime Minister, Sir John Major, is quoted as observing: 'In every single sphere of British influence, the upper echelons of power in 2013 are held overwhelmingly by the privately educated or the affluent middle class.'[18]

The 2014 report identifies that 71% of UK senior judges are educated at independent (private) schools, 23% at grammar schools and just 4% at comprehensive schools;[19] 99% attended university, of which 75% went to Oxbridge[20] and 94% at a Russell Group University[21] (which includes Oxbridge).[22]

The solution offered by the report is that universities should 'use contextual admissions to gain a rounder picture of a student' and 'engage with a wide range of schools to raise aspiration of attainment'.[23] In other words, the solution is predicated on the notion of getting more individuals into the elite institutions, which in a law school context means more people into Oxbridge and Russell Group institutions; institutions in which the students might find themselves at the UK equivalent of the 'Coffee Houses' described by Turner and Manderson. Law students as the hunted rather than the hunters.

What, one might therefore ask, is so special, and so distinct about these institutions? What do they do differently from the rest of the sector that makes their graduates so 'employable'. Logically, one might assume that these institutions

18 Commission on Social Mobility and Child Poverty, *Elitist Britain?* (2014), https://www.gov.uk/government/uploads/system/uploads/attachment_data/file/347915/Elitist_Britain_-_Final.pdf p6 (accessed 18 September 2015).

19 Ibid., 71.

20 Oxford or Cambridge University.

21 Commission on Social Mobility and Child Poverty, n. 18, p. 72.

22 The Russell Group describes itself as representing '24 leading UK universities which are committed to maintaining the very best research, an outstanding teaching and learning experience and unrivaled links with business and the public sector': see: http://www.russellgroup.ac.uk/home/ (accessed 7 June 2015).

23 Commission on Social Mobility and Child Poverty, n. 18, p. 67.

must place tremendous emphasis on so-called 'employability skills'[24] or on vocationalism.[25]

The Solicitors Regulation Authority currently lists thirty-six authorised providers of the Legal Practice Course (LPC), just five of whom are Russell Group institutions.[26] The Bar Standards Board indicates that thirteen institutions offer the Bar Professional Training Course (BPTC) and just one – Cardiff – is a member of the Russell Group.

This is a rather crude indicator of whether an institution is more likely to be more vocational in nature, but it does provide some limited insight. There is a need for research exploring differences between law schools, their culture and curriculum.

Those that seek to orientate themselves towards a vocational agenda do not therefore seem to be the institutions that the Milburn Report believes more students ought to be aspiring to, if they want to succeed in the legal profession. Moreover, Turner and Manderson's research suggests that the most employable feature one can have is to hold the badge of being within an elite community.

Regulating legal education and the professions

The role of legal education and the form it takes has long been argued, and (re)negotiated by academics and the profession. Who 'owns' legal education is a question locked in a symbiotic relationship with the question of what the purpose of legal education is.[27]

Fitzgerald has suggested that this lack of clarity forms one body of long-established criticism and debate within the legal education community.[28] That we seem to be in the same position over twenty years after she made that argument suggests she may have had a point.

Flood has argued that there is an inexorable move in the world towards the Americanisation of legal education through the widespread adoption of the JD

24 Strevens et al have suggested that responding to this agenda can be of value for those students who will not be able to get places at 'Magic Circle' elite law firms, and instead can help orientate and prepare students for provincial firms (particularly in the context of a commoditisation of legal services). See: Strevens, C, Welch, C and Welch, R, 'On-line Legal Services and the Changing Legal market: preparing Law Undergraduates for the Future' (2011) 45(3) *The Law Teacher* 328–47.

25 It is interesting to note the Washington and Lee University School of Law experiment in the United States with a 'vocational model'. For details of the Washington and Lee initiative see http://law.wlu.edu/thirdyear/ (accessed 11 June 2015). See Richard Moorhead's blog for commentary from a UK perspective at http://lawyerwatch.wordpress.com/2013/06/27/letr-ii-employability-may-not-be-what-really-employers-want/ (accessed 11 June 2015). Moorhead notes the assumption of practitioners to want to have practical skills. However, a law school that seemingly gave legal practitioners precisely what they wanted found that the employment options for their graduates got worse. James Moliterno (Faculty member of W& L Law School) has sought to explain the rationale behind this development in 'The Future of Legal Education Reform' (2013) 40 *Pepperdine Law Review* 2–26. The university motto of *Non incautusfuturi* (not unmindful of the future) seems particularly apt.

26 Twenty-four institutions, all of who offer undergraduate law degrees.

27 See for example: Gower, L C B, 'English Legal Training' (1950) 13 *Modern Law Review* 137–205.

28 Fitzgerald, M F, 'Stirring the Pot of Legal Education' (1993) 27(1) *The Law Teacher* 4–35.

degree over the LLB because of the JD's perceived greater practice orientation.[29] For Flood, UK legal education is clearly at risk of being 'left behind'. Flood is one of many academics who have contributed to research exploring the desires of the profession and the impact that it has and may have on legal education,[30] yet it should also be noted that whilst the JD arguably has a greater practice orientation than the LLB (subject to how an institution configures the LLB), it is based on the student already holding a degree, already having been exposed to a broader education. The question is not therefore merely whether a programme ought to be vocational or more academic, but is also about whether law views itself as something 'after' academic training or whether it can be foundational academic training in itself.

Further, the desires of the profession have arguably been overtaken by regulatory change. Since the Legal Services Act 2007 fragmented the profession into representative and regulatory functions,[31] this is arguably even more the case and is the context in which legal reform in the aftermath of the 2013 LETR takes place.

In the aftermath of the report, the professional bodies have embarked on a process of change the implications of which will take some time fully to understand. The Joint Academic Stage, once the body designed to ensure that law degrees met the required standards of both the Bar and the solicitors' profession, has gone. Yet this was a body that Boon and Webb argued could act as a potential body to regulate the competing demands of the profession and academia.[32] One potential referee for Twining's 'tug of war' has gone and there are no obvious alternative candidates.

Whilst the LETR Report certainly did not preclude a liberal or socio-legal education, the responses to it and the reforms to legal education have been determined largely by professional legal practice.[33]

Liberal education and the binary divide

As has already been noted, the liberal law school not only seeks to position itself at a distance (rather than removed) from the professions, but also recognises that

29 Flood, J, 'The Global Contest for Legal Education', in Westwood, F and Barton, K, *The Calling of Law: The Pivotal Role of Vocational Legal Education* (Farnham: Ashgate, 2014) 13.

30 See for example: Ashford, C, 'Legal Education and the Academic-Commercial Nexus' (2004) 38(1) *The Law Teacher* 80–92; Boon, A, Duff, E and Shiner, M, 'Career Paths and Choices in a Highly Differentiated Profession: The Position of Newly Qualified Solicitors' (2001) 64(4) *Modern Law* Review 563–594; Boon, A, *Practitioner Perspectives on Legal Education and Training*, UKCLE Project, http://www.ukcle.ac.uk/research/projects/ boon.html (accessed 8 June 2015); Sherr, A, 'Legal Education, Legal Competence and Little Bo Peep (1998) 32(1) *The Law Teacher* 37–63; Boon, A, Flood, J and Webb, J, 'Postmodern professions? The Fragmentation of Legal Education and the Legal Profession' (2005) 32 *Journal of Law and Society* 473–92.

31 Ching, J, Maharg, P, Sherr, A and Webb, J, 'An Overture for Well-Tempered Regulators: Four Variations on a LETR Theme' (2015) *The Law Teacher*, http://www.tandfonline.com/doi/abs/10.1080/03069400.2015.1035866 (accessed 8 June 2015).

32 Boon and Webb, n. 9, 89–90.

33 Guth and Ashford, n. 7, 5–19.

it might come in a number of different forms. Perhaps by definition, liberal law schools – with the freedom and creativity the name suggests – are going to vary from one to another, dependent upon their own established discourse and creative input. Nonetheless, as briefly discussed, one might view institutions as more at one end of the vocational/liberal spectrum than the other, and this is disproportionately along binary lines, those that are the so-called 'new' universities created as a result of reforms in 1992, and those that have longer histories as university law schools.

Although there has been some discussion of the post-binary divide within higher education, it is largely at an institutional level rather than at the level of the law school, department or faculty.[34]

The last large study of UK law schools was published in 2005,[35] yet Broadbent and Sellman[36] note that we can tell a lot about the differences between law schools via their efforts to recruit and how they position themselves through their websites. They recently observed a contrast between the former polytechnic law schools and the 'old sector'. They argue that whilst the pre-1992 sector retains a focus on research and their national and international character, the 'new' universities are more likely to emphasise teaching and a local character.

Subsequent to his Lord Upjohn Lecture, Lawton observed that the legal education of the 1950s offered 'an astonishingly narrow intellectual training',[37] again apparently suggesting that what the profession has wanted, and continues to want is a more liberal approach to legal education, and therefore a more 'old sector' approach.

Even in a distinctively professional context, Sullivan et al have described how law school provides 'the single experience that virtually all legal professionals share. It forms minds and shapes identities'.[38]

In a detailed study of twenty-six US-based law teachers considering 'exceptional learning', the study found that responses tended to focus on skills, 'legal skills' or 'professional skills' which might include drafting, the synthesis of material and so on.[39] Legal training in a US context might therefore be expected to focus much more on these narrow skills, reflecting, as Flood noted and mentioned earlier, the greater vocational nature of the JD. Yet in a more UK context, we might be more mindful of the role legal education can have in forming minds and shaping identities, taking its place more clearly among the social sciences.

34 See Pratt, J, *The Polytechnic Experiment 1965–1992* (SRHE/Open University Press, 1997) *passim* and Gledhill, J, 'The Modern English Universities', in Warner, D and Palfreyman, D (eds), *The State of UK Higher Education* (SRHE/Open University Press, 2001) 95–102.

35 Harris, P and Beinhart, S, 'A Survey of Law Schools in the United Kingdom, 2004' (2005) 39(3) *The Law Teacher* 299–366.

36 Broadbent, G and Sellman, P, 'Great Expectations? Law Schools, Websites and "the Student Experience"' (2013) 47(1) *The Law Teacher* 44–63.

37 Moore, n. 13, 127.

38 Sullivan, W M, Colby, A, Wegner, J W, Bond, L and Shulman, L S, *Educating Lawyers: Preparation for the Profession of Law* (San Francisco: Jossey-Bass, 2007) 6.

39 Schwartz, M H, Hess, G F and Sparrow, S M, *What the Best Law Teachers Do* (Cambridge: Harvard University Press, 2013).

All three UK scholarly societies for law – the Association of Law Teachers, the Society of Legal Scholars and the Socio-Legal Studies Association – are members of the Academy of Social Science, and support the Campaign for Social Science, suggesting a desire by these organisations to be part of the broader community of academics.

The Campaign for Social Science recently described social science as 'disciplined curiosity about the arrangements by which people live together' and argued that 'applied curiosity widens and deepens bodies of knowledge about markets, states and institutions, and about groups, attitudes and behaviour'.[40] Whichever part of the sector a law school finds itself in, these statements offer an insight into how law might more clearly position itself and thus serve the legal profession rather than serve the needs the legal profession might think it has.[41]

Bottomley argued in 1997 that we need – as a body of legal scholars – to challenge the 'myths and demons of our own making', and suggesting three hydra-heads that needed to be confronted. She argued that black-letter law is itself challengeable as a stable fixed concept and forms part of a discussion about what law is and where the boundaries should be fixed; she also challenged presumptions we might have about students, arguing that 'on simple statistics, the majority of undergraduate law students will not become lawyers. Yet we continue to teach them as if that is the focus of our mutual endeavour'.[42]

Moreover, Bottomley asserts that 'we have been unable to persuade the legal profession that a law degree should be the only route into the practice of law'.[43] At a time of increased pathways and the potential deregulation of pathways into the profession, Bottomley's almost two-decade-old observation is even more true today than when she first made it. What does, however, bind these new pathways together is an emphasis upon legal skills.

Legal skills

Law has arguably positioned itself as special, as a subject of value beyond others. In 1938, Lord Wright asked why law seems to offer such a key role, why it is that those legally trained find themselves in places of key civic import. He answered:

> 'It is true that lawyers have bulked large in the highest political and administrative positions, in the Cabinet, in the great public departments, in local

40 Campaign for Social Science, *The Business of People: The Significance of Social Science Over the Next Decade* (London: Sage, 2015) 11–12.

41 See more generally on boundary work between law and society, practitioner and client as intrinsic to the juridicial field: Sommerlad, H, 'Socio-Legal Studies and the Cultural Practice of Lawyering', in Feenan, D (ed.), *Exploring the 'Socio' of Socio-Legal Studies* (Basingstoke: Palgrave Macmillan, 2013) 187. Also see Hunter, C (ed.), *Integrating Socio-Legal Studies into the Law Curriculum* (Basingstoke: Palgrave Macmillan, 2012).

42 Bottomley, A, 'Lessons from the Classroom: Some Aspects of the "Socio" in "Legal" Education', in Thomas, P A (ed.), *Socio-Legal Studies* (Aldershot: Dartmouth Publishing, 1997) 178.

43 Ibid., 179.

> government. This would seem to indicate the worth of a legal training. It is true also that law in its own way covers the whole range of human activity; there is no side of life which it does not touch. And the student of law must know the course of national history under which it developed, he must appreciate the affinity of its ideas with the social, moral and economic ideas alongside of which it developed. Law upholds the equality of all men, it impartially regards the proud and the lowly; humanity is its essential characteristic.'[44]

For Wright, law was something that binds together the state and humanity. Yet, in more recent times, we have perhaps shifted law's identity to being a skill, to 'think like a lawyer'.

Yet, clarity quickly proves elusive when one seeks to understand what 'thinking like a lawyer' actually means. For Lord Denning, there was but one skill that a lawyer required: a command of language:

> 'All my prizes from the age of 11 were for English. I have them still, bound in handsome leather, with the school crest and the date AD 1569. The titles in succession are the Great Authors, Macauley, Carlyle, and Milton.'

Denning added that by reading these and other texts, he was provided with 'a wide vocabulary of words, and an understanding of the meaning attached to them'.[45] Once more, the apparent 'uniqueness' of law ought to be a broad education. Moreover, it is seemingly something that does not necessarily involve legal rules, cases and statute at all.

The post-war period in legal education has also been characterised by the growth in 'skills-based' education that goes well beyond that envisaged by Denning.[46] Historic moots have expanded internationally; we have seen the emergence of negotiation competitions and a huge deepening of clinical legal education.[47] The mass expansion of legal education in the 1960s and 1970s saw a similar expansion in the use of clinical legal education – particularly in the United States – as concern grew about the social purpose of legal education,[48] providing a response to social and political need as much as a vocational one. When law schools respond to any agenda it seems, we do so for complex reasons

44 Wright, R, 'The Study of Law' (1938) 54 *Law Quarterly Review* 185–200.

45 Denning, A, *The Discipline of Law* (London: Butterworths, 1979) 7.

46 See more generally: Garvey, J B and Zinkin, A F, 'We Must Make Law Students Client-ready', in Westwood, F and Barton, K, *The Calling of Law: The Pivotal Role of Vocational Legal Education* (Farnham: Ashgate, 2014).

47 See for example: Bloch, F (ed.), *The Global Clinical Movement: Educating Lawyers for Social Justice* (Oxford: Oxford University Press, 2011); Kerrigan, K and Murray, V (eds), *A Student Guide to Clinical Legal Education and Pro Bono* (Basingstoke: Palgrave Macmillan, 2011); and Giddings, J, *Promoting Justice Through Clinical Legal Education* (Melbourne: Justice Press, 2013).

48 Sullivan et al, n. 38, 7.

that manage to blend the vocational with broader socio-legal agenda, many of which might logically be more traditionally aligned with the liberal law school.[49]

Conclusion

Law schools have become adept at blending the apparent needs of the legal profession, or rather a perceived 'vocational' agenda with that of a social, political and even arguably moral purpose to varying degrees.

Yet when considering responding to the needs of the legal profession, the agenda has typically been based on what the legal profession – the typically male, white and privileged profession – tells us that it needs as a stakeholder within legal education.

Law schools have been less forthcoming in identifying and then telling the profession what it needs, and why it needs it. Yet change is coming. Packer and Ehrlich[50] as long ago as 1972 observed an America becoming more urban, more post-industrial and more service-orientated, and predicted increased commoditisation and technological transformation. More recently, Susskind has similarly pointed to technology as transformative for the sector[51] and how it can be even more so in the context of commoditisation.[52] Such change of itself generated shifts to apprenticeships and alternative career structures long before the introduction of the Legal Services Act 2007, and long before the 2013 LETR and the regulatory responses to it.[53]

When the legal profession is prompted for its thoughts, it reflects its perspective today just as much as Lawton did in his 1980 Lord Upjohn Lecture. It is today likely to be a male, white and privileged perspective that seeks to define its legal education needs in relation to those qualities. Cultural capital remains a key driver and thus, as Kennedy[54] noted in his 1983 polemic, the system of legal education recreates the power and structures of what has gone before. Even change is reduced to the appearance of change. The technology apparently sweeping through the sector coupled with apprenticeships has the potential to offer increased entry to the legal profession. Yet, one must ask the question, who are these routes for? They are arguably for the very people that the Milburn Report, discussed earlier, believes need a more liberal, broader education rather than one narrower and 'vocation' focused. The legal profession gets what the legal profession wants, but it cannot help but want the wrong thing.

49 Guth and Ashford, n. 7, 5–19.

50 Packer, H L and Ehrlich, T, *New Directions in Legal Education* (New York: McGraw-Hill Book Company, 1972) 6.

51 Susskind, R, *The Future of Law: Facing the Challenges of Information Technology* (Oxford: Oxford University Press, 1996) and Susskind, R, *Transforming the Law: Essays on Technology, Justice and the Legal Marketplace* (Oxford: Oxford University Press, 2000).

52 Susskind, R, *Tomorrow's Lawyers: An Introduction to Your Future* (Oxford: Oxford University Press, 2013).

53 Ashford, n. 30, 80–92. Also see Ashford, C, 'The 21st Century Law School: Choices, Challenges and Opportunities Ahead' (2006) 3 *Web Journal of Current Legal Issues*, http://www.bailii.org/uk/other/journals/WebJCLI/2006/issue3/ashford3.html (accessed 18 September 2015).

54 Kennedy, D, *Legal Education and the Reproduction of Hierarchy: A Polemic Against the System* (New York: New York University Press, 2004).

19 Twenty-second Lord Upjohn Lecture 1993

The Lord Chancellor's Advisory Committee on Legal Education and the Legal Profession*

Lord Griffiths of Govilon M.C.

In the year 1773 King George III of England, being rather short of funds, ordered a census to be taken of his new American colonies with a view to raising further taxation. The Clerk to Grafton County in New Hampshire replied in the following terms:

> 'Your Majesty, Grafton County supports some two thousand five hundred and sixty souls mostly engaged in the pursuit of agriculture. But we count among our number five doctors, seven blacksmiths, fifteen wheelwrights, twenty-six preachers and one hundred and forty teachers and students at our new college of education. We have not one lawyer for which we seek to take no credit but give thanks to an almighty and merciful providence.'

Little changes: and you might perhaps be tempted to draw the inference that it was this attitude towards lawyers that led the Government to name April Fool's Day 1991 for the commencement of the labours of its newly appointed Advisory Committee on Legal Education and Conduct. I, however, prefer to regard it as either an unhappy coincidence or a hitherto unsuspected sense of bureaucratic humour; for in fact the majority of the Advisory Committee are not lawyers and bring a wide spectrum of experience to bear on issues which lawyers may tend to see in a rather narrow focus conditioned by centuries of legal tradition.

This evening I wish to give you an account of our work in the two different but to some extent overlapping areas of our responsibility. The Courts and Legal Services Act 1990 has breached the monopoly hitherto employed by the solicitors' profession in litigation and by the Bar in the right to conduct advocacy in the higher courts. But it has not created a market overt where anyone can set up his stall regardless of his skill, experience or integrity. The Act provides that anyone wishing to exercise lawyer's skills must belong to a professional body that will

* This article is an abridged version of the lecture delivered as the twenty-second Lord Upjohn Lecture at King's College, London on 14 May 1993.

impose and enforce suitable training and conduct regulations (as a condition of granting to their members a right to conduct litigation or to act as an advocate). The Act preserves the rights of solicitors and barristers as they were at the date of the passing of the Act but if they seek any new rights, or if any other body seeks rights to litigation or advocacy, they have to engage in a most stately gavotte before they are finally achieved, and it is our place in the dance which is the first area of our responsibility about which I wish to speak. I shall turn later to our responsibilities in the field of education.

I have always found it easier to talk, and indeed to think, in terms of practical examples rather than abstract conceptions, so I will turn to one of the actual applications with which we have been dealing in our first two years. On the first day of our existence there dropped through our letter-box the Law Society's application to grant rights of audience in the higher courts to solicitors. The Committee's first duty is to consider the terms of the application and to advise the applicant, the Law Society, whether in their opinion it needs amendment. In practical terms this means first whether the education and training requirements are adequate and second whether the rules of conduct are acceptable. But we also have to look at the application from a wider perspective and consider the effect that it might have upon the proper administration of justice.

We therefore decided that this being the first and obviously a major application it would be wise to consult publicly. This we did and during the time that this took we embarked upon a wide series of visits to solicitors' offices, barristers' chambers and courts at all levels to inform ourselves of the present operation of the legal system, taking the view that it is not wise to start advising on the alteration of the system before you understand its present operation.

After our small but dedicated and highly competent secretariat had produced an analysis of the result of the consultative process we divided into two sub-committees, the one to consider the education and training content of the application and the other the rules of conduct. Wider aspects of the impact on the administration of justice we always debated in the full committee. Let me illustrate this by a reference to a part of the Law Society's application which we advised they should not pursue and which advice they have accepted. The Law Society's original application proposed that immediately on qualification a solicitor should have rights to appear in pleas of guilty in the Crown Court and also in all appeals to the Crown Court. There were two quite distinct reasons that led us to advise against this extension of rights. In the first place looking at the matter solely as a matter of education and training the Law Society required no compulsory training in advocacy before qualification, and we could not recommend that persons who might be wholly untrained should be at liberty to represent the public in the Crown Court where grave consequences might attend any shortcomings in the presentation of the case. There was also another aspect of the problem. Our system of oral adversary trial is dependent upon there being a sufficient supply of competent advocates to present both sides of the case. As with all professional skills, advocates develop with experience and they must start by gaining that experience with the simpler and less serious cases. Now the

Law Society were also proposing to grant rights to solicitors to conduct contested cases in the Crown Court, but only if they had had considerable experience in the lower courts and had passed a further examination and undertaken further training. But suppose a considerable number of solicitors had said to themselves 'We don't want to undertake any further training as advocates but we will do all pleas of guilty in the Crown Court'. There would then dry up the work that one expects will be available to aspiring advocates to gain the experience that leads on to greater skill, and it might result in higher court advocates being forced to run before they could walk which could not be in the general interest of the administration of justice.

I will not descend to too much detail but the education and training which the Law Society originally proposed for the grant of rights of audience in the higher courts did not appear to the Committee to be sufficient and we so advised the Law Society. Since then there have been discussions with the Law Society on this issue culminating in the setting-up of a joint working party of members of the Committee led by Professor Richard Card and the Law Society which gave detailed consideration to the nature of the examination and the course which solicitors should pass before being granted advocacy rights in the higher courts. This has been a most fruitful exercise; the Committee is now satisfied with the package and has so advised the Law Society.

Now let me return to the dance. The Law Society has to consider the Committee's advice but it does not have to accept it. After considering the Committee's advice the Law Society will then make a formal application to the Lord Chancellor and the Lord Chancellor then refers the application to both the Advisory Committee and to the Director General of Fair Trading who will advise on the competitive aspects of the application. If the Law Society has amended its application in accordance with our advice our task at this stage is simple – we advise the Lord Chancellor that the application should be granted. If, however, the Law Society chooses not to accept or not to accept parts of our advice then we have to take another look at the application and decide whether those parts of our advice which have not been accepted are so fundamental that in our opinion the application should not be granted and so advise the Lord Chancellor. The Lord Chancellor then decides whether or not the application should be granted. If he decides against the application that is the end of the matter – the application fails. If, however, the Lord Chancellor is in favour of the application the dance continues. The application then has to be considered by the designated judges, that is the Lord Chief Justice, the Master of the Rolls, the President of the Family Division and the Vice-Chancellor the Head of the Chancery Division. It is only if all are in favour of the application that it succeeds; any one of the judges can veto the application. So you see it is a formidable and time-consuming process, but we are after all making far-reaching changes to a system that has existed for centuries.

We have also received applications from the Crown Prosecution Service and the Government Legal Service for their lawyers to exercise rights of audience in the higher courts, and applications from other bodies seeking specific rights of audience for non-lawyers. Different considerations have to be taken into account in respect of these, as with the application for employed lawyers to exercise higher court advocacy rights on behalf of their employers. We do not favour this at present, but are having discussions with the Law Society and Bar to see if progress can be made.

We are also acutely conscious of the difficulty of forecasting the impact of change and we regard it as one of our functions to attempt to manage change so that it will improve but not destroy the present fabric of justice. At times this will mean moving forward cautiously and monitoring the effect of what has been done rather than jumping in with both feet and hoping for the best. The difficulty of forecasting the effect of change is illustrated by the controversial question of the cab rank rule which requires a barrister to accept any brief within his competence. The Law Society resisted a rule of conduct that imposed the cab rank rule on solicitor advocates arguing that it was impractical to impose it upon a partnership structure and would result in many solicitors who might otherwise have become higher court advocates declining to do so and thus limiting rather than increasing the available choice of advocate. Those who support the cab rank rule warn in the strongest terms that if the solicitor advocates are able to pick and choose whom they will represent it may well result in a few powerful firms of solicitors cornering the best advocates who will only be prepared to represent the rich and strong, leaving the poor and weak to go to the wall. The majority of the Committee were not persuaded that permitting solicitor advocates to practice without the constraint of the cab rank rule would have such a disastrous consequence for justice in this country. Nevertheless, it would be exceedingly foolish to close one's eyes to such a possibility and as a part of the concept of managing change we intend to monitor the effect of extended rights of audience, and as part of that exercise we will consult annually with the Law Society and the Bar. The Law Society have themselves proposed that they consult the Committee on the following question:

> 'In view of trends and developments in the market for advocacy services, are there any further steps which the Society should take, including the adoption of new rules, in order to promote access to advocates and the availability of advocacy services.'

In addition, with the advice of Dr. Shapland and in consultation with the Law Society and the Bar, we are considering commissioning research into the present pattern of advocacy services, and how it may be affected by any additional rights of audience. The present position is that the Law Society have our advice on their application and we await to see the final form in which it is submitted to the Lord Chancellor.

I will now turn to educational issues. Our first real problem with legal education came with the Bar Council's application to amend their rules governing entry to the Inns of Court School of Law. At present the only route to qualification to practice at the Bar involves attending and passing the Inns of Court School's vocational course, that is leaving aside for the moment the possibility of transferring from the solicitors' profession. Historically, the Bar has maintained an open door policy, setting fairly minimal standards of educational attainment as a condition of call to the Bar. Some years ago this was tightened up by requiring at least a second class degree as a condition of entry to the Inns of Court School, Bar Final Course. For a time this filter worked and kept the applications for a place at the school within manageable numbers. But as the law schools in the universities and polytechnics expanded so the numbers of those attaining second class degrees increased, and to these were added those students with non-law degrees who had qualified through the common professional examination (CPE) route. Finally the Inns of Court School was overwhelmed by the number of applications of those qualified for a place. With a capacity at a pinch of about 1,000 but ideally of little more than 800, they were faced with the likelihood of 2,000 applications. Something had to be done, and as an emergency measure they determined that they must set a limit of 1,000 places. Guaranteed places would be awarded to those with Firsts and 2:1s in law or who had passed the CPE and all 2:2s in law were to be on a first-come, first-served basis. But as this involved altering the rules that governed education and training for the Bar they had to obtain consent to the alteration of their rules through the process I have already described. And so it was that they submitted their first-come, first-served proposals to us with the assurance that it was a temporary emergency measure whilst they sought to devise a selection procedure to apply in the future. We approved the emergency measure, and had to approve a slightly better version for a second year. It was really Hobson's choice, but it made us acutely aware of the difficulties the Bar faced if they continued to run the only professional law school that gave access to a career at the Bar.

The present situation is that we have approved a further alteration to their rules that enables the school to limit their number to 800 and to introduce selection techniques for a period limited to three years. I know that active consideration is being given to the possibility of franchising vocational training to other providers but such solutions cannot be introduced overnight. The complexity of the problem is also compounded by the limited number of pupillages available for those who do pass the vocational course and, of course, pupillage, that is learning on the job, is a necessary part of the training for practice at the Bar. Questions have to be asked about the wisdom of providing many more places on vocational courses than the number of available pupillages. Is it better to have the filter at the first stage of entry to vocational training, that is entry to the Inns of Court School of Law, or at the second stage, that is at pupillage? At the moment the Bar have placed the filter at the first stage and it is to be hoped that those who pass the course will all be able to find pupillages; from what we hear, however, some who pass the course are now finding difficulty in obtaining pupillage. If of course much greater numbers came forward from the vocational course or courses many more would fail to obtain pupillages and perhaps feel resentful that they had wasted a year and a great deal of money on the vocational course. The alternative argument is that those who undertake the vocational course all know that the number of pupillages is limited and if they want to take the chance of obtaining one they should not be deprived of the opportunity by restricting the number of places on the vocational course. There are no easy answers to these questions but they are some of those that we shall have to consider in the review of legal education upon which we have now embarked.

If this review is to be meaningful we must work closely and openly with both academic and professional lawyers. My experience so far makes me confident that we shall be able to do so. We have already received much valuable guidance from the deliberations of the Standing Conference on Legal Education. The Standing Conference was inaugurated as the result of an initiative by Professor Roy Goode and Professor Peter Birks to provide a forum in which academic lawyers and professional lawyers would continue to meet and discuss those issues previously debated in the old Lord Chancellor's Advisory Committee on Education. The Conference meets twice a year in the premises of the Advisory Committee. It pursues its own agenda and it is in no way the creature of the Advisory Committee but they do let me sit in as Chairman, and Alistair Shaw, our Secretary, and Professor Patricia Hassett, our Educational Secretary, also attend. Her place will be taken when she returns to her university appointment in the United States this summer by Kim Economides from Exeter. We have benefited greatly from Professor Hassett's wisdom and experience; we are very fortunate that Kim Economides will be joining us in her place. In this way we have had an insight into some of the issues of current concern in legal education which we can share with other members of the Committee and which will help us on the learning curve upon which we have now embarked. As a small practical illustration of the value of the conference it was as a result of a conference discussion that the Bar amended its first-come, first-served procedure so that those who had passed the CPE examination did not have preference over two law graduates unless they had obtained a 2:1 in their other degree.

As I am sure most of you know, we commenced our review by issuing a consultation paper in broad terms designed to search out the major issues of concern and contention in the field of legal education. We are very grateful for the response and we are currently engaged in the mammoth task of analysing these replies from which we hope to gain a broad picture of the current thinking of those engaged in teaching law. At the same time the members of the Committee have been visiting law schools throughout the country to see for themselves what is going on, on the ground. Again I would like to take this opportunity to express our thanks and appreciation for the way in which our visits have been organised and for the warm reception we have received. We are particularly grateful for the opportunity to talk confidentially to the students in the absence of staff. This was invariably an illuminating experience but of course my lips are sealed.

This July we are going to hold our first conference on legal education, which will be attended by all members of the Advisory Committee, members of the Standing Conference and some 30 other distinguished teachers of law and other guests. We shall take stock of the results of the consultation process and seek to identify the vital issues on which the review must concentrate. Thereafter I anticipate the different issues will be considered in the first place in a number of working parties, that there will be further consultation upon them and that they will be considered in further conferences. We have also started to commission research on educational issues and we are actively considering what further areas of research should be pursued in the light of the responses we have received to the initial consultation.

We are at the moment only on the threshold of the review. It will be a time-consuming process and unfortunately we cannot devote ourselves to it exclusively for we have also to deal with all our other responsibilities and most members of the Committee are themselves in full time occupations. For example we have to advise on the appropriate standards of training and conduct for those who are not solicitors and wish to act as probate practitioners and we are anticipating applications in this field from the Institute of Legal Executives, the Council of Licensed Conveyancers and the Institute of Chartered Accountants, and there may well be others. But we must have a target for the completion of the legal education review; this we have set at three years and I very much hope that with your good will and co-operation it will be achieved.

We are of course acutely aware of the problem of funding or perhaps it would be more accurate to say lack of funding for legal education. Legal education is the Cinderella in the queue for funding and the excellent report by Professor Bernard Jackson for the British and Irish Law Education and Technology Association (BILETA) has shown how urgent is the need for a more realistic appreciation of the need for student lawyers to be trained in the use of computers and word processors and the expenses that this involves. We are also aware that public funding is drying up for the vocational stage of training, with the result that many students are unable to proceed beyond the academic stage. We have already had one discussion on funding with the Department for Education to inquire into the likelihood of any immediate change in the present position – I have, I fear, no good news for you. The review will have to look most carefully at funding and with a realistic eye because it is of little value to produce a product that no one can afford. On the other hand we must not be inhibited from going public in our annual report if we are satisfied that the government is not allocating legal education a fair slice of the educational cake.

I am now taking off my hat as chairman of the Advisory Committee and I will finish by expressing a few entirely personal opinions. I do not believe that extending rights of audience to solicitors would present a serious threat to the existence of the Bar, so long as we resolve disputes through oral adversarial procedures. When I look at those areas of law such as planning law, employment law and family law, where so much of the work is in chambers and before tribunals where solicitors already have full rights of audience, I see a thriving independent Bar. Barristers are specialist sub-contractors and just as the building contractor calls in the specialist sub-contractor rather than keeping electrical or plumbing specialists on his permanent staff, so I believe most solicitors will find it more economical and efficient to use the specialist Bar rather than trying to cover the whole field by an in-house advocacy department. New Zealand is an interesting analogy. All lawyers obtain a dual qualification and have rights of audience in all courts but a lawyer can declare that he intends to practise solely as a member of the Bar and act as an independent referral advocate. So, far from the Bar withering on the vine; whilst the legal profession has doubled in size since the war the Bar has increased tenfold and you see the same pattern in many Australian states.

The threat to the Bar will come not through extension of rights of audience but through the ever increasing length of trials and the prolixity of some of their advocacy. Oral adversary trial may soon be seen as too expensive and too time consuming a way of settling disputes. The search for alternative dispute resolution has already begun and I foresee it growing apace with many of the cases that are presently tried or arbitrated being settled in the future by mediation procedures. When I took office as President of M.C.C. I found that they were heading for a law suit with the builders of the Compton and Edrich stands. The stands were excellent but they were completed a year late and we and the Test and County Cricket Board had lost a lot of money in ticket sales. Naturally the contractors disclaimed responsibility blaming the delay on many factors such as inadequate drawings, changes in design, ground conditions and so forth. It was for me a novel experience being a client. But I was a client with a difference: I knew that if this dispute went the full distance it would drag on for years during which it would make huge demands on the time of the club staff and the costs would almost certainly escalate to a sum that far exceeded anything that was in dispute between the parties. So we sat down with the contractors, negotiated directly and settled it. It was the only sensible thing to do because the alternative was an appallingly cumbersome and prohibitively expensive form of litigation. We are already introducing far more written material into trials in place of oral testimony and speeches and I foresee that ere long we will introduce a limit to the time allowed for oral submissions on appeals. Let us hope that we can take measures to bring the length of trials back under some form of control. If we cannot then the only alternative will be to abandon that form of trial and search for alternative procedures.

As for education, I am concerned that we should not become a nation of lawyers. I would prefer us to be a nation of traders for thereby is the wealth created to improve living standards. A balance has to be struck between producing sufficient lawyers to serve real needs and to protect real rights and an overproduction of lawyers many of whom will only survive by the promotion of shoddy litigation and the over-complication of every commercial transaction. So I would not like to see a wholly uncontrolled expansion of law schools and I think some attempt should be made to decide upon the level of lawyering that is healthy in our society.

And lastly, I would like to see lawyers complete a common education and all start with a period in general practice before holding themselves out at the Bar as independent specialists. I have always thought it unfair to require a young undergraduate to choose which branch of the profession he or she preferred to enter when barely halfway through a university career. I also think great benefits would be gained by young lawyers through having more contact with clients before becoming specialist advocates or advisors and it would promote a greater understanding between the two branches of the profession. These are a few of my heretical thoughts. Thank you for your kind attention.

20 Response: From Gavotte to Techno – But the Dance Goes On

John Hodgson

The gavotte which Lord Griffiths referred to was a metaphorical description of the protracted, convoluted and highly formal procedure for securing a change to the competences of a branch of the legal profession under the Courts and Legal Services Act 1990. Lord Griffiths had been involved as chairman of the Lord Chancellor's Advisory Committee on Legal Education and Conduct (ACLEC) in the procedures for the granting of extended rights of audience introduced by the Act.

Initially, the relationship between legal education and training and dancing was literal rather than metaphorical. In the heyday of the Inns of Court in the sixteenth and seventeenth centuries, when they rivalled universities as suitable 'finishing schools' for the sons of the nobility and gentry, as well as providing the initial and continuing education of barristers, serjeants and judges, dancing, at least of the formal, courtly description, was an integral part of the curriculum. Subsequently the metaphorical use is particularly appropriate. A dance should involve two or more participants collaborating on a complex, rhythmically challenging task to achieve a harmonious conclusion, which may even include an end product, such as the plaited sword of some folk dancers. Not all dancing is successful. The partner with two large left feet is regrettably common. In some cases the elaborate costumes, and the sheer complexities of the process, may seem counter-productive. In a slightly different usage of the word 'dancing' it can suggest opponents shadowboxing, moving around each other and looking for the opportunity to gain advantage. Without trying to strain the metaphor too far, examples of all these aspects can be seen in the history of legal education and qualification for practice over the past century or so.

We perhaps need to remind ourselves that until relatively recently, the organisation of the legal profession, including its educational and qualification arrangements, was very much seen as a matter for the profession itself. There was remarkably little intervention by the state. The Inns of Court were proudly independent private corporations. In the dog days of the eighteenth and early nineteenth centuries, their contribution to legal education was probably fairly minimal; the only formal requirement was 'keeping terms', which effectively meant dining in Hall on a set number of occasions, with the opportunity for conversation with established practitioners, and possibly mooting or other similar exercises. However, an advocate who wished to make a career was very much responsible for developing his own knowledge. Solicitors, in the Courts of Chancery, attorneys, in the Common Law Courts, and proctors, in the Probate, Divorce and Admiralty jurisdiction, acquired their title by apprenticeship, with some rudimentary supervision by the courts of which they were officers. They thus acquired knowledge from their predecessors rather than through a formal process.

The Victorians changed this, but largely through the activities of the professions themselves. The solicitors/proctors/attorneys, initially at a local level, and subsequently at a national one, sought to improve and protect their position. The three professions were merged and all took the title 'solicitor' following the reform of the court system in the Judicature Act 1873, which created the unified Supreme Court (in the original sense of the High Court and Court of Appeal). The institution of a formal qualification and certification allowed action to be taken against those who had the temerity to hold themselves out as legal advisers without that qualification. The proceedings of provincial law societies until relatively recently, certainly after the Second World War, were largely taken up with discussion of how to proceed against such unlicensed 'hedge lawyers' and also those who were offending professional etiquette by overzealous promotion or 'touting'.

The Bar had also, by the end of the nineteenth century, modernised its approach, and instituted examinations.

Prior to the nineteenth century the university study of law had focused initially on civil and canon law, and after the Reformation the emphasis remained on civil law together with elements of international law. Cambridge, for instance, did not appoint its first professor of English law until 1800, and did not commence teaching an undergraduate law degree until 1858. Before that, Cambridge doctors of law did practise extensively in the civil law-based Probate Divorce and Admiralty jurisdictions, but there was little other connection between academia and legal practice.[1] By the end of the nineteenth century the law was being taught in a number of universities, but generally to very small numbers of students. Some of these might go on to practice, but the law degree was entirely optional.

By the middle of the twentieth century both branches of the profession had established a two-part examination system. The first part concentrated on what we would today call the academic stage, namely the basic principles of English law: contract, tort, land law, criminal law and constitutional law. Even equity and trusts was not regarded as core until somewhat later, and of course EU law only became relevant following accession in the 1970s. It became accepted that a law degree, at least one which covered the required subjects, could be offered in lieu of taking the first part of the examination, although when the law faculty at the University of Nottingham commenced after the Second World War its classes typically contained a small number of undergraduates reading for a degree,

1 See http://www.law.cam.ac.uk/about-the-faculty/history-of-the-faculty.php (accessed 21 April 2015).

coming predominantly from the then colonies and Dominions, and a majority of local articled clerks auditing the lectures as preparation for their Solicitors Part One examination. The second part of the examinations focused more closely on elements of practice, litigation and advocacy for the Bar, conveyancing and probate for solicitors in particular, and did not attract exemptions.

Particularly following the Robbins expansion of higher education in the 1960s, graduate entry to the professions became the norm, although the alternative route into the solicitors profession of five-year articles remained available, and many, if not most, barristers were graduates of non-legal disciplines who took a conversion course.

This entire process was undertaken almost entirely on a self-regulated basis. The Lord Chancellor and senior members of the judiciary exercised a degree of oversight. Under section 2 of the Solicitors Act 1974, the Law Society was empowered to make training regulations which required the concurrence of the Lord Chancellor, Lord Chief Justice and Master of the Rolls and consultation with the Home Secretary and any advisory committee he might designate. While the body that is now the Law Society was initially incorporated by Royal Charter in 1845, the profession was not really put on a statutory footing until the second half of the twentieth century, and the process was only completed by the 1974 Act. The Act did, however, provide for self-regulation within a statutory framework and subject to judicial oversight. At this stage the Bar was still wholly self-regulating under the oversight of the judges.

In the 1980s it began to be suggested that the organisation and operation of the legal profession as a self-regulating interlocking set of monopolies was not operating in the public interest. In particular it was considered that allowing a greater degree of competition, both by allowing members of the same profession to advertise to a greater extent and by extending the scope of the work of professions would benefit the public by making legal services more widely available at more competitive prices without compromising quality. At the same time, the debate over the relationship between academic legal education and professional education in the narrow sense began to intensify.

There had been considerable scrutiny of legal education prior to the enactment of the Courts and Legal Services Act 1990. This started with the Ormrod Report.[2] This recommended that legal education should comprise an academic stage (in principle a law degree), a professional stage (including both a vocational course and work-based learning, but not articles or pupillage as such) and continuing professional development. This reflected the current reality, but the report focused on the need to develop and improve the professional stage.[3] This

2 *Report of the Committee on Legal Education*, Cmnd. 4595 (1971).

3 Progress with fulfilling the requirements of the Ormrod Report was monitored by the Royal Commission on Legal Services ('the Benson Report'), Cmnd. 7648 (1979) and the report of the Marre Committee, *Report of the Committee on the Future of the Legal Profession, A Time for Change* (1988). Although these resulted in further impetus to the changes which were fought, they did not significantly affect the overall framework.

resulted in the development of the Law Society's Final Examination, and amendments to the Bar Finals. During the period of operation of ACLEC, one of the principal topics of discussion was whether there could be common professional legal education. Eventually this was rejected, and the pattern of legal education remained broadly that proposed by Ormrod, although articles of clerkship/training contracts and pupillage remained part of the process. Vocational education for solicitors was decentralised with the establishment of the Legal Practice Course (LPC) in the early 1990s. Approved providers took full responsibility for their own courses operating within a specification laid down by the Law Society. The Bar Vocational Course (BVC), which had been introduced some years earlier at the Inns of Court School of Law, was similarly opened to approved providers in 1997. There was, however, a broad consensus that an academic stage (qualifying law degree or CPE), vocational stage (LPC or BVC), and practical stage (training contract or pupillage) represented the essential and appropriate structure for legal education for the professions. Indeed, one signal achievement of the *First Report on Legal Education and Training* produced by ACLEC[4] was to restate that a law degree should be seen as the basic underpinning qualification for a lawyer: 'A lasting achievement of the Ormrod Committee was to establish beyond question that the law should be a graduate profession, and to give the universities a clear and crucial role in providing intellectual foundations for intending lawyers.'[5] ACLEC itself proposed: 'the starting point is that law must continue to be *a graduate profession*. This would normally be by way of a *qualifying law degree* although, consistent with our philosophy of wide access, a route must also exist for mature candidates with appropriate experience . . . to qualify as lawyers, and for non-law graduates to convert to law.'[6] The main thrust of this First Report was towards an increasing measure of common vocational education, although nothing significant eventually came of this.

What is significant, looking back at the activity of ACLEC after some two decades, is the intensity of the scrutiny which was undertaken in the public interest. Lord Griffiths describes in graphic detail the complexities involved in the application for higher rights of audience lodged by the Law Society as soon as ACLEC commenced operation. The review of legal education and training conducted by ACLEC was equally rigorous. It was of course comprehensive, in the sense that the report considered education and training for both solicitors and barristers, although not in any detail that of legal executives or members of other specialised legal professions. As the report makes clear, a wide range of expertise was enlisted, and extensive consultation took place. A comparative study was made of a number of other jurisdictions.

We now move forward to the brave new world of the twenty-first century. In the early years of the millennium the solicitors' profession conducted a lengthy,

4 ACLEC, 1996.
5 Ibid., p. 26.
6 Ibid., p. 32 (emphasis in original).

but at the time largely abortive, Training Framework Review. The essential premise was that there needed to be greater flexibility in routes to qualification, to allow for greater diversity. The initial proposals were extremely radical: '[T]he consultation paper maps out nine possible routes to qualification which include a continuous pathway integrating academic, vocational and work based learning. It is possible to imagine other routes, and the consultation paper does not preclude them.'

To avoid frightening too many horses, the consultation paper is firm on at least some of the parameters. The profession will continue to be all graduate. All aspirants must be taught ethics. The pathways to qualification should include elements of academic, vocational and work-based learning in law. However, two key issues are ducked. The paper is vague on the degree of specialisation which will be permitted before qualification. Further, it does not lay down a minimum period for the training period as a whole.[7]

However, while there were incremental developments in the LPC, the more radical changes were shelved.

At the same time, Sir David Clementi was producing his *Report of the Review of the Regulatory Framework for Legal Services in England and Wales.*[8] Essentially, this recommended that the regulatory functions of the various professional bodies should be separated from their representative functions, and that there should be an overarching 'super regulator'. Effect was given to these recommendations in the Legal Services Act 2007. The Legal Services Board (LSB) was established as the super regulator. Section 1 of the Act specified a number of regulatory objectives:

(a) protecting and promoting the public interest;
(b) supporting the constitutional principle of the rule of law;
(c) improving access to justice;
(d) protecting and promoting the interests of consumers;
(e) promoting competition in the provision of services within subsection (2);
(f) encouraging an independent, strong, diverse and effective legal profession;
(g) increasing public understanding of the citizen's legal rights and duties;
(h) promoting and maintaining adherence to the professional principles.

By virtue of section 4 the LSB is also responsible for:

(a) the regulation by approved regulators of persons authorised by them to carry on activities which are reserved legal activities, and
(b) the education and training of persons so authorised.

7 N. Johnson, 'At the point of qualification: reflections on the Law Society's Training Framework Review', Directions 2004, UKCLE, http://78.158.56.101/archive/law/resources/directions/previous/issue8/johnson/index.html (accessed 25 May 2015).

8 (2004), http://webarchive.nationalarchives.gov.uk/+/http://www.legal-services-review.org.uk/content/report/index.htm (accessed 25 May 2015).

Initially, the existing arrangements for legal education and training continued, albeit under the auspices of the new regulators, principally the Solicitors Regulatory Authority (SRA) and the Bar Standards Board (BSB). These bodies, together with ILEX Professional Standards,[9] commissioned the Legal Education and Training Review (LETR) in 2011. Among the principal recommendations made by the LETR in 2013 were:

> '*Recommendation 1*
>
> Learning outcomes should be prescribed for the knowledge, skills and attributes expected of a competent member of each of the regulated professions. These outcome statements should be supported by additional standards and guidance as necessary.
>
> *Recommendation 2*
>
> Such guidance should require education and training providers to have appropriate methods in place for setting standards in assessment to ensure that students or trainees have achieved the outcomes prescribed.
>
> *Recommendation 3*
>
> Learning outcomes for prescribed qualification routes into the regulated professions should be based on occupational analysis of the range of knowledge, skills and attributes required. They should begin with a set of "day one" learning outcomes that must be achieved before trainees can receive authorisation to practise. These learning outcomes could be cascaded downwards, as appropriate, to outcomes for different initial stages or levels of LSET. Learning outcomes may also be set (see later) for post-qualification activities.'

Further, if the public is entitled to expect a single level of competence across at least the range of reserved activities and common core skills, there will need to be some co-ordination in setting threshold levels of competence. This does not mean that different pathways or qualifications must adopt common learning processes, or that qualifications cannot be set above the threshold, but it does mean that different approaches must have at least equivalent effect. It is recommended that, to assure an appropriate underlying standard, the threshold for authorisation should be at not less than level 6. Further, longer term, a national framework for the sector would simplify decisions about transfer between professions and qualification routes, and about partial authorisation. It will facilitate the development of specialist activity-based qualifications or accreditations. It could also provide a single framework to support progression from paralegal to authorised practitioner.

9 Now CILEX Regulation.

> '*Recommendation 4*
>
> Mechanisms should be put in place for regulators to co-ordinate and co-operate with relevant stakeholders including members of their regulated profession, other regulators, educational providers, trainees and consumers, in the setting of learning outcomes and prescription of standards.
>
> *Recommendation 5*
>
> Longer term, further consideration should be given to the development of a common framework of learning outcomes and standards for the legal services sector as a whole.'[10]

The LSB responded to the LETR by publishing statutory guidance.[11] Paragraph 9 states:

> 'This framework does not explicitly cover education and training requirements but, as with all regulatory tools, we see a need for regulators to take a risk based and outcomes approach in this area. This is supported by the recommendations within the LETR and is reflected within this guidance.'

The guidance goes on to indicate that educational arrangements should be outcomes based, i.e. focusing on what the professional needs to know and be able to do at qualification, and there is a strong emphasis on the plurality of routes and providers.[12]

Following the publication of the LETR Report and the LSB guidance, the SRA and BSB have proceeded to reconsider what is required by way of competences for admission to the specific professions they regulate. The SRA has now finalised its Statement of Solicitor Competence.[13] This is intended to indicate what any solicitor is competent to do as at the point of qualification. The statement itself is not particularly controversial. However, it has been accompanied by a 'Statement of Legal Knowledge'.[14] This purports to set out 'the knowledge that solicitors are required [to] demonstrate at the point of qualification'.

It is, to be frank, a mess. It is simply a list of topics, some of which equate to the existing Foundations of Legal Knowledge, contained in the Joint Statement on Qualifying Law Degrees. Others relate to the present content of the LPC. Apparently, all solicitors must know in detail about taxation, which is the third

10 LETR Executive Summary, http://letr.org.uk/the-report/executive-summary/executive-summary-english/index.html (accessed 25 May 2015).

11 'Guidance on regulatory arrangements for education and training issued under section 162 of the Legal Services Act 2007', http://www.legalservicesboard.org.uk/what_we_do/regulation/pdf/20140304_LSB_Education_And_Training_Guidance.pdf (accessed 28 May 2015).

12 Ibid., Outcomes 1 and 2.

13 See http://www.sra.org.uk/solicitors/competence-statement.page (accessed 25 May 2015).

14 See http://www.sra.org.uk/knowledge/ (accessed 25 May 2015).

heading, including income tax, capital gains tax, inheritance tax, corporation tax and VAT. They must also know about criminal law and litigation (heads 8 and 9), but they are not required to know anything about family law or employment law.

Of much greater concern is the fact that the SRA appears to be behaving in an autarkic manner in relation to the process for qualification. On each occasion when legal education has been reviewed, from Ormrod to the LETR, there has been an assumption that law is a graduate profession. This does not exclude alternative routes into the profession, but does assume that a lawyer requires the necessary intellectual development associated with being qualified at Level Six of the QAA Framework for Higher Educational Qualifications.[15] When the SRA consulted on these statements, it was challenged on whether it agreed that the solicitors' profession should be an essentially graduate one, and to identify the level at which the various elements of legal knowledge would be assessed. Although the SRA acknowledged these challenges in its responses to the consultation, it has not responded substantively. In further consultations on the implementation of the new scheme, it is clear that the current thinking of the SRA is heavily influenced by the Training Framework Review. Consultations with the profession have highlighted the desirability of an apprenticeship-based route to qualification, broadly equivalent to the old five-year articles. This was a theme in the early stages of the Training Framework Review. In consultations with academia, the SRA has indicated that its preferred method of assessment is not to create approved programmes, or to authorise providers, but to establish its own assessments. The model for these assessments appears to be the existing Qualified Lawyers Transfer Test. There is, however, an essential difference between a mechanism designed to ensure that a qualified lawyer has the necessary specific knowledge to practice in a particular jurisdiction, and the initial qualification mechanism. By definition the qualified lawyer seeking homologation is already a qualified lawyer. The new entrant does not come with any such guarantee.

The difficulty here is that the LSB guidance appears to proceed from the assumption that diversity and flexibility are primary ends and goals in themselves.

This can be traced back to another Lord Upjohn Lecture, that delivered by David Edmonds, the then Chair of the LSB, in 2010:[16]

> 'I have a hypothesis. My hypothesis is that dialogue and interplay isn't happening at the level that it should. Some go further and say that the current framework is simply not fit for purpose. If that's right – and it is what I hear consistently from educationalists and practitioners alike – then there is

15 See http://www.qaa.ac.uk/publications/information-and-guidance/publication/?PubID=2718#.VWOMIU9Viko (accessed 25 May 2015).

16 See http://www.legalservicesboard.org.uk/news_publications/speeches_presentations/2010/de_lord_upjohn_lec.pdf (accessed 28 May 2015). This is an edited version of the Lecture which also appears as Ch. 7 of this volume.

a clear need for the current education and training arrangements to develop at a much quicker pace to keep up to date with the challenges lawyers will face day in, day out in the future.'

Later he said:

> 'A single magic bullet for education and training is no more credible than a single business model for firms or chambers. In fact, we are already seeing plurality through different and equally effective ways of delivering the same outcomes – for example academic study versus so called "clinical legal education" versus on the job experience for those entering the profession via further rather than higher education.'

This is a category error. The primary objective should be to ensure quality, not diversity.

Lord Neuberger made precisely this point in his 2012 Lord Upjohn Lecture:[17]

> 'What then is the purpose of legal education and training? The LETR suggested an answer to that question, "The primary objective of the Review is to ensure that England and Wales has a legal education and training system which advances the regulatory objectives contained in the Legal Services Act 2007, and particularly the need to protect and promote the interests of consumers and to ensure an independent, strong, diverse and effective legal profession."
>
> I am afraid that that is not a good start. It is true that legal education and training should be consistent with the regulatory objectives specified in the 2007 Act. But those objectives also include improving access to justice, promoting competition in the provision of legal activities, increasing public understanding of the citizen's legal rights and duties, and promoting and maintaining adherence to the professional principles, which include acting in the best interests of clients, and independence in the interests of justice. It is worrying that the Review decided to describe its fundamental aim as directed to only two of the regulatory objectives, the interests of consumers, and a diverse and effective legal profession.'

It is important to ensure that all those with the ability, motivation and attributes have the opportunity of pursuing a legal career. However, the steer given by the LSB, the focus of the LETR, the statutory guidance and the way in which these have been interpreted, in particular by the SRA, indicate a troubling vacuum at the centre of the regulatory process,

The reason for outlining what the SRA is currently proposing is to indicate this relative lack of effective control. The regulatory structure within which Lord

17 'Reforming Legal Education', https://www.supremecourt.uk/docs/lord-neuberger-121115-speech.pdf (accessed 28 May 2015) and reproduced in Ch. 3 of this volume.

Griffiths was operating, and which he describes in his lecture, does contain a very substantial amount of externality. The final responsibility for approval of changes to legal services, and to legal education lay with an expert body (the Lord Chancellor[18] and the senior judges) which consulted widely, took advice from a range of experts, and produced substantive reasoned recommendations. By contrast, the SRA has consulted to a strictly limited extent, and has not explained why it has approved its statements unaltered despite substantial criticisms, particularly of the Statement of Legal Knowledge.[19] While there has been some involvement of external expertise, the basis upon which advice has been sought and the precise role of the advisers are not readily apparent.[20]

Part of the difficulty appears to be that the SRA seems to conceive that it has a very narrow role as a regulator. It is concerned to protect the public interest. It does not have any remit to promote or support the solicitors' profession as such. This is a crucial weakness of the separation between the representative and regulatory functions. It can be argued that the present situation, where there are two tiers of regulator, with the LSB supervising the individual professional regulators, is inappropriate. It is fair to say that the history of the performance by the various professional bodies in relation to complaint handling has been undistinguished, but it appears that this aspect of professional regulation has been allowed to dominate to the exclusion of all others. A profession and its members have a considerable investment in the standing of that profession. The regulatory and prudential functions underpinning that profession should facilitate this. At the moment they do not. While it is likely that many large solicitors' firms will continue to recruit law graduates, and will expect them to undertake something broadly equivalent to the LPC, in order to ensure that their qualification is equivalent to that of a New York attorney, an Australian solicitor or a German *Rechtsanwalt*, it is not at all clear that the SRA has any clear idea of how the average potential entrant to the profession is expected to proceed. Some solicitors' firms have embraced modern apprenticeships, often for fee earners who they do not expect to become fully qualified, but the majority are unlikely to do so. If the SRA is serious that it is not minded to establish a structure of qualifications and authorise providers to deliver courses preparing for them, unfavourable comparisons will inevitably be drawn with the CILEX qualification, which is clearly articulated, can be undertaken either by a law degree or as a wholly work-based qualification, and has a much more rational knowledge base for any given practitioner. It appears that

18 Who at the time was, and was expected always to be, both a lawyer and a senior politician.

19 The analysis of responses is at file:///C:/Users/John/Downloads/Competence%20Statement%20consultation%20response%20(1).pdf (accessed 28 May 2015). Specifically, para. 66 details a number of responses stressing the importance of the required knowledge being as a graduate level. The SRA has not dealt with this at all.

20 They are listed in Appendix 1 of the consultation document: http://www.sra.org.uk/sra/consultations/competence-statement.page (accessed 29 May 2015). However, the remit the advisers were given is not stated.

solicitors will have to know 'everything about more or less everything', while legal executives are able to focus on a body of knowledge relevant to a practice area.

Initially, the SRA and the BSB proceeded in consultation with each other 'with the aim of producing a common structure'.[21] However, this proved impracticable[22] so each has proceeded separately. In spring 2015 the BSB issued its proposed Professional Statement for consultation. This does not appear to be particularly controversial. In summer 2015 it opened a further consultation on the education and training framework to support this.[23] It proceeds on the assumption that the Bar is a graduate profession and will continue to require a law degree or a graduate conversion qualification.[24] The BSB proposes to rely on the QAA Benchmark Statement for law[25] in particular in relation to legal skills.[26] It proposes to move away from prescribed core subjects and to require that 'students should demonstrate **knowledge and understanding of the basic concepts and principles of public and private law within an institutional, social, theoretical and transnational context**'.[27] By so doing, the BSB has ensured that the Bar remains within the mainstream of international legal professions. It is also taking a moderate approach, which recognises that mere topic knowledge is less significant than the intellectual ability to apply and deploy knowledge in context.

The essential difficulty is that neither the super regulator, the LSB nor the individual regulators for particular professions, such as the SRA and BSB, are primarily concerned with educational issues. Education is a means to an end so far as their outcomes-based, day-one competence statements are concerned. It is inconceivable that a major legal profession would be able to deconstruct its qualification process in this way if there were a proper independent and expert regulator of legal education, as recommended by ACLEC.[28] The modern structure, while it has multiplied the layers of regulation, does not seem to have improved it.

Lord Griffiths' stately gavotte has moved beyond more modern dance forms such as techno; so far as the solicitors' profession is concerned it is rapidly becoming a dance of death.

21 Future Bar Training Consultation: The Professional Statement https://www.barstandardsboard.org.uk/media/1661549/professional_statement_consultation.pdf (accessed 20 August 2015) para 20.
22 Ibid.
23 Consultation on the Future of Training for the Bar: Academic, Vocational and Professional Stages of Training, https://www.barstandardsboard.org.uk/media/1676754/fbt_triple_consultation_9_july_2015.pdf (accessed 20 August 2015).
24 Ibid., paras 18, 57, 84.
25 http://www.qaa.ac.uk/publications/information-and-guidance/publication?PubID=2966#.VdXicvlVhHw (accessed 20 August 2015) (The BSB reference is to an earlier draft for consultation).
26 BSB, n2, para 84.
27 Ibid., para 83 (original emphasis).
28 ACLEC, n. 4, Ch. 7. The specific recommendations were largely overtaken by the establishment of the QAA, which initially undertook reviews at the subject level. Now that the Quality Assurance Agency has discontinued such reviews, it would be timely to revisit the recommendations of the ACLEC Report.

21 Eleventh Lord Upjohn Lecture 1981

The Teaching of the Law and Politics[1]

J.A.G. Griffith

I begin this lecture by assuming that members of this Association accept that, save in the most arcane and remote fastnesses of the law, it is not possible to disentangle law from politics. Or, to put the matter at a much lower level, that no man or woman should pass out of a polytechnic, college or university with the label of a law degree around his or her neck without being well acquainted with the general character of political life in this country. Ideally, of course, he or she should have much more than that. But I assume you agree that the minimum is a necessity.

I have to admit that in this respect lawyers like myself may appear to be in a special position. I read the other day in a book on the sociology of law or socio-legal studies that only in recent years had law been taught in a social or political context. This view was advanced to justify the teaching of those specially named areas of study. To me the statement made no sense at all, not because I am a public lawyer but because when I was an undergraduate at the London School of Economics between 1937 and 1940 I sat at the feet of men like Kahn-Freund, Robson, Ivor Jennings and Harold Laski, and anyone who attended their lectures and seminars was left in no doubt about the social context of law. Later, at the beginning of my teaching career in 1946, I taught, amongst most things, criminal law and international law and jurisprudence. As I had no specialist knowledge of at least two of these subjects I expect I taught them poorly. I was 28 years of age at the time, and that was about the average age of those post-war undergraduates, mostly being men and women who had been unable to complete their degrees before the war. I began my very first lecture – it was at Aberystwyth – by saying that I assumed they knew very little and that I had largely forgotten what I had learned so that we would have to co-operate in a joint effort to defeat the examiners of whom I was not one. Two years later when I returned to the London School of Economics as a lecturer, the average age of the class had dropped to about 19. This gave me more confidence, not necessarily well-placed or deserved. But during none of those early years, whether as an undergraduate before the war

1 This lecture was delivered as the eleventh Lord Upjohn Lecture at King's College, University of London on 6 November 1981.

or as a lecturer subsequently, did it ever occur to me that politics and law were separate matters. It took a little longer for tort and contract and property to be treated as common law subjects having considerable political significance. But, for a public lawyer, the connection, almost the identification, of these two major disciplines, was inevitable and obvious.

Our obligation as law teachers to consider law and politics as two ways of looking at the same thing is particularly necessary because of the most curious state of the study of politics as a separate discipline in this country. Here I should be a little careful because I cannot claim to be familiar with the teaching of politics in more than a few polytechnics and universities. But I will venture a few generalisations about the teaching of politics and I will be surprised if they are inaccurate.

In my experience, courses of lectures on politics for degrees in politics, or political science, or government, or whatever it is called, concentrate on these three main areas, in roughly equal proportions. These are, first, the history of political thought from Plato and Aristotle through the mediaeval Schoolmen to Machiavelli, Hobbes, Locke, Rousseau, Hegel, Kant, Bentham and, possibly, Marx; second, some aspects of comparative government; and, third, the political institutions of modern Britain. Now the unbelievable characteristic of these courses is that none of them considers the study of law to be an integral part. I am not talking about the occasional funnelling off of students to attend occasional courses on legal subjects put on either *ad hoc* or otherwise by law lecturers for the so-called benefit of students of politics. I am talking rather of the almost total failure of politics tutors to understand that a knowledge of the principles of law is an essential part of each of these three main divisions. How is it possible to understand, for example, the great events of the seventeenth century without a study of the part played not merely by lawyers like Coke but by the law itself? It is not possible to understand what is happening in French or Italian politics today without appreciating the position of the judiciary in those countries. And how can a lecturer compare the function of those judiciaries with that of the judiciary in this country when he is ignorant of the nature of the judicial process in this country? I would go further and suggest that lecturers in comparative politics may actually know more about the judiciary in France and Italy than they know about the judiciary in the United Kingdom. As to political institutions in the United Kingdom, lectures are given in politics courses on the Executive and on Parliament. But the third great arm of state power – the Judiciary – receives little or no treatment. And more important still, the close relationship, in the politics of the United Kingdom, between the functioning of the Executive and the functioning of the Judiciary, is virtually ignored. What politics student has ever heard of judicial review of administrative action? What politics lecturer has ever taken down a Law Report from the shelf or read a statute?

One result of this extraordinary state of affairs is that there is virtually no discussion in departments of politics of contemporary political problems. For how can you discuss the problems of immigration, of sex and race discrimination, of housing, of town and country planning, of public health, of police powers and of industrial relations unless you understand the law on these matters? Where will you find any of these matters considered? Only in faculties of law or faculties of social administration. In no other country of Europe could such a situation arise. In every other European country, law is seen as an integral part of such studies and scholars who have not received a training in the law soon set about acquiring the necessary expertise. This acquisition is not so difficult. In the USA the position is more similar to that of continental Europe than to the United Kingdom.

The other day I looked through some recent issues of the journal *Political Studies*. Out of 322 books there reviewed I found five which had some connection with legal studies; out of 30 articles, there were three. All this means that the teaching of political science in faculties supposedly devoted to that purpose concerns itself with political philosophy and with political institutions but quite omits the substance of politics. It is concerned with concepts, with forms and with procedure. It wholly lacks substance. It is as if one taught medicine without anatomy, or theology without the text. This is the context, whether in university or polytechnic, in which we teach law. And it is a context which places on our shoulders the burden of explaining to our students, and indeed to the students of other faculties, including the faculty of politics, how it is that a knowledge of law in its widest application is essential to an understanding of the society in which we live.

This leads me to speak briefly about two cognate matters which interest some of our colleagues and those of other disciplines: the sociology of law and social-legal studies. Although some find little help in attempts to define the areas which these two matters deal with – and so to separate them – I think there is a gain in clarity if we make the attempt. I understand the sociology of law to mean the study of society through the institutions and practices and philosophies of law. It is a branch of sociology in exactly the same terms as we speak of the sociology of religion, for example. We look to see what we can learn about the society we live in by examining the law. On the other hand socio-legal studies are concerned to look at the law and how it operates by considering its social implications and consequences. It is a branch of legal studies and I have already said enough to indicate why I believe – and I would expect all of you to believe – that to view law in any other way is constricting and misleading.

The sociology of law, however, is more difficult to evaluate. It takes very many forms. That book I recently read on law and sociology began with two chapters on the relationship of structuralism to law. Neither author thought the relationship existed: one because he said he knew nothing about law and the other because he knew little about structuralism. The third chapter sought connections between Max Weber and law. The fourth was on functionalism, the fifth on Marxism, the sixth on the Frankfurt School, the seventh on the principle of exchange as a basis for the study of law, the eighth on law as a social phenomenon, the ninth on the symbolic dimension of law and social control, the tenth on law from a phenomenological perspective and the eleventh on ethnomethodological approaches to socio-legal studies.

Some of the writings on the sociology of law I do not find easy. Probably there are two reasons for this. One is the strictly pedantic way in which I was brought up in the use of the English language. I believe some sociological writing is unnecessarily obscure. I will not say wilfully obscure. But it is too Latin for me. The second and more substantial reason is that I am by nature and instinct a positivist and I find too much of this writing undirected. But I mention the sociology of law to praise it, not to bury it. I am sure that law and sociology are as close as law and politics. And all I am saying is that there seem to me to be certain philosophical, and indeed sophistical, dangers and difficulties which we need to be on guard against.

At this point I will absent myself from objectivity for a while and speak about some of the matters which particularly interest me in the teaching of law and politics. As I shall be dealing with familiar subjects, I claim no originality. But most of the best things in controversy are the oldest, if only because political controversy in the end is concerned with what people believe, what they seek to achieve, and how they behave. And human beings do not change so much over the centuries.

Knowing that these questions are familiar to you, I could frame my discussion in oblique language with allusions predominating over substantive statements, implications and inferences taking precedence over facts and concrete arguments. But I confess I am not much given to such devices. I will not claim, as Mark Antony did, that I am only a plain blunt man if for no other reason than that you would immediately and naturally suppose that I was about to be both obscure and devious. But I do prefer to speak simply if I can, more particularly because I believe most worthwhile arguments can be expressed straightforwardly.

The first question closely involving law and politics is one of which I spoke some months ago at a conference of public lawyers which I believe some of you attended. That certainly precludes me from repetition but I hope you will forgive me if I briefly summarise the argument. I do not in any event flatter myself that those who were at the conference are likely to remember much I said on that occasion.

I spoke of the argument about rights. The argument is not whether certain propositions about the relationship between those exercising political power as rulers and those who are subject to these rules are good or bad. The argument is about the origin and nature of these propositions. The natural lawyers argue that it is possible to enunciate certain principles about individual freedom *vis-à-vis* the political rulers which can be expressed as fundamental, innate, human rights. Their opponents (of whom I am one and who, for shortness, may be called positivists) say that there are no such rights, that to speak of natural law in this connection is a mystification and that history and present practice show that the issue is not legal but essentially political.

May I make clear that I am anti-authoritarian by instinct, by upbringing and by experience. I deeply distrust all those who exercise political power. And it is because of this that I distrust natural lawyers who, I believe, give a legitimacy to the exercise of political power which I wish to deny. Authoritarianism is in the heart of politics and authority is in the heart of law. But sometimes authoritarianism also is in the heart of law. We strive (or say we strive) to control authoritarianism by the use of law only to find that the authoritarians are using law to extend their tyranny. We strive (or say we strive) to make democratic institutions to control authoritarianism only to find that those institutions are being used to give an appearance of legitimacy to the use of force.

It is fashionable, especially amongst lawyers, to claim that fictions are valuable and that we abandon them at our peril. But this fashion rests on the assumption that we, the sophisticates, know a fiction when we see one and use it intelligently but that others believe that fiction to be true. And that it is better thus. Bread and circuses can become quite expensive. Fictions are cheap. But they can prove quite costly when the illusion disappears. It seems to me that one of the more dangerous fictions of our time and one that may prove to be very costly is that individuals have personal, inherent, natural rights.

This is principally because those who are neither lawyers nor politicians do not distinguish legal rights from political rights. We know the difference. We know that a legal right is something vested in a person which a court of law will uphold – unless indeed it is successfully challenged by an even bigger and better legal right We know also that a political right is a shout, a protest, above all a *claim*. And I have argued elsewhere that we would do better not to speak of rights unless we mean legally established rights. We may of course speak properly of a claim to a legal right.

I find there is a common belief that examination questions, whatever other peculiarities and complexities they may display, should be clear, should not admit of ambiguity. I remember seeking to get a question accepted by my colleagues which asked, 'What Price Local Government Reform?' They wouldn't let me have it because they said – rightly – that it had more than one meaning. Another of my failures was, 'Why Public Law?'.

I was tempted to put that last question to you. But amongst its many meanings there are so few to which I know even an approximate answer that even an informal address on such a subject would result merely in an exposition of my widespread areas of ignorance and lack of understanding. The old definition of the specialist was that he knew more and more about less and less. I find that I know less and less about less and less, which will lead me only to know nothing about nothing.

I am not therefore going to attempt to answer the question, 'Why Public Law?'. But I am very briefly going to suggest that the question is answerable along one of two lines, of two philosophies, and that for myself I cannot see how a choice is to be avoided. The subtitle of the Song of Roland was 'Christians are Right, Pagans are Wrong'. It is not perhaps quite as simple as that. But the re-emergence of the religious writers – like Ronald Dworkin and John Rawls – makes old rationalists like me stir our weary limbs. For it seems to me that if Dworkin and Rawls are the answer, the question must be wrong. So it is with the new natural lawyers. I confess myself amazed and bewildered at the enthusiasms aroused by John Rawls's *A Theory of Justice*. I cannot see how it has come to support such an industry unless it be that our modern jurisprudents are frightened of the great problems raised by thinking about the relations of law to the modern world of over-population, economic collapse, terrorism and the rest that they have fled to the safety of conceptual moral philosophy. It was bad enough in the old days when political systems were intellectually constructed on the basis of two men and two women on a desert island, or on the basis of social contracts which were remarkable only for their wholly metaphorical character. It is interesting that the social contracts of Rousseau and of Harold Wilson had this in common: that despite their legal phraseology their essence was wholly political. Over 150 years ago, Jeremy Bentham said:

> 'It is impossible to create rights, to impose obligations, to protect the person, life, reputation, property, subsistence, liberty itself, except at the expense of liberty.'

The proposition that every law is contrary to liberty,[2] though as clear as evidence can make it, is not generally acknowledged. On the contrary, those among the friends of liberty who are more ardent than enlightened, make it a duty of conscience to combat this truth. And how? They pervert language; they refuse to employ the word *liberty* in its common acceptation; they speak a tongue peculiar to themselves. This is the definition they give of liberty: *Liberty consists in the right of doing everything which is not injurious to another.* But is this the ordinary sense of the word? Is not the liberty to do evil liberty? If not, what is it? What word can we use in speaking of it? Do we not say that it is necessary to take away liberty from idiots and bad men, because they abuse it? According to this definition, I can never know whether I have the liberty to do an action until I have examined all its consequences. If it seems to me injurious to a single individual, even though the law permit it, or perhaps command it, I should not be at liberty to do it. An officer of justice would not be at liberty to punish a robber, unless, indeed, he were sure that this punishment could not hurt the robber! Such are the absurdities which this definition implies. What does simple reason tell us? Let us attempt to establish a series of true propositions on this subject.

The only object of government ought to be the greatest possible happiness of the community. How stands the truth of things? That there are no such things as natural rights – no such things as rights anterior to the 'establishment of government – no such things as natural rights opposed to, in contra-distinction to, legal: that the expression is merely figurative; that when used, in the moment you attempt to give it a literal meaning, it leads to error, and to that sort of error that leads to mischief – to the extremity of mischief . . . *Natural rights* is simple nonsense: natural and imprescriptible rights rhetorical nonsense – nonsense upon stilts'.[3] So much for a small part of what I said at that earlier conference. But where do we go from there? The doctrine of inalienable human rights, and the idea of justice, provide a basis on which a philosophy of law can be constructed. And on that philosophic basis we may go on to build a political position and so to

2 Those laws must be excepted by which restrictive laws are revoked, laws which *permit* what other laws had forbidden.

3 'Anarchical Fallacies', re-published in Vol. 2, *Collected Works*, edited by John Bowring.

know what we must do. But if, as I am inviting you to do, we regard that doctrine of human rights as a mirage and that idea of justice as insubstantial and largely subjective, what are we to put in their place?

First, we must note that Rawls and Dworkin start from an assumption that everyone in the society has an adequacy of material goods. We had better start from the assumption that this is false, and we should have no difficulty in establishing our position. In other words we had better begin by looking at our society as it is. If we look at our own society, we see that it is essentially oligarchic and authoritarian in terms both of government and of the distribution of wealth. We see that this leads, naturally and inevitably, to conflicts and strains which are endemic and, however much they are changed in subject-matter over the centuries, have many constant characteristics. We see that in our society the interests of those few who control our economy appear to conflict with the interests of the many. And we call all this, in industrial and economic terms, capitalism. When, however, we look outside our society to societies where private capitalism has been overthrown and replaced, we find that there oligarchy and authoritarianism have persisted, even grown stronger.

It seems to me, and here I speak simply because the idea is simple as well as being trite, that the only way to resolve this difficulty, the only way to move from private capitalism without falling into state capitalism, the only way to avoid replacing one form of oligarchy and authoritarianism with another form of oligarchy and authoritarianism, is by a real and considerable extension of democratic, representative control in virtually all kinds of institutions – industrial, governmental, professional, educational, legal, etc. I will not spell this out for you because it is so trite. But it is a difficult and a revolutionary solution. It is difficult primarily because it does necessarily require a much greater degree of involvement of many, many people and this is not our tradition. But I suspect it is not our tradition because the opportunity has never been offered. Nevertheless we must remember that not everyone is as interested in politics as we are. Many people prefer fishing. But if involvement were seen to lead to genuine and effective improvements in the quality of life, then I have no doubt that much greater participation would ensue. I do not need to give you a lecture on the evils of alienation in our society. Its remedies are not easy but somehow they must be achieved if we are to avoid catastrophe. Out of democratic participation, especially industrial democracy, would emerge a different set of values and standards which would determine the nature of rights and the concept of justice. Apart from this extensive development of democratic involvement, I can see no way in which we can make progress.

I turn now to a different contemporary argument. It is about the meaning and relevance of that slippery concept: the Rule of Law. As you know, there has lately broken out like a political rash upon the white skin of the pure body of the law a disagreement amongst heavyweights in the political camp. E.P. Thompson's argument (*Whigs and Hunters* and a Haldane lecture) is that, although on very many occasions the law is indeed a tool used by the ruling class to impose its will and its value on the ruled, it is also more than that. Consequently, to regard law merely as part of the superstructure is an over-simplification. Legal rights are enjoyed also by the ruled, who will seek to enforce those rights in the courts and who will sometimes do so successfully. Although he does not use the word (he speaks of 'practices'), Thompson could have strengthened this part of his argument by noting that one of the three main sources of law has long been recognised as custom, and also that legal rights may be acquired by usage, i.e. by prescription. Thompson also argues that if law is evidently partial or unjust, it soon loses its attribute as a legitimating agent. Consequently, its content is often modified to the advantage of the ruled.

Moreover (and this again is a point Thompson could have made more of), every law defines its own limits and this is so even where a law, made by the rulers, enlarges their own power. He could have drawn a distinction here between statute law and common law. The latter tends always to be less precise and so the limits of any powers it gives to the rulers are less well defined. This can be seen today particularly in relation to police powers of arrest, questioning, search and seizure. No rulers whose main aim is to increase their powers (or at least not to allow those powers to be diminished) would seek to turn those police powers into statutory form (e.g. by enacting the Judges' Rules). The clarification of statute law carries a similar danger for rulers. The recognition of this, rather than the side winds of the Blunt affair, probably account for the withdrawal of the Protection of Official Information Bill. The initial attack on that Bill was such that the Government may have realised that they would have had to give way on one or two important provisions in the Bill. Rather than do this, they preferred the imprecisions of the existing legislation. Thompson also refers (in explaining the attitude to law in the eighteenth century) to the revolutionary inheritance from the sixteenth and seventeenth centuries which opposed centralised power; also to the Whiggish rhetoric about freeborn Englishmen; and to the struggles over *habeas corpus*, juries, rights of the press, etc., which, he says, 'cannot be seen as the products of bourgeois cunning but as products of successive struggles'. There is a radical bourgeois tradition of the individual against the state.

Perry Anderson (*Arguments within English Marxism*) makes these criticisms of this argument. First, that the most despotic states have typically had comprehensive legal codes and have ruled by laws. For Anderson this makes Thompson's distinction between arbitrary power and the rule of law 'far less obvious than Thompson supposes'. Anderson also criticises Thompson (rightly in my opinion) for suggesting that in 1832 'rather than shatter their own self-image and repudiate 150 years of constitutional legality, they [the rulers] surrendered to the law'. Anderson's main criticism of this is that Thompson takes constitutional law for the whole of law. I doubt if the rulers in 1832 thought of themselves as surrendering to the law at all. Faced with the popular demand for the Bill, they yielded to it for a variety of reasons, but surely, for almost all the rulers, 1832 was a tactical withdrawal from which, they hoped, not too much harm could come. Others, at that time, no doubt saw 1832 as a first step only. My own view is that the significant reforms which took place between 1830 and 1870 (during which period the regulatory state was founded) owed less to 1832 than to other factors. The questions seem to be two. First, to what extent basic structure and super-structure is a useful metaphor to use for the Marxist analysis of the function of law in eighteenth century or present-day society? And this question is part of a very much wider argument about structuralism, Althusser, historical materialism. etc. Second, metaphors apart, what is the function of law in present-day society, and how is it to be analysed as part of the political, economic and social context?

If I, as a lawyer, were asked to consider this second question, I would begin by saying that law is inevitably two-faced in operation. It confers power by creating rights but in so doing it defines and therefore limits the extent of the power and of the rights. Governments give themselves power by legislation but they remain constrained within the limits of their power. Thompson refers to the revolutionary inheritance from the sixteenth and seventeenth centuries but the argument is stronger. It was Bracton who said: '*Rex non debet sub hominesed sub deoetlege*'. I agree with Anderson that the phrase 'the rule of law' is generally too ambiguous to be helpful. What is old learning is that certainly in a democratic society (that is, a society where certain people are selected by a wider electorate to govern and can be dismissed by that electorate) laws bind the rulers as well as the ruled. And Bracton is authority for saying that the law may also be seen as binding even on a non-democratic ruler. The idea that lawmakers are bound by their own laws is clearly part of Roman and Greek law. Chief Justice Coke made the same point to the king in 1607 and James II learnt the same lesson the hard way in 1688. Tyrants are those who suspend and dispense with the laws which they find inconvenient. (In this particular context, the 'rule of law' as a phrase is useful.) Laws, whether or not they are made by rulers for their own advantage, continue in force until they are repealed or fall into desuetude. This continuity of existence sometimes creates problems for rulers when circumstances change and the same law takes on a different meaning, or the rulers change their policy. The phrase 'in contemplation or furtherance of a trade dispute' which bestowed rights on trade unionists has a different look about it in 1981 from that which it had when first enacted many years ago. And a government in 1981 which wants to diminish the rights now implicit in that phrase is faced with the necessity of enacting positive limitations on words which have acquired more than a little sanctity (for trade unionists). This causes political embarrassment.

This last example is an example of the long existence of the radical movement for the individual's rights against the state or of the continuing challenge of the ruled to the ruler. This perennial conflict has resulted in many victories and many defeats on both sides. But over the last 150 years it has emerged as the challenge of organised labour to organised capital. In terms of the law, it has been shown in the battle for the establishment of trade unions, in the recognition of the right to strike, and in the protection of both trade unionists from the rulers of the common law (both civil and criminal). If the structuralists are insisting on the proposition that law is only the manifestation of the will of the rulers and nothing more then they vastly oversimplify the truth. The law is a set of rules made at different times for different purposes and often reflects compromises in that perennial struggle between rulers and ruled. If, on the other hand, all that the structuralists are saying is that the rulers have in their hands, as lawmakers, a very powerful weapon which they frequently and consistently use to seek to promote their own interests, then they are stating an obvious truth.

It may be that the argument between Thompson and Anderson on this matter is never properly joined because each is emphasising an aspect of the truth which is not inconsistent with that of the other. Thompson emphasises the continuity of the law and its occasional value to the cause of the ruled. Anderson emphasises the power of the rulers to make new laws in their own interest. So put, there is no contradiction. Thirty years ago I tried to clarify the way in which this phrase, 'the Rule of Law', is used. I suggested that there were five common usages of the phrase. First, it meant simply that the law rules. But this is ambiguous. It could either be contrasted with a state of chaos or anarchy or with a state ruled by laws rather than by the unpredictable and capricious dictates of one man or group of men.

Both of these were largely hypothetical situations rather than descriptions of political realities. Second, the Rule of Law might mean that society should be governed by established principles so that the actions of the Administration were foreseeable. We know that the extent to which this is possible is limited because of the inevitability of the discretionary exercise of powers. This meaning of the Rule of Law is thus a political position in disguise, as is shown by Dicey's definition that the Rule of Law means the absolute supremacy or predominance of regular law as opposed to the influence of arbitrary power, and excludes the existence of arbitrariness, of prerogative, or even of wide discretionary authority on the part of the government.

Third, and like the second, is the contention that the Rule of Law requires or demands certain political values to be upheld, for example, the payment of compensation in certain circumstances following government action. Of these three meanings, the first is hypothetical, and the second and third are statements of what the proponents thought to be politically desirable. The other two meanings are that the powers of the Administration are derived from statutes or from the prerogative and that individual rights cannot be infringed without the authority of one or other of these sources of power; and that, as a corollary, the law, as it exists at a particular moment, binds the Administration. Indeed, every time a government obtains new powers by way of legislation, it by the same act prescribes the limits of those powers.

From all this I conclude that we can say no more about the Rule of Law than a few simple propositions. First, laws are things not words. If we break them, certain consequences may follow, including being deprived of personal freedom of movement or indeed of life itself. Second, and subject to many important and practical exceptions, laws are binding on our masters as on ourselves. If our masters are very powerful they may be able to set aside some laws from time to time but usually they will find it politic to submit to them or to change them in accordance with constitutional processes. At the time E.P. Thompson was talking about, Walpole was powerful but not overwhelmingly so. His writ did not run through all levels of society or all institutions. So it is not surprising that there were acquittals from prosecutions brought under the Black Act. Third, and by the same token, officials and bureaucrats sitting in public offices may be constrained if they seek to exert authority which they have not got. The powers they have are reasonably explicit. The parts of their authority and so of their limits are named and may be discovered. Perhaps I may be excused a personal indulgence, as a last example. When the first edition was published of my little ewe lamb (as Lord Hailsham would say), *The Politics of the Judiciary*, its reception was curious if not altogether unexpected. Some people clearly believed that at last I, as wolf, had emerged from lamb's clothing and shown myself to be the dangerous extremist they had long suspected me to be. One of my colleagues at LSE, not a lawyer, even suggested that my attitude to law was indistinguishable from that of the Baader-Meinhof group. Essentially the charge here was of subversion, though the individual and I have remained on good speaking terms and he recently told me that he did not intend to review the second edition which came out – this is a commercial break – last month. I was sorry to hear this as his attack had been much publicised and made many people buy the book to see whether they should burn it. At the other extreme were those, most of them practitioners in the profession, who adopted a world-weary approach and denied, quite rightly but a little more forcibly than was perhaps necessary, that the argument was old hat, not to say tedious. Others again disputed its particular conclusions on particular areas with more or less persuasiveness. I even had a few positively abusive letters from members of the Bar, written from a particular political position. All this was cheering stuff. It also exemplified a sad academic truth. I have written two or three books which could I think fall into the category of 'learned', though I hope they were not as dull as that sounds. I spent years of my life on them, often helped by collaborators. I sweated blood and guts – but they sold little. Along comes this small effort, written off the top of the head, largely for fun, and it sells 20,000 copies in three years. As Belloc said of an author: His sins were scarlet but his books were read. It is a funny old world.

However, I digress. What I wanted to say was that I had only one major disappointment about the reception of the first edition: that no one – not even Lord Devlin – examined the validity of the central proposition: that, in our system, judges must act politically and cannot act neutrally because they are constantly required to determine where the public interest lies. I would have been interested to see a position developed which argued that the limits of that judicial discretion were so tight that the exercise of the discretion could not properly be called political. But no one took that or any comparable line. Of course, shortly after the book came out, we had all the fun and games between the Court of Appeal and the House of Lords over *NWX v Woods*, *Express Newspapers v McShane* and *Duport Steels v Sirs* which may have made alternative analyses of the political nature of the judicial function more difficult to sustain. It was interesting to be presented with yet another example of the pathetic fallacy of nature imitating art. In giving a public lecture I always like to end rather sooner than the pessimists in the audience expected. On the principle of seeking to promote the greatest happiness of the greatest number, such a course is enhanced by its general popularity.

I have touched on a few matters which to me seem important. But that is largely idiosyncratic. You may very well and very properly consider that I have not spoken about many more considerable areas in this vast subject. Some few of you may be surprised that, given the title of my talk, I have not mentioned methods of teaching. But I do not presume to teach other members of this guild of teachers and scholars to which we all belong any lessons in technique. All good teaching is based on observation: that is, by watching the class and seeing whether what we are saying is being received (for example, whether most of them are awake most of the time) and understood. And then trying to discover why we are failing. Though we may learn a lot from watching the masters of our trade, in the end we have to find our own solutions, because our failings are our own. I believe that as teachers – not law teachers, not polytechnic or college teachers, not university teachers but simply as teachers – we belong to a trade or a profession which makes very great demands on us, is very difficult to do well, and that each of us is infinitely capable of improvement. I also believe that students would profit and the educational system in this country would profit if this ridiculous binary distinction were abandoned.

But that is another story.

22 Response: But It Still Goes On

The Teaching of Law and Politics in 2015

Anthony Bradney

Introduction

Thirty-three years after Griffith's Lord Upjohn Lecture matters should be different; 33 years later they are different.

The academic context

Griffith gave his lecture in an era where the idea of any link between law and politics had only been recently accepted in most university law schools.[1] In his lecture Griffith observes that his own undergraduate course at the LSE had assumed this connection.[2] However, the unusual nature of the law school at the LSE up until the 1970s has been widely noted.[3] In his history of the LSE Dahrendorf writes of the exceptional character of a law department in which academics from the 1930s onwards had been happy to see themselves as social scientists, noting specifically that Griffith was well-aware of the unconventional character of the department.[4] Law in those years in the LSE was not law in universities in general.

Thirty-three years ago law schools in the United Kingdom were not what they are now.[5] 'Academic law remained a fairly moribund, amateurish profession

1 If indeed it had been. The place of politics does not seem to have figured highly in legal academics' research agenda at this time. Thus, for example, the index for the *Law Quarterly Review* Volumes 1–100, volume 100 being published in 1984, has less than a page of entries under the heading 'Politics'. In contrast the heading 'Practice and Procedure' goes on for over four pages.

2 J Griffith, 'Eleventh Lord Upjohn Lecture 1981: The Teaching of Law and Politics' (1982) 16 *The Law Teacher* 1 at 1.

3 See, for example, M Adler and J Simon, 'Stepwise Progression: The Past, Present and Possible Future of Empirical Research on Law in the United States and United Kingdom' (2014) 41 *Journal of Law and Society* 173 at 184–5.

4 R Dahrendorf, *LSE: A History of the London School of Economics and Political Science 1895–1995* (Oxford University Press, 1995) pp 205 and 387. On the LSE's law school from the 1920s to the 1940s, see R Gwynedd Parry, *David Hughes Parry: a Jurist in Society* (University of Wales Press, 2010), Chs 2–4. See also C Glasser, 'Radicals and Refugees: The Foundation of the Modern Law Review and English Legal Scholarship' (1987) 50 *Modern Law Review* 688 at 694–5.

5 There is no general history of university legal education in the United Kingdom. However, for evidence of the general situation within university law schools until the 1970s, see F Cownie and R Cocks, *'A Noble Occupation!': The History of the Society of Legal Scholars* (Hart Publishing, 2009), Chs 1–7.

throughout the first half of the twentieth century.'[6] As late as 1975 Bridge had asserted that '[i]f academic lawyers are honest they will admit that there is still too little research being done'.[7] By the early 1980s the situation was beginning to improve. Nevertheless, Griffith still delivered his lecture at a time when research in university law schools was underdeveloped and socio-legal research a novelty. In 1987, five years after Griffith had given his lecture, Wilson commented that:

> 'the words "English legal scholarship" though high sounding have a similar function to the words "disposable paper cup". Each adjective strengthens the message that one cannot expect much in terms of long term quality or utility from it.'[8]

Traditional doctrinal legal scholarship, then dominant within UK law schools, with its '"*strong internalist*" point of view' focusing on an explication of legal rules based purely on an analysis of judgments and legislation, afforded Griffith little succour in his attempt to link law and politics.[9]

In his lecture, Griffith strongly favoured socio-legal studies as an approach to legal studies; 'to view law in any other way is constricting and misleading'.[10] However, at the time of his lecture socio-legal studies had yet to achieve the degree of prominence as a research paradigm that it has since gained. Harris in his 1983 survey of socio-legal research is somewhat more optimistic than Griffith was in his lecture about the then inter-play between the academic disciplines of law and political science. Whilst Griffith had noted the paucity of material about law in the journal *Political Studies* Harris observed that *Public Administration* 'regularly publish articles that consider the administration of laws in their political and bureaucratic contexts'.[11] Why Griffith selected *Political Studies* as a test case for the interplay between politics and law at the time is slightly mysterious. Apart from *Public Administration* Griffith might also have looked at *The Political Quarterly* whose joint founding editor was his LSE colleague, William Robson. In an article on the foundation of

6 N Duxbury, *Jurists and Judges: An Essay on Influence* (Hart Publishing, 2001) p 71.

7 J Bridge, 'The Academic Lawyer: Mere Working Mason or Architect?' (1975) 91 *Law Quarterly Review* 488 at 494.

8 G Wilson, 'English Legal Scholarship' (1987) 50 *Modern Law Review* 818 at 819.

9 M Bódig, 'Legal Theory and Legal Doctrinal Scholarship' (2010) 23 *Canadian Journal of Law and Jurisprudence* 483 at 494 (emphasis in original). Jones, in a defence of such scholarship past and present, writes of the '[r]igorous analysis of (then) case law and (now) statutory and case law, to discover true principle' (G Jones, '"Traditional" Legal Scholarship: A Personal View' in P Birks (ed), *Pressing Problems in Law: Volume 2: What Are Law Schools For?* (Oxford University Press, 1996) p 9). See also R Cotterrell, *The Sociology of Law* (2nd edn, Butterworths, 1992) p 2; C McCrudden, 'Legal research and the Social Sciences' (2006) 122 *Law Quarterly Review* 632 at 633; and, more generally, S Perry, 'Interpretation and Methodology in Legal Theory' in A Marmor (ed), *Law and Interpretation: Essays in Legal Philosophy* (Clarendon Press, 1995).

10 Griffith, n 2, p 3.

11 Ibid., p 2. D. Harris, 'The development of socio-legal studies in the United Kingdom' (1983) 3 *Legal Studies* 315 at 333.

The Political Quarterly Robson wrote that his appointment as joint editor was because of, inter alia, his expertise in administrative law, labour legislation and law reform.[12] In 1982 article titles in the *The Political Quarterly* included 'Inspecting Prisons', 'Police Discretion', 'Police Powers', 'The Finger on the Policeman's Collar', 'The Law Lords and the Needs of Contemporary Society' and 'Who are the Police?'. Harris's view of the state of relations between political science and law therefore seems to have been more accurate than that of Griffith. Nevertheless, the general position of socio-legal studies in law schools was poor. Even by 1997, Hutter and Lloyd-Bostock were suggesting that 'socio-legal studies is, in many aspects, still in its infancy'.[13] Law schools in 1982 thus did not offer the most propitious intellectual climate to argue for the intimate connection between law and politics.

The situation in the present day could scarcely be more different. If socio-legal studies is understood simply as the acknowledgement that the study of law must include the use of techniques and methods taken from the social sciences and humanities and cannot attend solely to judgments and legislation analysed on their own terms socio-legal studies now dominates research done in law schools in the United Kingdom.[14] In very broad terms, in acknowledging the necessity to study law as a human artefact rather than as a self-contained set of rules, legal research now assumes the connection between law and politics. Current debate is not about whether there is such a connection; it is about its nature.

Judges and politics

We know little about what judges thought about the connection between law and politics at the time that Griffith gave his lecture. The constraints of the Kilmuir Rules as well as a general culture of judicial reticence meant that extra-judicial writing was relatively restricted compared with the present era.[15] A restricted

12 W Robson, 'The Founding of the Political Quarterly' (1970) 41 *The Political Quarterly* 1 at 9.

13 B Hutter and S Lloyd-Bostock, 'Law's Relationship with Social Science: The Interdependence of Theory, Empirical Work, and Social Relevance in Socio-Legal Studies' in K Hawkins (ed), *The Human Face of Law: Essays in Honour of Donald Harris* (Clarendon Press, 1997) p 38.

14 F Cownie, *Legal Academics: Identities and Culture* (Hart Publishing, 2004) pp 54–8 and McCrudden, n 9, pp 642–645. For a contrary view, asserting that doctrinalism still prevails, see D Howarth, *Law as Engineering: Thinking About What Lawyers Do* (Edward Elgar, 2013) p 149. However Howarth, unlike Cownie, provides no empirical evidence to support his view. In any event Howarth argues for the desirability of what he sees as a new research agenda which would 'reconnect legal research with empirical social science research': p 167.

15 For the foundation of the Kilmuir Rules, see A Bradley, 'Judges and the media – the Kilmuir Rules' [1986] *Public Law* 283. When he became Lord Chancellor in 1987 Lord Mackay decided not to enforce the Kilmuir Rules (D Oliver, 'Politicians and Courts' (1988) 41 *Parliamentary Affairs* 13 at 17). Evidence for the general culture of the senior judiciary lies partially in the fact that Kilmuir said that he acted with the approval of the Lord Chief Justice, The Master of the Rolls and the President of the Probate, Divorce and Admiralty Division (Bradley, p 38). Other judges also commented on the general need for judicial silence in public; see, for example, Lord Radcliffe quoted in P Atiyah, 'Judges and Policy' (1980) 15 *Israel Law Review* 346 at 357. See further J Young, 'The Politics of the Human Rights Act' (1999) 26 *Journal of Law and Society* 27 at 35–6.

amount of writing does not mean that there was no writing.[16] Whilst much of this writing was of a technical or mundane nature some material that was published did relate to the matters pertaining to the connection between law and politics.[17] Perhaps the most noteworthy example of this was Patrick Devlin's book *The Judge*, a collection of previously published lectures, which he, in his preface, describes as 'thoughts on different facets of a single aspect, which is the place of the judge in the political life of the country. What part does he play in the government of it?'[18]

Nonetheless, at the time when Griffith gave his lecture there is a general paucity of judicial comment on the subject of the connection between law and politics.[19] Similarly those few academics at the time who sought to understand the working of the judicial mind did not look at the connection between law and politics. Thus, for example, Paterson's book on the Law Lords, published in 1976, based upon interviews he conducted with both existing and retired Law Lords, notes the possibility of the legislature being a reference group for the Law Lords, and thus a potential connection between law and politics, but does not analyse this further.[20] Griffith's lecture is therefore given in what was largely a vacuum as regards the judges' own known views on the connection between law and politics.[21]

Academics now work in an era where not only have the Kilmuir Rules been abandoned but extra-judicial writing by the judges is widely publicised by the courts themselves, with both the Supreme Court and the Court of Appeal having websites that detail judicial speeches.[22] Whilst much of this material is focused on technical matters a considerable quantity relates directly to the connection that there is between law and politics. Thus, for example, the judges themselves describe their work, in their extra-judicial writing, as being 'the weakest and least dangerous department of government', debate, this time in both extra-judicial writing

16 A notable example of this is B Harvey (ed.), *The Lawyer and Justice* (Sweet and Maxwell, 1978) which brought together 14 essays, 12 of which were from serving judges.

17 See, for example, Lord Edmund-Davies, 'Judicial Activism' (1975) 28 *Current Legal Problems* 1.

18 P Devlin, *The Judge* (Oxford University Press, 1979) p vii. Devlin was a retired Law Lord when he gave these lectures.

19 One exception to this is Devlin's 'Judges, Government and Politics', which is in large part a review and response to Griffith's book *The Politics of the Judiciary* (P Devlin, 'Judges, Government and Politics' (1978) 41 *Modern Law Review* 501 at 505–11).

20 A Paterson, *The Law Lords* (Macmillan, 1976) p 9.

21 Which is not to say that academics were not writing about judges and politics. Thus, for example, in the preface to his monograph on judicial policy arguments, Bell writes '[m]y aim in this book has been to analyse the judicial function in contemporary government' (J Bell, *Policy Arguments in Judicial decisions* (Clarendon Press, 1983) p v). Other contributions to this debate published within a few years of Griffith's lecture include J Hackney, 'The Politics of Chancery' (1981) *Current Legal Problems* 113 and R Stevens, *Law and Politics: The House of Lords as a Judicial Body, 1800–1976* (Weidenfeld and Nicolson, 1979). The latter was reviewed by Griffith. In his review Griffith wrote that 'this book . . . is not about law and politics. It is about the attitudes of certain judges to their task of adjudication' (*Spectator*, 11 August 1979, p 19).

22 See https://www.supremecourt.uk/news/speeches.html; http://www.judiciary.gov.uk/you-and-the-judiciary/going-to-court/court-of-appeal-home/speeches/ (accessed 20 August 2015).

and in their rulings, the desirability of the doctrine of parliamentary sovereignty and, again in both extra-judicial writing and their rulings, vaunt, or not, the value of the notion of fundamental rights as a constitutional protection.[23] In the present era the nexus between law and politics is clear to judges and is publicly discussed by judges; how then could it not now be obvious to academics? Given this change it is unsurprising that the academic literature on the judiciary now assumes the connection between law and politics and seeks to analyse its workings. Thus, for example, the penultimate chapter of Paterson's 2013 book *Final Judgement: The Last Law Lords and the Supreme Court*, is entitled 'The Dialogue with Other Branches of Government'.[24] The subject-matter of Griffith's lecture is thus now seen as being central to a conversation that the senior judiciary are involved in.

'Religious rights'

Thus far the changes that have occurred since Griffith's lecture have been ones that have made it easier in the present day to make the broad case about law and politics he made than it was at the time he gave his lecture. However, we now need to turn to matters where the reverse is so.

In his lecture Griffith argues against both notions of natural law in general and what he terms 'religious writers' such as Rawls and Dworkin in particular.[25] To look at the jurisprudential arguments that he raises lies outside the scope of this chapter. What, however, is relevant is the change in the legal landscape for his arguments. For Griffith what is crucial is the distinction between legal rights and both political rights and natural rights; that political rights are simply claims and natural rights are, borrowing Bentham's phrase, 'nonsense upon stilts' whilst legal rights are rights which a court will uphold.[26] Here the changes in the landscape that are important are the Human Rights Act 1998 and the judicial notion that predates it – the idea of fundamental rights.

In the strictest sense rights found in the Human Rights Act 1998 are what Griffith would have recognised as legal rights.[27] However, to see them simply in that way is

23 Lord Steyn, 'The Weakest and Least Dangerous Department of Government' [1997] *Public Law* 84; see, for example, Lord Hope, 'Sovereignty in Question – A View from the Bench' (2011), http://www.supremecourt.uk/docs/speech_110628.pdf (accessed 20 August 2015); T Bingham, *The Rule of Law* (Allen Lane, 2010) Ch 12 (although it should be noted that Lord Bingham had retired from the Supreme Court by the time he published this book); and Lady Hale, Lord Hope and Lord Steyn in *Jackson v Attorney General* [2006] 1 AC 262 at 302, 303 and 318; see, for example, Sir John Laws, 'Constitutional Guarantees' (2008) 29(1) *Statute Law Review* 1; Lord Sumption, 'The Limits of Law' (2013), http://www.supremecourt.uk/docs/speech-131120.pdf (accessed 20 August 2015); and Lord Hoffmann in *R v Secretary of State for the Home Department ex p Simms* [2000] 2 AC 115 at 131.

24 A Paterson, *Final Judgement: The Last Law Lords and the Supreme Court* (Hart Publishing, 2013) Ch 7.

25 Griffith, n 2, p 5.

26 Ibid., pp 4–5.

27 Thus, for example, Campbell sees the Act as an example of an attempt 'to concretize or positivize human rights by rendering them more specific and justiciable' (T Campbell, 'Human Rights: A Culture of Controversy' (1999) 26 *Journal of Law and Society* 6 at 9).

to ignore both the rhetorical force that they have and their philosophical underpinnings. Feldman, for example, comments that '[t]he Human Rights Act 1998 is . . . not an ordinary statute' whilst Nicol observes that 'the HRA was not intended solely for judicial consumption. Rather, the government's avowed aim in introducing it was to engender a pervasive rights culture, embracing all institutions of governance'.[28]

Rights in the Human Rights Act 1998, with their direct source in the European Convention on Human Rights (again legal rights in the strict sense), have both a different position and a different provenance to rights in a standard statute. The Act is plainly pertinent to the subject-matter of Griffith's lecture. As Ewing writes, 'the Act . . . represents an unprecedented transfer of political power from the executive and the legislature to the judiciary'.[29] However, it is not a change that reflects what Griffith thought the place of the courts in politics ought to be. His remarks in his lecture about 'religious writers' are general but in an earlier article he had been more specific rejecting the arguing against in the desirability of a Bill of Rights.[30]

The notion of fundamental rights raises, for the purposes of this chapter, very similar issues to those noted earlier with respect to the Human Rights Act 1998. Since they are so similar the concept can be dealt with more shortly. One difference between the notion of fundamental rights and the Human Rights Act should, however, be noted. Whilst the Human Rights Act does exist as a statute only some judges have written in support of the notion of fundamental rights; its very existence therefore is somewhat equivocal. Some judges do see a utility in the notion of fundamental rights. For those judges the idea is fairly clear, at least in broad terms:

> 'Parliamentary sovereignty means that Parliament can, if it chooses, legislate contrary to fundamental principles of human rights . . . But the principle of legality means that parliament must squarely confront what it is doing and accept the political cost. Fundamental rights cannot be overridden by general or ambiguous words . . .'[31]

Like the rights in the Human Rights Act, the rights are legal in Griffith's terms, and exist independent of the Act, but they are also, again in Griffith's terms, 'religious' in their nature.[32] Unsurprisingly Griffith was critical of those who support the idea.[33] The idea changes the connection between law and politics in a manner that was objectionable to Griffith.

28 D Feldman, 'The Human Rights Act 1998 and constitutional principles' (1999) 19 *Legal Studies* 165 at 180; D Nicol, 'The Human Rights Act and the politicians' (2004) 24 *Legal Studies* 451 at 452.

29 K Ewing 'The Human Rights Act and Parliamentary Democracy' (1999) 62 *Modern Law Review* 79 at 79.

30 J Griffith, 'The Political Constitution' (1979) 42 *Modern Law Review* 1 at 14.

31 *R v Secretary of State for the Home Department ex p. Simms* [2000] 2 AC 115 at 131.

32 Thus, for example, one of the proponents of the notion, Sir John Laws, had written about the existence of the idea long before the Act. See, for example, Sir John Laws, 'Is the High Court the Guardian of Fundamental Rights?' (1992) 18 *Commonwealth Law Bulletin* 1385.

33 See J Griffith, 'The Brave New World of Sir John Laws' (2000) 63 *Modern Law Review* 159 and J Griffith, 'The Common Law and the Political Constitution' (2001) 117 *Law Quarterly Review* 42.

The rule of law

Griffith's lecture concerned itself in part with the rule of law. However, at the time he wrote the principle of the rule of law was rarely referred to directly in judicial argument.[34] In the modern era judges regularly raise the idea of the rule of law in support of their arguments.[35] The highpoint in the use of such argument to date is to be seen in *Jackson v Attorney General*. In this case Lord Hope argued that '[t]he rule of law enforced by the courts is the ultimate controlling factor on which our constitution is based', whilst Baroness Hale suggested that '[t]he courts will treat with particular suspicion (and might even reject) any attempt to subvert the rule of law by removing governmental action affecting the rights of the individual from all judicial scrutiny'.[36]

In *Jackson*, Lord Steyn, like Baroness Hale and Lord Hope, doubted the efficacy of the traditional concept of parliamentary sovereignty.[37] Unlike them he did not explicitly refer to the idea of the rule of law to support his arguments. However, in a subsequently published article, like his judgment in *Jackson* based in part on Lord Hailsham's book *The Dilemma of Democracy* and which took as its theme similar ideas to those which he had put forward in *Jackson*, Lord Steyn argued that '[t]he greater the arrogation of power by a seemingly all-powerful executive which dominates the House of Commons, the greater the incentive and need for the judges to protect the rule of law'.[38]

It seems clear that the notion of the rule of law motivated Lord Steyn's objection to the notion of parliamentary sovereignty in *Jackson* as much as it did the views of Baroness Hale and Lord Hope.

For Griffith in his lecture the idea of the rule of law was a 'slippery concept'.[39] For some of the present-day judiciary the idea has become a powerful tool which involves them 'counterposing to the idea of the sovereignty of parliament the idea of the rule of law'.[40] As with 'religious rights' the new usage makes more manifest the nexus between law and politics and draws the senior judiciary directly into

34 The Lexis database of All England Law Reports records the use of the notion of rule of law as a legal argument in only five cases in the few years prior to 1982.

35 The Lexis database of All England Law Reports records 15 cases where this argument is used in the first six months of 2014.

36 *Jackson v Attorney General* [2006] 1 AC 262 at 305 and 318.

37 Ibid., p 302.

38 Lord Steyn, 'Democracy, the rule of law and the role of judges' (2006) *European Human Rights Law Review* 242 at 247.

39 Griffith, n 2, p 6.

40 V Bognador,'The Liberal Party and the Constitution' (2007) 54 *Journal of Liberal History* 46 at 49. For the most complete analysis of this juxtaposition, see J Jowell, 'Parliamentary Sovereignty under the New Constitutional Hypothesis' [2006] *Public Law* 562.

an analysis of this connection.[41] However, it seems unlikely that Griffith would welcome the new political role that some of the judiciary have sought to arrogate to themselves.

Teaching

All of the above would seem to suggest that there is a radical schism between the past and the present. In terms of the analysis of the relationship between law and politics there is much to support such a position. However, such analysis was not the title that Griffith gave to his lecture; instead, the lecture was entitled 'The Teaching of Law and Politics' and it was to the matter of teaching that he turned in his final two paragraphs.

Consideration of Grifftth's remarks on teaching would, at least superficially, suggest that the notion of the disjunction between past and present is continued even in this final section of his lecture. 'All good teaching', asserts Griffith, 'is based on observation: that is, by watching the class and seeing whether what we are saying to them is being received . . . and understood'.[42] Such scant analysis, unsupported by any reference to relevant literature, seems to be a world away from an era in which neophyte academics receive compulsory training in techniques of teaching and journals are replete with material on how to teach courses, including courses about law and politics.[43] This is not to imply that such courses necessarily improve the quality of teaching; their existence does, however, suggest a closer and more nuanced attention to the importance of teaching, at least in, to use Trow's terminology, the public life of the university.[44]

All of the above would seem to suggest that the most accurate response to Griffith's lecture is summed up in the title of Robert Graves' volume of memoirs published after the first world war, *Goodbye to All That*; that things have changed vastly in a wide variety of ways in the 33 years between his lecture and the present

41 Not all senior judges see an opposition between the notions of parliamentary sovereignty and the rule of law. See, for example, T Bingham, *The Rule of Law* (Allen Lane, 2010) Ch 12. In *Jackson v Attorney General* Lord Bingham had noted the existence of the potential constitutional problem of 'the Commons, dominated by the executive, as the ultimately unconstrained power in the state'. He concluded his opinion with the observation that '[t]here are issues here which merit serious and objective thought and study. But it would be quite inappropriate for the House in its judicial capacity to express or appear to express any opinion upon them, and I do not do so': *Jackson v Attorney General*, n 36, pp 286–7.

42 Griffith, n 2, p 10.

43 On both current courses on teaching offered to new academics and on possible future developments in such courses see F Cownie, 'Twining, teachers of law and law teaching' (2011) 18 *International Journal of the Legal Profession* 121 at 126–36. See also H James, 'Supporting new law teachers – a study to determine needs' (2009) 43 *The Law Teacher* 200. On teaching law and politics see P Abrahams, 'We the People and Other Constitutional Tales: Narrative and Constitutional Meaning' (2007) 42 *The Law Teacher* 247.

44 On the distinction between the public life of the university, mission statements and the like, as compared with the private life, what goes on in actual seminars and lectures, see M Trow, 'The Public and Private Lives of Higher Education' (1975) 104 *Daedalus* 113.

day. In fact a more accurate reaction is to be found in the title of Graves' later collection, *But it Still Goes On*.[45]

The degree of attention that law schools pay to the study of law and politics has increased dramatically since 1982, as has the political role of the senior judiciary. Whether the teaching of the interaction of law and politics has changed is a moot point. Teaching is part of, again to use Trow's terminology, the private life of universities. Observing it and analysing it is thus difficult. However, scrutiny of textbooks can serve as a proxy for scrutiny of teaching. Textbooks may not be closely related to the teaching in some individual courses. Nevertheless, if there were no general relation between textbooks and the nature of teaching done in courses there would be no purpose is setting them, buying them or reading them. Their very existence and their content thus say something about the nature of teaching.

In his lecture Griffith refers only to one court judgment. Elsewhere his references, sometimes brief and sometimes lengthy, are to theorists from Plato to Perry Anderson. By contrast public law textbooks in the present day remain much more things about legal rules. Cases and statutes figure heavily in footnotes. References to writers from outside law schools are relatively rare and relatively brief. Grand debates about politics may be alluded to but they are peripheral to the main thrust of the textbook's task. If they are books about law and politics, and many are, they are more about law than they are about politics. In our research law schools may now believe that public law is 'a discourse of political right' but in our teaching we largely take a different approach.[46] The fact that textbooks have tables of cases and statutes but not bibliographies is hugely significant. The content of such books may now be more sophisticated than it was at the time Griffith gave his lecture but their basic form seems to have changed very little. Whilst in our research the majority of UK legal academics have followed the path favoured by Griffith and have become socio-legal in their approach, teaching appears to have lagged behind. In this important sense little has changed since 1982. Research into law and politics now seems to be much more in accord with Griffith's lecture; teaching law and politics is still stuck in the past.

45 For an account of the complicated history of, and motivations behind, *Goodbye to All That* and also the later volume *But it Still Goes On*, see R Graves, *Robert Graves: The Years with Laura, 1926–40* (Macmillan, 1991).

46 M Loughlin, *Foundations of Public Law* (Oxford University Press, 2010).

23 Twenty-fifth Lord Upjohn Lecture 1996

The Integration of Teaching and Research in the Law Department[1]

Dawn Oliver Q.C.

University law schools are currently in a state of some suspense. Our submissions for the latest research assessment exercise (RAE) were sent off some weeks ago and we await the results at the turn of the year. On those results will hang: funding decisions by the Higher Education Funding Council (HEFCE); the ability of departments to attract good students, especially for postgraduate work; the ability to attract and retain research active staff; and the ability to attract funds for research from the Research Councils, the grant giving charities and other sources. So most university law departments feel themselves to be under pressure to do well in the RAE. But the fact of the matter is that by no means all law departments or all law teachers engage to any great extent in research activity.[2]

Until the abolition of the binary divide and the reorganisation of the funding of universities that followed it the former polytechnics were not eligible for funding for research from HEFCE, so their research activity had to be conducted within the funding for teaching – squeezed in as a side line, so to speak – or else it had to be funded through the award of grants or contracts. Much excellent research, often applied, was conducted in the former polytechnics – and is conducted in the new universities – but the history of funding and status still affects the level of research activity in the new universities.

My purposes in this lecture are, first, to look at the evidence about the relationships between the activities of teaching and research in law schools and the pros and cons of combining the two. I shall consider the position of departments for whom HEFCE funding for research may not be available. I shall suggest that, where teaching and research are combined, there are some hard and sometimes risky decisions to be made about the management of the two activities and in particular about how, and how much, teaching takes place and the division

1 This lecture was delivered as the twenty-fifth Lord Upjohn Lecture at the Inns of Court School of Law on 17 May 1996.

2 Leighton, Mortimer and Whatley found that 35 per cent of staff in law departments in new universities did not engage in research as compared to 4 per cent in old universities. Overall 60 per cent of principal lecturers (in new universities and colleges of further education) were engaged in research: P. Leighton, T. Mortimer and N. Whatley, *Today's Law Teachers: Lawyers or Academics?* (1995), at p. 38.

of resources between undergraduate and postgraduate teaching. I shall also try to face up to some unpleasant truths, in particular the likelihood that the underfunding of universities will continue and the likelihood, as I see it, that HEFCE funding for research will not be available to all universities or all law departments. Research funding in England and Wales is almost certainly going to be increasingly selective. An Ivy League (as *The Times* was calling it earlier this week)[3] may be developing as foreign governments grade universities, thus affecting the recruitment of overseas students. The recent Harris Report calls for a two-tier postgraduate system in which HEFCE funds for research students would be targeted at departments who score 3 or above in the RAE.[4] And the National Academic Policy Advisory Group (see later) has recently called for research funds to be concentrated on the most research active institutions.

This is a difficult issue for me to discuss. I am very conscious that my audience contains many law teachers who are faced with the possibility of having to work in departments with poor staff-student ratios and without HEFCE research funding; I am also very conscious of the fact that my university, UCL, would probably be in the Ivy League of universities if one were to develop. This makes me singularly unqualified to give this lecture. I want to take this opportunity to say that I would very much regret the withdrawal of research funding from some universities and law departments, and that in daring to look that possibility in the face I should not be taken to condone it.

Relationships between teaching and research

[. . .]

I take research for HEFCE purposes to mean 'the advancement of learning, the discovery of new knowledge or of new associations between events or phenomena already known'.[5]

The orthodox view among academics (at least in the old universities which, as we have noted, benefited from the old dual support system in receiving public funds to conduct research) is that research and teaching enhance one another. The Robbins Report put it very elegantly – and at length. Their view can be captured in the following extract:

> 'It is of the essence of higher education that it introduces students to a world of intellectual responsibility and intellectual discovery in which they are to

3 'Top universities forced into new Ivy League', *The Times*, 13 May 1996.

4 The review of postgraduate education, led by Professor Martin Harris, Vice-Chancellor of Manchester University, was commissioned jointly by HEFCE, the Standing Committee of Principals and the Committee of Vice-Chancellors and Principals and published on 15 May 1996.

5 The definition adopted by the National Academic Policy Advisory Group (NAPAG) in its report, *Research Capability of the University System* (The Royal Society, 1996), at p. 5. The members of the NAPAG are the British Academy, the Conference of Medical Royal Colleges, the Royal Academy of Engineers and the Royal Society.

play their part . . . There is no borderline between teaching and research; they are complementary and overlapping activities.'[6]

In their Policy Document *Commitment to Scholarship and Research in Universities* in 1993 the National Conference of University Professors stated that 'The scholarship of discovery which should prevail (in universities) is purposeful in several ways: it contributes not only to the stock of knowledge but also essentially to the intellectual climate of a university and thereby to the quality of teaching' (at p. 13) and 'scholarship and research are indispensable complements of university teaching' (at p. 14). 'Higher education cannot afford to lose its tradition of scholarship, which rewards students with insights into the continual development and unfolding of knowledge' (at p. 15).[7]

On the other hand Durham and Oldham report that at the SRHE Leverhulme seminar in 1981 the generally accepted wisdom that teaching and research are intimately related was challenged and most participants in the seminar agreed that there was no evidence to support it.[8] No doubt the position varies from discipline to discipline, but recent Research Assessments and the first Teaching Quality Assessments do seem to provide evidence that the two activities enhance one another, at least in relation to *legal* research. However, it is also clear that good teaching *can* take place in departments with little or no research activity.[9]

6 *Report of the Committee on Higher Education* ('Robbins Report'), HMSO, Cmnd. 2154, 1963, paras 555, 557.

7 National Conference of University Professors, *Commitment to Scholarship and Research in Universities* (NCUP, Newcastle on Tyne, 1993).

8 F. Durham and G. Oldham in G. Oldham (ed), *The Future of Research* (1982), at p. 215

9 The HEFCE *Report on Quality Assessment 1992–1995* (1995) found that assessment reports identified 'Broad and flexible curricula that are well matched with aims and objectives and are informed by up-to-date scholarship and research' and 'Well qualified and committed staff, whose teaching is underpinned by scholarship and research' (at p. 11) among characteristics that peer assessors associated with excellent education across the sector and across subjects. And that Report's comparison of RAE Ratings and Quality Assessment Excellent Judgments (Table 10) found that all Law Departments placed in grade 5 in the 1992 RAE achieved a rating of Excellent in the Teaching Assessment, 86 per cent of Departments with a research grade of 4 were rated Excellent, and 60 per cent of those with a research grade of 3. Eight per cent of those with a research grade of 2 were rated Excellent in teaching, and none of those with a research raring of 1. If we look at the matter the other way round – the percentage of law schools rated Excellent that had strong research ratings – we find that 28 per cent of those rated Excellent were in grade 5 in research, 33 per cent in grade 4 research, and 33 per cent in grade 3. Six per cent were in grade 2. We shall see later this year whether the latest research assessment confirms that there are correlations between high quality research and excellent teaching. The Advisory Committee on Legal Education and Conduct (ACLEC) has recently recognised the importance of staff being involved in research and scholarly activity: *First Report on Legal Education and Training* (1996), at para. 338.

The recent National Academies Policy Advisory Group (NAPAG) report to which I referred earlier, *Research Capability of the University System*,[10] observes that, with the end of the old dual support system 'the tacit assumptions that university teaching and research are inseparable, and that universities need to have research money if they are to provide high-quality university teaching'[11] are gone. This, it seems to me, raises questions about the nature of a university – questions which were inevitable when the old binary line was abolished and institutions without strong records in research became universities.[12]

But why, exactly, are teaching and research supposed to go well together? In preparing for this lecture I asked colleagues in my department about the benefits and disbenefits their teaching brought to their research, and vice versa. Without exception all of those who replied to my questionnaire felt that teaching was beneficial to their research, and their research was beneficial to their teaching. Not one would have wanted to work in a research-only institution or a teaching-only institution. None of the ways in which they find the two activities to be mutually beneficial are very surprising but it may be informative to set them out briefly here.[13]

The benefits to researchers of the process of teaching are often not appreciated. They include the experience that explaining things to students can help to clarify one's own thoughts and compel a researcher to formulate thoughts and tentative conclusions in a concrete, presentable form; teaching keeps one up to date; it highlights researchable issues and maintains the critical attitude that is necessary to research. Teaching frequently raises issues of difficulty which would not have been noticed, and it enforces a wide view of the subject as a counterweight to the specialisation that research often involves. And teaching helps test research hypotheses and findings. In LLM teaching in particular one's research is exposed to critical comment, especially where there are students from other jurisdictions and other disciplines in the class. Students can often contribute new insights into areas of research and give helpful feedback. In other words, students are invaluable sounding boards for researchers. Teaching can also bring academics into contact with other research active colleagues, and this can stimulate ideas, research and collaboration. This is especially the case in postgraduate teaching in the University of London LLM, for example, where courses are shared, often with members of other London university law schools, or other disciplines.

10 See n. 5.

11 Ibid., at p. 12.

12 We should note in passing that it seems that the United Kingdom differs from other European countries in this commitment to combining research and teaching. I do not know what theories of learning inform teaching in continental law schools, though it seems that the staff student ratios are far worse there than here, that learning is seldom very participative, and that students are expected to do far more for themselves than is the case with students in English universities.

13 A full account would take too long.

As far as the other side of the coin – the benefits of research to students – is concerned, many of the points mentioned can clearly be applied equally the other way round. Research activity can also generate primary source materials for teaching, and original insights into the subject; it can provide examples, applications, case studies, data, sometimes theory to explain and illustrate legal processes. A researcher has more to say to the students than what is in the textbooks. Research can furnish the issues for assessment by examination.

[. . .]

An especially important point in my view is that the research activity of teachers should shape students' attitudes to scholarship generally. It can assist the development of students' ideas and detached critical analysis; it can boost their analytical training. It helps to increase students' enthusiasm for discussing the acquisition of knowledge and ideas through research. It can bring home to perceptive students that knowledge is not static, that all answers are provisional and no solution final. Another way of putting it, used by one member of the department, was that 'one shares one's puzzlement with students'. Not all students, of course, welcome this, but recognition of puzzlement as legitimate is, I suggest, something that students need to learn.

One way of testing assertions of the benefits of combining research and teaching is against the views of students. What do students consider to be the most important qualities of a good teacher? Do they attach any importance to research? Qualities mentioned by our students in the (admittedly paltry) response to my survey were to do with intellectual qualities, including knowledge of the subject, and personality and attitude. Qualities in the first category included intellectual coherence, clarity, strong analysis, knowledge. Qualities in the second category included an open ear, patience, interest in students, ability to transfer knowledge, ability to maintain interest, enthusiasm, an ability to share and demonstrate personal opinions, and an ability to encourage student participation.[14]

It must be obvious to all of us that not all of the qualities of a good teacher depend on research activity, and nor is an excellent knowledge of the subject always essential in a teacher. A new teacher who has not yet built up much

14 This list of qualities of a good teacher contrasts with those given by Ramsden, for instance, in his important work on teaching in higher education, which did not mention intellectual coherence, strong analysis and knowledge: P. Ramsden, *Learning to Teach in Higher Education* (1992), at p. 89. This point illustrates the tendency in much writing about teaching methods and the learning experiences of students to overlook or undervalue the expertise of the teacher in the subject, and to focus instead on qualities of personality and process and the acquisition of skills. The aspect of learning that involves acquiring knowledge and understanding that are only available from a teacher possessing them is given scant if any attention in much of the literature on the art of teaching, which seems to assume that the subject is unproblematically there and somehow the tutor need only be a step ahead of the students as long as he or she is creating good learning experiences through participative methods and so on and the students are acquiring skills. This does not, it seems to me, recognise the advantages of the integration of teaching and research, especially at advanced levels of teaching.

research can have many of the qualities of a good teacher, though he or she may not have the excellent knowledge of a subject students expect or hope for. Most of us can remember being only a few pages ahead of students some of the time when we started to teach, and yet our teaching may have been good or at least adequate for the purpose, if we had the other qualities referred to. We need to admit, I think, that some teaching, especially in the first year of a law degree, does not require excellent knowledge of a subject.[15] I consider this point to be important because it bears on the pressure on every teacher to be active in research all the time that can make life unnecessarily uncomfortable for some teachers and departments.

I think we also need to admit that there can be disadvantages and problems where teachers are combining teaching with research activity. Pressures of time can lead staff to devote less of their effort to teaching, preparation, marking, etc. than they should. Researchers may assume that students have greater background knowledge than in actual fact they do and impose too great a workload on students. They may be too wrapped up in their latest projects and difficult issues and so spend insufficient time ensuring that the students understand the basics. Some teachers may communicate to students their view that teaching is an inferior activity to research and that teaching distracts them from their 'real' work.

To summarise my position, then, before moving on to considering matters of management, I suggest that research often benefits from teaching activity (save for the time pressures that teaching imposes). This benefit is often overlooked. Students, I believe, benefit from being taught, at least some of the time, by researchers, and this is the ideal. But at intermediate – or undergraduate – level, as long as the students are receiving some experience of the Robbins world of intellectual responsibility and intellectual discovery[16] from some of their teachers, it is probably better to be taught by good non-research teachers than by poor teachers who are good researchers. As students progress through undergraduate degree courses it becomes increasingly beneficial for them to have contact in their learning experiences with active researchers.[17] At advanced levels of study, especially in some specialised subjects and in taught Masters degrees, students no longer need to acquire skills (though of course skills can be honed indefinitely).

Students will be wanting to get to grips with the substance of subjects. At this level it may be that only a researcher can teach. Here it is probably better to be taught by a poor teacher with expertise in the subject than not to be offered the subject at all. That is not to condone poor teaching, but to be realistic about the

15 Though lack of an *adequate* knowledge can of course leave students with positive misunderstandings and undermine student confidence in themselves and their tutor.

16 See Robbins Report, n. 6.

17 As one member of my department put it, 'some difficult, highly theoretical subjects can only be learned and deeply understood through the experience of observing a great scholar talking about a subject and thinking creatively out loud'.

difficulties of finding people with the qualities of both good teachers and strong researchers in some subject areas.

As we all know, there are pressures at work which are damaging to both teaching and research, especially in law departments, which are often treated by their universities as sources of cheap teaching for large numbers of students.[18] With deteriorating staff student ratios,[19] the emergence of the consumer student who makes increasing demands for contact hours, assessed work, handouts and good results, and the time-consuming bureaucratic demands of audit, quality assessment and quality assurance, it is easy for staff morale to suffer. The quality of teaching suffers too and research activity is squeezed in various ways – research is time consuming, but it can wait from day to day in a way that teaching and administration cannot. The funding regimes operated by HEFCE impose often unnecessary or unrealistic pressures on law departments. We could do with clearer criteria from HEFCE about, for instance, what level of non-research active, or not very research active, staff is tolerable in a top class department, which still has to assign to some of its members jobs that make research activity difficult to sustain, such as being dean, head of department (or both), faculty tutor and so on.

The position of departments who do not receive HEFCE research funding

Given the pressures we are all under, I fear that quite a number of law departments – probably those rated at 2 in the RAE – will have to face up to the fact that they will in future receive little or no funding for research from HEFCE. Others will have to face up to the fact that, though their research is strong, it will not be adequately funded by HEFCE.

I think it would be very regrettable if substantial numbers of law schools were put in the position that no scholarly research at all is taking place there because of inadequate funding. The students cannot experience the Robbins world of intellectual discovery in a research-free environment. However, I think it would be wrong to assume that, in the absence of HEFCE research funding, no research activity will be possible in a department. In practice it is possible to conduct scholarly research in law at relatively low cost when compared to many other disciplines. Depending on the sort of research, much can be achieved with time and access to the right sort of library. Before the end of the binary divide many polytechnic law teachers conducted excellent research, without the equivalent of HEFCE support. Of course the cuts in government funding and increases in

18 ACLEC in its First Report (n 9) urges universities to take account of needs of law schools: at para. 3.39.

19 In the 'Other Social Studies' in which law is placed staff student ratios have deteriorated from 13.5 to 17.8 between 1988–89 and 1993–94: the position of law is usually much worse than this (see NAPAG Report, n. 5).

student numbers make this especially difficult nowadays but, as a natural optimist, I would not want to concede the point that research is not possible without HEFCE funding.

A difficulty in departments where little or no research activity is taking place is that staff may become demotivated, and their teaching may suffer. Research, as we have seen, adds spice to teaching. The recent NAPAG report on *Research Capability of the University System*[20] comes up with a proposal that part of the HEFCE research funding that currently goes to departments rated at 2 in the RAE ought to go instead into professional development and teaching (PDT). This fund, it suggests, should be targeted at departments with staff student ratios above the national average which did not enter the most recent RAE. The money could be used to reduce staff student ratios (presumably through the recruitment of additional staff) thus providing staff with time to keep abreast of their subjects, and to contribute to the support of staff through library and laboratory resources for teaching, staff training and the costs of academic collaboration with other institutions.

I have no doubt that the implicit acceptance in these proposals that university teaching can take place in a research-free environment will be challenged. But, as NAPAG observes, the assumption that universities need to have research money if they are to provide high-quality university teaching has already been rejected with the changing of the status of polytechnics to universities. I do not see any government returning to the old position that research funding should be available to all universities – it is too expensive. But the potential benefits of the PDT proposal should not be drowned in calls for the impossible – research funding for all. It could well be that if the pressure to engage in research were removed from departments meeting the above criteria, staff morale, especially of those who do not really wish to be research active, would rise and with it the quality of teaching. Staff would no longer need to feel that they were inadequate or letting down their departments because they were not producing research. Resources could become available to enhance the learning experiences of students through staff training or the purchase of equipment – computer access for computer assisted learning – for instance. The 'mission drift' that NAPAG complains of, which pushes institutions into research when historically they had other, worthy and comfortable missions, could cease. And, as I have already indicated, some research could still take place in those departments.

Managing the integration of teaching and research

Even where money is available to support teaching and research, management matters to the effective integration of the two activities. Good teaching (or, more accurately, good learning experiences) and good research do not just happen.

20 Note 5.

There is not the space to say much about this here, and in any event much of what is needed if the integration of teaching and research is to be well managed is obvious. The institutional ethos – at university and departmental levels – is crucial, and has to support the integration of teaching and research; teaching should provide outlets for research activity and this may mean channelling resources into LLM teaching in preference to LLB teaching; quite ruthless measures may have to be taken by the university, the department and individual academics to concentrate resources in the integration of research and teaching and in particular to protect high quality research potential and research activity from the encroachments of teaching and, especially, administration.

And, for me a very important point, students should be made to take a high degree of responsibility for their own learning. There is currently, as I have indicated already, a problem of a consumer culture and dependency among students, and too often tutors give in to this. It is manifested in law students expecting – and often receiving – far more contact hours than students in other humanities subjects normally receive. Students will often assume that the tutor is there to provide them with the answer to questions, whereas most of us do not think that is our job – and anyway we prefer to ask questions to which there is no definite answer. A consumer culture is also evident where students expect to be provided with study packs of materials that are in fact obtainable in libraries (packs of unobtainable material are obviously different and strongly to be recommended): preparation of these packs can consume valuable time that tutors could more profitably use in research.

There is general agreement in the literature on university teaching methods that the focus should be on the *learning experiences of students* rather than *the teaching activities of tutors*, and that students should learn to be independent and take responsibility for their own learning.[21] I agree. This is what a liberal education should be about.[22] The Advisory Committee on Legal Education and Conduct (ACLEC) in its First Report indicates that the consensus from their respondents was that law should be a liberal discipline.[23]

But it is my belief that in fact, despite greatly improved teaching methods, the quality of the student learning experience has deteriorated in many respects over the last, say, 15 years, because we have given in to consumer demands and not insisted on students taking this responsibility. The deterioration in student learning experience is not, in my view, just because of deteriorating staff student ratios and units of resource. I feel that, very much in the spirit of the times, many teachers tend to underestimate the ability of students to go deeply into a manageable amount of material themselves, but to overestimate the ability of students to cover

21 See Ramsden, n. 14, Chs 6, 8, 9, 10.

22 I have argued out elsewhere the extent to which a liberal law degree is in fact vocational: D. Oliver, 'In defence of the liberal law degree' in P. Birks, ed., *Reviewing Legal Education* (1994).

23 Note 9, at para. 2.2.

a lot of material. This produces a vicious circle. We tend – some of us at least – to give students more and more information, contact hours and handouts. But we find that we get less back from them in the way of knowledge, understanding and depth than they are capable of; and so we are tempted to lower our expectations of them and give them more attention. And so we relieve them of responsibility and take it upon ourselves. And it is often the most conscientious teachers who do this – and in so doing they damage their own research activity.

This concentrating of resources on teaching contributes substantially to the tensions and pressures we law teachers are under in trying to be excellent in our teaching *and* research.[24]

This problem of 'spoon-feeding' students results in part from the fact that the subject matter of law has increased enormously over the years. The literature only gets bigger, and enthusiastic teachers want their students to know about it. But the acquisition of large quantities of substantive knowledge – at least at undergraduate level – should not be the primary aim.

A strategy designed to shift the focus from teaching to learning should shift responsibility for the learning process from staff to students; it should mean that teachers' concerns should not be with transferring large quantities of information, delivering a set of lectures which express the tutor's matured view of the subject and ensuring that students get a good set of notes from the lectures which will enable them to answer questions in the forthcoming examination (which is what many of us instinctively want to do, and what the more senior of us experienced ourselves as students). Teachers should be concerned to ensure that the learning experience of students is active not passive, recognising that understanding is more important than rote learning of material, that depth is more important than breadth, that superficial learning is not desirable, and that students should acquire research skills and skills of analysis, synthesis and so on.[25] ACLEC has recently endorsed active learning arrangements (though acknowledging that they make heavy demands on resources[26]). But if this is to be achieved it will be essential to ensure that the coverage in a subject is not so broad that depth of study and understanding are impossible (ACLEC accepts this too).

For this kind of active learning experience, students do not require large numbers of contact hours. They require *quality* contact hours and a realisation of what is expected of them – a point made earlier. So I believe that some of the pressures that make research hard to conduct can be reduced with benefits to students as well as to teachers by requiring students to take a high degree of responsibility for their own learning and reducing the responsibilities of tutors in this regard.

24 And, again in my view importantly, it also contributes to the complaints that many employers make about law graduates, that too often they are not capable of doing independent research and their understanding is superficial.

25 See for instance Ramsden, n. 14; Birks, n. 22; R. Mager, *Preparing Instructional Objectives*, 2nd edn (1991).

26 Note 9, at paras 2.4, 3.38, 4.20.

But getting students to change their attitudes is hard, and it will not of itself solve many of the problems of integrating teaching and research and encouraging research activity. Many potentially excellent researchers need to learn how to manage their own research activity. They may need to develop their own short, medium and long term research plans, perhaps in consultation with a mentor, so that their energies are not dissipated across too wide a range of interests. They need to be realistic about their own abilities – again a mentor may help here. They may need help in judging whether the time is right to embark on writing an ambitious book (which can lead to people getting hopelessly bogged down) or whether it is better to concentrate on high quality articles. Most of us have to learn to say no to some invitations to write and research that will undermine our own strategies. But we also need to know when to seize good opportunities for research that do represent departures from the plan. Managing research at an individual level is not easy, and much will depend on the research culture of the department and the university.

A research culture doesn't just happen, it has to be cultivated. As Goddard has put it:

> '(Researchers) will only flourish in organisations that nurture and sustain (their) talent – through creating a lively intellectual milieu, encouraging multidisciplinary perspectives, providing specialist technical and administrative support, offering career development prospects and ensuring accountability for research funding.'[27]

Mutual confidence between staff, a supportive sense of academic community, study leave, flexibility in teaching, opportunities to teach to research interests, and so on all feed into it.

It is easy for there to be a lack of congruence between research activity and the ethos of teaching which inhibits the mutual benefits which they should bring to each other. Twining, in his account of the University of Rutland,[28] has highlighted how many subliminal (and some strongly liminal) messages can convey unintended messages about the value of academic activity to students. For instance, requiring all students (regardless of nationality and regardless of their career intentions) to take all the 'core', prescribed by the professions, emphasising the links with the professions that the school has established, focusing career advice on practice, not requiring students to take non-practical subjects – all of these could seem to negate the value of research in the sense we are using the word (the advancement of learning, the discovery of new knowledge or of new associations between events or phenomena already known) which requires an academic

27 *The Times Higher*, 15 March 1995. John Goddard is Dean of the Faculty of Law, Environment and Social Sciences, University of Newcastle, and member of the Association of Directors of Research Centres in the Social Sciences (DOROSS).

28 W. L. Twining, *Blackstone's Tower. The English Law School* (1994).

to be deeply reflective and concerned with theory, policy and the like and not simply with practicalities and vocational training.

A visit to QCL

[...]

Round up

The pressures are towards turning us into teaching and research machines. It would be easy to lose sight of the importance of the world of intellectual responsibility and intellectual discovery that is so central to universities in such an inhospitable climate. I regret that is it unlikely to be possible financially for all law schools to receive HEFCE funding for research in future. That need not mean the end of research activity in those law schools. But it could well demoralise teachers and damage the learning experience of students, unless resources are made available to enhance teaching and improve the quality of life and working conditions of teachers. It would be truly disastrous if research funding were withdrawn and no additional provision were made for staff and students in poorly provided-for departments.

For those departments who do receive research funding the battle to integrate teaching and research will not be over in the foreseeable future. Success in doing so requires the right institutional ethos and careful management of teaching and research. Law departments, like all university departments, are, I am afraid, living through very hard times.

24 Response: Fostering Curiosity

The Importance of Research and Teaching in Law Schools

Jessica Guth

It is striking that, with nothing more than a few tweaks, Dawn Oliver's Lord Upjohn Lecture on the integration of teaching and research in law schools could have been delivered today. Can it really be true that in nearly two decades almost nothing has changed? As I write, law schools have recently received the 2014 Research Excellence Framework results and have thus been released from the 'state of some suspense' in which Oliver wrote, as law schools then awaited the results of the 1996 Research Assessment Exercise.[1] It remains true that there are many excellent law teachers who do not engage in research activity to any significant extent and it is also still true that new universities on the whole carry out research activities which are more applied, teaching-focused and still seen as less valuable. Other debates about the pressures of workload for (legal) academics, students as customers and whether or not law is a vocational discipline are all so familiar to me that it is hard to believe they were penned almost 20 years ago – a year before I started my law degree in fact.

The debates may not have changed but they have become more nuanced and our understanding of what legal education is, what research is and what teaching is has also developed. In addition the higher education (HE) landscape and the legal services market have changed, some would say dramatically. The purpose of this chapter is therefore to challenge some of Oliver's assumptions about research and teaching: I do not, as Oliver does, regard teaching and research as completely distinct and competing activities; I do not see the same tensions between them in terms of management and I see no reason why even the most vocationally oriented course (or student) cannot be research led or informed.

The integration of teaching and research in the law department

'Whilst the *idea* of the university as a community of scholars engaged in the dispassionate pursuit of truth may never have accorded precisely with the

1 Oliver, D. (1996), 'The Integration of Teaching and Research in the Law Department', *The Law Teacher* 30(2), 133–49. See also Chapter 23 in this volume.

reality, any semblance of the *idea* now seems to have gone forever as the market assumes centre-stage and governments seek to deploy universities for instrumental ends'[2]

The market has certainly taken over. Oliver wrote in the context of a reduction in HEFCE funding for research with many departments, particularly in new universities, possibly not receiving any; of significantly lower research activity in new universities than in old, of an increase in a consumer culture and linked to that, a deterioration in learning experience; and of there being a focus on substantive knowledge sacrificing depth and understanding for breadth and memorising. She also notes the increase in student numbers and impact of staff student ratios as well as the introduction of fees and the considerable pressures on the academic workload. Most, if not all, of those concerns are familiar to us now.

Curiosity: alternative views on teaching and research

Oliver's lecture never fully articulates how she understands the relationship between research and teaching. She is clearly aware (and perhaps agrees) that some see teaching as something which gets in the way of our real work – research. This, in today's HE marketplace certainly but maybe also in the past, makes no sense at all. The balance may be wrong but research and teaching are both part of what academics do and what universities are for. In my view, in a world where everything is about the marketplace and we have to teach ethics rather than expect ethical behaviour, we have a duty as law teachers to embed research into our courses; to base our arguments and teachings on well-researched and well-thought-through evidence, to counter the information age where any question can be answered at the click of a button but is rarely understood. We also have a duty to show the impact of law, both positive and negative, and we have a duty to foster critical minds. Integrating research into our teaching is one way to do this. However, even if your view of our duties is different from mine, embedding research in teaching exposes students to the intellectual endeavours we thrive on and the curiosity we experience when we realise we have stumbled on something interesting we do not yet fully understand.

Before I go any further, I need to be clear about what I mean when talking about linking research and teaching. 'There is a view that the link between teaching and research is what makes university education distinctive.'[3] This is a point that Oliver seems to accept but she goes no further and this lack of exploration

2 Thornton. M. (2012), *Privatising the Public University: The Case of Law*. Oxford: Routledge, at p. 2.
3 Schapper, J. and Mayson, S.E. (2010), 'Research-led teaching: moving from a fractured engagement to a marriage of convenience', *Higher Education Research & Development* 29(6), 641–651 at 644. See also Brown, R.B. (2005), 'Why Link personal research and teaching?', *Education and Training* 47(6), 393–407.

has implications for the arguments she makes. Perhaps the first point to note is that '[w]hether legal academics should research and what can constitute that research are and always have been deeply contested questions'.[4] In the US context Tamanaha has suggested that 'an age old drift has bedevilled law schools from their initial implantation in universities up through the present. Law students attend law school to learn how to become lawyers. Law professors are academics'.[5] This issue is not unfamiliar to the English context, though perhaps less acute given the differences in legal education between the two jurisdictions. Cownie for example found that:

> 'Research has come to play an increasingly important part in the culture of academic law, and the type of research which is valued appears to be changing, with less emphasis upon research which is oriented towards practitioners.'[6]

The point thus is that research is an integral part of university law schools and in fact one of what has been described as the 'twin peaks of excellence',[7] the other being teaching. However, just because an organisation, in this case a law school, is engaged in two or more activities, in this case teaching and research, does not automatically mean that there has to be a link between those two activities. The question that therefore needs to be asked is this:

> 'What are the motivations for [bringing teaching and research more closely together]? Is this just a bid on the part of research-intensive universities to prop up the research enterprise, or a cry from less research-focused institutions to ensure that a wedge is not drawn between research and teaching institutions?'[8]

Or put differently: Why should our teaching be influenced by (our) research and vice versa?

I will return to my attempt at answering that question later. First, however, it is worth noting that the literature in this area mostly avoids the question. Cretchley and colleagues simply state that '[t]he notion that teaching and research are complementary activities is entrenched in academic history and ideology'[9] and

4 Bradney, A. (2003), *Conversations, Choices and Chances: The Liberal Law School in the Twenty-First Century*. Oxford: Hart Publishing, at p. 109.
5 Tamanaha, B.Z. (2012), *Failing Law Schools*. Chicago: University of Chicago Press, at p. 54.
6 Cownie, F. (2004), *Legal Academics. Culture and Identities*. Oxford: Hart Publishing, at p. 141.
7 Schapper and Mayson, n. 3, at 641.
8 Brew, A. (2005), 'Preface', in Jenkins, A., Breen, R. and Lindsay, R. (eds), *Reshaping Teaching in Higher Education*. London: Kogan, x–xi, at p. x.
9 Cretchley, P.C., Edwards, S.L., O'Shea, P., Sheard, J., Hurst, J. and Brookes, W. (2014), 'Research and/or learning and teaching: a study of Australian professors' priorities, beliefs and behaviours', *Higher Education Research & Development* 33(4), 649–69 at 650.

Coate et al, considering the writing available in this area, come to the conclusion that '[t]his developing literature is strong on rhetoric and light on the empirical nature of the relationship between teaching and research'.[10] They also note that '[i]f teaching and research are as inseparable as many participants claimed, the lack of explicit strategies to promote this synergy is interesting'.[11] What is clear, is that the relationship between research and teaching is very complex and that complexity is not acknowledged by Oliver in her lecture. This leads to a number of assumptions which are implicit in what Oliver says about the benefits of linking research and teaching, the challenges of making those links and the managerial issues which arise. She does what many others have also done and confuses research-led teaching and researcher-led teaching[12] or at least does not explicitly distinguish them. She also does not draw a distinction between research-led and research-informed teaching. But these distinctions are important because they can signal very different expectations to both staff and students as to how the activities carried out within law schools are conceived, linked and valued. As Coate et al rightly note:

> 'Teaching and research can exist in a range of relationships with each other, and these relationships are shaped by the value-orientation of academic staff and the management of available resources.'[13]

The relationships are complex and have to be negotiated by academics on the ground. Schapper and Mayson identify a 'large gap between institutional rhetoric of research-led teaching, accepted research findings and the reality that confronts academic staff who seek to make meaningful linkages between the two'.[14] This gap is, in my view, at least partly because we have failed to engage with the complexity of what the various relationships imply and we have not fully recognised or accepted that

> 'to develop closer links between research and teaching requires a well researched, sophisticated, broad based understanding of what research-led teaching is across diverse university contexts . . .'[15]

However, I have avoided 'the why question'. In acknowledging the complexities of the relationships between research and teaching I have not yet engaged with why we should seek to build positive relationships between research and teaching in law schools. I turn to this now.

10 Coate, K., Barnett, R. and Williams, G. (2001), 'Relationships Between Teaching and Research in Higher Education in England', *Higher Education Quarterly* 55(2), 158–74 at 159.
11 Ibid., at 162.
12 Schapper and Mayson, n. 3, at 646.
13 Coate, Barnett and Williams, n. 10, at 172.
14 Schapper and Mayson, n. 3, at 642.
15 Ibid., at 647.

> 'Healy (2005a) [. . .] has reported that students perceive clear benefits from staff research, including enthusiasm, credibility, and the reflected glory of being taught by nationally and internationally known researchers.'[16]

So one argument as to why it might be worth encouraging researcher-led teaching, that is teaching that is delivered by people who are active researchers in that particular field, is that students like it. This is not, however, a reason to try and encourage other links between research and teaching which do not depend on the researcher themselves actually delivering the teaching related to their specialist topic. There are additional, and perhaps better reasons as to why links between research and teaching are valuable.

Bradney notes that 'Because human beings are reasoning beings, human beings are researching beings' and goes on to suggest that to foster reasoning and researching gives our students the best possible chance to, quoting Nussbaum, 'call their minds their own'.[17] Samarasekera states '[t]he human spirit thrives on discovery. We must integrate discovery into all aspects of learning'.[18] So one argument for making links between research and teaching, for introducing students to research – our own, that of colleagues or published work – or in fact simply the idea of research is that as human beings we will thrive on the discoveries which are to be made through such introductions. Cownie reported that in her research, '[t]he majority of respondents were involved in research, and were enthusiastic about it, particularly the opportunity it provides for the satisfaction of intellectual curiosity'.[19] The majority of her respondents thrived on their research. This is something we should share with students.

This is perhaps what Healy, cited earlier, discovered the students respond to when they talk of enthusiasm. So as well as helping our students to thrive, engagement with research may also increase their level of engagement with their studies generally and help them to enjoy their intellectual journey. It may foster their curiosity. Embedding research into teaching – whether that is our own work or that of others – allows us to show students that law is ever changing, evolving and that we do not have all the answers, in fact we do not have all the questions. It can show students that most areas of law are highly contested, that there is no right

16 Wuetherick, B. and McLaughlin, L. (2011), 'Exploring Students' Perceptions of Research in the Learning Environment: A Partnership to Enhance Our Understanding of the Undergraduate Student Experience', in Little, S. (ed.), *Student-Staff Partnerships in Higher Education*. London: Bloomsbury, at p. 190. Healy, M. (2005), 'Linking teaching and research: exploring disciplinary spaces and the role of enquiry based learning', in Barnett, R. (ed), *Reshaping the University: New Relationships Between Research, Scholarship and Teaching*. London: Society for Research into Higher Education and Open University Press, at pp. 67–78.

17 Bradney, n. 4, at 118; Nussbaum, M. (1997), *Cultivating Humanity: A Classical Defence for Reform in Liberal Education*. Cambridge: Harvard University Press, at p. 293.

18 Samarasekera, I. (2005), *Installation Address*. Edmonton: Office of the President, University of Alberta. Cited in Wuetherick and McLaughlin, n. 16, at 185.

19 Cownie, n. 6, at 202.

answer and that the study of law, far from being the pursuit of a right answer, is the pursuit of argument and critical thought.

As well as doing that, engaging with research allows students to see for themselves the demands of academic study and the rigour required for such an intellectual endeavour. We encourage our students to read widely, build their arguments carefully and provide evidence of their argument throughout their work. We do not always hold ourselves to the same standards when preparing teaching materials or delivering teaching sessions. Using research and explicitly referring to it in our materials and in our delivery sets a good example. Research, as Bradney notes, mirrors what we ask students to do:

> 'Research in the liberal law school makes the same demands of the academic as are made of the student except that the academic sets their own questions and their permanent residence in the law school allows for a more developed answer. In both cases of teaching and learning and that of research a liberal education involves no more and no less than the concentration of curiosity.'[20]

If that is accepted, and you may of course disagree with me that we should be delivering a liberal legal education, then research should influence our teaching because it is through engagement with research that students develop an understanding of law that goes beyond learning legal principles and how to apply them.

In a world where answers to most questions can be found in minutes by the click of a button but where issues are rarely fully understood, never mind thought through, highlighting academic research and explaining the process behind that research is crucial. Exposure to research can instil in students a more detailed and more nuanced understanding of legal principles and their application and, depending on the type of research, the impact of those legal provisions in certain context.

Ian Ward, quoting both Bradney and, interestingly Dawn Oliver herself, puts it like this:

> 'A liberal legal education, it has been argued, should seek to engage the sensitivities of law students. And it should be critical; a law student should not merely *know* or *know how to* but *understand* why things are as they are and how they could be different.'[21]

20 Bradney, n. 4, at 121.

21 Ward, I. (2009), 'Legal Education and the Democratic Imagination', Learning in Law Annual Conference Keynote Address, at 3: original footnotes omitted but see Bradney, A. (1999), 'Liberalising Legal Education', in Cownie, F. (ed), *The Law School: Global Questions, Local Issues*. London: Ashgate; and Oliver, D. (1994), 'Teaching and Learning Law: Pressures on the Liberal Degree', in Birks, P. (ed), *Reviewing Legal Education*. Oxford: Oxford University Press, at p, 78.

This is particularly the case if we agree that 'the university is among the few custodians of the quality of culture and intellectual sustainability and depth'.[22] Of course you may not agree that this is what law schools should be about. You may not consider a liberal legal education to be important and you may take a more vocational approach to legal education preferring to focus on the training of lawyers. If that is the case then maybe students do not need to understand why things are as they are and how they could be different; maybe knowing and knowing how to are sufficient for them to become little worker drones in large firms. However, I doubt it because finding solutions to often complex legal problems requires lawyers to think in a particularly logical, clear but also very creative way and if you are only taught to know legal rules and how to apply them rather than how to really think about them, you are likely to lack the creativity required.

There is an even more compelling reason to insist on students engaging with research and one which is linked to my own affinity to socio-legal research.[23] Ian Ward, writing in the context of terrorism, our legal response and our conceptualisation of civil liberties, writes this:

> 'If we are indeed serious about the role of HE in general, and legal education in particular, as a vehicle for nurturing the ideals of a liberal democracy, no matter how much we might choose to squabble about the niceties of particular ideas of liberalism, and indeed liberty, we must recognise an overarching responsibility to ensure that our students are encouraged to think long and hard about these challenges; not just their legal efficacy, the appropriateness of counter-terrorist measures as legal or extra-legal instruments, but also the broader consequences for the political society in which we live, and the culture which sustains it. The case for crossing cultural and disciplinary boundaries, in order to resuscitate our democratic imagination, has rarely, I would suggest, been stronger.'[24]

This paragraph can, in my view, be applied to most if not all major (legal) challenges facing us today, from climate change to economic crises to the erosion of human rights and the increasing securitisation of our lives. If we do not introduce students to a wide range of thinking, we cannot begin to hope that they will be able to put their minds to complex problems which their generation and generations to come will inherit.

Healy also notes drawbacks to research and teaching links: 'Disadvantages reported by students included staff unavailability, the lack of involvement

22 Pillay, G. (2008), 'Valuing higher education', Keynote Lecture delivered at the Society for Research into Higher Education, Liverpool, December 2008. Available at http://www.srhe.ac.uk/conference2008/download/KeynoteAddressProfGeraldPillay.pdfat page6 (accessed 6 July 2015).

23 Guth, J. and Ashford, C. (2014). 'The Legal Education and Training Review: Regulating Socio-legal and liberal legal education?, *The Law Teacher*, 48(1), 5–19.

24 Ward, n. 21, at 17.

in research activities and staff research taking priority over their learning'.[25] Demands on our time are many and varied and we need some way to decide how we prioritise our work. For some academics that undoubtedly means that research work takes precedence over other work – including work which benefits students. The balance of academic work changes over time generally but also for individual academics over their careers and over the academic year but the importance of research seems ever present. Coate et al put it like this: 'The volumes and values of academic activities are not static and have shifted over time, although the high value accorded to research has been a conspicuous pattern for half a century at least'.[26] Schapper and Mayson argue that academics may have to serve more than one master: 'From a policy perspective, contradictory demands are made on academics caught in the political contest between the institutional value of research *vis a vis* the community's demand for teaching'.[27] So while universities and other academics assign value based on someone's research profile, the communities which universities serve are more interested in what is offered to students. This can create tensions and those tensions need to be managed.

'The assumption that good researchers will also be good teachers has been described as a myth of higher education, and so too is perhaps the belief that research enhances teaching.'[28] Even if it is a myth that research necessarily enhances teaching, we should still try to link research and teaching, and I have set out earlier why. However, it does mean that we need to think about how we link the two activities. Does it mean that there is no longer a place for academics whose contribution comes purely from research, nor for academics who do not engage in research but focus on teaching students? This would not make sense. Not all of us are good at both and you do not have to be good at one to be good at the other. The extent to which law schools can and do ask their researchers to teach based on their research or ask their teachers to base their teaching on research (whether their own or not) or to introduce students to the notion of research within the curriculum must largely be determined by the law schools themselves. This should not be a decision which is based purely on resources, though resources will of course be a factor. It is a far more fundamental question about what the purpose and value of a law degree is and what the ethos and culture of the law school should be. In making such decisions it should always be remembered that 'Academic Freedom means freedom for us to do our work. It also means allowing other academics freedom to do their work'.[29] So while we

25 Healy, M. (2005), 'Linking teaching and research: exploring disciplinary spaces and the role of enquiry based learning', in Barnett, R. (ed), *Reshaping the University: New Relationships Between Research, Scholarship and Teaching*. London: Society for Research into Higher Education and Open University Press, at pp. 67–78.

26 Coate, Barnett and Williams, n. 10, at 1163.

27 Schapper. and Mayson, n. 3, at 646.

28 Coate, Barnett and Williams, n. 10, at 172; Terezini, P.T. and Pascarella, E.T. (1994), 'Living with Myths. Undergraduate Education in America', *Change* 28–32.

29 Bradney, T. (2003), 'On Academic Freedom', *The Reporter*, No. 26 Spring, 1–2.

must recognise that teaching and research are valuable to all law schools, the relationship between the activities is likely to be fluid and very dynamic and vary from law school to law school.

I have so far presented the relationship as rather one way. I have talked about research-led or research-informed teaching; I have assumed that it is the research that influences teaching. I have said nothing about how the relationship works the other way around:

> 'there is no suggestion that teaching might be valued independently from or even alongside research. Elton (2001) also notes that in this debate there is never a suggestion that research is best conducted in a teaching environment.'[30]

This perhaps tells us something about the value placed on the activities. It perhaps suggests that research is the superior one. This chimes with experience of academics, particularly those seeking promotion. 'If research is more highly valued and rewarded than teaching, academics may be less inclined to spend time on curricular developments or pedagogical approaches.'[31] This is problematic for two main reasons. First, we have noted that the integration of research into teaching is complex and that for it to be effective it needs to be well thought out. This takes time – time academics seeking career advancement might feel is better spent actually doing research rather than thinking about how it can best be included in teaching. Second, it creates a divide between those academics who are focused mainly on research and those who are focused mainly on teaching (and puts those who try and do both in an impossible position). It establishes a hierarchy which is misplaced. This hierarchy is not only applied within institutions but also between institutions with those who achieve significant scores in whatever research assessment mechanism exists at the time, being seen as more prestigious and generally better than those who do not. This sort of hierarchy allows Dawn Oliver to suggest that research funding should be (and of course is) concentrated in certain institutions allowing them to focus on research while others focus on teaching – a notion which is stated very clearly in the US context by Tamanaha: 'Especially at lower-ranked schools where graduates have lower expected income, the students should not be made to bear the costly burden for faculty research'.[32] While I agree that students should not bear the cost, this is not the argument I wish to make here. The point is the distinction between low and high ranking schools and the students within them. Given the case made earlier for the integration of research into teaching, it should be evident that all law students should benefit from it, not just those who, largely by winning in

30 Schapper and Mayson, n. 3, at 646; Elton, L. (2001), 'Research and teaching: Conditions for a positive link', *Teaching in Higher Education* 6(1), 43–56.

31 Coate, Barnett and Williams, n. 10, at 170. See also Cownie, n. 6.

32 Tamanaha, n. 5, at 61.

the lottery of birth, secure places at elite law schools. It should also be clear that engagement with research should not be confined to students on postgraduate degrees. But research is expensive and resources are finite. Add to that the fact that students are paying for their higher education (not their degrees – yet!) and that other income, particularly income which is directly for legal research, is very limited, we do need to answer some serious questions about research and how it is funded, or more broadly, how universities are funded. Engaging with this important debate is sadly beyond the scope of the chapter.

Dawn Oliver's argument is based on an elitist view of what research is and how it links to teaching. Her view is shaped by the position she holds in a research-intensive elite institution but it is not a view that is helpful to legal academics and law students across the country. An alternative view which sees learning, teaching and research as something that is a collegial endeavour and one which academics and students contribute to, allows us to see the value of research in teaching and teaching in research:

> 'In order for this model of staff-student partnership to succeed, the hierarchy that is implicitly built into the organization of universities must be challenged, as must the definition of who can legitimately be a scholar. While "inclusive" does not mean equal, Brew argues that it does mean "valuing the contributions of each person no matter what their level of prior understanding and knowledge" (Brew 2006, p163). We must critically reflect on the ways in which we enable not only undergraduate students, but also postgraduate students and contract instructors, to be a part of this scholarly community.'[33]

Not all law teachers are researchers. Even those who are, do not necessarily research in areas where they teach or teach in areas they research. It is therefore not always easy to use our own research in teaching. In addition, if we are teaching in areas where we are not also research active there might be little incentive to search out research work in order to use it in our teaching. We might simply not be interested enough in the subject or we might simply not have the time. The days where we all just teach our specialist subjects, if they ever existed, are over. Many of us teach on core undergraduate courses and many perceive there to be little scope for introducing research into such teaching. Students do not yet know enough, so the argument goes, to understand the research. They need to learn more law before they can make sense of the research on it. This is a stance which Oliver seems to support. However, it strikes me as flawed.

It is possible to make use of research in all our teaching. It does not have to be our own research work; it can be any research on the issues we are trying to teach (it also does not have to be legal research of course; there are many disciplines where work is carried out which is of relevance to law students). Good teaching

33 Wuetherick and McLaughlin, n. 16, at 194–5; Brew, A. (2006), *Research and Teaching: Beyond the Divide*. New York: Palgrave MacMillan.

surely requires us to go beyond a textbook in a given topic and to familiarise ourselves with the debates, issues and, yes, the research in that area. We perhaps do not need to become experts on every aspect but we do need to do what we ask our students to do: read widely and justify our arguments using the evidence available to us – which includes research. In Coate et al's research 'a final year undergraduate engineering student suggested that non-research-active staff teach students to pass exams, whereas research active staff teach students the subject'.[34] Surely we should be aiming to teach our students the subject.

The notion that undergraduate students, and particular first year students, do not know enough law to be able to understand research makes no sense – taking this to its logical conclusion it would mean that any legal research should only be engaged with by people who hold law degrees and who have a good understanding of the particular area of law already. That is nonsense. Research can make law more interesting and exciting and therefore more accessible to students. Engaging with research can throw up questions for students or highlight issues which they can follow up and will lead to a better understanding of law. This does mean that we 'may be required to re-evaluate [our] curriculum using the concept of learning as the link between research and teaching'.[35] This is particularly so as reading journal articles and understanding research is a skill and it is one that our students do not magically possess or develop just because we give them a journal article to read. We therefore need to think carefully about what research we introduce them to, what published material we ask them to read and how we present information to students. We need to explain what research is, why we get excited about it, why it is important and what it can tell us. Without that, students are not likely to fully appreciate the difference between reading a research paper on the rule of law and the Wikipedia entry on the same topic.

Curiosity: not good for cats, great for students[36]

This chapter has sought to respond to a number of the points raised and assumptions made by Dawn Oliver in her Lord Upjohn Lecture. It has challenged the idea that research should perhaps be concentrated in some elite institution and focused on postgraduate teaching. It has done so by setting out why research-informed/led teaching is important and why it is important at all levels. The chapter has also highlighted some important questions which the HE community must address, not least how HE is to be funded in the future in order to safeguard all activities taking place in universities. If HE generally and legal education specifically are about learning in a broad sense then we need to find a way to

34 Coate, Barnett and Williams, n. 10, at 166.
35 Schapper and Mayson, n. 3, at 649.
36 Adapted from the TV Programme *Numb3rs* (2005): Dr Larry Fleinhardt in season 2, episode 8: 'Curiosity. Not good for cats, great for scientists'.

channel our students' curiosity; we need to allow them to follow it in the same way that we seek to follow our own. We need to share our curiosity with them and we need to get excited about our learning together. Brown and Atkins suggest that research is sometimes described as 'organized curiosity' whereas teaching is 'organized communication'.[37] However, I would argue that teaching and research are both about curiosity and about communication and that, as Einstein told us, 'the important thing is not to stop questioning. Curiosity has its own reason for existing'.[38]

37 Brown, G. and Atkins, M. (1998), *Effective Teaching in Higher Education.* London: Routledge, at p. 5.

38 Attributed to Albert Einstein on various websites including 'Famous Quotes', http://www.famous-quotes-and-quotations.com/ (accessed 18 May 2015).

Index

Note: Page numbers followed by 'n' refer to notes.

academics: bridging gap between practitioners and 102, 165; out of touch 175; status 137; undertaking teaching and research 231, 247–8, 249–50
access courses 48
access to justice 14, 40, 74, 91, 111, 200; and legal education reform 40–1; at proportionate cost 108–10
Access to Justice Act 1999 106
Access to Justice Report 105–6
access to legal education 38, 166, 180–1, 194 *see also* widening participation in higher education
accident claims 117, 128–9
accountability 33–5, 144
administrative law teaching 174–5
admissions, university 50, 172–3
Advisory Committee on Legal Education and Conduct (ACLEC) 6, 31, 33, 188–95, 205, 236; application process stages 190; audit society discourse 34–5; Bar application to amend rules of entry to Inns of Court School of Law 191–3; cab rank rule 191; CPS application 190; discussion and rejection of common training 199; failure of 33, 36; Government Legal Service application 190; law established as a graduate profession 199; Law Society application 189–90; managing change 191; and public interest 36, 199; review of legal education 193–4; shift from teaching to learning 237
Advocacy Training Council 82
after-the-event (ATE) insurance premiums 106–7
Aimhigher 47, 50
air crashes, expert evidence in 118–19
Alternative Business Structures (ABS) 74, 75, 79, 168–9
alternative dispute resolution (ADR) 41, 126, 128, 142, 169, 170, 195
American colonies 188
Americanisation of legal education 182–3
Anderson, P. 214, 216
apprenticeship: CILEX qualification 16–17; cognitive 16, 17; forms of 15–16; integrated models of 38; new forms of 81, 87, 93, 187, 203; or professional identity and values 16, 19; of skills and practice 16, 17–19; solicitors' 203, 205
Arthurs, H. 35–6
assessment: BPTC 94, 127, 130–1; HEFCE *Report on Quality Assessment 1992–1995* 230n; SRA review of 203
Association of Law Teachers 97, 155, 185; appreciation of Upjohn as President 8–9
Atkin Committee 1936 27n, 30, 31, 32, 37
authoritarianism 210–11, 213

Bar: application to ACLEC 191–3; and CILEX qualification 17; consultations with ACLEC 191; contribution to legal education in 16th-19th centuries 196–7; Gandhi on training for 121–2; inequalities in obtaining pupillages 70, 166; post-initial qualification training, proposal for 38–9; public law training 99; rejecting common training with solicitors 22, 36, 38, 167; routes to qualification in mid 20th century 198; specialisms 158; standards of scholarship

in academia and at 158, 165; suggested reform of qualification route for 17, 21–2, 38–9; threats to 194–5; training and CPD review 82; training in 1930s 171–2; training in 1974 122–3; vocational training in 1977 159–61
Bar Professional Training Course (BPTC): aptitude test 94; assessment 94, 127, 130–1; authorised providers of 182; availability of pupillages following 22, 38, 70, 192; clinical developments 133–4; drafting 128–9; knowledge areas 131; learning in response to civil procedure reforms 127–30; numbers enrolling 75, 163; student satisfaction 131–2
Bar Standards Board (BSB) 87, 127, 201; reform following LETR 76, 82, 94, 167, 202
Bar Vocational Course 82, 164, 165, 199
Barnard, D. 21, 22
barristers: educational background 52; growth in numbers of 75, 163–4, 167; widening of services offered by 167
Bentham, J. 212
boundaries between different types of lawyer, collapsing of 77
Browne Review of Higher Education 57, 61, 65
Bruges 12–13
bundles, preparation of 126
business, law as 92

cab rank rule 191
Cable, V. 45
Calvino, I. 41
Campaign for Social Science 185
Caparo Industries Plc v Dickman (1990) 100
careers advice 63
Carnegie Foundation of the Advancement of Teaching 14–15, 38; three forms of apprenticeship 15–16
case management conferences 106, 108, 126
case management reform 105–6, 107, 125, 126
charters 138
child poverty 46
CILEX qualification 16–17, 205
City Law School (formerly Inns of Court School of Law) 121; BPTC training in response to civil procedure reforms 127–30; real-client clinical learning 133
Civil Evidence Act 1968 114, 115, 117, 119
civil litigation, cost of 106, 111; importance of proportionality 108–10; Jackson Reforms 106–8, 124, 168
civil procedure: growing focus on ADR 169; Jackson Reforms 106–8; Woolf reforms 98–9, 105–6, 124–6
Civil Procedure Rules (CPR) 98–9; case management reform 105–6, 107, 125, 126; development 105–6; overriding objective 105–6, 124–5; pre-action protocols 125; Rules of Evidence 98–9; track allocation 125
clearing for university admissions 50, 60–1
Clegg, N. 45
Clementi, D. 73, 200
clinical education 18; BPTC 133–4
co-ordination and consistency problems in legal education 31–3
Coate, K. et al 243, 247, 250
Coffee Houses in Canada 180–1
cognitive apprenticeships 16, 17
College of Law 80, 159, 165
commercial practice: emergence of 32; focus on 40, 76, 77, 166
commercialism and maintenance of professional standards 102, 105
Commitment to Scholarship and Research in Universities 230
Committee Report 1846 30, 31
Common Professional Examination (CPE) 162, 192, 193, 199
common training 21–2, 36, 38–9, 161, 167; ACLEC discussion and rejection of 199; co-ordination and consistency problems 195
competence 34–5, 39, 201–2
conditional fee agreements 105, 106, 111, 169
consistency and co-ordination problems in legal education 31–3
constitutional law 174, 197, 214
consumerism 65, 73
consumers, students as 64–7, 234, 236
contact time 138, 236, 237; and value creation 153
continuing professional development (CPD) 39, 78–9; critique of LETR recommendations for 93; SRA reform of 95

contractual interpretation 101, 111
control of legal education 29, 33–4, 35–6, 37, 199; and public interest 35–6
corporate law firms 40–1, 111
costs of legal training 17, 36, 40–1, 93, 160, 163
Courts and Legal Services Act 1990 33, 106, 188–9, 196, 198
cross-examination 116, 117; of 'own witness' 114–15
Crown Prosecution Service (CPS) 22, 190
cultural capital 47, 187

damages-based agreements (DBAs) 107, 111, 169
damages for non-pecuniary loss 100–1
Data Protection Act 1998 (DPA) 140
Dearing Report 43, 50
delivery of education and training, flexibility in 81, 93
democratic control 213
Denning, Lord 55, 97, 186
Devlin, Lord 217, 222
diaries 117
Diploma in Legal Practice 18
disability legislation 140
disadvantaged students: financial support 47–8, 49–50, 51; GCSEs 45; Helena Kennedy Foundation and support for 51; in higher education 44; poverty of aspiration 44; widening participation for 44–7, 51
discrimination legislation 140
diversity 19–20, 56–7, 80–2, 137, 179–82
diversity of practice, increasing 76–7, 77–8
divorce petitions 116, 117
documents, interpretation of 101
Doll, R. 120
drafting, teaching of 128–9
Dworkin, R. 211

economic benefits of higher education 54–5, 69
Edmonds, D. 10, 12, 72–84, 85, 86, 95, 203
Education Maintenance Allowance (EMA) 47–8
education, sound, a requirement for legal practice 172–3
educational background in legal profession 52, 181
Edwards, Judge H. 101–2
elitism 46, 55
employment, graduate 69–70
employment tribunals, students representing clients at 133
ethics 19, 88, 91–2, 111; conflict between commercialism and professional standards 102, 105; teaching 78, 79–80, 102, 111
ethnic minorities in legal profession 19–20
European Court of Human Rights 100
evidence and procedure 114–15
expert evidence 118–19; resolving disagreements over 119

fact-finding 113–20; cross-examination 114–15, 116, 117; evidence and procedure 114–15; expert evidence 118–19; judges 119–20; recollection and observation 117–18; techniques 115–16
First Report on Legal Education and Training 199
Flood, J. 182, 183, 184
forensic science 119
foundation degrees 67
fragmentation of academic and professional education 29, 30–1, 165, 167
Freedom of Information Act 2000 (FOIA) 140
freedom of speech guarantees 139–40
fundamental rights 223–4
funding: cuts for civil and criminal work 106, 167, 169; for legal education 29, 32, 166, 194; support for disadvantaged students 47–8, 49–50, 51 *see also* research funding
future of legal profession 73, 88–90, 94–5, 167–70

Gandhi, M. 121–2
gavotte 189, 196
globalisation and working across different jurisdictions 169–70; languages useful for 175–6
globalised markets, delivery of legal services in 75–6
Goddard, J. 238
good teaching 226, 230, 232–3, 247, 249–50

Graduate Diploma in Law (GDL) 16, 111, 162; content reform 17–19; enrollment numbers 75; online study for 81; questions over 'core law' syllabus 166
graduate jobs 69–70
graduate profession, law established as 199

Harford, T. 12
Heil v Rankin (2000) 100–1
Helena Kennedy Foundation 48, 51, 63
Higher Education Funding Council (HEFCE) 228, 229, 234, 241; *Report on Quality Assessment 1992–1995* 230n
history of English legal education reform 25–37
Human Rights Act 2008: impact of 110–11; law schools and teaching on 99–100, 104, 111; nature of rights in 223, 224

ICS v. West Bromwich Building Society (1997) 111
ILEX Professional Standards 82, 83, 87
implementation of reform, difficulties with 37
industrial accident cases 117
Inns of Court School of Law (subsequently City Law School): application to amend rules of entry 191–3; Bar training in 1974 122–3; Gandhi on studying at 121–2; vocational training in 1977 159–61
insurance cover, universities 139
international law firms 111
international law, teaching 75, 172, 197, 207
Invisible Cities 41

Jackson Reforms 106–8, 124, 168; and costs of civil litigation 106–8; and proportionality 108–10
Jackson v. Attorney General (2006) 225
Joint Academic Stage 183
The Judge 222
judges: change in role from umpire to decision-maker 122; educational background 181; extra-judicial writing 222; as fact-finders 119–20; and politics 217, 221–3, 225–6; references to rule of law 225–6
Judicature Act 1873 197
judicial review of education law 141
Judicial Studies Board 99

Kennedy, H. 43
Key Information Sets (KIS) 61, 62, 65
Kilmuir Rules 221, 222
Kinnock, N. 44
knowledge: fundamental requirements 159; and principles analysis in study of law 156–7; vs. skills distinction 150–4; and skills review 17–19; solicitors' Statement of Legal Knowledge 202–3, 205; technology and disruption of delivery 153

languages, teaching of 175–6
Latin 173
Law and Learning 35
law degrees: costs of 17, 160, 163; debate on value of 155–6, 163; 'dumbing down' concerns 152; as entry to legal profession 162, 198, 199; growth in popularity of 57–8, 163, 164–5; non-practitioners with 101, 111, 164, 169; numbers of graduates 75, 101, 155, 163, 164, 195; online 81; Ormrod Report and control over 33–4; providers 155, 163
law schools: in 1980s 219–20; administrative law teaching 174–5; admissions 172–3; catering for non-practitioners as well as practitioners 101, 104, 111, 164, 169; collaboration between practice and 18, 179; constitutional law teaching 174; contrast between pre and post 1992 university sector 184, 228, 240; 'core law' to be studied 159, 166–7; CPR training 99, 104, 111; developing professional identity and values 19; diffusion of control and impact on 29; distinction between law as practiced and taught in 157–9; ethics, teaching of 78, 79–80, 102, 111; extent of practical teaching 159; facts, study of 157; fragmentation of professional and academic education 29, 30–1, 165, 167; funding 29, 32, 166, 194; future developments 102, 168–70; gaps in teaching 174–5; human rights training 99–100, 104, 111; increase in subject matter 237; independent identities 157, 179; knowledge and analysis in study of law 156–7; knowledge and skills reform 17–19; knowledge vs. skills distinction 150–4; languages, teaching of 175–6; learning experiences of students 153–4, 233, 235, 236–7; liberal 103–4, 179, 245–6; a more

broad-based approach required 100–1, 111; 'out of touch' academics in 175; political studies in 219–21, 227; requirement for a sound education prior to entry 172–3; research and teaching in 229–34, 235–9, 240, 241–50; scholarship standards at Bar and in 158, 165; selection of candidates for 172–3; shift to an outcomes approach 167; social context of studies 157; 'tug of war' in aspirations of 178–9; US 101–2; value judgements and human rights training 99–100, 104, 111
Law Society: application to ACLEC 189–90; consultations with ACLEC 191; establishment 198; rejecting common training with barristers 22, 36, 38, 167; resisting cab rank rule 191
learning experience of students: decline in quality of 236–7; seeking to improve 153–4, 233, 235
Learning Works 43
legal aid 74, 91, 96, 106, 111, 169, 175
Legal Disciplinary Partnerships 77
Legal Education and Training Review (LETR): areas omitted from 92–4; BSB reform following 76, 82, 94, 167, 202; collaboration between professional bodies 39–40; commissioning of 200; continuing professional development (CPD) 39, 93; final Report 87–8, 201–2; limitations of first phase 42; LSB statutory guidance in response to 202; missed opportunities 88, 90; not fit enough for new purpose 89–90, 91–2; primary objective 87, 204; principal recommendations 87–8, 201–2; purpose of education and training according to 13–14; questioning 'fit for purpose' discourse 11–12; SRA reforms following 82, 94–5; SRA response to report 92; testing hypothesis that training is not fit for purpose 10–11; understanding raison d'être of legal profession 12–13
Legal Education Association 31, 37
Legal Education Council 7, 42, 87
legal practice: bridging gap between academics and 102, 165; collaboration with academia 18, 179; distinction between law as taught and 157–9; future of 73, 88–90, 94–5, 167–70; increasing diversity 76–7, 77–8; specialisation 76, 77, 78, 158; students inadequately prepared for 91–2
legal practice course, city firms establish own 103
Legal Practice Course (LPC) 28n, 164, 165, 199; authorised providers of 182; critique of 91, 93; numbers enrolling 75; online version 81; problems in progressing beyond 70; reform 21, 22, 82, 200
legal rights 211, 214, 223, 224
Legal Services Act 2007 13, 33, 36, 39, 72, 79, 88, 183, 200
Legal Services Board 72; concerns of 85–6; consensus on review 82–3; making a review work 83–4; outcomes approach, shift to 166–7; problems with primary objectives of 203–4; regulatory objectives 72, 200; statutory guidance following LETR 202; two-tier system of regulation 205
Legal Services Consultative Panel 33
legal services market: changing 73, 75–7, 88–90; critique of LETR review of 88, 90; separation of regulated legal professions from 90
legislation, volume of 76–7
letters 117
liberty 212
lifelong learning 43, 47
litigants in person 111
LLM 231
London School of Economics (LSE) 207, 219
Lownds v. Home Office (2002) 4, 109, 110

Major, J. 181
Manderson, D. 180, 181
Marre Committee 33, 36
mature students 57
MBA course 21
mediation procedures 143, 169, 195; teaching 128
medical evidence 119
Milburn Report 20, 181, 182
model for legal education 15–16, 30–1, 38, 167, 198–9

National Academies Policy Advisory Group (NAPAG) 231, 235
National Conference of University Professors 230
National Student Survey (NSS) 3, 62, 65
National Students Forum 138
natural rights 212–13, 223

necessity, concept of 109
New Zealand 194–5
non-law graduates/graduates in legal profession debate 155–6, 163
non-practitioners with law degrees 101, 111, 164, 169
non-university route into legal profession 16–17; CILEX qualification 16–17, 205; LETR Report recommendations 87, 93; paralegal services 29–40, 168; solicitor apprenticeships 203, 205; technology and enabling of 81, 187

observation, unreliability of 118
Office for Fair Access 49–50, 57, 68
Office of Fair Trading (OFT) 62
Office of the Independent Adjudicator for Higher Education (OIA) 141–2, 143–4
online: degrees 81; dispute resolution 170; learning 150, 153
oral testimony 117–18, 195
Ormrod, Lord Justice 113–20, 122
Ormrod Report 75, 165; advisory function recommendations 32–3; Arthurs' discussion of control and public interest 35; discussion of vocational training 34, 36, 165, 199; fundamental knowledge requirements in law degrees 159; issues of accountability and control 33–4, 35; legal education recommendations 30–1, 33, 162, 198–9; post-review structure 37; separate vocational training for barristers and solicitors 36; university control of legal education 34, 199
Osman v UK (2000) 100
outcomes approach, LSB shift to 166–7
outcomes focused regulation (OFR) 90–1

paralegal workforce 39–40, 41, 79, 168; LPC and BPTC qualified candidates working in 70
part-time students 66, 67, 81
partnerships between professional services 75–6, 77
Paterson, A. 222, 223
personal injury claims 106–7, 173
plurality, increasing 76–7, 77–8
political journals and articles on law 209, 220–1
political rights 211, 223
politics and law: failure to teach both together 208–9; integrated subjects 207–9; judges and 217, 221–3, 225–6; law schools and teaching of 219–21, 227; legal research connecting 220, 221; and rights 210–13, 223–4; textbooks on 227
The Politics of the Judiciary 6, 217
polytechnics: divide between old sector universities and former 68, 184, 238; expansion of law teaching 32, 67; research in former 228, 234–5, 240
popularity of law 57–8, 163, 164–5
postgraduates 68–9; bridging gap between training and 81; flexibility in delivery of education and training 81; LLM 231; numbers of 56n, 57n; two-tier research system 229
poverty of aspiration 44
pre-action protocols 125
pre-trial reviews 106, 108
pro bono legal services 103, 104, 111–12; students offering 133
professional development and teaching (PDT) 235
professional identity and values 16, 19
professional standards: commercialism and maintenance of 102, 105; training in 103, 105
project management skills 91
proportionality 108–10
Protection of Official Information Bill 214
psychological contract 146–7
public interest 14, 35–6, 40, 200, 217
pupillages: difficulties in obtaining 22, 38, 70, 192; inequalities in acquiring 70, 166
purpose of legal education and training 14–15; LETR view on 13–14

quality assurance (QA) 34–5

Race Relations (Amendment) Act 2000 140
Rawls, J. 211
recollection and observation 117–18
recruitment methods of Canadian law firms 180–1
reform of legal education 10–23, 37–41; access to justice challenge 40–1; continuing professional development (CPD) 39; and forms of apprenticeship 15–16, 38; increasing diversity 19–20;

knowledge and skills 17–19; need for collaboration between professional bodies 39–40; non-university route into legal profession 16–17; practical 'skills curriculum' 18; professional ethics, teaching of 19; professional identity and values 16, 19; purpose of legal education and training 13–15; vocational training, need for 20–1; vocational training, possible changes to 21–2, 38–9
reform of legal education, history of English 25–37; accountability and control 33–6; consistency and co-ordination problems 31–3; fragmentation of academic and professional education 30–1; implementation of reform 37; major reviews, impact on legal education system 26–7; major reviews prior to LETR 25–6; profession's shaping of reform agenda 28–9; and public interest 35–6; reliance on external triggers for change 27–30; tendency of policy makers to shift problems onto educational institutions 29–30
regulation: and changing legal service market 73, 75–7, 88–90; changing regulatory landscape 73–4; and CPD 78–9; and diversity and social mobility 80–2; and education 74–8; led reforms 82; making a review work 83–4; and professional ethics 78, 79–80; and reserved activities 80; review 82–3; two-tier system of 205 *see also* Bar Standards Board (BSB); Solicitors Regulation Authority (SRA)
religious rights 211–13, 223–4
Report of the Committee on Legal Education see Ormrod Report
Report of the Review of the Regulatory Framework for Legal Services in England and Wales 200
Report on Quality Assessment 1992–1995 230n
research: academics and balancing of teaching and 238, 247–8, 249–50; alternative views on teaching and 241–50; cultivating a culture of 238; departments not receiving HEFCE funding 234–5; in former polytechnics 228, 234–5, 240; integral to delivering a liberal legal education 245–6; managing integration of teaching and 235–9, 240–1, 249–50; politics and 220, 221
research assessment exercises (RAE) 137, 228, 229, 230n, 235
Research Capability of the University System 231, 235
research funding 234; departments not receiving HEFCE 234–5; in former polytechnics 228; idea to reroute to PDT 235; increasingly selective nature of 229
research, relationship between teaching and 229–34; benefits to students 232–3, 244–6, 248–50; complexity of 243; disadvantages in 233–4, 246–7; embedding research in teaching 241, 249–50; gap between rhetoric and reality 243; and good teaching 226, 230, 232–3, 247, 249–50; hierarchical divide 248; as mutually beneficial 229–31, 242–3; pressures of funding regimes 234; qualities of a good teacher 232–3; reasons to build positive relationships 243–6
reserved activities 80, 88, 93, 168
responsibility for own learning 236–7
retention rates 50, 57, 60
rights: argument about 210–13; distinguishing political from legal 211; fundamental 223–4; and Human Rights Act 223, 224; legal 211, 214, 223, 224; natural 212–13, 223; political 211, 223; religious 211–13, 223–4
road accidents, expert evidence in 119
Robbins Report: and barriers to participation 59; intellectual responsibility and discovery 229–30, 233, 234, 235; notion of student life 55–6; on teaching and research relationship 229–30; widening participation in higher education 32, 55, 56, 67
Rule of Law 213–18; common usages of phrase 216; function of law in present day society 215; individual rights against state 215; lawmakers bound by own laws 215–16, 216–17; and political role of judges 217, 225–6; revolutionary inheritance from 16th and 17th century 214; Thompson, Anderson's critique of 214, 216; Thompson's argument 213–14, 216; trade unions and 215
Rules of Evidence 99
Rules of Procedure 99
Russell Group universities 166; aspiring to 181–2

Sedley, Lord Justice 99, 100, 102
selection of candidates for law school 172–3
self-regulation 72, 198
Simmons & Simmons 21
skills 78, 185–7; apprenticeship 16, 17–19; changing requirements for legal 76–7, 173, 175–6; vs. knowledge distinction 150–4; training in law degrees 18
social change 73
social mobility 80–2; in action 52, 53; Coalition government strategy for 45–6; in legal profession 55
social welfare practice, emergence of 32
Society of Legal Scholars 163, 185
Society of Public Teachers of Law (SPTL) 163
socio-legal studies 156, 164, 166, 207, 209–10, 220, 221, 227
solicitors: 19th century establishment of qualification and certification 197; combined courses for barristers and 161; growth in numbers of 75, 163–4, 167; mid 20th century routes to qualification 197–8; reform of qualification route for 17, 21–2; rejection of common training with barristers 22, 36, 38, 167; training contract 21, 70, 75, 79, 93, 166, 199; Training Framework Review 199–200, 203; widening of services offered by 167
Solicitors Act 1974 198
Solicitors Regulation Authority (SRA) 73, 201; apprenticeship route 203, 205; assessment review 203; co-operation with IPS for alternative qualification route 17; demonstrating a lack of effective regulatory control 204–5; narrow view of regulatory role 205; process for qualification 203; proposals for core law studies in law degrees 166; reform following LETR 82, 94–5; response to LETR Report 92; Statement of Legal Knowledge 202–3, 205; Statement of Solicitor Competence 202
specialisation 76, 77, 78, 158
Statement of Legal Knowledge 202–3, 205
Statement of Solicitor Competence 202
statements of claim 117, 128–9
Steyn, Lord 225
student contract: based on consumer choice and satisfaction 144; education and questioning suitability for a 142; formation 137–9; general law applying to 139–41; lost opportunity for a standard 138; and OIA/ombudsman jurisdiction 141–2; OIA preferable to 143–4; purpose 136–7; unpopular with British students 138–9
student finance system: communicating facts of 48–50; misconceptions over reforms 47
student learning experience: decline in quality of 236–7; seeking to improve 153–4, 233, 235
students: benefits of engaging with research 232–3, 244–6, 248–50; choice 57, 60; consumer 64–7, 234, 236; expectations, 2015 147–50; mature 57; part-time 66, 67, 81; responsibility for own learning 236–7; satisfaction on BPTC 131–2; technology in lives of 148, 149, 150; variables affecting individual experiences of university 58–60 *see also* disadvantaged students; university-student relationship, general law applying to
subjects studied at university 57–8
Sutton Trust 46, 50

teaching, good 226, 230, 232–3, 247, 249–50
technical law 91
technology 73; and alternative career structures 81, 187; and automation of legal processes 168; disruption of knowledge delivery 153; in lives of students 148, 149, 150; use in legal learning processes 149, 151, 153
Templeman, Lord 97
textbooks on law and politics 227
Thatcher, M. 179–80
A Theory of Justice 211
Thompson, E.P. 213–14, 216; Anderson's critique of 214, 216
track allocation 125
training contract, solicitors 21, 70, 75, 79, 93, 166, 199
Training Framework Review 199–200, 203
trust 80
'tug of war' in legal education 178–9
tuition fees 47; impact of cap on 61–2
Turner, S. 180, 181
Twining, W. 7, 26n, 32n, 178–9, 226n, 238

The Undercover Economist 12
Unfair Contract Terms Act 1977 139
Unfair Terms in Consumer Contracts Regulations 1999 139
United States of America: approach to legal education 15, 21; law schools 101–2; legal qualifications 182–3; research and teaching in law schools 242, 248
universities: access to most selective 46, 55; admissions 50, 172–3; clearing 50, 60–1; collaboration with schools and colleges 50; contact time 138, 236, 237; contact time and value creation 153; contrast between pre and post 1992 sector 68, 184, 228, 238, 240; expenditure on legal advice and litigation 141; financial support and fee waivers 49–50; increased responsibilities for professional education 29–30, 34; increasing responsibility for vocational training 29–30, 34, 165; individual student experiences, variables affecting 58–60; insurance cover 139; Key Information Sets (KIS) 61, 62, 65; knowledge vs. skills distinction 150–4; and provision of information 61–4, 138; retention rates 50, 57, 60; Russell Group 166, 181–2; social selecting at 46, 55; study of law prior to 19th century 197; subjects studied 57–8; unofficial advice on 63–4
University of Cambridge 52, 171, 197
University of East London (UEL) 53
University of London 37, 231
University of Nottingham 197–8
University of Rutland 238
University of Strathclyde 18
university-student relationship, general law applying to 139–41; data protection 140; on disability 140; on discrimination 140; on eviction from student lodgings 140; freedom of information 140; freedom of speech guarantees 139–40; judicial review 141
Upjohn, Lord 8–9

value judgments, requirement for 100–1, 104, 111
value of a law degree, debate on 155–6, 163
vocational training: accountability and control of 34–5, 37, 199; Bar application to amend rules of entry for 191–3; for the Bar in 1977 159–61; catering for non-practitioners as well as practitioners in law schools 104–5; concentrated outside Russell Group universities 181–2; cost and access problems 36, 166, 194; difficulties in running a combined course for barrister and solicitors 161; ethics training 19; forces likely to influence future developments in 168–70; fusion of barristers' and solicitors' 21–2, 36, 38–9, 161, 167, 195, 199; involvement of practitioners 160; lessons learned 160–1; LETR recommendations 87; need for 20–1; Ormrod Report discussion of 34, 36, 165, 199; possible changes to 21–2, 38–9; proposals leading to two standards in solicitors' 103; separate training for barristers and solicitors 36, 167; separation of academic and 29, 30–1, 165, 167; skills courses 18; universities having increasing responsibility for 29–30, 34, 165 *see also* Bar Professional Training Course (BPTC); Bar Vocational Course; Legal Practice Course (LPC)

widening participation in higher education: Coalition government social mobility, fair access and 45–6; for disadvantaged students 44–7, 51; drive under New Labour 43–4; examples of 52–3; flexibility in delivery of education and training 81, 93; and graduate employment 69–70; and institutional differences 68; and investing in lifelong learning 47; and mass higher education 67; minority groups 56–7; policy setbacks to 47–8; and provision of information by universities 61–4; student finance communications 48–50; and students as consumers 64–7; subjects studied 57–8; taking higher degrees 68–9; tuition fees 47, 61–2; university admissions reform 50; work experience, internships and placement 68
Willetts, D. 45
Wilson, G. 220
women in legal profession 19, 175, 179–80
Wood, D. 82
Woolf Reforms 98–9, 105–6, 124–6
Wright, Lord 185–6

Yorke, M. 57

For Product Safety Concerns and Information please contact our EU representative GPSR@taylorandfrancis.com
Taylor & Francis Verlag GmbH, Kaufingerstraße 24, 80331 München, Germany

www.ingramcontent.com/pod-product-compliance
Ingram Content Group UK Ltd.
Pitfield, Milton Keynes, MK11 3LW, UK
UKHW022223190926
475702UK00003B/479
* 9 7 8 1 1 3 8 8 1 2 5 8 1 *